11th EDITION

Luckey's Hummel Figurines & Plates

Identification and Value Guide

CARL F. LUCKEY

© 1997 by

Carl F. Luckey

Published by

700 E. State Street • Iola, WI 54990-0001
Telephone: 715/445-2214

Please call or write for our free catalog.
Our toll-free number to place an order or obtain a free catalog is 800-258-0929
or please use our regular business telephone 715-445-2214 for editorial comment and further information.

ISBN: 0-89689-119-4

Printed in the United States of America

DEDICATED TO

Sister Maria Innocentia (Berta) Hummel
1909-1946

For her legacy of love and joy

Millions of people around the world have delighted in the
artistic genius and love of this extraordinary woman.

As one famous obituary stated:
"The gift of her art was the priceless endowment of Joy...".

TABLE OF CONTENTS

ACKNOWLEDGMENTS

In the 20 years I have been writing about M.I. Hummel collectibles, I have met an enormous number of very helpful people in the ongoing task of taking pictures and gathering data. There are so many, in fact, that have helped that it is not practical to attempt naming them all. There are some, however, that have given me so much, including their friendship, that it would be unforgivable not to name them.

Extra special thanks have to go to Rue Dee and Judy Marker and to Pat and Carol Arbenz for their unselfish sharing, patience and hospitality over all these years.

Thank you Don Stephens and the Village of Rosemont, Illinois, for allowing me to photograph your extraordinary collection for this book. A special thanks with a laurel wreath goes to Betty Rossi, director of the museum housing this collection, for putting up with me, a bunch of equipment and variously photographers, publishers and others underfoot, on more than one occasion. You graciously accepted an inconvenient intruder.

Others who directly contributed to this and previous editions in some way or another are Margaret Caddis, Prestwick, Scotland; Nancy M. Campbell of Lerner Publications, Minneapolis, MN; C.C. Campbell; Dona Danziger of The Clay Works, Exmore, VA ; Reg Eastop, Cheshire, England; Jean Dixon, Jeffersonville, IN; Beverly Edmondson, Bristol, PA; Ursula Ehman of the Hummel Museum, Inc., New Braunfels, TX; Gwen Fletcher, Covina, CA; Yvonne Flory, Orange, CA; Dick Gabbe of H&G Studios, West Palm Beach, FL; , Bernadette Galliker of ARS AG, Zug, Switzerland; Alfred Hummel of the Berta-Hummel-Museum, Massing, Germany; Richard Hyll, St. Croix, U.S. Virgin Islands; William H. Jones, Ronkonkoma, NY; Marci Karales of Schmid, Randolph, MA; Gabriela Kuster of ARS AG, Zug, Switzerland; Beatrix Laurent of ARS AG, Zug, Switzerland; Margaret Long, Annapolis, MD; John E. Martin, Columbus, OH; Betty McNair, Hackensack, NJ; Jacques Nauer of ARS AG, Zug, Switzerland; Jerry Northam, Hoopeston. IL; Doris Smith, Seattle, WA; Sieglinde Schoen Smith,of the Hummel Museum, Inc., New Braunfels, TX; Dana Stannard M. of Hawthorne, Niles, IL; Mona Star, Port Richey, FL; Cathy Crist Talcott of the Hummel Museum, Inc., New Braunfels, TX; Gwen Toma of the M.I. Hummel Club, Pennington, NJ; Linda Thuman, North Tonawanda, NY; Vera Young, Kansas City, MO.

AUTHOR'S NOTE

It's hard for me to believe that I have been writing about M.I. Hummel figurines and related items for twenty years now, and that this is the eleventh edition of a book I had trouble selling to a publisher when I first proposed writing it back in 1976. That first edition was 300 pages long. By the time the ninth edition came out in 1992 it had grown to 450 pages: a full fifty percent! Because I am writing this long in advance of the release of this edition, I have no idea of its page length but suspect if it were to be reduced to the old 5" x 8-1/2" format, it would exceed the ninth edition by a significant percentage. This is a good gauge of the amount of increase in knowledge with regard to the hobby over the years. With each new edition I have attempted to correct any misconceptions and mistakes in the previous edition and to present you with any additional information that has been uncovered since its release. Little was written about M.I. Hummel collectibles prior to the first edition of this book and some of the written guidance that was available was either erroneous or misleading. This was not due to any attempt to profit through the presentation of spurious data, but simply due to the very limited resources at the time. I and the majority of other writers and collectors who have joined the ranks have steadfastly tried to ferret out all the correct data and present it to you, the collector, so that you may enjoy the world of Hummel through the fun and excitement of new finds and additions to your collections. While we are on the subject of information, I urge you to read the next section. It will tell you how to use this book to your best advantage. If you use the book without reading how to use it, you may be led astray and make mistakes. It is sort of like trying to put the bicycle together on Christmas Eve without referring to the directions.

Over my years of research and travel, photographing collections and rare finds and picking the brains of dealers and collectors, I have noticed that there are many collectible items related to Hummel figurines, plates, etc., that could make interesting additions to a Hummel collection. I have also noticed a growing interest in these items and therefore have expanded the book's purview to include a selection of them.

Much of the information has come directly from those of you who buy, read and use this book. You have been an important part in making the book the resounding success it has been over the years. I hope you will continue to help me as you have in the past. In addition to hearing from thousands of collectors and dealers through the years, I also frequently hear from estate appraisers who have found a cache of Hummel items and people who discover, as a result of seeing my book, that they have a Hummel item or two. Consequently I have been able to uncover many new (old) pieces and add much data to my bulging research files. I can never have enough, so keep it coming. This message is especially true for you dealers and former dealers. If you have boxes or overflowing file cabinets with old literature and catalogs, ship them to me. I am interested in *anything* connected to Goebel, Hummel or not. Good quality photos are preferred, but snapshots are welcome. Please see Appendix A for directions on describing and photographing Hummel items. By all means try it. You may be surprised at the results.

Please do not ask me to appraise from lists or photographs. I used to try to do them all, but time no longer allows me that luxury.

Do write if you wish. I cannot promise to acknowledge every single letter, but will attempt to do so, as numbers allow. I hope you will remember to enclose a stamped, self-addressed envelope (SASE). That goes a long way toward encouraging a response from any author. **Please do not attempt to call me on the telephone.** My telephone number is unlisted, but there is a Carl F. Luckey in the book. That is my father's telephone number. He is retired and doesn't need the hassle of numerous telephone calls. My number has been listed for the past twenty years of my writing career. I did not want to remove it from the directory, but with several hundreds of thousands of my many books about collectibles out there, each containing my address, you can imagine how often my phone began to ring, day and night, weekdays and weekends. I just had to do it. I love to talk, but I have to work!

Happy Collecting!
Carl F. Luckey
Route 4, Box 301
Killen, AL 35645

OTHER BOOKS BY CARL F. LUCKEY

Old Fishing Lures and Tackle (Editions 1-4)
Collector Prints, Old and New
Guide to Collector Prints
The Art of Ferrandiz
Price Guide to Silver and Silverplate and Their Makers
Luckey's Hummel Figurines and Plates (Editions 1-10)
Norman Rockwell Art and Collectibles
Antique Bird Decoys
Collecting Antique Bird Decoys and Duck Calls (Edition 2)
Depression Era Glassware (Editions 1-3)

INTRODUCTION

The interest in Hummel figurines continues to grow with every passing year. Of course, there have been collectors of Hummel figurines and related articles since very soon after they were first offered by Goebel at the Leipzig Trade Fair in March of 1935, but the past seventeen years have seen an incredible surge of interest.

Values skyrocketed for the first ten or twelve of those years, but settled down in the mid-1990s. Indeed, some values have decreased, but these are the exception rather than the rule. In the last few years many collector values of the pieces have more or less leveled off, and others have grown steadily.

The book is for anyone with an interest in the world of Hummel art: the dealer, the collector, anyone owning one or two figurines or someone just contemplating beginning a collection. It is important to state that even though every effort is made to ensure its completeness and accuracy, neither this book nor any other can be an absolute authority at this time. Too much is still unknown. There are too many diverse opinions and too many unknown circumstances surrounding the history of the development, production and marketing of the early Hummel pieces, new variations still being found, pieces not yet uncovered but known to have been produced at least in prototype, and last but not least, unquestionably genuine M.I. Hummel figurines showing up that were never believed to have existed.

This is a collector's guide — just that and no more. It is a *guide,* to be used in conjunction with every bit of other information you may be able to obtain. To that end I not only recommend that you obtain all the other books and publications you can, but list the titles and brief descriptions of them and, when possible, an address where you might obtain them.

The information in this book was obtained from many of the same sources available to collectors, dealers and other writers. It is a compendium of information gleaned from historians, old company and dealer pamphlets, brochures and publications, dealers and collectors themselves, shows and conventions and distributors and writers, and hopefully it will prove useful to all such contributors.

The book contains a short history of W. Goebel Porzellanfabrik, the company that makes Hummel figurines; a biographical sketch of Sister Maria Innocentia Hummel (the artist from whose works virtually all the designs are taken); an explanation of the trademark system and other markings found on the figurines; a glossary of terminology; a description of production techniques; and most important of all, a comprehensive listing of all the pieces themselves. In the tenth edition and this eleventh edition the listings have been considerably expanded to include much information that was not in the first nine editions. Each listing contains at least one photograph of each piece when possible, detailed descriptions of color and mold variations and photos of them when available, current production status, sizes found and available, other remarks of interest, cross-references when of interest, a current market value range and the latest Goebel factory recommended retail price list at the back of the book.

MUSEUMS
AND
INSTITUTIONS

CHAPTER ONE

MUSEUMS AND INSTITUTIONS

THE HUMMEL MUSEUM

This beautiful new facility opened in 1992 in New Braunfels, Texas, just north of San Antonio. It houses, among other things, an approximately 350-piece collection of original paintings and drawings by Sr. Maria Innocentia Hummel, of which fifty have never been published. The collection is on loan from the Nauer family of Switzerland. The Nauer family association with M.I. Hummel goes back four generations to the days when their publishing company was first contacted by the Siessen Convent regarding the publishing of some of Sr. Maria Innocentia's work.

On display is a large exhibit of the current figurines and related collectibles produced by the W. Goebel Porzellanfabrik company, as well as related articles, but the major objective of the museum is to present the artist and exhibit her original art.

To define the artist, her studio and other aspects of her convent life have been recreated. There are also plans for a childrens' art room where young visitors will be encouraged to draw what they have seen in the museum. This is an appropriate and living memorial to her love of children.

Any lover of things Hummel must pay a visit to The Hummel Museum. The address is 199 Main Plaza, New Braunfels, Texas. Mail inquiries to P.O. Box 31100, New Braunfels, Texas 78131-1100. The museum office telephone number is (210) 625-5636. There is a toll-free information line that provides information about on-going museum activities, 1-800-456-4866. Museum hours are 10:00 a.m. to 5:00 p.m., Monday through Saturday and 12:00 noon to 5:00 p.m. on Sundays.

Exterior of The Hummel Museum, New Braunfels, Texas.

Interior view of The Hummel Museum, New Braunfels, Texas.

Interior view of another part of The Hummel Museum.

THE DONALD E. STEPHENS MUSEUM (GOEBEL AND M.I. HUMMEL GALLERY)

The reason for the two names above is that at present there is the Donald E. Stephens Museum only. The Goebel and M.I. Hummel Gallery has been in the planning for about four years. In the fall of 1996 the Volume 20, No. 2 issue of the M.I. Hummel Club *Bulletin Board* said it was "...soon to be constructed..." in Rosemont, Illinois. It is to be located on the grounds of the Exposition Center in the Village of Rosemont, a suburb of Chicago, only five minutes from O'Hare International Airport.

The new 15,000-square-foot building will be large enough to accommodate the Stephens Collection, a display of all current M.I. Hummel products, a facsimile Goebel factory that demonstrates the fashioning of the figurines, a display of other Goebel products, special exhibits and shows, a retail store and an auditorium.

The Donald E. Stephens Museum was opened in 1986 in the Exposition Center. Stephens, long-time mayor of Rosemont, donated his magnificent Hummel collection to the village in 1984 for the purpose of establishing a museum. The museum is probably the largest public display in the world of both the current-production M.I. Hummel items and the old and rare pieces. The collection does not stop there, however: it is constantly expanding. With guidance from the board of directors and with Stephens' expert consulting, the museum continues to seek out and acquire rare pieces.

The Donald E. Stephens Museum is open to the public. The address is Rosemont/O'Hare Exposition Center, South Lobby, 5555 North River Road, Rosemont, Illinois 60018. Museum hours are 9:00 a.m. to 5:00 p.m. Monday through Friday and 10:00 a.m. to 2:00 p.m. on Saturdays. Because of construction and other activities, it is advisable to call first: (847) 692-4000.

Architectural rendering of The Goebel and M.I. Hummel Gallery.

Exterior view of the Donald E. Stephens Museum in Rosemont, Illinois.

Interior view of the Donald E. Stephens Museum.

DAS BERTA-HUMMEL-MUSEUM IM HUMMELHAUS

This museum was opened in July 1994. It is located in the Hummel home in Massing, Bavaria, and was the birthplace of Berta Hummel and her home, before she took her vows to become a nun.

The museum, directed by her nephew Alfred Hummel, houses the largest exhibit of Hummel figurines in Europe. More important is the large collection of paintings and drawings the artist accomplished before entering the convent. The museum and a related pre-existing company have been responsible for the production of several M.I. Hummel collectibles, which are listed elsewhere in this volume.

The museum address is: Das Berta-Hummel-Museum im Hummelhaus, Strasse 2,D - 84323 Massing, Germany. The museum hours: Monday through Saturday, 9:00 a.m. to 5:00 p.m., Sunday 10:00 a.m. to 5:00 p.m.

A view of the entry to the Berta-Hummel-Museum in Massing, Germany.

THE SIESSEN CONVENT-HUMMELSAAL

Sister Maria Innocentia's convent maintains an exhibit of many of her original drawings and paintings. If you are lucky you may be able to see her renderings of the Stations of the Cross in the adjacent chapel. A selection of Hummel postcards and small prints is offered for sale. There is also the opportunity to see her final resting place in the convent cemetery. The convent is a regular stop on the annual club-sponsored tours.

The convent is located just three kilometers out of Saulgau, Southern Germany. The address is Kloster Siessen, D-88348 Saulgau, Germany. The hours of operation are : Monday morning is closed; 2:00 p.m. to 4:00 p.m. Tuesday through Saturday, 10:00 to noon and 2:00 p.m. to 4:00 p.m. on Saturday and 1:30 p.m. to 4:00 p.m. Sunday, 1:30 p.m. to 4:00 p.m. It is best to phone ahead in case of religious celebrations or other unscheduled closings.

SISTER MARIA INNOCENTIA (BERTA) HUMMEL 1909-1946

Sister of the Third Order of Saint Francis
Siessen Convent, Saulgau, Germany

The story of the Hummel figurines is unique. It is practically required reading for those with an interest in the artist, her work and the resulting three-dimensional fine earthenware renditions, the famous Hummel figurines.

These charming but simple figurines of boys and girls easily capture hearts. In them we see, perhaps, our son or daughter, sister or brother, or even ourselves when we were racing along the paths of happy childhood. When you see the School Boy or School Girl you may be taken back to your own school days. Seeing the figurine Culprits could bring back the time when you purloined your first apple from a neighbor's tree and were promptly chased away by his dog. You will delight in the beauty of the Flower Madonna or The Little Shepherd. You will love

An interior view showing some of Berta Hummel's artwork.

An interior view showing childhood and family photos of Berta Hummel.

them all with their little round faces and big questioning eyes. These figurines will collect you and, if you have the collecting tendency, you will undoubtedly want to collect them. You may ask yourself what artist is behind these beguiling figurines. Who is the person with the talent to portray beauty and innocence with such simplicity? The answer is Berta Hummel, a Franciscan sister called Maria Innocentia.

M.J.Hummel ®

Facsimile of the well-known M.I. Hummel signature.

Berta Hummel was born on May 21, 1909, in Massing in lower Bavaria about 40 miles northeast of Munich. She grew up in a family of two brothers and three sisters in a home where music and art were part of everyday life. In this environment her talent for art was encouraged and nourished by her parents.

She attended primary school between 1915 and 1921. During these early years she demonstrated the great imagination so necessary for an artist. She created delightful little cards and printed verses for family celebrations, birthdays, anniversaries and Christmas. Her subjects were almost always the simple objects with which she was familiar: flowers, birds, animals and her friends. In her simple child's world she saw only the beautiful things around her.

When she finished primary school she was enrolled in the Girls Finishing School in Simbach in 1921, in order to nurture and train her talent further and to give her a wider scope of education and experience. Here again her artistic talent was recognized and upon finishing it was decided that she should go to a place where she could further cultivate that talent and realize her desire to pursue art as a vocation. In 1927 Hummel moved to Munich, where she entered the Academy of Fine and Applied Arts. There she lived the life of an artist, made friends and painted to her heart's content. Here at the Academy she acquired full mastery of art history, theory and technique. It was here also that she met two Franciscan sisters who, like herself, attended the Academy.

There is an old adage that art and religion go together. Berta Hummel's life was no exception. She became friends with the two sisters and began to think that this might be the best way to serve. Over time she decided to join the sisters in their pilgrimage for art and God, in spite of the fact that she had been offered a position at the Academy.

For a time Hummel divided her days between her talent for art and her love for humanity and hours of devotion and worship. Then she took the first step into a new life of sacrifice and love: after completing her term as a novice she took the first vows in the Convent of Siessen on August 30, 1934, at the age of 25.

Although Berta Hummel (now Sister Maria Innocentia) gave her life over to an idea she thought greater than any worldly aspiration, the world became the recipient of her wonderful works. Within the walls and the beautiful surroundings of the centuries-old convent, she created the paintings and drawings that were to make her famous. Within these sacred confines her artistic desires enjoyed unbounded impetus.

Little did her superiors dream that this modest blue-eyed artist who had joined their community would someday win worldwide renown. Much less did they realize what financial assistance Hummel's beloved convent would derive from her work as an artist.

During World War II, in 1945, after the French had occupied the region, the noble-minded artist's state of health was broken. On November 6, 1946, at age 37, despite the best care, God summoned her to His eternal home, leaving all her fellow sisters in deep mourning.

Today the M.I. Hummel figurines, modelled according to Sister Maria Innocentia's work, are known all over the world. They are her messengers, bringing pleasure to many, many people.

W. GOEBEL PORZELLANFABRIK

The company was founded in 1871 by Franz Detleff Goebel and his son William Goebel in an area very near Coburg in northern Bavaria. Once known as Oeslau, the village is now known as Rodental. Initially the company manufactured slates, pencils and marbles, and after 1879 it was well into the production of porcelain dinnerware and beer steins. By the mid-1910s a third generation, Max Louis Goebel, had taken the helm of the company and they had begun manufacturing fine earthenware products. His son Franz Goebel became active in the company and the two of them developed a line of porcelain figurines that was well accepted on the international market. Upon Max Louis' death in 1929 Franz took over the running of the company along with his brother-in-law Dr. Eugen Stocke, a trained economist, who was the financial manager of the operation.

By the early 1930s Goebel had gained considerable experience and expertise in fashioning products of porcelain and fine earthenware. Sister Maria Innocentia's art came to the attention of Franz in December of 1933 in Munich, in the form of religious note cards for the Christmas and New Year seasons. These cards were brand new publications of her art by Ars Sacra Josef Muller Verlag. (This company has since evolved into arsEdition, well known to collectors of prints and postcards of Hummel art.) Remarkably, it was in March of the same year that the Siessen Convent had made an unsolicited inquiry of the Josef Muller firm regarding the possibility of reproducing their Sister Maria Innocentia's art.

Once Franz Goebel saw the cards in Munich he conceived the idea of translating them into three-dimensional figurines. He sought and gained permission from the convent and Sister Maria Innocentia Hummel. The original letters rest in the Goebel archives. The letter granting Goebel permission stated plainly that all proposed designs must be pre-approved before the product could be manufactured. This is true to this day: the convent still has the final say as to whether a proposed design is in keeping with the high standards insisted upon by M.I. Hummel.

After Franz Goebel gained permission for the company to produce the figurines it took about a year to model the first examples, make the first molds, experiment with media and make the first models of fine earthenware. They presented the first figurines at the Leipzig Trade Fair in 1935. They were a great success, and by the end of 1935 there were forty-six models in the new line of Hummel figurines.

Production of Hummel figurines and practically everything else in the Goebel lines slowly dwindled during the years of World War II, and toward the end of the war production had ceased altogether. During the American Occupation the United States Military Occupation Government allowed Goebel to resume operation. This of course included the production of their Hummel figurines. During this period the figurines became quite popular among U.S. service men in the occupation forces and upon their return to the States many brought them home as gifts. This engendered a new popularity for Hummel figurines.

Today W. Goebel Porzellanfabrik maintains a large factory complex in Rodental where they manufacture, among many other things, M.I. Hummel figurines and related articles. They maintain a very nice visitor center where they welcome collectors. Visitors are shown a film and then conducted on a short tour to view the manufacturing process in a special demonstration room.

COLLECTORS' GUIDE

COLLECTORS' GUIDE

BUYING AND SELLING

Finding and Buying M.I. Hummel Collectibles

The single most important factor in any collecting discipline is knowledge. Before you spend your hard-earned funds to start or expand a collection it is incumbent upon you to arm yourself with knowledge. If you've bought this book you have made a good start. Now you must study it, learn from it and refer to it often when you're on your hunt. But don't stop there. In chapter 3 is a list of other books and publications dealing with the subject. Some are out of print and no longer readily available, but others are easy to obtain. Get them and study them as well. Be sure you get the latest edition.

In today's market there are many sources, some quite productive and some not so productive, as is true of any collectibles field. Supply and demand is a very important factor in the world of Hummel collecting. We have been through some extraordinary times. Twenty-three years ago I owned a retail business that sold, among other things, Hummel figurines and plates. I had a very difficult time obtaining them in any quantity, never had a choice of pieces and often went for weeks with none in stock. As I remember, we had to order an assortment and there were three monetary levels of assortments. In addition it was often two to three months between ordering them and taking delivery. This was true of almost every retail Hummel dealer in the country. While the rule is still generally no choice for the smaller dealers, production increases have improved over the years to where the number you have to select from at your local dealer is usually pretty good.

Although I was a small dealer I was known to local collectors, and when my small shipment arrived it was usually gone in a matter of days. There was a time in the late 1970s and early 1980s that dealers not only couldn't meet collectors' demands, but kept lists of collectors and what each collector was looking for. The result was most of their stock was pre-sold. What was left would sometimes literally be fought over.

As many of you know, I try to attend most of the shows and conventions that feature Hummel. I will never forget the crowds in those early years of the surge in Hummel popularity. Frequently the dealers would literally be cleaned out before half the show was over, leaving booths empty of all but tables and display fixtures. Even my book was snatched up so rapidly at one show, I was left with none to sell after the first day.

Our economic times have changed all that, but the good news is that the collector now has many sources from which to choose. This is particularly true if you are not specializing in the older trademark pieces. These can be readily found in gift shops, jewelry stores, galleries and shops specializing in collectibles. Even the popular new TV shopping programs feature Hummel figurine sales from time to time. They are also available by mail-order from various dealers around the country, many of whom also deal in the old trademark pieces. The best way to find them is by looking in the various antique and collectible publications (names and addresses of these are listed elsewhere in the book). Many of them have a classified ad section where dealers and collectors alike offer Hummel figurines and related pieces such as plates. The most productive sources, if you can get to them, are the large annual gatherings of dealers and collectors held around the country. Especially if you're trying to find the older-marked pieces, these shows can be a goldmine. But even if you're a collector of the new pieces, attending the shows is fun and a good learning experience. They usually offer lectures and seminars by experts and dealers, all of whom are subject to much "brain-picking" by crowds of collectors. You also have the opportunity to meet other collectors and learn from them. Just be sure to pick the ones with this book under their arm: they are obviously the smartest!

Other than at shows and by mail-order, you can find old trademark pieces in those shops that sell both new and old pieces. There are a few around the country. With the increased awareness of the value of the older mark pieces it is very unlikely but still possible that some smaller, uninformed shops could have a few pieces bearing older trade-

Sometimes there would be 40 or 50 tables like this at a show, all practically empty by the last day.

marks, bought some years ago for sale at whatever the current retail price is for the newer ones.

Bargains? Yes, there are bargains to be found. Sometimes you get lucky at auctions if no one else is looking for the particular figurine you have picked out. That would be a rare occurrence at an all-Hummel auction. Estate auctions and sales and country auctions would be your best bet. By far the best source for bargains are flea markets (especially in Europe), junk shops, attics, basements, relatives, friends, acquaintances and neighbors. In short, anywhere one might find curious old gifts, castaways, etc. For instance, a few years ago I discovered that one of my neighbors has eight older pieces bearing the Full Bee trademark.

These engaging little figurines have, for over 50 years now, been considered a wonderful gift or souvenir. There are so many motifs you can almost always find one that fits a friend's or relative's particular personality, profession or avocation. Until recently they were also relatively inexpensive. So "bone up," and start looking and asking. You may find a real treasure.

The Price to Pay

The province of this book is primarily Hummel figurines and related articles. The preponderance of these collectibles are made by W. Goebel Porzellanfabrik (hereinafter called Goebel) and most of those covered here bear trademarks other than the one currently being used by the company. It is always nice to have a listing of what is currently being produced by Goebel along with the suggested retail prices. There is one printed in the back of the book, but a more portable version printed by Goebel should be available at your nearest dealer.

Licenses have been granted to companies other than Goebel to produce various other items. Most but not all of these items utilize a two-dimensional Hummel design motif. The first and earliest were those who were licensed to produce prints and postcards. Many companies used these prints by applying them to such things as framed pictures, wall plaques and music boxes. These and the more recent releases have yet to develop much of a secondary collector market. For this reason, you will see few of them in this book with a quoted collector value.

There are several factors that influence the actual selling price of the old and the new. The suggested retail price list, released by the company periodically, addresses those pieces bearing the current production trademark. Each time the list is released it reflects changes in the retail price. These changes (usually increases) are due primarily to the basic principle of supply and demand, economic influences of the world money market, ever-increasing material and production costs, the American market demand and last, but certainly not least, an expanding interest in Germany and the rest of the European market.

The list does not necessarily reflect the actual price you may have to pay. Highly popular pieces in limited supply can go higher and some of the less popular pieces can go for less. This has been the case more in the recent past than now, but the phenomenon still occurs.

The value of Hummel figurines, plates, etc. bearing trademarks other than the one currently being used in production is influenced by some of the same factors discussed above, to a greater or lesser extent. The law of supply and demand comes into even more prominent light with regard to pieces bearing the older trademarks, for they are no longer being made and the number on the market is finite. More simply, there are more collectors desiring them than there are available pieces. Generally speaking, the older the trademark the more valuable or desirable the piece. One must realize, however, that this is not a hard and fast rule. In many instances there are larger numbers available of pieces bearing an older mark than there are of pieces bearing later trademarks. If the latter is a more desirable figure and is in much shorter supply, it is perfectly reasonable for it to be more valuable.

Another factor must be considered. The initial find of the rare International Figurines (see chapter 5) saw values shoot up as high as $20,000 each. At first the figures were thought to exist in just eight designs and in only one or two prototypes of each. Over the years several more designs and multiples of the figurines have been found. While they are still quite rare, most bring less than half of the original inflated value. So you see, values can fall as the result of an increase in supply of a rare or uncommon piece. This situation can be brought about artificially as well. If someone secretly buys up and hoards a large quantity of a popular piece for a period of time, the short supply will drive the value up. If that supply is suddenly dumped on the market, demand goes down. This has happened more than once in the past, but not so much now.

Yet another circumstance that *may* influence a fall is the re-issue of a piece previously thought by collectors to be permanently out of production. This has happened because of collectors' past confusion over company terminology with regard to whether a piece was permanently or temporarily withdrawn from production. Many collectors wish to possess a particular item simply because they like it and have no interest in an older trademark version. These collectors will buy the newer piece simply because they can purchase it for less, although recent years have seen the last of the older trademarked pieces go for about the same. It follows naturally that demand for an even older trademark version will lessen under those circumstances.

You may find it surprising that many of the values in the old trademark listing are less than the values reflected in the current Goebel suggested retail price list. You have to realize that serious collectors of old mark Hummel collectibles have very little interest in the price of or the collecting of those pieces currently being produced, except where the list has an influence on the pricing structure of the secondary market. As we have seen, demand softens for some of the later old trademark pieces. That is not to say that those and the current production pieces are not valuable. Quite the contrary. They will be collectible on the secondary market eventually. Time must pass. Make no bones about it, with the changing of the trademarks and the passing of time will come the logical step into the secondary market. The principal market for the last two trademarks is found in the general public, not the seasoned collector. The heaviest trading in the collector market in the past couple of years has been in the Crown and Full Bee trademark pieces. The Stylized Bee and Three Line trademark pieces are currently remaining stable and the Last Bee trademark pieces are experiencing a stagnant market.

Selling M.I. Hummel Collectibles

There is an old saying in the antique and collectibles world that goes like this: "You buy at retail and sell at wholesale." While this is true in some cases, it is most assuredly (and thankfully) not the rule. The axiom can be true if you *must* sell and the only ready buyer is a dealer whose percent discount equals or exceeds the amount your item has appreciated in value. This can also be true if you have consigned your piece to an auction, although auctions usually allow you to set a reserve. A reserve is the lowest price you will sell. If bidding doesn't reach your reserve you still owe the auctioneer his fee, but you get your item back.

There are several other methods of selling, each of which has its own set of advantages and disadvantages.

Selling to a Dealer

The have-to-sell scenario above is an obvious disadvantage, but selling to a dealer will in most cases be a painless experience. If you have been fortunate in your acquisitions and the collection has appreciated considerably, it may also be a profitable encounter. If you are not near the dealer and have to ship, then you run the risk of damage or loss.

Running Sales Ads in your Local Newspaper

Selling to another collector in your local area is probably the easiest and most profitable way to dispose of your piece(s). There is the advantage of personal examination and no shipping risks.

Running Sales Ads in Collector Publications

This is probably the other best way to get best price, as long as the sale is to another collector. The same shipping risks exist here also, and you do have to consider the cost of the ad.

Answer Wanted Ads in Collector Publications

The only risk beyond the usual shipping risks is the possibility of the buyer being disappointed and wishing to return the pieces for a refund.

Local Dealers

If you are fortunate enough to have a dealer near you, they may take consignments for a percentage.

Utilize Collector Club Services

The M.I. Hummel Club runs a Collector's Market for members, where items wanted and items for sale are matched by a computer program. There is no charge for this service beyond membership dues. The club also periodically conducts mail auctions. The address is Dept. CM, M.I. Hummel Club, Goebel Plaza, P.O. Box 11, Pennington, NJ 08534. You must be a member, so if you need the enrollment forms call 1-800-666-2582 or use the membership form in the back of this book.

The Hummel Collector's Club, Inc. publishes a quarterly newsletter in which they run sales and wanted ads, free of charge to members. You respond to these ads by mailing your response to the club. They then forward the response, unopened, to the individuals running the ad. The address for membership is Hummel Collector's Club, P.O. Box 257, Yardley, PA 19067-2857. If you need a membership application write to them or call toll free at 1-888-5-HUMMEL (1-888-548-6635).

PITFALLS YOU MAY ENCOUNTER

The determination of the authenticity of the piece in question is fairly easy in the greatest majority of instances. If you have no reason to suspect the piece of being a fake or forgery and it somewhere bears the incised M.I. Hummel signature, it is probably genuine. In a few instances the piece is simply too small for the incised signature to be placed on it without defacing it. Under these circumstances the company usually places a paper or foil sticker where it is least obtrusive. Often these are lost from the piece over the years, but these small items are few in number and usually readily identifiable by the use of the incised mold number and trademark.

By carefully studying the section on how Goebel utilizes mold numbers on the M.I. Hummel pieces you will gain much more insight into correct identification.

Be ever alert to the trademarks found on pieces and how to interpret them (see "History and Progression of Trademarks"). It is a complicated and sometimes confusing system, and you must know how marks are used and what they mean in order to know what you are buying.

Variations are rampant (see individual listings) in both size, coloration and mold, and you may think you are buying one thing when you're actually getting something quite different.

Concerning the value of broken but expertly restored pieces, they are generally worth one-half or less than the current value of the unbroken "mint" pieces. This value is entirely dependent upon the availability of unbroken mint pieces bearing the same mold number, size designator, and trademark. In the case of a rare piece, however, it is often worth almost as much as the mint piece if expertly restored, due simply to its scarcity. (See the list of restorers in "Care, Protection and Display.")

Crazing is another important factor to keep in mind. Please refer to "Care, Protection and Display" for further discussion of this matter.

Detecting Restored Pieces

It is sometimes difficult or impossible for the average collector to detect an expert restoration of a Hummel figurine or article. The two most reliable methods are (1) examination by long-wave ultraviolet light and (2) examination by X-ray. Until very recently one could rely almost 100% on ultraviolet light examination, but some restorative techniques have been developed in the past few years that are undetectable except by X-ray examination.

Examination by X-ray

Access to X-ray equipment might prove difficult. If you have a good friend who is a doctor or dentist with their own equipment you might be able to get your X-ray by reimbursing expenses. A crack otherwise invisible to the naked eye may appear where the piece has been restored. If the piece does exhibit such a feature, it is safe to assume it is a restored piece. There are some restoration marks, however, that may not show up, so the X-ray examination is not foolproof. The latter represents state-of-the-art restoration.

Examination by Long-wave Ultraviolet Light

When an undamaged piece is exposed to this light, it will appear uniformly light purple in color (the value of the purple will vary with color on the piece). A crack or fracture with glue in it will appear a lighter color (usually orange or pink), patches will appear almost white and most new paint will appear a much, much darker purple.

Non-Hummel Items Made by Goebel

You need to be aware that from 1871, when the company was founded, until 1991, Goebel used the same trademarking system on just about all of its products. In 1991, they changed the system so that now there is a special trademark that is used exclusively on M.I. Hummel items. The older Goebel trademark found on an item is, therefore, not necessarily an indication that it is a Hummel design, only that it *might be*. For further identification use the guidelines described above. You would not believe how many letters I get from folks who think they have a rare Hummel item only to find that they have another of Goebel's many other products.

The reason for including this tea cup here is twofold: first, to illustrate the diversity of the products Goebel has produced and continues to produce. Second, to illustrate how the company used, until 1991, the same trademarks on all of their products. In 1991 they developed a special trademark to be used exclusively on Hummel items from then on.

Display plaque for the Goebel Friar Tuck series. The mold number "WZ 2" is incised and inked in, indicating it is a Mother Mold Piece. It bears the Stylized Bee (TMK-3) mark, a 1959 MID and measures 4-3/4"x 3-7/8".

A Norman Rockwell piece from Goebel. It bears the "ROCK 217" mold number, the Three Line (TMK-4) mark and measures 3-5/8" x 5-1/2".

Two examples of Shrine by Janet Robson. Each bears the Three Line (TMK-4) mark and the mold number ROB 422 incised and inked in, indicating there are Mother Mold Pieces. Both have the incised 1961 MID and measure 5-1/4".

The Seven Dwarfs from the Walt Disney series by Goebel: Snow White and the Seven Dwarfs. They bear various trademarks from Stylized (TMK-3) through the Last Bee (TMK-5) and measure from 2-3/4" to 3".

A non-Hummel figurine made by Goebel. Base markings: "FF 124/l" with a Full Bee trademark and Black Germany.

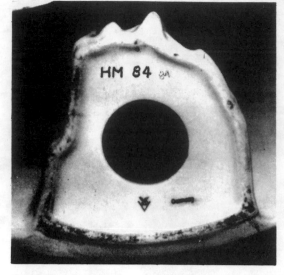

Base marking found on a non-Hummel Madonna made by Goebel. Note: the "HM" letter prefix (enhanced for reproduction with pen and ink).

With Goebel's M.I. Hummel products it is the rule that letter prefixes are not used. When a letter or letters are used they are almost invariably a suffix, placed **after** the incised mold number.

When Goebel marks a non-Hummel item, the mold number usually has a one, two or three letter prefix associated. Following are few examples of the many prefixes and what they mean:

Byj ... Taken from designs by Charlot Byj
Dis ... Taken from Walt Disney characters
FF ... Free standing figure
HM ... Madonna
HX ... Religious figurine
KF ... Whimsical figure

Rob ... Taken from designs by Janet Robson
Rock ... Taken from Norman Rockwell art
Spo ... Taken from designs by Maria Spotl

There are many more than listed here, and the pieces are just as well-made as are the Hummel items and are themselves eminently collectible. They are not Hummel art, however, so be sure before you buy.

There seems to be a developing market for some non-Hummel Goebel products such as the Charlot Byj "Red Heads" (as they are known) and the Little Monk or "Friar

This display plaque for the Charlot Byj Red Head series from Goebel bears the mold number "Byj 47," the Three-Line (TMK-4) mark, a 1966 MID and measures 4-5/8" high.

Plastic imitation of Hum 201, Retreat to Safety. Made in Hong Kong, it appears that the mold for this piece was taken directly from a genuine Hummel figurine.

A non-Hummel figurine made by Goebel. Base markings: Crown and Full Bee trademarks, "FF 124/1 B."

Tuck" pieces. There is already a well-developed secondary market for the Norman Rockwell and Walt Disney character figurines.

Fakes, Forgeries, Imitations and Copies

Fakes and Forgeries

As far as I have been able to determine, there are not yet many blatant forgeries on the market but, as noted earlier, we must be ever aware of the possibility.

Unfortunately there have been a few rather obvious alterations to the trademarks and to the figurines themselves, making them appear older or different from the norm and therefore more valuable. There have been additions or deletions of small parts (i.e. birds, flowers, etc.) to figures. Worse, one or two unscrupulous individuals have been reglazing colored figurines and other articles with a white overglaze to make them appear to be the relatively uncommon to rare all-white pieces. These can sometimes be detected by the serious collector, but it is best left to the experts. Should you purchase a piece that is ultimately proven to be one of these, I know of no reputable dealer who wouldn't replace your figurine if possible. At the very least, the dealer would refund your money.

Imitations, Copies and Reproductions of Original Hummel Pieces

Anyone interested in copies should consult the excellent book *Hummel Copycats* by Lawrence L. Wonsch (see chapter 3). Wonsch shows that the collecting of copycat M.I. Hummels can be fascinating and fun.

There are many reproductions and imitations of the original Hummel pieces, some better than others, but so far all are easily detectable upon the most casual examination if one is reasonably knowledgeable about what constitutes an original.

The most common of these imitations are those produced in Japan. They are similar in design motif but obviously not original when one applies the simplest of rules. See "History and Progression of Trademarks."

Take note of the photo above of Retreat to Safety (Hum 201). To look at the photo is disconcerting because

A plastic imitation Hummel of Hum 197, Be Patient. This is the first I have found with articulating arms.

This 3" imitation appears to be a combination of "Easter Time" and "Playmates." No markings.

A 7" imitation "Strolling Along."

These two 4-1/4" figures are made of plastic and are decidedly inferior. No markings found.

Six Herbert Dubler Figures.

the figure appears to be genuine. When you hold this particular copy in your hand, however, it feels very light and is obviously inferior. Beneath the base is the phrase "Made in Hong Kong." I purchased this plastic copy in a truck stop gift shop in a Midwestern state in 1979 for $3.95. It was probably worth about fifty cents at the time. Over the years I have seen many others. I am told there is a whole series of these plastic copies.

I have seen many other figurines and articles that are obvious attempts at copying the exact design of the genuine article. In every single instance it was immediately detectable as being made of materials and paints severely inferior to the quality exhibited by the real thing. Most are manufactured from a material similar to the plaster or plaster-like substance used in the manufacture of the various prizes one wins at the carnival game booth. Some of these actually bear a sticker proclaiming that they are genuine, authentic or original Hummel pieces.

The Dubler Figures

During World War II the Nazi government did not allow the Goebel company to carry on production of Hummel figurines. During this period a New York firm known as Ars Sacra (a subsidiary of todays Ars Edition in Munich) produced a small collection of figurines very much like the original designs and others in the Hummel style, but not copying any particular design. Those that were Hummel copies usually bore a 5/8" x 1" foil sticker, as reproduced here. They often also had "B. Hummel" and either "ARS SACRA" or "Herbert Dubler, Inc." associated with the signature. Either version was usually incised into the top or side of the base of the figurine. Frequently a copyright date also appears in the same area. In Wonsh's guide *Hummel Copycats* more than 20 of these Dubler figures are pictured. His research indicates the possibility that 61 of these figures were designed and perhaps made.

Most Dubler pieces were made of a chalk-like or plaster of paris-type substance, but a few were rendered in bronze and some have even been found cast in silver. They were ostensibly distributed in the United States by the Crestwick Company of New York. Crestwick later became Hummelwerk, an old U.S. distributing company

Reproduction of ARS SACRA sticker.

Large and heavy bronze figures on marble. Left measures 7" and the other 6-1/2". Incised at the rear of the figures is "Copyright 1942 Herbert Dubler, Inc."

owned by Goebel. They eventually evolved to the present Goebel operations in the U.S.

Another name associated with Dubler was "Decorative Figurines, Inc." These figurines, also made of plaster of paris, were almost exact copies.

These rather pitiful Hummel-like figures bear the inscription "Copyright 1947 Decorative Figurines Corp., the Dubler company."

The English or Beswick Pieces

These interesting pieces are intriguing in that some mystery surrounds their origin. They are usually known collectively as "The English Pieces" by collectors. There has been speculation in the past that they have some claim to legitimacy, but there has never been any hard evidence found to support that claim. The backstamp "BESWICK-ENGLAND" indicates they were made by an old and respected English porcelain manufacturer that was later bought out by Royal Doulton. Inquiries to Royal Doulton were fruitless for they could find no reference to the pieces in what records of Beswick that were obtained when they bought the company.

English/Beswick backstamp.

There have been twelve different designs identified with or without the Beswick backstamp, M.I. Hummel incised signature and other markings. The mold numbers are 903 through 914. The number 907 model has never been found. The list follows:

903 Trumpet Boy
904 Book Worm
905 Goose Girl
906 Strolling Along
907 ??????
908 Stormy Weather
909 Puppy Love
910 Meditation
911 Max and Moritz
912 Farm Boy
913 Globe Trotter
914 Shepherd's Boy

The figurines are shiny and brightly colored in the faience tradition. Most of them bear the inscription "Original Hummel Studios Copyright" in script letters (see drawings above) and some version of the Beswick backstamp. Most, but not all, also bear an incised M.I. Hummel signature along with the base inscriptions described above, and there have been some found with no markings at all. All are sought eagerly by many serious collectors. The collector value range of those bearing the signature is $800-1,000.

English/Beswick Strolling Along (906).

English/Beswick pieces. Left to right with their incised mold numbers: Meditation (910); Trumpet Boy (903); Puppy Love (909).

English/Beswick Shepherd's Boy (914).

English/Beswick Farm Boy (912).

HISTORY AND EXPLANATION OF TRADEMARKS

Since 1934-35 there have been several changes in the trademarks used by the Goebel company on M.I. Hummel items. In later years of production each new trademark design merely replaced the old one, but in the earlier years frequently the new design trademark would be placed on a figurine that already bore the older style trademark. In some cases a change from an incised trademark to a surface stamped version of the same mark would result in both appearing on the figure. The former represents a transition period from older to newer and the latter resulted in what are called "Double Crown." This section is meant to give you an illustrated guide to the major trademarks and their evolution to the trademark presently used on Goebel-produced M.I. Hummel items.

Many subtle differences will not be covered because they serve no significant purpose in identifying the era in which an item was produced. There are, however, a few that do help to date a piece. These will be discussed and illustrated. The dates of the early trademark changes are approximate in some cases, but probably accurate to within five years or so. Please bear in mind that the dates, although mostly derived from company records, are not necessarily as definite as they appear. There are documented examples where pieces vary from the stated years both earlier and later. A number of words and phrases associated with various trademarks can in some cases help to date a piece.

NOTE: It is imperative that you understand that the various trademarks illustrated and discussed here have been used by Goebel on *all* of their products, not just Hummel items, until about mid-1991, when a new mark was developed exclusively for use on M.I. Hummel items.

The Crown Mark (TMK-1, CM): 1934-1950

The Crown Mark (TMK-1 or CM), sometimes referred to as the "Crown-WG," was used by Goebel on all of its products in 1935, when M.I. Hummel figurines were first made commercially available. Subtle variations have been noted, but the illustration above is all you need to identify the trademark. Those subtle differences are of no important significance to the collector. The letters WG below the crown in the mark are the initials of William Goebel, one of the founders of the company. The crown signifies his loyalty to the imperial family of Germany at the time of the mark's design, around 1900. The mark is sometimes found in an incised circle.

Another Crown-type mark is sometimes confusing to collectors: some refer to it as the "Narrow Crown" and others the "Wide Ducal Crown." This mark was introduced by Goebel in 1937 and used on many of their products. They call it the Wide Ducal Crown mark, so we shall adopt this name as well to alleviate confusion. To date most dealers and collectors have thought this mark was never found on a M.I. Hummel piece. The author certainly has never heard of its occurrence. Goebel, however, in their newsletter *Insights* (Vol. 14, No. 3, pg. 8) states that the mark was used "...rarely on figurines" so we will defer to them and assume there might be some out there somewhere.

Often, as stated earlier, the Crown Mark will appear twice on the same piece, more often one mark incised and the other stamped. This is, as we know, the "Double Crown."

When World War II ended and the United States Occupation Forces allowed Goebel to begin exporting, the pieces were marked as having been made in the occupied zone. The various forms and phrases to be found in this regard are illustrated on page 32.

These marks were applied to the bases of the figurines, along with the other markings, over the years 1946-1948. They were sometimes applied under the glaze and often over the glaze. The latter were easily lost over the years through wear and cleaning if the owner was not careful. About 1948-49 the U.S. Zone mark requirement was dropped and the word "Germany" took its place. With the partitioning of Germany into East and West, "W. Germany," "West Germany" or "Western Germany" began to appear most of the time instead.

Until the early 1950s the company occasionally used a WG or a WG to the right of the incised M.I. Hummel signature.

Incised Crown
Mark

Stamped Crown
Mark

Wide Ducal Crown
Mark

M.J. Hummel © 〰

The Hummel signature as a base rim marking.

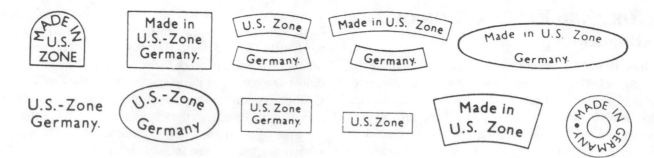

Various base markings from the 1940s.

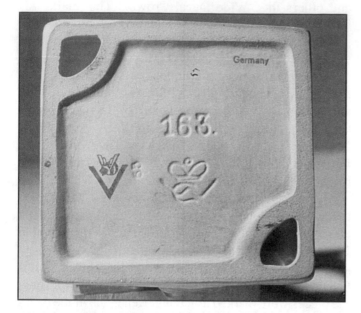

The base of Hum 163 illustrating the incised Crown Mark and the stamped Full Bee trademark. Note also the use of the decimal designator with the incised mold number.

When found the signature is usually placed on the edge of or the vertical edge of the base. Some have been known to confuse this with the Crown Mark (TMK- 1) when in fact it is not.

The Bee Marks: 1950-1979

In 1950 the Goebel company made a major change in their trademark. They incorporated a bee in a V. It is thought that the bumblebee part of the mark was derived from a childhood nickname of Sister Maria Innocentia Hummel, meaning bumblebee. The bee flies within a V, which is the first letter of the German word for distributing company, *Verkaufsgesellschaft*. The mark was to honor M.I. Hummel, who died in 1946.

The incised Full Bee

The Stamped Full Bee

There are actually twelve variations of the Bee marks to be found on Goebel-produced M.I. Hummel items, but some are grouped together as the differences between them are not considered particularly significant. They will be detailed as a matter of interest.

The High Bee

The Small Bee - Note that the bee's wingtips are level with the top of the V.

The Baby Bee

The Vee Bee

The Full Bee (TMK-2, FB): 1940-1959

The Full Bee mark, also referred to as TMK-2 or abbreviated FB, is the first of the Bee marks to appear. The mark evolved over almost twenty years until the company began to modernize it. It is sometimes found in an incised circle. The history of the transition and illustrations of each major change follows. Each of them are still considered to be the Full Bee (TMK-2).

The very large bee flying in the V remained until around 1956, when the bee was reduced in size and lowered into the V. It can be found incised, stamped in black or stamped in blue, in that order, through its evolution.

The Stylized Bee (TMK-3, Sty-Bee): 1960-1972

A major change in the way the bee is rendered in the trademark made its appearance in 1960. The Stylized Bee (TMK-3), sometimes abbreviated as Sty-Bee when written, as the major component of the trademark appeared in three basic forms through 1972. The first two are both classified as the Stylized Bee (TMK-3), but the third is considered a fourth step in the evolution, the Three Line Mark (TMK-4). It might interest you to know that Goebel re-used the Crown-WG backstamp from 1969 until 1972. It is not always there, but when it shows it is a small blue decal application. This was done to protect Geobel's copyright of the mark. It otherwise would have run out.

The Large Stylized Bee

The Large Stylized Bee. This trademark was used primarily from 1960 through 1963. Notice in the illustration that the "W. Germany" is placed to the right of the bottom of the V. The color of the mark will be black or blue. It is sometimes found inside an incised circle. When you find the Large Stylized Bee mark, you will normally find a stamped "West" or "Western Germany" in black elsewhere on the base, but not always.

Small Stylized Bee

The Small Stylized Bee. This mark is also considered to be TMK-3. It was used concurrently with the Large Stylized Bee from about 1960 and continued in this use until about 1972. Note in the illustration the "W. Germany" appears centered beneath the V and Bee. The mark is usually rendered in blue and it too is often accompanied by a stamped black West or Western Germany. The mark is sometimes referred to by collectors and dealers as the One Line Mark.

The Three Line Mark (TMK-4)

This trademark is sometimes abbreviated 3-line or 3LM in print. The trademark used the same stylized V and Bee as the others, but also included three lines of wording beside it, as you can see. This major change appeared in blue color.

Three Line Mark

The Goebel Bee or The Last Bee Mark (TMK-5): 1972-1979

Actually developed and occasionally used as early as 1970, this major change is known by some collectors as the Last Bee mark because the next change in the trademark no longer incorporated any form of the V and the bee. The mark was used until about mid-1979, when they began to phase it out, completing the transition to the new trademark in 1980. There are three minor variations in the mark shown in the illustration. Generally the mark was placed under the glaze from 1972-1976 and is found placed over the glaze 1976-1979.

Last Bee Mark

The Missing Bee Mark (TMK-6): 1979-1991

The transition to this trademark began in 1979 and was complete by mid-1980. As you can see Goebel removed the V and bee from the mark altogether. Many dealers and collectors lamented the passing of the traditional stylized V and bee and for a while called the mark the Missing Bee. In conjunction with this change, the company instituted the practice of adding to the traditional artist's mark the date the artist finished painting the piece. Because the white overglaze pieces are not usually painted, it would be reasonable to assume that the date is omitted on them.

Missing Bee Mark

The Hummel Mark (TMK-7): 1991-Present

In 1991 Goebel made a move of historical import. They changed the trademark once again. This time the change was not only symbolic of the reunification of the two Germanies by removal of the "West" from the mark, but very significant in another way. Until then they used the same trademark on virtually all of their products. The mark illustrated here is for exclusive use on Goebel products made from the paintings and drawings of M.I. Hummel. Other Goebel products will bear a different mark than that used on Hummel pieces.

Hummel Mark

Other Marks Associated with the Trademarks

There are marks in addition to the U.S. Zone marks already covered that are to be found on the bases and backs of Goebel Hummel items.

First of all there are several colors of marks that you may encounter. The colors found to date are black, purple, red, brown, green and blue.

The color blue has been used exclusively since 1972. There also have been several combinations of colors found.

The following list contains various words and marks found associated with the trademarks. There are probably more to be discovered, but these are representative.

W. Germany - by W. Goebel (in script)

Anniversary backstamp

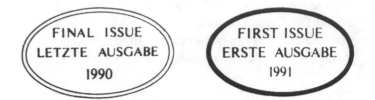

Final issue and first issue stamps

W. Germany - W. Goebel (in script)

W. Goebel mark in script

GERMANY - Copr. W. Goebel
Germany - by W. Goebel, Oeslau 1957
WEST GERMANY - *II Gbl. 1948
West Germany - OCCUPIED GERMANY
WESTERN GERMANY - Western Germany

First Issue, Final Issue and 125th Anniversary Backstamps

Starting in 1990 Goebel began stamping any newly issued piece with the words "First Issue," during the first year of production only. In 1991 they began doing the same thing during the last year before retiring a piece, by marking each with the words "Final Issue." The words are also accompanied by the appropriate year date. The stamps are illustrated for you here. The first piece to bear the Final Issue backstamp was Hum 203, Signs of Spring, in both sizes. The final issue pieces will also be sold with a commemorative retirement medallion hung around them.

Goebel's 125th anniversary was in 1996, and all figures produced in that year bear the special backstamp.

The Goebel Mold Number and Size Designator System

Mold Numbers

All Goebel-made Hummel items are made by the use of molds and each unique mold is assigned a number. The number is part of the mold and it, along with the size designator, becomes a part of the finished piece. It is generally incised on the underside of the base, but for practical reasons may appear elsewhere on the item.

Until the mid-1980s it was thought by most collectors that the highest mold number normally used in production was in the mid-400s. Time and extensive research by writers, dealers and serious collectors revealed, among other things, that the number in the Goebel design pool most likely exceeds 1000 by a great deal. A large number of these have not yet been put into production and those planned are designated Possible Future Editions (PFE) by Goebel. A few of these (presumably in sample form) have somehow found their way into the collector market, but the occurrence is exceedingly rare. When a PFE becomes a production piece, the earlier PFE example almost always bears an earlier trademark than the mark found on the production piece. It, therefore, retains its unique status. Of the remaining designs, some may be PFE's and some may never make it into the collection. The highest mold number used so far is 2002, but the next highest is only 795. There are many numbers below 795 that have not yet been used. There is no explanation for that 2002 as yet.

NOTE: Before we get into the explanation of the mold number system let's eliminate the source of one area of confusion. Some price lists (including the one from Goebel) show an odd letter or number preceded by a slash mark associated with some Hummel mold numbers. Example: Flower Madonna, 10/I/W. The "W" and the slash are price list indications that this piece is finished in all white. The actual mold number found incised on the piece is "10/1" only. The "/W," meaning white overglaze finish, and the "/11" or "/6," meaning the normal color finish, are the decor indicators found in some of today's price lists. Remember that they are not part of the mold number.

The Size Designator Portion of the Mold Number

While the mold number as discussed above was treated as separate from the size designator system, in reality the two comprise what is sometimes called the Hummel number (Hum number), but more commonly, the mold number. It seems complicated, but isn't really if you factor out Goebel's occasional departure from the rules.

The system has changed little over the years, but has been modified once or twice.

Beginning with the first piece in 1934-35 and continuing to about 1952, the first size of a particular piece produced was considered by the factory to be the "standard" size. If plans were to produce a smaller or larger version, the factory would place an "O" or a decimal point after the model or mold number. Frequently, but not always, the "O" would be separated from the mold number by the placing of a slash mark (/) between them. There are many cases where the "O" or decimal point do not appear. Apparently this signified that at the time there were no plans to produce other sizes of the same piece. In the case of Hum 1, Puppy Love, there exists only one "standard" size and no size designator has ever been found on the figure. It is reasonable to assume, however, that subsequent changes in production plans would result in other sizes being produced. Therefore the absence of the "O" or decimal point is not a reliable indicator that there exists only one standard size of the particular piece. In fact, there are some instances where later versions of a piece have been found bearing the "slash O," decimal point, and even a "slash I," which are smaller than the "standard" for that piece. In some cases the decimal point appears along with the slash mark. I have seen the figurine Village Boy (Hum 51) marked thus: "51./O." It could be that when they changed to the slash designator, they just didn't remove the decimal from the mold, but how do you explain the decimal point following the "O"?

The factory used Roman numerals or Arabic numbers in conjunction with the mold numbers to indicate larger or smaller sizes than the standard.

The best way for the collector to understand the system is by example. The figure Village Boy (Hum 51), has been produced in four different sizes.

Example 51/0

The number 51 tells us that this is the figurine Village Boy and the "/0" indicates that it is the first size produced, therefore the standard size. In this case the size of the piece is roughly 6". The presence of the "/0" (or of a decimal point) is also an indication that the figurine was produced sometime prior to 1952.

As discussed earlier, not all the figures produced prior to 1952 were designated with the "slash 0" or decimal point, but if present it is a great help in beginning to date a figure. The one exception currently known is the discontinuance of the use of the "slash 0" designator on Hum 353, Spring Dance. It was produced with the 353/0 mold and size designator about 1963, taken out of current production later and recently reinstated once more.

By checking the reference for Hum 51, you will note there exist three more sizes: Hum 51/I/O, Hum 51/3/0 and Hum 51/1. Roman numerals are normally used to denote sizes larger than the standard and Arabic numbers indicate sizes smaller than the standard. When utilized in the normal manner, the Arabic number is always found to the left of the "O" designator. There are two exceptions to this norm, one specific, the other general. The specific known exception is Heavenly Angel, Hum 21/0/1/2. This is one of only two known instances of the use of a fractional size designator. The last two numbers are incised and read as one-half (1/2). The general exception is the occasional use of an Arabic number in the same manner as the Roman numeral. The Roman numeral size indicator is never used with the "O" designator present, and the Arabic number is never normally used without the "O" designator. Therefore, if you were to find a mold number 51/2, you would know to read it 51/II and that it represents a piece larger than the standard.

Note: After the mold for Hum 218 (Birthday Serenade), the use of the "slash 0" size designator was eliminated. The mold number (51/II) does not exist. It is used here for illustrative purposes only.

Example 51/1

As before, the number 51 identifies the piece for us. The addition of the "/1" tells us that this is larger figure than the standard. In this case it is about one inch larger.

Example 51/2/0 and 51/3/0

Once again we know the identity of the piece is Hum 51, Village Boy. In both cases there is an Arabic number, the mold number and the "/0," therefore we can assume both are smaller than the standard. The 51/2/0 is smaller than 5" and the 51/3/0 is even smaller still.

The "O" and decimal point size designators are no longer in use. Keeping in mind the cited exceptions, we can usually assume that a figure with the mold number and no accompanying Arabic or Roman numerals is the standard size for that model. If the mold number is accompanied by Roman numerals the figure is a larger size, ascending to larger sizes the higher the numeral.

There seems to be no set standard size or set increase in size for each of the Arabic or Roman numeral size designators used in the collection. The designators are individually specific to each model and bear no relation to the designators on other models.

Additional Designators

There are a number of pieces in the collection: table lamps, candy boxes, bookends, ashtrays, fonts, plaques, music boxes, candleholders, plates and sets of figures, some of which have additional or different designators. A list follows, with explanations of how each is marked.

Table Lamps are numbered in the traditional manner. Some later price lists show the number preceded by an "M." Example: M/285.

Candy Boxes (Candy Bowls) are covered cylindrical deep bowls, the cover being topped with one of the Hummel figures. They are numbered with the appropriate mold number for the figure and preceded with the Roman numeral 111. Example: "111/57" is a candy box topped with Hum 57, Chick Girl.

Bookends are both large figures with provisions for weighting with sand and smaller figures placed on wooden bookend bases. The only sand-weighted bookends are the Book Worms. The designation for a bookend is accomplished by placing A and III after the assigned Hummel mold number for the bookends. Example: Hum 61/A and Hum 61/B are a set of bookends utilizing Hum 58 and Hum 47, Playmates and Chick Girl. These are the current designations. In some cases if the figurines are removed from the bookend bases they are indistinguishable from a regular figurine.

Ashtrays are numbered in the traditional manner.

Fonts are numbered in the traditional manner. Exception: There is a font, Hum 91 (Angel at Prayer), in two versions. One faces left, the other right. They are numbered 91/A and 91/B respectively.

Plaques are numbered in the traditional manner.

Music Boxes are round wooden containers in which there is a music box movement, topped with a traditional Hummel model that rotates as the music plays. The catalog and price list number for the music box is the Hummel number for the piece on the box followed by the letter "M." If the figure is removed from the top it will not have the "M" but will be marked in the traditional manner.

Candleholders are numbered in the traditional manner. They sometimes have Roman numerals to the left of the model designator in price lists. These indicate candle size: I = 0.6 cm, II = 1.0 cm.

Plates are numbered in the traditional manner. To date, none have been produced with the size designator, only the mold number.

Sets of figures are numbered with one model number sequence and followed by the designation /A, /B, /C ... /Z, to indicate each figure is part of one set. Example: The Nativity Set 214 contains 15 Hummel figures, numbers 214/A, 214/B, 214/C, and so on. In the case of Nativity Sets there are some letters that are not used. The letters I and Q are not utilized because of the possibility of confusing them with the Roman numeral I or Arabic I and 0.

Some Additional Notes on Special Markings

Sets

Any time there have been two or more pieces in the collection that were meant to be matched as a pair or set, the alphabetical listings A through Z are respectively applied to the Hummel mold numbers in some way. Exception: Sometimes called the "Little Band" are the three figures: Hum 389, Hum 390 and Hum 391. They do not bear the A, B, C designating them as a set. The piece actually entitled "Little Band" is Hum 392, an incorporation of these three figures on one base together. References to the "Little Band" and the "Eight Piece Orchestra" are occasionally found in price lists that include Hummel Numbers 2/0, 1/I, 89/I, 89/II, 129, 389, 390 and 391. A charming group, but not officially a set.

Mold Induction Dates

The year date incised on the base of many M.I. Hummel pieces is the source of much confusion to some collectors. The year date is the mold induction date (MID). The MID is the date the original mold for that particular piece was made and not the date the piece was made. It bears no relationship whatsoever with the date of making the item, only the mold. As a matter of fact there are many molds that are years old and still being used to make figures today. The MID doesn't always appear on the older pieces, but all those currently being made will have it.

Example of a mold induction date (MID)

THE MAKING OF M.I. HUMMEL FIGURINES AND PLATES BY GOEBEL

The question most asked by those uninitiated to the Hummel world is "Why do they cost so much?" It is not an unreasonable question and the answer can be simply that they are handmade. That, however, really doesn't do justice to the true story. The making of Hummel pieces is immensely complex; truly a hand operation from start to finish. The process requires no less than seven hundred steps! Those few of you who have been lucky enough to visit Goebel's northern Bavaria facility know how complicated the operation is. Others of you who have seen the Goebel film and/or visited the facsimile factory on its 1985 U.S. tour have a pretty good idea.

To call the facility a factory is misleading, for the word factory causes the majority of us to conjure up an image of machinery and automated assembly lines. It is not that at all. It is an enormous artists' and artisans' studio and workshop complete with friendly relaxed surroundings including good music, hanging baskets and potted plants. In short, it is a pleasant place to create and work. It is packed with highly trained and skilled artists and craftsmen. Each of them must undergo a full three-year apprenticeship before actually taking part in the fashioning of the figurines and other items that are made available to the collector. This apprenticeship is required no matter whether the worker is a mold-maker or painter. Each specialist in the process must understand the duties of the others.

Goebel's Master Sculptor Gerhard Skrobek sculpting the figurine Ring Around the Rosie, Hum 348. Photo courtesy M.I. Hummel Club

There is insufficient space to elaborate on all seven hundred steps involved, so I have grouped them into six basic areas: Sculpting the Master Model, Mother or Master Mold Making, Molding the Pieces, Bisque Firing, Glaze Firing, and last, Painting and Decorating (decor firing).

1. Sculpting the Master Model

It is estimated that there are 1200 to 1500 M.I. Hummel artworks from which Goebel may choose to render into a three-dimensional figurine or other item. Once a piece of art is chosen a master sculptor fashions a model in a water-based Bavarian black clay. This is a long process during which the artists must not just reproduce the art but interpret it. They must visualize, for instance, what the back of the piece must look like and sculpt it as they think M.I. Hummel would have rendered it. Once the wax model is deemed acceptable it is taken to the Siessen Convent where it is presented for approval or disapproval. If the preliminary model is approved it is then taken back to Goebel for the next step.

2. Master or Mother Mold Making

A figurine cannot be made from a single mold because of its complexity. Therefore, after a very careful study of the wax model, it is strategically cut into several pieces. Some figurines must be cut into as many as thirty pieces for molding. For example, Hum 396 (Ride into Christmas)

Body of Goose Girl embedded in wax on oval base. Preparatory to surrounding with flexible plastic for containing the plaster of paris after pouring.

Result of the pouring of plaster of paris. The wax body has not yet been removed. Note the key slots. The one on the right is still in process of being carved out.

had to be cut into twelve separate pieces and Hum 47 (Goose Girl) into seven.

Using the Goose Girl's seven pieces, we continue. Each of the seven are placed on a round or oval base and secured with more clay. The base is then surrounded by a piece of flexible plastic that extends above the piece to be molded. Liquid plaster of paris is then poured into it. The dry plaster of paris is removed, resulting in an impression of the part. This process must be repeated for the other six parts. After each of the seven parts are molded the result is fourteen separate mold halves. From these are made the mother (sometimes called master) molds. These are made from an acrylic resin. The mother molds are cream-colored and very durable. It is from the mother molds that the working molds are made. The plaster of paris working molds can be used only about twenty times, at which time a new set must be made from the mother molds.

Before full production of a new figure is commenced, a few samples are made. The figure must again be carried to the Siessen Convent for approval, rejection or recommendations for changes. Once final approval is given, the piece is ready for production. That could be immediately or years later.

The Master or Mother Mold.

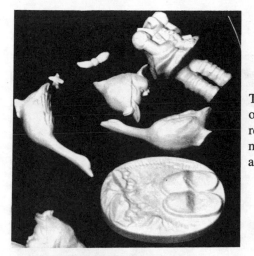

The seven pieces of Goose Girl after removal from the molds and prior to assembly.

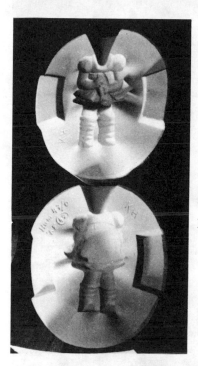

The two halves of a plaster of Paris working mold. Note the keys left and right. These insure accuracy of fitting the two halves together for pouring the piece.

3. Molding and Assembly of the Pieces

All the pieces in the collection are made of fine earthenware, consisting of a mixture of feldspar, kaolin and quartz. It is the finest earthenware available. Both porcelain and earthenware come under the definition of ceramic. Add just a bit more kaolin and the earthenware would become porcelain. Goebel chooses to use earthenware because of its inherent softness. That softness is considered best for Hummel items.

The liquid mixture of the three ingredients plus water is called slip. The slip is poured into the working molds and left for a period of time. The porous character of the plaster of paris acts like a sponge and draws moisture out

of the slip. After a carefully monitored time the remaining slip is poured out of the mold, leaving a hollow shell of the desired thickness. The parts are removed from the molds and while still damp are assembled, using the slip as a sort of glue. The assembled piece is then refined: all seams and imperfections are removed and the more subtle areas are detailed. The piece is then set aside to dry for about a week.

4. The Bisque Firing

Bisque is fired, unglazed ceramic. The dry assembled pieces are gathered together and fired in a kiln for eighteen hours at 2100 degrees Fahrenheit. This results in a white, unglazed bisque figurine.

The assembled, refined piece prior to bisque firing.

The tinted piece prior to glaze firing

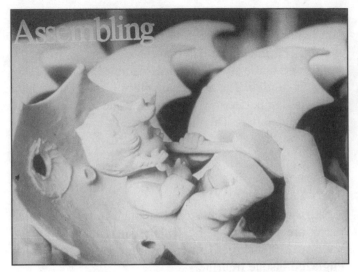

Assembling the cast parts prior to drying and bisque firing. Umbrella Girl, Hum 152/B. Photo courtesy M.I. Hummel Club.

Pouring the slip into the mold. Photo courtesy M.I. Hummel

Refining the assembled pieces prior to the first firing.

Several hundred assembled figurines just prior to the bisque firing. The various racks and shelves upon which they rest are called "furniture."

A row of kilns at the factory

Appearance of the Goose Girl after bisque firing. Photo courtesy M.I. Hummel Club.

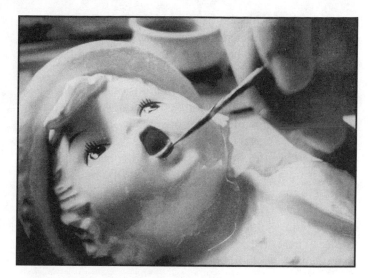

Hand-painting a face. Photo courtesy M.I. Hummel Club.

5. The Glaze Firing

The bisque-fired pieces are then dipped into a tinted glaze mixture. The glaze is tinted to assure that the whole piece is covered with the mixture. The tint is usually green, therefore any uncovered area will show up white. The dipped pieces are then fired at 1872 degrees Fahrenheit. When removed from the kiln after cooling, they are a shiny white.

6. The Painting and Decorating

The colors are mixed in small amounts and given to the painters only as needed. Some of the colors react to each other upon firing, so oftentimes the item must be painted with one or a few colors and fired before others

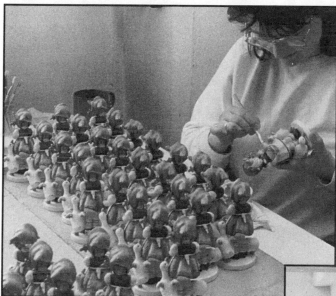

One of the final steps of decorating prior to decor firing.

One of the light and cheerful studios where artists paint the figurines.

can be applied. This results in multiple decor firings before the pieces are finished. In some cases up to ten separate firings are required before they are finished and ready for distribution.

As you can see now, the making of the pieces is a long, involved and painstaking operation. As noted earlier there are 700 separate operations, the workers are highly trained and experienced, and there are twenty-five different quality control inspection points. In spite of this each figure is unique because it is the result of a manual operation. No matter how a piece is assembled or painted, no matter how experienced a worker is, he or she is still a human being, inherently incapable of creating identical copies. That is part of the magic. Each piece is a joy, each unique, each a handmade work of art.

CARE, DISPLAY AND PROTECTION

Caring for Your Collection

Direct sunlight

The first consideration is the potential damage from direct sunlight. It can wreak havoc on just about any type of collectible, including kiln-fired colors on the pieces and the decals under the glaze. Once this occurs the damage is irreversible. Some of the older figurines are much more susceptible to this than the newer ones. A few have discolored somewhat due to environmental and atmospheric pollution. In the early years the pigments used in the paints, while the finest available at the time, were not as durable and lasting as those used today and were more sensitive to the caustic elements of air pollution.

Crazing

Crazing is defined as fine cracks in the glaze of ceramics, normally unintentional, resulting from the unequal shrinking of the glaze and the body of the object. It is manifest as a "crackle-look" finish or a fine, intricate web of what appear to be cracks in the glaze of a ceramic piece. This phenomenon is apparently inherent in the ceramic arts and is most likely to occur in older pieces, but can occur in newer ones as well. In the introduction of *World Ceramics* (1968, Hamlyn Publishing Group, Ltd.) editor Robert J. Charleston says "A glaze must be suited to the body of the pot which it covers, or it may crack..." Fired earthenware is quite porous and can absorb moisture if not *completely* covered by a suitable glaze. It is of paramount importance that the earthenware body and its glaze expand and contract uniformly. If they don't it can result in crazing. Heretofore

it had been thought that crazing was irreversible, so some accept its presence as an aesthetic charm. In fact, in some circles it is accepted as proof of antiquity. Most all ancient Chinese ceramics exhibit crazing.

In recent years ceramicists have been studying crazing to discover whether it might be reversible after all. It now seems that the malady is curable. Those of you who are members of the Hummel Collector's Club, Inc. are already aware of this. In 1996 they announced in their newsletter that they had found a company that had developed a procedure for the reversal of crazing, for whom they are presently acting as an agent. They and one other company claiming successful reversal of crazing are listed below. If you wish to use their services be sure to understand their terms, conditions, guarantees and cost before proceeding.

Crazing and its Effect on Collector Values. Another very important aspect to crazing is how it can affect the collector value of a piece. As stated before some collectors don't mind crazing unless it is apparent to the extent that it detracts from the inherent beauty or appeal of the figurine. In 1996, Dorothy Dous of the Hummel Collector's Club, Inc. published in the club newsletter a chart that is a subjective quantification of the amount of crazing and the corresponding percentage devaluation of a Hummel figurine. I have spoken to other dealers and they all feel that the Dous chart is a realistic evaluation of a crazed piece. It is predicated upon an observation of the piece in question with normal vision (presumably the naked eye or with corrected vision) from a distance of eighteen (18) inches. There are three levels of condition:

None ... No apparent crazing.

Light ... No crazing visible from a distance of eighteen inches.

Severe ... Crazing visible to the naked eye from a distance of eighteen inches.

These conditions are further defined as to the percent of devaluation according to the following criteria:

Crazing Location	Percent Devaluation	
	Light	Severe
Beneath base only	25%	30%
On top of base only	35%	40%
Beneath and top of base only	45%	50%
Figurine only, excluding face	50%	55%
Figurine only, including face	60%	65%
Total figurine excluding face	70%	75%
Total figurine including face	75%	80%

Example: Viewing a figurine worth $450 from eighteen inches you observe that crazing is not apparent anywhere on it. When you examine it more closely, however, you detect some crazing beneath and on top of the base. Under this system the piece would be considered to have *light* crazing and be devalued by 45%. If it is devalued by 45%, it is, therefore, worth 55% of its value in uncrazed condition.

Collector Value = .55 x $450 = $247.50

Values After Craze Reversal. Most collectors seem quite pleased with their figurines after craze reversal and would not consider them worth any less than if they were in normal uncrazed condition. All figurines undergoing this process are noticeable improved, most often resulting in complete elimination of crazing. There is a very small chance that a bit of crazing may still detectible in some cases upon close examination. The other result is that often the figurines will come through the process with a slightly higher sheen. This should not bother most collectors. The collector value of de-crazed pieces is, in the final analysis, a subject conditional to the individuals involved. Most dealers and collectors, however, consider the value to be that of a normal unprocessed piece of comparable uncrazed condition.

Some Display Tips to Help Prevent Crazing. While no one can guarantee the prevention of crazing nor of its re-occurrence after craze reversal, there are some precautions that you should be aware of.

1. Heat or cold can exacerbate crazing tendency, so avoid any circumstances where your pieces would be subject to heat or cold extremes.
2. A sudden change in temperature can do the same thing.
3. Avoid air pollution if possible.
4. Avoid excessive handling.
5. When cleaning by immersion in water or any other solution, try to prevent entry through air-holes. Tape them or otherwise block them somehow. If you do get liquid inside, allow the pieces to air dry for a long time before placing them back on display. Be sure to remove whatever you used to block the airholes.

Cleaning

A simple periodic dusting of earthenware or ceramic pieces is always a good idea, but occasionally they may need a little freshening up. Through the M.I. Hummel Club Goebel sells an M.I. Hummel Care Kit that consists of two specially formulated cleaning solutions and some brushes, all designed specifically with earthenware, ceramic and porcelain collectibles in mind. It also includes an instruction booklet.

Should you not wish to order the kit you can still clean your items. Use your kitchen sink or a similar large vessel. Line it with a towel or other soft material to minimize the possibility of breakage when handling your figure. Make up a solution of barely warm water and a mild soap such as baby shampoo. Cover the airhole(s) with tape or by some other method. Dip the piece in the solution and scrub gently with a very soft toothbrush or similar soft bristle brush, all the while holding it over the towel-lined sink. Rinse it off here also. It may take more than one washing if the piece is heavily soiled. Dab it with a soft, absorbent cloth and place on the same type of surface to air dry. Should you be unable to avoid getting water inside the figure, it may take quite some time to dry out.

Many knowledgeable dealers and collectors use strong detergents without harm, but I would be reluctant to use them as they may contain chemicals or other harsh additives that could be incompatible with the finish. At the very least, you may lose some of the base markings.

If while handling your figures you notice a tinkling or rattling sound, don't worry. When the figure is being made sometimes a small piece comes loose inside the figure and rattles around. Sometimes, depending on the shape and design of the figure, you can stop this by injecting a little household glue into the interior of the figure through the airhole(s) and shaking it until the rattle stops. Place it on its side until it dries. Presto! No more rattle.

Cleaning paper collectibles beyond dusting is not recommended. If you are fortunate enough to own an original drawing or painting, proper archival framing and care of the frame is recommended. Best advice? Don't touch it. Leave the cleaning of such things to the professionals.

Displaying Your Collection

The display of your collection is limited only by your imagination. This section is not meant to help you with display ideas, but to give you some practical information and guidance for displaying your collection safely and securely.

One of the first considerations is the strength of the display case, if you choose to go that route. I will never forget photographing a large collection many years ago that was displayed in several antique china cabinets and etageres. It was indeed elegant, but every time I opened a door or moved a figurine all the others rattled or shook. It was nerve-racking, to say the least. The point is, be sure that your display unit is strong enough to hold your collection safely. Remember, a large group of earthenware figurines can be very heavy.

Remember also the severe damage that direct sunlight can inflict on just about any type of collectible. Try to avoid displaying on a mantle if there is ever a fire in the fireplace. You can cause severe damage to any framed artwork placed there.

Protecting Your Collection

Safeguards

We have discussed the strength factor with regard to the display fixture. Another consideration should be security. Certainly if there are any innocent but mischievous little hands about, keep the displays out of their reach and cabinets latched or locked. The most important consideration should be security. This is especially true if you have a significant and/or large collection.

After you have given the usual attention to normal home security there are some things you need to consider with respect to your collection. No matter how tempting or flattering, turn down any media attention to your collection. This is a red alert to thieves and yes, there are Hummel thieves. Most thefts take place from display tables set at shows and vehicles used to transport them to and from such events, but there have been instances of home burglary and armed robbery in the home. Keep knowledge of your collection among family and friends. If you don't have a home security system consider installing one. Fairly inexpensive do-it-yourself systems have been developed. Some are even wireless, eliminating the need to run wires all over the house. Whether or not you are handy with this sort of thing, the best route may be a professionally installed system. It's your call.

What To Do When It's Broken

How you react to breakage depends upon the nature of the item and its value, intrinsic or sentimental. If you attach great meaning to the piece but it is a relatively inexpensive item, you could simply glue it back together. If it has great sentimental value and you have the wherewithal, by all means have it professionally restored. If you have damaged a very rare or valuable piece, it might be worth having it professionally restored. Restoration can be expensive and take quite some time so you must first decide whether it is worth the trouble and more importantly, whether the piece will be worth as much or more than the cost.

There are three types of restoration: cold repairing, firing and bracing. The method used in the greatest majority of cases where Hummel figures are concerned is cold repairing (except in the case of craze reversal). Cold repairing is the least expensive of the three and the results are very good. You will probably not be able to detect the repairs with the naked eye. Examination by X-ray and/or long-wave ultraviolet light is the only way to detect a professionally restored piece of earthenware or porcelain.

In selecting a restorer a personal visit to the shop is advisable. There you can look over work that is in process and maybe even see a few finished restorations. Many professionals keep a photo album of their work as well. Ask for some references, get an estimate for the job and find out how long a wait there is. In most cases, a long wait (we can be talking months here, folks) means many people on the list, and that is usually an indication of a good reputation. The best way to be sure is to get a recommendation from a friend or trusted dealer.

The following list of general restorers is a combination of the list provided by the M.I. Hummel Club and a list I have developed over the last twenty years. It is by no means complete, for there are dozens more around the country doing competent, professional restorations. Over the years I have heard from or spoken to dealers and collectors who have not been satisfied with the work or service of some of them, while on the other hand I have heard praise from others regarding the same restorers. In fairness to all of them, I cannot be responsible for recommendations and therefore offer only the list. The general restorers are listed alphabetically by the state in which they are located. Those two companies that have come to my attention as being capable of crazing reversal are listed first.

Restorers

THE CLAY WORKS (offers crazing reversal)
4058 Main Street
P.O. Box 353
Exmore, Virginia 23350
(757) 414-0567

CRAZEMASTERS (offers crazing reversal)
c/o Dorothy Dous
Hummel Collector's Club, Inc.
1261 University Drive
Yardley, PA 19067-2857
(215) 493-6705 (Ask for Bob)

Arizona

CHINA AND CRYSTAL CLINIC
Victor Coleman
1808 N. Scottsdale Road
Tempe, AZ 85203
1-800-658-9197

California

ATTIC UNLIMITED
22435 E. La Palma
Linda, CA 92686
(714) 692-2940

CERAMIC RESTORATION
Gene Gomas
Manteca, CA
(209) 823-3922

MR. MARK R. DURBAN
P.O. Box 4084
Big Bear Lake, CA
(714) 585-9989

FOSTER ART RESTORATION
711 West 17th Street
Suite C-2
Costa Mesa, CA 92627
1-800-824-6967

HOUSE OF RENEW
27601 Forbes Road, Unit 55
Laguna Miguel, CA 92677
(714) 582-3117

JUST ENTERPRISES
2790 Sherwin Ave., No.10
Ventura, Ca 93003
(805) 644-5837

GEPPETTO'S RESTORATION
Barry J. Korngiebel
31121 Via Colinas, No. 1003
Westlake Village, CA 91362
(818) 889-0901

MARTHA A. McCLEARY
14851 Jeffrey Road, No. 75
Irvine, CA 92720
(714) 262-9110

PORCELAIN REPAIR BY JOAN
San Diego, CA
(619) 291-6539

RESTORATIONS BY LINDA
Linda M. Peet
1759 Hemlock Street
Fairfield, CA 94533
(707) 422-6497
By Appointment Only

VENERABLE CLASSICS
645 Fourth Street, Suite 208
Santa Rosa, CA 95404
(707) 575-3626

Colorado

HERBERT KLUG
2270 South Zang Court
Lakewood, CO 80228
(303) 985-9261

NYLANDER STUDIOS
1650 South Forest Street
Denver, CO 80222
(303) 758-4313

Connecticut

WALTER C. KAHN
76 North Sylvan Road
Westport, CT 06880
(203) 227-2195

Florida

A FINE TOUCH
William R. York
5740 Lakefield Court
Orlando, FL 32810
(407) 298-7129

ERIC BECKUS
4511 32nd Avenue North
St. Petersburg, FL 33713
(813) 533-4288

ROBERT E. DiCARLO RESTORATION
P.O. Box 16222
Orlando, FL 32861
(407) 886-7423

LOUGHLIN RESTORATION STUDIO
Indian Beach Circle
Sarasota, FL 34234
(813) 355-7318

THE OLD COBERG, INC.
Markus A. Paetzold
1300 Tyrone Blvd.
St. Petersburg, FL 33710
(813) 343-1419
By Appointment Only

RESTORATIONS OBJECTS D'ART
Eric W. Idstrom Company
12500 SE Highway 301
Belleview, FL 32620
(904) 245-8862

MAISON GINO, INC.
Ginette or Irving Sultan
845 Lincoln Road
Miami Beach, FL 33139
(305) 532-2015

Illinois

J.B. SERVICES
John and Betty Bazar
2302 Sudbury Lane
Geneva, IL 60134

REPAIR AND RESTORATION
Doe Lasky
Oak Park, IL
(708) 386-1722

SIERRA STUDIOS
37 W 222
Rt. 64, State 103
St. Charles, IL 60175

WAYNE WARNER
Route 16, Box 557
Bloomington, IL 61704
(309) 828-0994

Iowa

MAXINE'S LTD.
7144 University Avenue
Des Moines, IA 50311
(515) 255-3197

Massachusetts

ROSINE GREEN ASSOCIATES
45 Bartlett Crescent
Brookline, MA 02146
(617) 277-8368

THE SHROPSHIRE
J. Kevin Samara
274 South Street
Shrewsbury, MA 01545
(508) 845-4381

New Jersey

BAER SPECIALTY SHOP
259 E. Browning Road
Bellmawr, NJ 08031
(609) 931-0696

ELY HOUSE
118 Patterson Avenue
Shrewsbury, NJ 07701

RESTORATION BY DUDLEY, INC.
47 Stanford Avenue
P.O. Box 345
West Orange, NJ
(201) 731-4449

RESTORATION BY LOUIS
Route 6, Box 340
Hyatt Road
Branchville, NJ 07826
(201) 875-2274

New Mexico

WEST HAUS
Katherine Ann West
1227 San Jose Avenue
Santa Fe, NM 87505
(505) 983-2917

New York

CHINA AND GLASS REPAIR
STUDIOS
282 Main Street
Eastchester, NY 10709
(914) 337-1977
or
P.O. Box 598
Somers, NY 10589
(914) 628-5531

RICHARD GERHARDT
66 Jayson Avenue
Great Neck, NY

IMPERIAL CHINA
22 North Park Avenue
Center, NY 11570
(516) 764-7311

RESTORATION UNLIMITED
Donna Curtin
3009 West Genesee Street
Syracuse, NY 13219
(315) 488-7123

CERAMIC RESTORATION OF
WESTCHESTER, INC.
Hans-Jurgen Schindhelm
81 Water Street
Ossining, NY 10562
(914) 762-1719

Ohio

COLONIAL HOUSE ANTIQUES
AND GIFTS
22 Front Street, Terrace Park
Berea, OH 44017
(216) 826-4169

OLD WORLD RESTORATIONS
347 Stanley Avenue
Cincinnati, OH 45226
(513) 321-1911
1-800-878-1911

WIEBOLD STUDIO, INC.
413 Terrace Place
Cincinnati, OH 45174
(513) 831-2541

Pennsylvania

H.A. EBERHARDT AND SONS, INC.
2010 Walnut Street
Philadelphia, PA 19103
(215) 568-4144

A. LUDWIG KLEIN AND SON, INC.
683 Sunnytown Pike
P.O. Box 145
Harleysville, PA 19438

THE KRAUSES
97 W. Wheeling Street
Washington, PA 15301
(412) 228-5034

South Dakota

D & J GLASS CLINIC, INC.
Route 3, Box 330
Sioux Falls, SD 57106
(605) 361-7524

Texas

SHARON LEWIS
1010 West Monroe Street
Austin, TX 78704
(512) 441-9985

Virginia

THE CLAY WORKS
4058 Main Street
P.O. Box 353
Exmore, VA 23350
(757) 414-0567

Canada

J&H CHINA REPAIRS
8296 St. George Street
Vancouver, British Columbia
Canada V5X 3C5
(604) 321-1093

ARTWORK RESTORATION
30 Hillhouse Road
Winnipeg, Manitoba
Canada R2V 2V9
(204) 334-7090

CLASSIC ART RESTORATION
875 Eglinton Avenue West
Toronto, Ontario
Canada M6C 3Z9
(416) 787-4794

Cataloging and Insuring Your Collection

As the value of your collection increases through acquisition and appreciation, the extent of possible loss increases. Just about everyone carries some amount of homeowners or household goods insurance against loss due to fire or natural disaster, but few collectors actually have enough. Many people don't realize that if there is any coverage at all for collectibles, it is severely limited. Most companies require a separate schedule for collectibles, listing each item individually, and others will offer a special policy. Discuss this with your local agent. As for establishing a value for each piece, you can pay for an appraisal by a knowledgeable dealer in your area or, that not being possible, ask your agent if he will accept the values listed in this book. I know many do, for I have been contacted by them on various occasions for up-to-the-minute valuations on collections. The market has become fairly stable so a one-year-old value is usually close to the current market, and this book rarely goes over two years without being updated.

You will need to catalog your collection for the insurance company and for your own peace of mind. A record of your collection, especially if it includes photographs, will go a long way toward helping the law enforcement authorities in their investigation of a theft. It will also assure you of identification of your property in the happy case of recovery by the authorities.

You can also place a unique mark beneath the base to aid in identifying the items as yours. The thieves may or may not discover your mark and remove it. There is, however, an even better way to mark them. There is a black ray crayon on the security market that is invisible to the naked eye when used. The marking from it becomes visible under a black light (long-wave ultraviolet light).

Refer to Appendix A of this book for instructions on photographing your collection. Take the pictures and attach them to a written description of each piece including trademarks and any other marks found on the base. These will not usually be visible in the photos. Record the exact size and any other characteristic unique to your piece. Some put this information on the back of the photo itself. Whatever method you use, be sure to make a duplicate set to be kept in a safe deposit box or some other secure location away from your home or where you keep your collection. You don't want your catalog stolen or burned up with your collection. Your insurance company will very likely require an itemized list with description and value. Your safely stored photo catalog will be a big help to you and them in the case of a disaster. Don't forget to update the catalog with any new acquisitions and significant changes in value.

GLOSSARY

The following is an alphabetical listing of terms and phrases you will encounter in this book as well as other related books, references and literature during the course of collecting Hummel items. In some cases they are specific and unique to Hummel collecting and others are generic in nature, applying to other earthenware and ceramic and porcelain as well. Refer to this glossary whenever you read or hear something you don't understand. Frequent use of it will enable you to become well versed in collecting Hummel figurines and other related articles.

Airholes - Small holes under the arms or other unobtrusive locations to vent the hollow figures during the firing stage of production. This prevents them from exploding as the interior air expands due to intense heat. Many pieces have these tiny little holes, but often they are difficult to locate. Those open at the bottom usually have no need for these holes.

Anniversary Plate - In 1975 a 10" plate bearing the Stormy Weather motif was released. Subsequent anniversary plates were released at five-year intervals. 1985 saw the third and last in the series released.

Annual Plate - Beginning in 1971 the W. Goebel firm began producing an annual Hummel plate. Each plate contains a bas-relief reproducing one of the Hummel motifs. The first was originally released to the Goebel factory workers in 1971, commemorating the hundredth anniversary of the firm. This original release was inscribed, thanking the workers. At the same time the first in a series of twenty-five was released to the public. That series is complete and a new series begun in 1997.

ARS - Latin word for "ART"

ARS AG - ARS AG, Zug, Switzerland, holds the two-dimensional rights for many of the original M.I. Hummel drawings as well as the two-dimensional rights for reproductions of M.I. Hummel products made by Goebel.

Ars Edition - Ars Edition was formerly known as Ars Sacra Josef Mueller Verlag, the German publishing house that first published Hummel art, producing and selling postcards, postcard-calendars and prints of M.I. Hummel. Today Ars Edition GmbH is the exclusive licensee for publishing Hummel (books, calendars, cards, stationery, etc.) Owner: Mr. Marcel Nauer (grandson of Dr. Herbert Dubler).

Ars Sacra - Trademark on a gold foil label sometimes found on Hummel-like figurines produced by Herbert Dubler. This was a New York firm that produced these figurines during the years of WWII when Goebel was forbidden by the Nazi government to produce Hummel items. Ars Sacra is also the original name of the Ars Edition firm in Munich. Dr. Herbert Dubler was a son-in-law of Mr. and Mrs. Mueller, the owners of Ars Edition, formerly Ars Sacra, Munich. Although there was some corporate connection for a very short time between Mueller and Dubler there is no connection between the Mueller Ars Sacra firm and the Hummel-like figurines produced by Dubler under the name "House of Ars Sacra" or the statement "Produced by Ars Sacra". Please see the discussion on the Dubler figures elsewhere in this volume.

Artist's Sample - See Master Sample.

Baby Bee - Describes the trademark of the factory used in 1958. A small bee flying in a V.

Backstamp - Backstamp is usually the trademark and any associated special markings on the underside of the base, the reverse or back side of an item.

Basic Size - This term is generally synonymous with standard size. However, because the sizes listed in this book are not substantiated initial factory released sizes, it was felt that it would be misleading to label them "standard." "Basic size" was chosen to denote only an *approximate* standard size.

Bas-relief - A raised or sculpted design, as on the Annual Bells and the Annual Plates, as opposed to a two-dimensional painted design or decal.

Bee - A symbol used since about 1940 in various forms, as a part of or along with the factory trademark on Hummel pieces until 1979, when the bee was dropped. It was re-incorporated in the special backstamp used on the M.I. Hummel exclusive pieces.

Bisque - A fired but unglazed condition. Usually white but sometimes colored.

Black Germany - Term used to describe one of the various wordings found along with the Hummel trademarks on the underside of the pieces. It refers to the color used to stamp the word "Germany." Many colors have been used for the trademarks and associated marks, but black generally indicates the figure is an older mode; however, this is not an absolutely reliable indicator.

Bookends - Throughout the collection of Goebel-made Hummel items are bookends. Some are the regular figurines merely attached to wooden bookends with some type of adhesive. Some, however, are different. The latter are made without the customary base and then attached. The regular pieces, when removed from the wood, have the traditional markings. Those without the base may or may not exhibit those markings.

Candleholder - Some Hummel figurines have been produced with provisions to place candles in them.

Candy Bowl - See Candy Box

Candy Box - Small covered cylindrical box with a Hummel figurine on the top. Design changes have been made in the shape of the box or bowl over the years, as well as in the manner in which the cover rests upon the bowl. See individual listings.

Candy Dish - See Candy Box

CE - See Closed Edition

CN - See Closed Number

Closed Edition (CE) - A term used by the Goebel factory to indicate that a particular item is no longer produced and will not be placed in production again.

Closed Number (CN) - A term used by the Goebel factory to indicate that a particular number in the Hummel Mold Number sequence has never been used to identify an item and never will by used. A caution here: Several unquestionably genuine pieces have been found recently bearing these so-called closed numbers.

Club Exclusive - This refers to the products made for membership premiums and sale exclusively to members of the M.I. Hummel Club. Each of these bears a special club backstamp to identify it as such.

Collector's Plaque - Same as the dealer plaque except it does not state "authorized dealer," as most later dealer plaques do. Frequently used for display with private collections (see Dealer Plaque).

Crazing - A fine web-like cracked appearance in the overglaze of older porcelain and earthenware. It occurs on Hummel figurines from time to time, mostly on older pieces. Crazing was previously thought irreversible but recently a process has been developed to eliminate this phenomenon. See above section on crazing.

Crown Mark (CM, TMK-1) - One of the early W. Goebel firm trademarks. Has not been used on Hummel figurines and related pieces since sometime around 1949-50.

Current Mark - For many years this was a term describing the trademark being used at the present time. It has become a somewhat confusing term, for what is current today may not be tomorrow. Most collectors and dealers have come to use a descriptive term such as the "Crown Mark" or the use of trademark number designations such as Trademark #1 (TMK-1) for the Crown Mark for instance. The number designation is usually shortened to "Trademark One" when spoken or "TMK-1" when written.

Current Production - Term describing figurines, plates, candy boxes, etc. supposedly being produced at the present time. They are not necessarily readily available, because the factory maintains the molds, but doesn't always produce the figure with regularity.

Dealer Plaque - A plaque made and distributed by the Goebel firm to retailers for the purpose of advertising the fact that they are authorized dealers in Hummel figurines and related articles. The plaques always used to have the "Merry Wanderer" figure incorporated into them. Earlier models have a bumblebee perched on the top edge (see Collector's Plaque). In recent years the figurine associated has not always been the "Merry Wanderer." For more detailed information see the listing for Hum 187.

Decimal Designator - Many earlier Goebel Hummel figurines exhibit a decimal point after the mold number, ie: "154." This is ostensibly to mean the same thing as the "slash" mark (/). The use of the slash mark means that there is another, smaller size of the piece either in existence, planned or at least in prototype. There is another theory that the decimal is to make it easier to clarify the incised mold numbers and to help determine whether a number is, for instance, a 66 rather than a 99. The decimal is not always found alone with the number. Some examples the author has observed are 49./0., 51./0. and 84./5.

Display Plaque - see Collector's Plaque and Dealer Plaque

Doll Face - See Faience

Donut (Doughnut) Base - Describes a type of base used with some figures. Looking at the bottom of the base, the outer margin of the base forms a circle or oval, and a smaller circle or oval within makes the base appear doughnut-like.

Donut (Doughnut) Halo - The only figures on which these appear are the Madonnas. They are formed as a solid cap type, or molded so that the figure's hair protrudes through slightly. The latter are called Donut Halos.

Double Crown - From 1934 to 1938 there were many figures produced with two Crown WG marks. This is known as the Double Crown. One of the crowns may be a stamped crown and the other incised. Pieces have been found with both trademarks incised (see above section on trademarks). Thereafter only a single Crown Mark is found.

Embossed - An erroneous term used to describe incised (see Incised).

Faience (Doll Face) - Faience is defined as brilliantly glazed, bright-colored fine earthenware. More commonly called "Doll Face" pieces by collectors, this describes the few Hummel figurines that were made by Goebel in the early days of paint and finish experimentation. Several have made it into collectors' hands. Refer to the color section for illustrations of a few.

Fink, Emil - Emil Fink Verlag, Stuttgart, Germany. A publisher of a limited number of postcards and greeting cards bearing the art of M.I. Hummel. All U.S. copyrights of cards published by Fink Verlag are owned by ARS AG, Zug, Switzerland.

Font - A number of pieces have been produced with a provision for holding a small portion of holy water. They can be hung on the wall. Often referred to as Holy Water Fonts.

Full Bee (TMK-2) - About 1940 the W. Goebel firm began using a bee as part of their trademark. The Full Bee trademark has been found along with the Crown trademark. The Full Bee is the first and largest bee to be utilized. There were many versions of the Full Bee trademark. The first Full Bee is sometimes found with (R) stamped somewhere on the base.

Germany - (W. GERMANY, West Germany, Western Germany) - All have appeared with the trademark in several different colors.

Goebelite - This is the name the Goebel firm gives to the patented mixture of materials used to form the slip used in the pouring and fashioning the earthenware Hummel figurines and other related Hummel pieces. Not often heard.

High Bee - A variation of the early Bee trademarks wherein the bee is smaller than the original bee used in the mark and flies with its wings slightly higher than the top of the V in the trademark.

Hollow Base - A base variation. Some bases for figures are solid and some are hollowed out and open into a hollow figure.

Hollow Mold - An erroneous term actually meaning Hollow Base, as above. All Hummel pieces are at least partially hollow in finished form.

Holy Water Font - See Font

Hummel Mark (TMK-7) - This mark was introduced in 1991. It is the first trademark to be used exclusively on Goebel products utilizing M.I. Hummel art for its design.

Hummel Number or Mold Number - A number or numbers incised into the base or bottom of the piece, used to identify the mold motif and sometimes the size of the figure or article. This designation is sometimes inadvertently omitted, but rarely.

Incised - Describes a mark or wording which has actually been pressed into the surface of a piece rather than printed or stamped on the surface. It is almost always found beneath the base.

Indented - See Incised

Jumbo - Sometimes used to describe the few Hummel figurines that have been produced in a substantially larger size than the normal range. Usually around 30". (See Hum Nos. 7, 141, 142.)

Light Stamp - (See M.I. Hummel.) It is thought that every Hummel figurine has Sister M.I. Hummel's signature stamped somewhere on it, but some apparently have no signature. In some cases the signature may have been stamped so lightly that in subsequent painting and glazing all but unidentifiable traces are obliterated. In other cases the signature may have been omitted altogether. The latter case is rare. The same may happen to the mold number.

Limited Edition - An item that is limited in production to a specified number or limited to the number produced in a defined period of time.

Mahlmuster - See Master Sample.

Master Sample - This is a figurine or other item that is the model from which Goebel artists paint the newly fashioned piece. The Master Sample figurines usually have a red line painted around the flat vertical portion of the base. It is known variously in German as the Mahlmuster, Master Zimmer, Muster Zimmer or Originalmuster. There is another notation sometimes found on the base: "Orig Arbt Muster." These are abbreviations for the German words Original Working Model.

Master Zimmer - See Master Sample

M.I. Hummel (Maria Innocentia Hummel) - This signature, illustrated below, is supposed to be applied to every Hummel article produced. However, as in Light Stamp above, it may not be evident. It is also reasonable to assume that because of the design of a particular piece or its extremely small size, it may not have been practical to place it on the piece. In these cases a small sticker is used in its place. It is possible that these stickers become loose and are lost over the years. The signature has been found painted on in some instances but rarely. It is also possible to find the signature in decal form, brown in color. From the late 1950s to early 1960s Goebel experimented with placing the signature on the figurines by the decal method, but abandoned the idea. A few of the pieces they tried it on somehow found their way into the market. Collectors should also take note of the fact that sometimes the signature appears as "Hummel" without the initials. This is also seldom found.

Mel - There are a few older Hummel figurines made by Goebel that bear this incised three-letter group along with a number. It is supposed that they were prototype pieces that were never placed in production, but at least three were. Please turn to the description of the Mel pieces elsewhere in this volume for an in-depth discussion.

MID - See Mold Induction Date

Missing Bee Mark (TMK-6) - In mid-1980 the Goebel company changed the trademark by removing the familiar "bee" mark collectors had grown accustomed to associating with M.I. Hummel items. It came to be known as the "Missing Bee" mark (TMK-6) for a while.

Model Number - See Mold Number

Mold Growth - There have been many theories in the past to explain the differences in sizes of figurines marked the same and with no significant differences other than size. The explanation from Goebel is that in the earlier years of molding, the molds were made of plaster of paris and had a tendency to wash out and erode with use. Therefore successive use would produce pieces each being slightly larger than the last. Another possible explanation is that the firm has been known to use more than one mold simultaneously in the production of the same figure and market them with the same mold number. The company developed a synthetic resin to use instead of plaster of paris in 1954. While this is a vast improvement, the new material still has the same tendencies although to a significantly smaller degree.

Mold Induction Date (MID) - The actual year the original mold was made. Often the mold is made, but figures are not produced for several years afterward. The MID is sometimes found along with other marks on older pieces but not always. All pieces currently being produced bear an MID.

Mold Number - the official mold number use by Goebel unique to each Hummel item or motif used. See section on the explanation of the mold number system elsewhere in this volume for an in-depth discussion.

Mother Mold Sample - When Goebel proposes a new figurine the piece is modeled, a mother mold made, and usually three to six sample figures are produced and then painted by one of Goebel's master painters. These are for the convent and others to examine and either approve for production suggest changes or reject, as the case may be. Typically never more than six to eight of these are produced. Sometimes the final approved models are marked with a red line and placed into service as a master sample for the artists. Although the mother mold samples do not necessarily have the red line, they are identifiable by the black ink within the incised mold number.

Mould - European spelling of Mold.

Muster Zimmer - See Master Sample

Narrow Crown - Trademark used by the W. Goebel firm from 1937 to the early 1940s. To date this trademark has never been found on an original Hummel piece.

One-Line Mark - See Stylized Bee

Open Edition - Designates the Hummel figurines presently in production or in planning. It does not mean all are in production, only that it is 'open' for production. Not necessarily available.

Open Number - A number in the numerical sequence of factory-designated Hummel model numbers that has not been used to identify a piece but may be used when a new design is released.

Out of Production - A confusing term sometimes used to indicate that an item is not of current production but may be placed back in production at some later date. The confusion results from the fact that some with this designation have been declared closed editions and others have been returned to production, thus leaving all the others in the classification in limbo.

Orig Arbt Muster - A marking sometimes found beneath the base of a figurine. It is the abbreviation for the German words roughly translated to mean "Original Working model."

Overglaze - See White Overglaze

Oversize - A term sometimes used to describe a Hummel piece larger than that which is currently being produced. These variations could be due to mold growth (see Mold Growth).

Painter's Sample - See Master Sample

PFE (Possible Future Edition) - A term applied to Hummel mold design that does exist, but has not yet been released.

Production Mold Sample - A piece that is cast out of the first production mold.

Prototype - This is a proposed figurine or other item that must be approved by those with the authority to do so. As used by Goebel it is further restricted to mean "the one and only sample," the first out of the mother mold. This is the one presented to the Siessen Convent for their approval/disapproval. See Mother Mold Sample.

Quartered Base - As it sounds, this is descriptive of the underside of the base of a piece being divided into four more or less equal parts.

Red Line - A red line around the outside edge of the base of a figurine means that the piece may have once served as the model for the painters.

Reinstated - A piece that is back in production after having been previously placed in a non-production status for some length of time.

Sample Model - A prototype piece modeled for the approving authorities. May or may not have gained approval. See Mother Mold Sample.

Secondary Market - When an item is bought and sold after the initial purchase, it is said to be traded on the secondary market.

Size Designator - Method of identifying the size of a figure. It is found in conjunction with the Hummel mold number on the bottom of the figure.

Slash Marked - From time to time a figure or a piece will be found with a slash or cut through the trademark. There are two theories as to the origin of this mark. Some think it is used to indicate a figure with some flaw or imperfection, although several figures with slash marks are, upon close examination, found to be in excellent, flawless condition. The other theory is that some figures are slash-marked to discourage resale of pieces given to or sold at a bargain price to factory workers.

Small Bee - A variation of the early Full Bee trademark wherein the bee is about one-half the size of the original bee.

Split Base - When viewing the bottom of the base of a piece it appears to be split into sections. Generally refers to a base split into two sections, but could readily be used to describe more than two sections.

Stamped - A method of placing marks on the bottom of a figure wherein the data is placed on the surface rather than pressed into it (see Incised).

Standard Size - As pointed out in the section on size designators, this is a general term used to describe the size of the first figure to be produced, when there are more sizes of the same figure to be found. It is not the largest nor the smallest, only the first. Over the years, as a result of mold design changes and possibly mold growth, all figures marked as standard are not necessarily the same size (see Basic Size above).

Stylized Bee (TMK-3) - About 1955 the traditional bee design in the trademark was changed to reflect a more modern "stylized" version. Also sometimes called the "One-Line Mark."

Temporarily Withdrawn - Similar to Out of Production, but in this case it would be reasonable to assume that the piece so described will be put back into production at some future date.

Terra Cotta - Literally translated from the Latin it means "baked earth." A naturally brownish-orange earthenware.

Three Line Mark (TMK.4) - A trademark variation used in the 1960s and 1970s.

Underglaze - A term describing anything that is found underneath the glaze as opposed to being placed after the glazing.

U.S. Zone or **U.S. Zone Germany -** During the American occupation of Germany after World War II the Goebel company was required to apply these words to their products. After the country was divided into East and West Germany in 1948 they began using "West Germany" or "Western Germany." The various configurations in which these words are found are illustrated in the above section on trademarks.

White Overglaze - After a piece has been formed a clear glaze is applied and fired, resulting in a shiny, all-white finish.

CHAPTER THREE

REFERENCES
AND
ORGANIZATIONS

REFERENCES AND ORGANIZATIONS

RECOMMENDED BOOKS FOR COLLECTORS

Aaseng, Nathan. *The Unsung Heroes: Unheralded People Who Invented Famous Products.* Lerner Publications Company, Minneapolis, Minnesota 55401. Eight people are included in this book for young readers. Among them are the inventors of Coca Cola, McDonald's hamburgers and vacuum cleaners. "Sister Maria Innocentia's Gift, M.I. Hummel Figurines" is the relevant chapter.

Arbenz, Pat. *Hummel Facts.* Misty's Gift Gallery, 228 Fry Blvd., Sierra Vista, Arizona 85635. A reprint collection of all Mr. Arbenz' columns for *Plate Collector* magazine. Indispensable to the collector. Although inexpensive, it is out of print and difficult to find. You might try contacting Arbenz: he may have a few copies.

Armke, Ken. *Hummel: An Illustrated Handbook and Price Guide.* Published by Wallace-Homestead, a division of Chilton Book Company, c/o Krause Publications, 700 E. State St., Iola, WI 54990. 1995. This full-color guide is of much practical use to the collector. Well researched, well written and interesting.

ArsEdition. *The Hummel.* Verlag Ars Sacra Josef Mueller, Munich, Germany, 1984. A 78-page, full-color hardcover book, full of illustrations by Sister M.I. Hummel and light verse.

Authentic Hummel Figurines. Copyright by W. Goebel, Rodental, Germany. An illustrated catalog that was for many years published by the company. Out of print.

Ehrmann, Erich and Robert L. Miller (special contributor). *Hummel, The Complete Collector's Guide and Illustrated Reference.* Portfolio Press Corporation, Huntington, NY 11743. 1976. Ehrmann, publisher of *Collectors Editions* magazine, and Miller,

acknowledged expert and owner of one of the world's largest Hummel collections, have collaborated to present this large work. As a reference it is invaluable to collectors.

Ehrmann, Erich W., Robert L. Miller and Walter Pfeiffer. *M.I. Hummel: The Golden Anniversary Album.* Portfolio Press Corporation, Huntington, NY 11743. 1984. A beautiful book full of color photos and much good information for collectors.

Guide for Collectors. Copyright by W. Goebel, Rodental, Germany. Available through the M.I. Hummel Club, P.O. Box 11, Pennington, NJ 08534-0011. A beautiful, large-format, full-color catalog of the current Goebel M.I. Hummel collection including closed editions. It is updated periodically.

Hotchkiss, John. *Hummel Art.* 3rd ed. Wallace-Homestead Book Co., c/o Krause Publications, 700 E. State St., Iola, WI 54990. 1982. A full-color handbook that essentially updates the first and second editions. Out of print.

Hummel, Berta and Margarete Seeman. *The Hummel Book.* 17th ed. W. Goebel, Rodental, Germany, 1992. This copyright is today with ARS AG, Zug, Switzerland.

Hunt, Dick. *Goebel Miniatures of Robert Olzewski.* 595 Jackson Ave., Satellite Beach, FL. Hunt's Collectibles.

Koller, Angelica. *The Hummel.* Released by ArsEdition in 1995, this book describes Berta Hummel's childhood and her life as a nun. It also explains her theory of art and includes many full-color reproductions of her art. Hardcover, 141 pages. Available through your dealer or the M.I. Hummel Club.

Luckey, Carl F. *Luckey's Hummel Figurines and Plates.* 11th ed. Books Americana, c/o Krause Publications, 700 E. State St., Iola, WI 54990. 1997. The most comprehensive collector's reference on the market today. Not only does it cover all of the W. Goebel Porzellanfabrik three-dimensional M.I. Hummel figurines and related items, but also all of the hundreds of other available Hummel collectibles. Crammed full of great pictures and useful and fascinating information. 450 pages. Available at most booksellers or from Carl F. Luckey, Rt. 4, Box 301, Killen, AL 35645, for $27 post paid.

M.I. Hummel Album. Portfolio Press Corporation, 1992. A beautiful full-color reference showing most of the figurines ever made. Of particular interest is the illustration of many possible future editions (PFE). A Goebel publication. See your dealer or contact the M.I. Hummel Club.

Miller, Robert L. *Hummel.* Portfolio Press Corporation, Huntington, New York 11743. 1979. This is a supplement to the original *Hummel, the Complete Collector's Guide and Illustrated Reference* by Ehrmann and Miller.

Miller, Robert L. *M.I. Hummel Figurines, Plates, More* ... 6th ed. Portfolio Press Corporation, Huntington, NY 11743. 1995. A well- organized and handy reference by this noted collector.

Plaut, James S. *Formation of an Artist, The Early Works of Berta Hummel.* Schmid Brothers, Inc., Randolph, MA, 1980. This softbound book is actually a catalog of the 1980-82 tour of an exhibition of paintings, drawings, photographs and a tapestry from the collection of the Hummel family.

Schwatlo, Wolfgang. *M.I. Hummel Collector's Handbook.* Schwatlo GMBH, D65522 Niedernhausen, Postfach 1224, Germany, 1994. This full-color handbook is of great value to the collector. It concentrates on the many variations that can be found and includes color photographs. A must for the serious collector.

Schwatlo, Wolfgang. *M.I. Hummel Collector's Handbook with Prices.* Schwatlo GmbH, D-65522 Niedernhausen, Postfach 1224, Germany, 1996. An update of Schwatlo's 1994 book. This edition has been expanded to include many other related collectibles. It is full-color and bilingual. A very useful book for the serious collector.

Struss, Dieter. *M.I. Hummel Figuren.* Weltbild Verlag GmbH, Augsburg, Bavaria, Germany, 1993. A full-color hardbound collector's guide (in German).

Wiegand, Sister M. Gonsalva, O.S.F. *Sketch Me Berta Hummel.* Reprinted by Robert L. Miller and available at most dealers or from Mr. Miller at P.O. Box 210, Eaton, Ohio 45320.

Wonsch, Lawrence L. *Hummel Copycats.* Wallace-Homestead, c/o Krause Publications, 700 E. State St., Iola, WI 54990. 1987. A superb treatment of the hundreds of copies of M.I. Hummel figurines over the years and around the world.

VIDEOTAPES

A Hummel Christmas. Cascom International, Inc., 806 4th Ave. So., Nashville, TN 37210. 1995. An enchanting production about 30 minutes long, this video boasts a masterful blend of rare figurines, original M.I. Hummel art, special effects and Christmas music. This is a must-have video for the Christmas season for any lover of Hummel figurines and art.

M.I. Hummel Marks of Distinction. A historical look at the progression of M.I. Hummel backstamps from the beginning to the current mark. Available from the M.I. Hummel Club.

The Insider's Guide to M.I. Hummel Collecting. Bottom Line Productions, Inc., 1994. This one-hour video features M.I. Hummel Club spokesperson Gwen Toma in an excellent presentation of the various marks and backstamps that be found on the figurines and related items. An excellent overview of how they are produced is given, as well as an explanation of how the figurines are painted by Goebel Master Artist Sigrid Then. The greatest part of the video is given over to a charming sequence by Bob and Ruth Miller, who give you a personal tour of some of the more rare and interesting pieces in their famous collection. Available from the M.I. Hummel Club.

The Life of Sister M.I. Hummel. Produced by W. Goebel. This is a striking 25-minute treatment of Berta Hummel's life. Available from the M.I. Hummel Club.

PERIODICALS

The following is a list of periodicals you may find useful in collecting Hummel figurines.

Antiques Journal (monthly)
P.O. Box 1046
Dubuque, Iowa 52001
Has occasional articles about Hummel collecting and ads for buying and selling Hummels.

The Antique Trader Weekly (weekly)
P.O. Box 1050
Dubuque, Iowa 52001
Occasional Hummel articles and extensive ads for buying and selling Hummel items.

Collector Editions (quarterly)
170 Fifth Avenue
New York, NY 10010
Has occasional Hummel column.

Collectors Journal (weekly)
Box 601
Vinton, Iowa 52349
Has ads for Hummel buying and selling.

Collectors Mart (bimonthly)
15100 W. Kellogg
Wichita, Kansas 67235

Collectors News (monthly)
606 8th Street
Grundy Center, Iowa 50638
Has ads for Hummel buying and selling and occasional Hummel articles.

Collectors' Showcase (bimonthly)
P.O. Box 6929
San Diego, California 92106

The Tri-State Trader (weekly)
P.O. Box 90
Knightstown, Indiana 46148
Has ads for Hummel buying and selling.

CLUBS AND ORGANIZATIONS

There are a few dealers and manufacturers who sponsor "collector's clubs." They are designed to market their products to a target audience. This is a good marketing technique that doubles as a means of educating collectors as to what artists and manufacturers are presently doing. The collector of M.I. Hummel items is lucky to have a couple of these. They are unique in that they are very large organizations and are very serious about keeping collectors informed. Both organizations offer a very valuable member figurine sales and wanted list. Membership in both is highly recommended.

The Hummel Collector's Club, Inc.
1261 University Drive
P.O. Box 157
Yardley, PA 19067
1-888-5-HUMMEL (Toll Free)

This club was established in 1975 by Dorothy Dous. She and her husband have developed the club into a very valuable organization for collectors of Hummel collectibles. Mrs. Dous (Dottie) writes an interesting quarterly newsletter that is lengthy, easy to read and crammed with information. The newsletter also includes a long list of members' for-sale, trade or wanted lists. The club acts as a gratis go-between for its members. Any collector would benefit by becoming a member of this organization

The M.I. Hummel Club
Goebel Plaza
P.O. Box 11
Pennington, NJ 08534-0011
(609) 737-8777, 1-800-666-2582 (Toll Free)

This club was founded by the W. Goebel firm in 1976 as the Goebel Collectors' Club and became the M.I. Hummel Club in the spring of 1989. The club publishes a beautiful and very informative full-color quarterly newsletter, *Insights,* which no collector should be without. Another advantage of membership is the renewal gifts each year, usually a figurine, and the chance to buy figures that are offered exclusively to members and are specially marked with the club backstamp. They also maintain a referral list of members' items for sale or wanted.

Plaque given to charter members of the M.I. Hummel Club.

Plaque given to charter members of the club on the occasion of their twentieth consecutive year of membership.

Local Chapters of the M.I. Hummel Club

At least 143 local chapters of the M.I. Hummel Club were active in 41 states and 4 provinces in Canada as of October 1996. There is even an International Chapter for members with the name "Hummel" as their surname or maiden name. If you are interested in joining a local chapter or starting one of your own, call or write the club in Pennington (address on page 57).

United States

Arizona
Northwest Valley (Sun City)
Roadrunner (Scottsdale)

Arkansas
Arkansas Traveler (Harrison)

California
Bumble Bee (Burbank)
Camarillo
Central Coast (Santa Maria)
Fresno
Heart of the Redwoods
Hollywood
Orange County
Pleasant Valley

San Bernardino (Yucaipa)
San Diego County
San Gabriel (Camarillo)
San Jose
Whittier

Colorado
Gateway to the Rockies (Aurora)
Loveland
Mile Hi (Denver)
Pikes Peak (Colorado Springs)

Connecticut
Rose City (Norwich)

Florida
Broward County (Hollywood)
Daytona Beach
Fivay (Hudson)

The old local chapter patch. The new ones read "M.I. Hummel Club." Many have their own custom patches made to more personally identify their chapter.

Ft. Lauderdale
Greater Zephryhills
Gulfview Coquettes (Holiday)
Greater Zephyrhills
Jacksonville
Ocala
Orlando Area
Palm Beach
Seven Rivers (Beverly Hills)
Suncoast (Palm Harbor)
Tampa Area

Hawaii
Aloha (Honolulu)

Illinois
Batavia Travelers
Gateway East
Greater Peoria Area
Illiana (Lansing)
LaGrange Park (Bridgeview)
McHenry County
N.W. Suburban (Palatine)
Springfield
Southern Illinois (Irvington)

Indiana
Danville
Hoosier Connection

Iowa
Quint Cities (Rock Island)
Siouxland Bees (Sioux City)

Kansas
Flint Hills (Americus)
Mo-Kan (Kansas City)
Kentucky
Oldham County

Louisiana
Cajun Collectors (Baton Rouge)

Maine
Nor'Easter (Lewiston)

Maryland
Pleasant Journey (Crownsville)
Silver Spring

Massachusetts
Cape Cod (Sandwich)
Neponset Valley (Dedham)
Pioneer Valley (Springfield)
Quabbin (Belchertown)

Michigan
Adventurous Anglers
Dearborn
Great Lakes (Dearborn)
Mid-Michigan (Flushing)
Niles
Saginaw Valley (Bay City)
Tri-County (Shelby Township)

Minnesota
Minneapolis/St. Paul (Eagan)
St. Cloud

Missouri
Gateway City (St. Peters)
Southwest Missouri
St. Louis Area
St. Louis Spirit of the River

Montana
Big Sky (Great Falls)

Nebraska
Lincoln
Omaha

Nevada
High Sierra (Reno)
New Hampshire
The Graniteer (Manchester)

New Jersey
Friendly Hands (NJ and NY)
Garden State (Maplewood)
Jersey Cape (Ocean View)

Ocean Pines (Whiting)
Raritan Valley (Piscataway)
South Jersey (Cherry Hill)

New York
Brookhaven (Babylon)
Great South Bay (Amityville)
Nassau-Suffolk (New Hyde Park)
Paumanok (Babylon)
Rochester (Hilton)
Tonawanda Valley (Attica)
Western NY (Buffalo)

North Carolina
Carolina Mountain Region
(Hendersonville)
Hornet's Nest (Concord)

Ohio
Firelands Area (Sandusky)
Greater Cleveland
Miami Valley (Dayton)
Queen City (Cincinnati)
Stark County Hall of Fame
Toledo
Western Reserve (Cleveland)
Youngstown/Hubbard

Oklahoma
OK Chapter (Oklahoma City)

Oregon
Cascade (Eugene)
Portland (West Linn)

Pennsylvania
Antietam Valley (Waynesboro)
Berks County (West Lawn)
Bux-Mont (Bucks & Montgomery
    Countys)
Central (Muncy)
Perkasie (Doylestown)

Philadelphia
Pittsburgh
Pocono (Stroudsburg)

Schuykill County (Pottsville)
York County (Spring Grove)

Puerto Rico
El Coqui (Guaynoba)

Rhode Island
Bristol County

South Carolina
Piedmont Carolinas (Fort Mill)

Tennessee
Knoxville

Texas
Alamo (San Antonio)
Brazosport (Lake Jackson)
Dallas Metroplex
Fort Worth
Gulf Coats (Houston)

Heart of Texas (Waco)
Museum Chapter of
  New Braunfels

Utah
Beehive (West Jordan)

Vermont
Burlington

Virginia
James/York Rivers
Northern Virginia (Fairfax)
Tidewater Area (Virginia Beach)

Washington
Belleview
Puget Sound (Kirkland)
Seattle-Tacoma

Wisconsin
Fox Valley (Fond du Lac)

Mad City West
Madison Capitol Collectors
Milwaukee

Canada
Alberta
Calgary
Edmonton (Sherwood Park)
British Columbia
Greater Vancouver (Langley)
Ontario
Trillium
Saskatchewan
Saskatoon
International

Club members with "Hummel" as
  their surnames or maiden
  names.
There is also a group of International
  M.I. Hummel Clubs in Europe.

OTHER HUMMEL COLLECTIBLES

OTHER HUMMEL COLLECTIBLES

The M.I. Hummel Club Exclusives

When the club was founded under Goebel sponsorship and management, as part of the benefits of membership the company began producing pieces that would be available only through the club. There are two types of these pieces. One is in the form of a membership renewal premium. For the past several years these have been figurines. The other is a redemption card(s) given to members each year, subsequent to renewal. The card(s) allows the member to purchase that year's exclusive offerings. They are available only through officially sanctioned dealers representing the club. Where practical, until early in 1989, each of these exclusive pieces bore the following inscription:

EXCLUSIVE SPECIAL EDITION
No. (1,2,3, etc) FOR MEMBERS OF THE
GOEBEL COLLECTOR'S CLUB

Concurrent with the transition from the old Goebel Collectors Club to the M.I. Hummel Club came a change in the club exclusive backstamp. The backstamp now incorporates a black and yellow Hummel bee within a lined half-circle with "M.I. Hummel" beneath the half-circle.

With only one exception, each of the redemption pieces has been based on an original M.I. Hummel drawing or painting. The exception was the redemption piece offered in the third year, a bust of Sister M.I. Hummel (Hu-3) designed by Goebel master sculptor Gerhard Skrobek and illustrated here.

M.I. Hummel Bust, Hu 3. Last Bee mark (TMK-5), incised 1978 MID, 5-3/4". This is *not* a Hummel piece, but one honoring her.

Base of Hum 479 (I Brought You A Gift) showing the new special club backstamp described above.

A most unusual club piece was offered in addition to the figurine for 1983-84 club exclusive. This was a miniature of the first exclusive club piece, Valentine Gift. It was made in the form of a tiny 1/2" figurine mounted in a 14K gold-plated cage hanging from a chain and worn as a necklace. It is easily removed from the cage for display as a free-standing figurine.

In 1986 a second M.I. Hummel miniature, What Now?, was introduced as an exclusive piece available to members.

Pins given to members of the M.I. Hummel Club (formerly the Goebel Collectors' Club) to commemorate the fifth, tenth, fifteenth and twentieth anniversaries of their membership.

4" plaque that was given to members upon joining until May 31, 1989.

The club published a calendar for members each year for a while.

What Now? (pendant).

The membership gift for 1990-91. Sterling silver pendant.

Valentine Gift miniature (pendant).

Morning Concert, Miniature, GMS 269-P. This is shown in the optional display dome and bandstand setting and also with the Goebel English-language miniature studio display plaque to the left. Note the dime on the right for scale. M.I. Hummel Club exclusive.

For the club year 1991-92 Goebel Miniatures created another miniature figurine exclusive for the club. This one is a 1" free-standing figurine, Morning Concert. It is supplied with an earthenware Bavarian Bandstand setting and a protective glass display dome and base. The release price was $175.

Goebel announced in 1984 that from that point on there would be a cut-off date for use of the redemption certificates, after which the pieces would no longer be available and the molds destroyed. Following here is a list of each of the exclusive club pieces and their respective cut-off dates. Those that do not bear regular Goebel Hummel mold numbers are illustrated and discussed at their appropriate location within the collection listing. The others are illustrated in this section.

Release Date	Name	Mold No.	Cut-off Date
1977-78	Valentine Gift	387	5/31/84
1978-79	Smiling Through (plaque)	690	5/31/84
1979-80	M.I. Hummel Bust	HU-3	5/31/84
1980-81	Valentine Joy	399	5/31/84
1981-82	Daisies Don't Tell	380	5/31/85
1982-83	It's Cold	421	5/31/85
1983-84	What Now?	422	5/31/85
1984-85	Valentine Gift (Miniature)	--	12/31/84
1984-85	Coffee Break	409	5/31/86
1985-86	Smiling Through	408	5/31/87
1986-87	What Now? (Miniature)	--	5/31/88
1986-87	Birthday Candle	440	5/31/88
**1986-87	Valentine Gift (6" plate)	738	5/31/88
1987-88	Morning Concert	447	5/31/89
**1987-88	Valentine Joy (6" plate)	737	5/31/89
1988-89	The Surprise	431	5/31/90
**1988-89	Daisies Don't Tell (6" plate)	736	5/31/90
1988-89	Daisies Don't Tell	380	5/31/90
*1989-90	I Brought You a Gift	479	5/31/91
**1989-90	It's Cold (6" plate)	735	5/31/91
1989-90	Hello World	429	5/31/91
1990-91	I Wonder	486	5/31/92
1990-91	Merry Wanderer (sterling silver pendant)	--	5/31/92
1991-92	Morning Concert (miniature w/display in dome)	--	5/31/93
1991-92	Two Hands, One Treat	493	5/31/93
1992-93	My Wish is Small	463/0	5/31/94
*1992-93	Lucky Fellow	560	5/31/94
1993-94	I Didn't Do It	626	5/31/95
*1993-94	A Sweet Offering	549/3/0	5/31/95
***1993-94	Sweet As Can Be	541	5/31/95
*1994-95	For Keeps	630	5/31/96
1994-95	Little Visitor	563/0	5/31/96
***1994-95	Little Troubadour	558	5/31/96

Release Date	Name	Mold No.	Cut-off Date
1994-95	Honey Lover (miniature on a gold chain)	--	5/31/96
1994-95	At Grandpa's	621	5/31/95
1995-96	A Story from Grandma	620	5/31/96
*1995-96	From Me to You	629	5/31/97
1995-96	Country Suitor	760	5/31/97
***1995-96	Strum Along	557	5/31/97
*1996-97	Forever Yours	793	5/31/98
1996-97	Valentine Gift Display Plaque (personalized)	717	5/31/98
***1996-97	One, Two, Three	555	5/31/98
1996-97	What's New?	418	5/31/97

*These are special edition pieces given to all old members who renewed. New members will get the figure for the year they first join.

**A four-plate series called the Celebration Plate Series.

***A Preview Edition. This figure will be offered to members exclusively, with the club backstamp for two years. Thereafter it will be a regular production figure with regular markings.

M.I. Hummel Dolls

The first Hummel dolls were made in 1950. At that time they were made outside of the Goebel factory by arrangement with another company. The first dolls had rubber heads and soft stuffed bodies, stood 16-1/2" tall, and were delivered to the Goebel factory to be dressed in hand-made clothing. Very shortly thereafter the composition of the body was changed (1951) to rubber also. Only six dolls were produced at first. In 1952 Goebel brought the entire production of the dolls in-house and added a smaller 10" size.

Over the years it became apparent that the rubber used in the dolls was unstable and the compound would sometimes break down. This breakdown is exhibited by overall deterioration of the head and body: areas sinking in or collapsing, cracking or a combination of any or all. By 1963 or 1964 the company changed the composition to rubber and vinyl according to their advertising at the time. The bodies are now all made of soft, durable material that is a type of polyvinylchloride (PVC).

There were about twelve different dolls of this type produced in a 10" (26 cm) size until 1983. At that point Goebel introduced a completely new line. These will be discussed on following pages.

NAME	SIMILAR TO
Bertl	Little Shopper
Gretl	Sister
Hansel	Little Hiker
Felix	Chimney Sweep
Radi-Bub	For Father
Mariandl	Unknown
Liesl	Unknown
Max	Unknown
Seppl	Boy with Toothache
Rosl	School Girl
Peterle	School Boy
Seppl	Unknown

Three current production Hummel dolls. Left to right: Carnival, Signs of Spring, Lost Sheep. All have Goebel earthenware heads and hands.

Over the years the company has called the dolls by different names and has also made an 8" version of some.

A 1976 catalog advertised the 8" dolls as:

NAME	SIMILAR TO
Vroni	Meditation
Rudi	Home from Market
Seppl	Boy with Toothache
Mariandi	None
Jackl	Happy Traveler (somewhat)
Rosl	Little Sweeper (somewhat)

The 1976 catalog also lists and illustrates a 10" baby doll in two different costumes (boy and girl), although it is not made completely clear whether or not they are Hummel dolls. The nine 10" dolls that were in production up until the introduction of the new line in 1983 were as follows:

NAME	SIMILAR TO
Felix	Chimney Sweep
Ganseliesl	Goose Girl
Gretl	Sister
Hansl	Brother
Peterle	School Boy
Radibub	For Father
Rosi	School Girl
Striekliesl	A Stitch in Time (somewhat)
Wanderbub	Merry Wanderer

All the heads of the girls and the boys were the same (two styles only). All the limbs were also the same. It is the costumes and accessories that made them different. Identification of the above Hummel dolls is made relatively easy by the presence of an incised M.I. Hummel signature and Goebel trademark found on the back of the neck of each.

Current Production Dolls

In 1983 the Goebel company announced a completely new line of M.I. Hummel dolls. The heads, hands and feet of the new dolls are made of the same or similar ceramic-type material as the figurines. The bodies are still of a soft, stuffed material. The new dolls are readily identifiable from the material of the heads, hands and feet but there are additional unmistakable identifying characteristics. They are 15" in height, each having the M.I. Hummel signature and the date of production year. The bodies will also carry a label containing the production date along with identifying remarks. The first four to be released were as follows: Postman, On Holiday, Boy from Birthday Ser-

enade, Girl from Birthday Serenade. They were released at a suggested retail price of $175 each and production was limited to the year 1984.

The dolls limited in production to the year 1985 were as follows: Lost Sheep, Easter Greetings, Signs of Spring, Carnival.

New dolls were released in 1996 and 1997. Little Scholar, 14" tall, was released in 1996 and School Girl in 1997. Each comes with a wooden stand. They have the usual porcelain head and limbs. They were released at about $200. Please turn to the Danbury Mint section for more on dolls.

Expressions of Youth Series

During factory tours or the promotional tour where a Goebel artist demonstrates the painting of a figure, Goebel officials noticed that people had a tendency to be drawn toward the figurines in the pure white, glazed stage of production. Something about the shiny pure white figurine was intriguing to them. Over the years collectors have also been drawn to the white overglaze pieces in the collection. Goebel decided to create a small collection of the white pieces with only the eyes, eyebrows and the lips rendered in color. So far only seven have been put into the collection:

HUM 2/I	Little Fiddler	7-1/2"
HUM 7/I	Merry Wanderer	7"
HUM 13/V	Meditation	13-1/2"
HUM 15/II	Hear Ye, Hear Ye	7-1/2"
HUM 21/II	Heavenly Angel	8-3/4"
HUM 47/II	Goose Girl	7-1/2"
HUM 89/II	Little Cellist	8"

These figurines are produced as an open edition, but methods of production and the extraordinary quality control required in their production will limit the number available. Each is identified beneath the base with the inscription "Expressions of Youth" in red, in addition to the trademark and other normal marks.

The Crystal Collection

In 1991 Goebel began producing twelve of the Hummel figurines in 24% lead crystal. They each bear the incised M.I. Hummel signature, although the signature is not visible in any of the three photographs accompanying. They also bear the Missing Bee (TMK-6) and the year date 1991. If Goebel continues to produce them it would be reasonable to assume that as the present stock runs out the new figures will be produced with the new Hummel Mark (TMK-7). The twelve are:

Apple Tree Girl	3-3/4"
Apple Tree Boy	3-3/4"
The Botanist	3-1/8"
For Mother	2-7/8"
Little Sweeper	2-1/8"
March Winds	2-7/8"
Meditation	3-1/2"
Merry Wanderer	3-1/2"
Postman	3-7/8"
Sister	3-7/8"
Soloist	3"
Village Boy	3"
Visiting an Invalid	3-1/4"

The observant among you may have counted the list above and found that it contains thirteen figurines, not twelve as previously stated. There were indeed only twelve when the last edition was written. In 1995 Goebel offered a special where if you bought the 141/3/0 and 142/3/0 sizes of Apple Tree Boy and Apple Tree Girl you would receive a matching crystal figurine free. Somewhere along the line they decided to add the crystal version of Apple Tree Boy to go along with the girl version.

Busts of M.I. Hummel

Only three Hummel busts have been produced. The first was large, 15" high, and fashioned in a white bisque finish. These were made primarily as display pieces for authorized dealers and were given to them. The number made is not known, but is likely to be fairly limited. First made in 1965, they have the incised mold number "HU 1" and the Three Line Mark (TMK-4). The second one to be made was a smaller version. The one in the photograph on page 69 measured 6-5/8" high. It has an incised mold number of "HU 2." As you can see it bears the incised signature on the base at front. Not visible is "1967 Skrobek" on the back of the base. It can be found in both the Three Line Mark (TMK-4) and the Last Bee (TMK-5) mark.

The third version appears to be the same as the "HU 2," but has the incised mold number "HU 3" and is painted in colors. It was limited to one year of production (1979-1980), during which it was an exclusive offering to the Goebel Collector's Club (now M.I. Hummel Club). It is found bearing the Last Bee (TMK-5) mark. It is illustrated on page 63.

Crystal Collection. Left to right: Little Sweeper, Soloist, For Mother, Sister, Village Boy, March Winds.

Crystal Collection. Left to right: The Botanist, Merry Wanderer, Apple Tree Girl.

Crystal Collection. Left to right: Postman, Meditation, Visiting an Invalid.

This is the "Hu 2" bisque finish bust of M.I. Hummel made for sale through dealers. This particular one was taken to a commercial mold ceramic operation, sprayed and fired, giving it this white overglaze finish. They were never produced by Goebel in white overglaze.

Wooden music boxes: 1987 (Ride into Christmas) and 1988 (Chick Girl).

Wooden music boxes: 1989 (In Tune) and 1990 (Umbrella Girl).

Wooden Music Boxes

A series of four music boxes was announced in late 1986. This was the first officially authorized hand-carved M.I. Hummel design in wood. Designed by Goebel and made in cooperation with the Anri Workshop carvers in Italy, the four designs were rendered in relief on the covers of the boxes. Each music box is accompanied by a sequentially numbered ceramic medallion made by Goebel. Each of the four is limited in production to 10,000. The four motifs are:

1987	Ride into Christmas	Release Price $389.95
1988	Chick Girl	Release Price $400
1989	In Tune	Release Price $425
1990	Umbrella Girl	Release Price $450

Example of the ceramic medallion that accompanied each Goebel music box

Plaques, Patches and Pins

Many collectors like to add related articles, sometimes called ephemera, to their collections. Various items made by Goebel as well as by other companies (with and without Goebel's knowledge and permission) have been made to commemorate events in the world of M.I. Hummel collecting. There are probably more than are listed here as this goes on constantly. There are a few unauthorized items that are too localized and small in number to precipitate a reaction from the company and probably others that are unknown to them for the same reasons. Whatever the case, the following lists and illustrations can give you a good idea of the type of thing that the collector may find.

Plaques

Year	Design	Event
none	Merry Wanderer	Free to each visitor to the Goebel factory 1977-May 31, 1989
none	Merry Wanderer	Free to each new member of the Goebel Collectors' Club. States Membership.
1979	Merry Wanderer	Hummel Festival, Eaton, Ohio
1980	Meditation	Hummel Festival, Eaton, Ohio
1981	Little Fiddler	Hummel Festival, Eaton, Ohio
1982	Goose Girl	Hummel Festival, Eaton, Ohio
1983	Little Fiddler (head)	Dealer Festival, January 6, 1983
1983	Merry Wanderer	South Bend Plate Collectors Convention, Goebel Facsimile Factory Display, South Bend, Indiana.
1983	Confidentially	M.I. Hummel Fiesta, Misty's Gift Gallery, Sierra Vista, Arizona
1983	Merry Wanderer	Archive Tour Spenser-Zaring, Ltd., Carefree, Arizona
1983	Merry Wanderer	Archive Tour Carol's Gift Shop, Artesia, California
1983	Merry Wanderer	Archive Tour, Henri's, Belmont, California
1985	Jubilee	Free to factory visitors
1985	Little Fiddler Head	Golden Anniversary Gala, January 6, 1985
1989	Rose	World's Fair of Hummels, Rosemont, Illinois, 1989
1991	text only	Commemorates the new M.I. Hummel backstamp (TMK-7)
1993	text only (back)	German language plaque clebrating an open house for club members at the factory on September 4, 1993
1997	Valentine Gift	Given to charter members of the M.I. Hummel Club commemorating the 20th anniversary

Patches

Year	Design	Event
1977	Merry Wanderer	Hummel Festival, Eaton, Ohio.
1978	Merry Wanderer	Hummel Festival, Eaton, Ohio.
1978	Silent Night w/ Black Child, Hum 31	Hummel Festival Eaton, Ohio
1979	Mountaineer	Hummel Festival, Eaton, Ohio.
1979	Singing Lesson (plate)	Collector's Exposition, Rosemont, Illinois
1980	Meditation	Hummel Festival, Eaton, Ohio.
1981	Little Fiddler	Hummel Festival, Eaton, Ohio.
1982	Goose Girl	Hummel Festival, Eaton, Ohio.
--	text only	"Goebel Collectors Club" LOCAL CHAPTER MEMBER NAME
1983	Confidentially	M.I. Hummel Fiesta Sierra Vista, Arizona
1988	Puppy Love	Bavarian Summer Festival, Eaton, Ohio
1988	text only	World's Fair of Hummels, Rosemont, Illinois

These two patches commemorate festivals held in Eaton, Ohio.

Many small plaques such as these are prepared by the factory for Goebel-sanctioned events.

The reverse of the two small plaques showing typical inscriptions.

Three of the plaques made especially for the U.S. tour of the Goebel Facsimile Factory and the Goebel Archive Tour. There are many others than just these three.

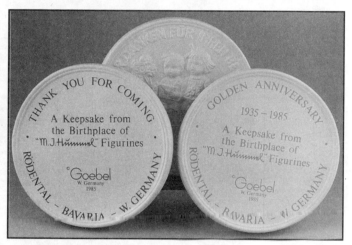

These 4-1/8" plaques are given to those who visit Goebel in Rodental. What is not generally known is the existence of the Golden Anniversary version shown on the right here. Normally printed in blue, the special version was printed in gold and given to visitors during 1985. The background shows the front of the plaque with Jubilee, Hum 416.

A special plaque commemorating the creation of the new Goebel trademark for exclusive use on Goebel M.I. Hummel collectibles. It came in a blue velvet presentation pouch.

Some of the many patches commemorating various Hummel events.

Pins

Year	Design	Event
--	Merry Wanderer	5 year membership pin for members of the Whitier, CA chapter.
1983	Confidentially	M.I. Hummel Fiesta Misty's Gift Gallery Sierra Vista, Arizona.
1982	text only	5 year membership pin for members of the Goebel Collector's Club.
1987	text only	10 year membership pin for members of the Goebel Collector's Club.
1988	Home from Market	Hummel Festival Volksmarsch. Eaton, Ohio.
1988	Friends	Hummel Festival Volksmarsch. Eaton, Ohio.
1989	Latest News	Hummel World's Fair Volksmarsch above without the Volksmarsch banner.
1989	Bumblebee on Rose	Created for the 1989 Chicago Show.
1991	Crossroads	Hummel Expo '91, Dayton, Ohio.
1992	Land in Sight	Miller's Hummel Expo '92, Dayton, Ohio (large badge).
1992	Merry Wanderer	15 year membership pin for members of the M.I. Hummel Club.
1997	Merry Wanderer	(from 20 year membership pin for the shoulders up) members of the M.I. Hummel Club.

Miscellaneous

Year	Design	Event
1986	Commemorative plaque	Goebel Fest (DeGrazia figure) Las Vegas, Nevada
1986	Mug (Chapel Time)	Goebel Fest, Las Vegas, Nevada
1992	On Our Way (metal in figure)	Miller's Expo '92, Dayton, Ohio
1993	Museum Building on Silver Plate Medallion	Opening of the new Hummel Museum, New Braunfels, Texas

Button given to attendees at the 1993 M.I. Hummel Club Convention.

Button from the Miller's Expo '92 in Dayton, Ohio.

Examples of cloisonne pins made to commemorate events in the Hummel collecting world. These have become

Metal Hum 472 (On Our Way) cast for the Miller's Expo '92 in Dayton, Ohio.

Base of the metal Hum 472 (On Our Way).

Above and left: Metal pins with Hummel designs produced for occasions of note.

Jewelry

In past years from time to time an individual or a company has produced jewelry utilizing M.I. Hummel design motifs. Goebel keeps tight control of licensing these days, but in the earlier years there were some who took advantage. One such effort turned into the Goebel Miniatures division of the company (see chapter 5). Refer also to the section on the M.I. Hummel Club exclusives for pictures of the pendants offered to the membership.

Most of the items are in the form of pins or brooches. Probably in excess of 50 of these have been produced. Quality has ranged from pot metal to silver and gold.

A few examples of brooches you may find are Little Hiker, For Mother, Retreat to Safety, and Umbrella Boy. There are many more.

Calendars

Goebel published the first calendar in 1951. It was made in the German language only. The following year the first English language version was published and until 1975, when the German language version illustrated the 1975 plate on the cover, the English calendar used the design from the previous year's German edition. In 1975 the cover of the German language calendar was the 1975 Annual Plate, so the next year's English edition illustrated the 1976 plate. The practice reverted to the German language design preceding the English language edition after that, with one other exception in 1964 and 1965. In 1989 the format of the calendars changed completely.

Goebel published a special calendar in 1985 to celebrate the fiftieth anniversary of M.I. Hummel figurines. This is apart from the annual series of calendars.

Another special edition calendar was published for 1987. This one was in commemoration of the tenth anniversary of the founding of the Goebel Collectors' Club (now the M.I. Hummel Club). This calendar is apart from the annual series of Hummel calendars.

The M. I. Hummel Annual Calendar Listing

Year	Language	Title
1951	German	Goose Girl
1952	English	Vacation Time
1953	German	Heavenly Protection
1954	English	
1954	German	Festival Harmony with Flute
1955	English	
1955	German	Candle Light candleholder
1956	English	
1956	German	School Girls
1957	English	
1957	German	School Boys
1958	English	
1958	German	Meditation
1959	English	
1959	German	Stormy Weather
1960	English	
1960	German	Book Worm
1961	English	
1961	German	Flower Madonna
1962	English	
1962	German	Telling Her Secret
1963	English	
1963	German	Little Tooter
1964	English	
1964	German	Saint George
1965	English	Goose Girl
1965	German	Spring Dance
1966	English	
1966	German	School Girls
1967	English	
1967	German	Duet
1968	English	
1968	German	Mail Coach
1969	English	
1969	German	Ring Around the Rosie
1970	English	
1970	German	To Market
1971	English	
1971	German	Stormy Weather (detail)
1972	English	
1972	German	Adventure Bound
1973	English	
1973	German	Umbrella Boy
1974	English	
1974	German	Happy Days
1975	English	
1975	German	1975 Annual Plate
1976	English	1976 Annual Plate
1976	German	The Artist
1977	English	
1977	German	Follow the Leader
1978	English	
1978	German	Happy Pastime
1979	English	

A Goebel calendar from 1978.

1979	German	Smart Little Sister
1980	English	
1980	German	School Girl
1981	English	
1981	German	Ring Around the Rosie
1983	English	
1983	German	Happy Days
1984	English	
1984	German	Merry Wanderer
1985	English	
1985	German	Thoughtful
1986	English	
1986	German	Auf Wiedersehen
1987	English	
1987	German	In Tune

(Note: From 1988 on the format was changed)

1988	English	In Tune
1988	German	Be Patient & Barnyard Hero
1989	English	
1989	German	Crossroads
1990	English	
1990	German	Ring Around the Rosie
1991	English	
1991	German	Home from Market & Globe Trotter
1992	English	
1992	German	A Fair Measure & Kiss Me
1993	English	
1993	German	Going to Grandma's
1993	English	
1994	German	Book Worm
1994	English	
1995	German	Umbrella Boy
1995	English	
1996	German	Sweet Music & Tuba Player
1997	English	

Goebel's 1985 calendar, in celebration of fifty years of Hummel figurines.

Goebel's 1987 calendar, a special edition in celebration of the tenth anniversary of the Goebel Collectors' Club (now M.I. Hummel Club).

CHAPTER FIVE

THE RARE AND THE UNUSUAL

THE RARE AND THE UNUSUAL

This section is devoted to the rare and to the not so rare, but unusual, items. The most famous of these is, of course, the International Collection. There are some others that are difficult to classify in the normal divisions of derivations of M.I. Hummel art and so they are placed here. Still others that could be placed with their respective normal production piece counterpart are more appropriately placed here because of a perceived special status. In some cases they will appear in both places and in other cases they will be cross-referenced.

EARTHENWARE

Faience or "Doll Face" Pieces

In 1986 a U.S. Army officer stationed in Germany discovered a most unusual Little Fiddler with the incised M.I. Hummel signature and the Crown trademark (TMK-1) in a German flea market. It was painted differently, with brighter colors than normal. Even more unusual was the china white face, hands and base and the very shiny glaze. Subsequent investigation not only authenticated the piece as genuine, but uncovered some new and interesting information with regard to the early history of the development of M.I. Hummel figurines. It seems that early on, while experimenting with different mediums, glazed porcelain was used. As far as is known, Goebel did not go into mass production of the porcelain pieces for it was found that the fine earthenware with a matte finish was more amenable to the true reproduction of the soft pastel colors used by M.I. Hummel in her artwork. What we do know is that they were produced in sufficient numbers for many to end up in private collections. Models and colors vary widely, but the majority reflect the normal colors. The piece the officer found had a bright blue coat, a red kerchief instead of the normal blue and a brown hat instead of black. The accompanying photo illustrates the difference between the normal and the faience pieces of the same era, but the difference can be more readily seen if you will turn to the examples shown in the color section. The faience variation can be found on Hum 1 through

The Little Fiddler figurine on the left is the faience piece. Note the very pale look to the face compared to the normal figure on the right. It has an incised Crown (TMK-1) mark that has been colored with green ink. The figure has a donut base and measures 10-15/16".

These two unusual Crown Marks shown here are often found incised on the underside of the base of the Doll Face pieces. The reason for the odd devices over the mark is as yet unexplained.

Hum 15. If found, these are valued about 20% higher than their Crown Mark (TMK-1) counterparts. It is unusual, but the faience pieces have been found bearing Full Bee and Stylized Bee marks as well. The difference between them is more readily seen in the color section.

How They Came to Be

In early experiments with the media and paints in which to render three-dimensional Hummel figures, porcelain was used. In the long run it was found that the inherent "whiteness" of fired porcelain would not lend itself to the rendering of the rosy cheeks so typical of M.I. Hummel's children in the paintings and drawings. They did, however cast, paint and fire the first fifteen of the designs in porcelain and took them along with the earthenware figures to the Leipzig Fair.

When they displayed the original forty-six figurines at the Leipzig Fair in 1935, they displayed the porcelain ones also. At the end of the fair it was the now-familiar earthenware pieces that proved the most popular. The porcelain pieces apparently languished in some storage area or another, but they obviously somehow made their way into the market. The individual faience pieces will be identified with their respective designs in the Goebel figurine listing.

The Terra Cotta Pieces

When Goebel displayed the original forty-six figurines they also displayed a number of them rendered in terra cotta, a brownish red unglazed earthenware. As with the porcelain pieces they did not prove to be popular and subsequently production of the terra cotta pieces was abandoned. There is no way of knowing how many designs and how many of each of the designs were made. What we do know is that they were apparently severely limited in number. For example: an unquestionably genuine terra cotta "Puppy Love" has been found with an incised "T 1" mold number and the M.I. Hummel signature, but it is the only one known to be in a private collection.

All known terra cotta pieces will be individually identified in the Goebel collection listing with their respective designs.

THE INTERNATIONAL FIGURINES

One of the most interesting and exciting aspects of collecting Hummel figurines and other related pieces is the omnipresent chance to discover a relatively uncommon or a significantly rare piece. This fortuitous circumstance has happened many times. It has often occurred as a result of painstaking research and detective work, but more often it is pure chance.

One such example is the story of the "Hungarians." A knowledgeable and serious collector of Hummel articles, Mr. Robert L. Miller, regularly advertises that he will buy original Hummel pieces in various collector periodicals around the world. He received a postcard from Europe

Unidentified as to country or mold number. 5", no apparent marks.

Mel. 9., BULGARIAN. Stamped Crown, 5-1/4".

BULGARIAN. The mold number on this example is not evident but is known to be 807. What is there is an incised "Bul. 2." and an incised Crown mark (TMK-1). It measures 5".

Hum 811, BULGARIAN. Double Crown Mark, 5-1/4".

Hum 808, BULGARIAN. Left: 808., double Crown Mark (TMK-1), donut base, 5". Right: No apparent markings, 4-15/16".

Hum 810, BULGARIAN. Both have the double Crown Mark (TMK-1) and measure 5-1/8".

Hum 812, SERBIAN. While similar in costume and pose, these two figures are obviously from different molds. Both have donut bases and measure 5-3/4".

Hum 812, SERBIAN. Base of one of the two in the previous photo showing the markings.

one day describing some Hummels an individual had for sale. After he obtained photographs of a few figurines it was obvious that some were familiar Hummel designs, but some were apparently in Hungarian costume. In relating his story to the author, Mr. Miller said he felt at first that they were probably not real Hummel pieces, but were attractive and he thought they might make a nice Christ-

mas present for his wife. He sent a check and after some thought he called the factory to inquire as to their possible authenticity. He was informed that they knew of no such figures. By the time the pieces arrived, however, he had begun to think that they might be genuine. Upon opening and examining them he saw that each bore the familiar M.I. Hummel signature! He again called the factory and

Hum 813, SERBIAN. Left: Incised Crown Mark (TMK-1), 5-3/4". Right: No apparent trademark, 5-3/4". There are some color decoration variations between the two.

Hum 813, SERBIAN. Shows markings beneath the base.

was told again they knew nothing of them but would investigate. A short time later he received a letter from the W. Goebel firm stating that the eight figurines were indeed produced by the factory as samples for a dealer in Hungary before the war and that they believed them to be the only eight ever produced. As most of us are aware now, many more have turned up since Mr. Miller's discovery. In fact something like twenty-six or more different designs have been found, representing many different countries. In the beginning they were thought to be unique and each of them commanded a price of $20,000. The old law of supply and demand came very much into play as more and

more were found. Today their value ranges from as low as about $4,500 to as high as about $12,000 for the very scarce and rare examples.

For several years these superb figures were erroneously referred to as the Hungarians, but they are now known as the Internationals because as time went by more and more were found wearing costumes from countries other than Hungary. Among them are Bulgaria, Serbia, Hungary, Czech, Slovakia and Sweden. There may yet be others found. The photos of the International figures here are also found in the color section.

So far there have been at least twenty-six unique models found. Counting variations and those figures that are different but bear the same mold number, there are at least thirty-six. When considering numbers missing in the sequence of those found so far, a conservative estimate of those left unfound would be twenty-five to thirty-five, but there is a distinct, however remote, possibility that upwards of 100 may yet be out there.

The following is a list of the different designs that have so far been found.

806	Bulgarian	Similar to Serenade
807	Bulgarian	Entirely different from other known Hummel designs. Could be a redesign of Feeding Time.
808	Bulgarian	Similar to Serenade
809	Bulgarian	Similar to Feeding Time. Has also been found with the Mel 9 designator.
810	Bulgarian	Entirely different from other known Hummel designs. There are four distinct paint variations to be found.
810	Bulgarian	Similar to Serenade
811	Bulgarian	Entirely different from other known Hummel designs.

812	Serbian	Entirely different from other known Hummel designs.
813	Serbian	Entirely different from other known Hummel designs.
824	Swedish	Similar to Merry Wanderer. The 824 has also been found with the "Mel 24" designator
825	Swedish	Similar to Meditation
831	Slovak	Similar to Serenade
832	Slovak	Similar to Meditation
833	Slovak	Similar to Serenade, but with a different instrument.
841	Czech	Similar to Lost Sheep
842	Czech	Similar to Goose Girl
851	Hungarian	Similar to Little Hiker
852	Hungarian	Entirely different from other known Hummel designs.
853	Hungarian	Similar to Not for You
853	Hungarian	Entirely different from other known Hummel designs. Boy with derby hat and flowers
854	Hungarian	Similar to the girl on the right in Happy Birthday
904	Serbian	Similar to Little Fiddler
913	Serbian	Similar to Meditation
947	Serbian	Similar to Goose Girl
968	Serbian	Similar to Lost Sheep

Hum 824, SWEDISH. Left: 4-5/8". Right: 4-3/4". Obviously inspired by the Merry Wanderer. The one on the right is really stepping out!

Hum 825, SWEDISH. Incised Crown mark (TMK-1) and a stamped Full Bee (TMK-2) trademark, black "Germany," 5".

Two variations on a theme. Left: Slovak dress. Mold number is not evident, but is known to be 831. There is an incised number that appears to be an 82 or 89. It measures 5-5/8". Right: The mold number is 806 and the figure measures 5" tall.

Two international versions of Lost Sheep that curiously have two different mold numbers. Left: Czechoslovakian costume with mold number 841. Stamped with Crown Mark (TMK-1) and measures 5-3/4". Right: Serbian dress with mold number 968 and a stamped Full Bee (TMK-2) mark, black "Germany," 5-1/2".

Hum 842, CZECHOSLOVAKIAN. Left: 842, stamped Crown Mark (TMK-1), 5-5/8". Right: 842, Full Bee (TMK-2), black "Germany," 5-1/2". Two obviously different molds.

Hum 832, country unknown. There is at least one other 832 design in Slovak costume. Markings are: incised Crown Mark (TMK-1) colored in blue. Measures 5-7/16".

A one-of-a-kind copy of one of the Internationals, Hum 851, in Hungarian dress. It was hand made for personal enjoyment by a talented artist many years ago.

Hum 852, HUNGARIAN. Incised Crown (TMK-1) and Full Bee (TMK-2) marks, 5".

Hum 851, HUNGARIAN. Left: Double Crown Mark (TMK-1), 5-1/4". Right: Incised Crown Mark (TMK-1) and stamped Full Bee (TMK-2) mark, black "Germany," 5-1/4".

Hum 853, HUNGARIAN. Incised Crown Mark (TMK-1), donut base, 5".

Two different international versions of Little Fiddler. Although they obviously reflect the same theme, the molds are very different. Left: No apparent markings. Measures 4-5/8". Right: Mold number 904 incised, Full Bee (TMK-2) mark, 5-1/4".

It was not generally known, but there was a tentative plan in the works to reissue thirty of the International designs in a larger size than the originals. It got to the sample phase and the plan was reconsidered and finally scrapped. Dealers and collectors lauded the decision to cancel the plan, as there was much speculation that such an issue would have a negative effect on one of the most exciting aspects of collecting M.I. Hummel items, i.e. the value of those known Internationals and those yet to be uncovered.

The Internationals were never part of the regular production line. Because they were never produced and released in large quantities, but only as a very limited number of sample pieces, they are quite rare.

Hum 854, HUNGARIAN. Double Crown Mark (TMK-1), 5"

Hum 913, SERBIAN. Left: Measuring 5-5/8", this figure has "MEL 1940 Unger" written in pencil beneath the base. No other marks apparent. Right: Mold number 913, registered trademark symbol, 5-1/4".

Hum 947/0., SERBIAN. Both have double Crown Marks (TMK-1). The left one measures 4-7/8" and the other, 5".

THE MEL PIECES

At least seven of a possible twenty-four or more of these interesting pieces are known to exist today. Some are more common than others but only on a relative basis. They are all scarce. Generally speaking, the rule of identification is that each of the pieces have the three-letter prefix "MEL" incised along with the mold number. It is now known that these were produced as samples only and marked with the last three letters of Hummel to identify them as such. Only two of these so far have been found with the M.I. Hummel incised signature and they are unique. The remaining pieces do not have the signature and therefore cannot be considered original Hummel pieces in the strictest sense. Their claim to authenticity otherwise is obvious.

Those positively identified as MEL pieces are:

Mel 1	Girl with Nosegay	$75
Mel 2	Girl with Fir Tree	$75
Mel 3	Boy with Horse	$75
Mel 4	Candy dish or box with a boy on the lid.	$6500-7500
Mel 5	Candy dish or box with a girl on the lid.	$6500-7500
Mel 6	Child in Bed candy dish or box.	$2500-3000
Mel 7	Child (sitting on lid of candy dish).	$6500-7500
Mel 9	International figure (Bulgarian, Hum 809)	
Mel 24*	International figure (Swedish, Hum 824)	

*This particular Mel piece bears the incised M.I. Hummel signature. The only one known exists in a private collection.

MEL 6, Child in Bed candy dish.

Three MEL pieces. Left to right: Mel 1, Mel 2, Mel 3. Each also has a black "Germany" beneath the base.

Of all these the first three are the most commonly found. It is a matter of interest that these three (Mel 1 through Mel 3) have subsequently been released as HUM 115, 116 and 117. The other Mel piece with the signature is only assumed to be so through an old Goebel catalog listing, for it does not have the Mel prefix in the mold number. It is unique, and the only one known exists in a private collection.

Some information suggests there may be more of these pieces to be found. For instance, there are missing numbers between nine and twenty-four, and factory records recount the modeling of Mel 4 and Mel 5, both candy dishes, one with a boy on top and the other with a girl.

METAL FIGURINES

Bronze or Brass

Pictured on page 88 are four metal Hummel figurines. In actuality they are the casting pieces from which the molds for the crystal figurines are cast. They are unique and a realistic secondary market value is impossible to assign. How they got into a private collection is unknown. As there are fourteen crystal pieces in this one collection, there is the possibility, however unlikely, that twelve more of these will be found. See the Crystal Collection, above.

The Miniature Collection

There is another division of Goebel, based in California, called Goebel Miniatures. They are the sole producers of the painted bronze miniature renditions of M.I. Hummel figurines.

There is an interesting story behind the formation of Goebel Miniatures. A few years before the division

Bronze casting pieces used for the crystal figurine molds.

Goebel Miniatures. Left to right: We Congratulate, Stormy Weather, Apple Tree Boy, School Boy, Little Sweeper, Merry Wanderer, a U.S. dime for scale.

Goebel Miniatures. Left to right: Little Tooter, Waiter, Accordion Boy, Little Fiddler, Baker, Goose Girl. A U.S. dime for scale.

Goebel Miniatures. Left to right: a German-language miniature display plaque, Visiting an Invalid, Postman, Ride into Christmas, a U.S. dime for scale.

Goebel Miniatures. Left to right: Doll Bath, a U.S. dime for scale, Busy Student.

existed, a talented artist named Robert Olszewski produced several miniature replicas of Hummel figurines in gold, innocently unaware of the need to obtain permission to do so. It is unlikely that the company would have allowed it and that's what makes the story interesting. Prior to Goebel finding out about his work and stopping him, he produced miniatures of each of the following five figurines: Barnyard Hero, Stormy Weather, Kiss Me, Ring Around the Rosie, Ride into Christmas.

He had also fashioned a very small number of solid gold bracelets with each one of the above miniatures attached. Those bracelets and the unauthorized miniatures have since become highly sought and, if sold, can command extraordinarily high prices.

Out of this incident came Goebel's recognition of Olszewski's talent and the fact that there was a market for the miniature figurines. It resulted in his association with Goebel and the creation of Goebel Miniatures with Olszewski as its head.

Goebel Miniatures has produced many other miniatures for Goebel, but our interest is in the series of miniatures of the M.I. Hummel figurines that have been made.

The Mail is Here miniature in clock tower display vignette. The clear protective dome has been removed.

The series is enhanced by the introduction of six separate little Bavarian buildings and settings that were connected by bridges. They were made to the same scale as the miniatures for their display. The settings are known as KinderWay.

The following is a list of all the miniatures produced:
Accordion Boy
Apple Tree Boy
Baker
Busy Student
Doll Bath
Dealer Display Plaque (English language)
Dealer Display Plaque (German language)
Goose Girl
Honey Lover (with pendant cage and chain)
Little Fiddler

Morning Concert Miniature, GMS 269-P. This is shown in the optional display dome and bandstand setting and also with the Goebel English-language miniature studio display plaque to the left. Note the dime on the right for scale. M.I. Hummel Club exclusive.

Ring Around the Rosie miniature on musical display. The clear protective dome has been removed. Suggested retail price: $675.

Little Sweeper
Little Tooter
The Mail is Here (display vignette with dome)
Merry Wanderer
Morning Concert (M.I. Hummel Club exclusive, display with dome)
Postman
Ride into Christmas
Ring Around the Rosie (musical display vignette with dome)
School Boy
Stormy Weather
Valentine Gift (M.I. Hummel Club exclusive)
Visiting an Invalid
Waiter
Wayside Harmony
We Congratulate
What Now? (M.I. Hummel Club exclusive)

The KinderWay Displays are as follows: Market Square Flower Stand, Countryside School, Wayside Shrine, Bavarian Cottage and Bavarian Village.

Goebel announced in early 1992 that the KinderWay Bavarian Village settings would be permanently retired, but more importantly, they announced that production of the M.I. Hummel figurine miniatures would be suspended indefinitely as of the end of 1992. They further stated in

the announcement *(Insights,* Vol. 15, No. 4, page 8): "Though the figurine miniatures have not yet been formally retired, there are currently no plans to resume production." There have been at least three produced since then as special editions. They are Ring Around the Rosie, The Mail is Here (Mail Coach) and Honey Lover.

The Mail is Here miniature. Underside shows the markings.

PLAQUES AND PLATES

The Jumbo Wooden Display Plaque

At least seven of these plaques have been found in recent years. They are each magnum sized (34" x 23", 20 lbs.), carved from wood and beautifully painted, duplicating the Hum 187 Display Plaque in a jumbo size.

The only identifying mark that could be found on the plaque was a curious "A" within a circle. The crossbar in the "A" appeared to be a bolt of lightening.

For several years the origin of this plaque remained elusive, giving rise to much speculation regarding the circle A mark. The "A" gave rise to the theory that the plaques were produced in the famous Anri Workshop in Italy. The character of the carving and painting seemed to be of the same style and quality as the famed woodcarvers'.

Some of the circle A marks were placed upside down on the back of the plaques and not rendered very clearly. This anomaly made the mark resemble the Goebel "Vee and Bee" trademark, giving rise to yet another theory that it might have been a Goebel product.

Both of these theories have since been discredited as the origin of the plaques has finally been traced. It seems that the manufacturer was a furniture company quite close to the Goebel factory in Oeslau (now Rodental), Germany. In fact, Goebel had these made by the company and Goebel artists painted them. When queried about them, the furniture company said they did indeed produce them, but have not done so for more than thirty years. It seems there was some sort of changeover in the type of production facility that resulted in the company halting the employment of the woodcarvers necessary to produce these plaques. No doubt the Goebel company would take a dim view of this endeavor these days in any case.

There is no record of how many plaques were made, but they are in short supply. They have been found both in Europe and the United States. The last one I know of was found in the U.S. Virgin Islands. Secondary market value is around $5000-6000.

The Factory Workers' Plate

This plate was produced for distribution to the Goebel factory workers involved in plate production, in commemoration of the tenth (1980) annual plate. Obviously it would have been produced in extremely low numbers since it was never intended for general distribution and retail sales. The quantity is reported to be sixty to one hundred. It is not rendered in bas-relief, as are all the other Goebel plates, but was made by utilizing the decal method. The design depicts the ten plates in miniature in a counterclockwise circle with the 1971 plate in the twelve o'clock position.

There are apparently three authorized and one unauthorized versions of this plate. The three legitimate versions are an uncolored plate, a single color wash on the illustrated plate and a single color illustrated plate with the inscription in a black rectangular box. The collector value of these three is $1200-1800.

Of some interest is the unauthorized version of this plate. It seems that someone produced a few of the plates in full color. When Goebel found out about this, they

Oversize Wooden Display Plaque. Its genuine Hummel normal-sized counterpart is placed in the foreground for size comparison.

The 1971-1980 Factory Workers Plate.

The Local Chapter Plaque

Pictured here is an example of a display plaque many collectors are not aware of. It is a modified Hum 187 Display Plaque that was made available for a short time to members of local chapters of the Goebel Collectors' Club (now the M.I. Hummel Club). It was personalized with the name of the member and the local chapter name.

Goebel Collectors' Club Chapter Plaque.

quickly put a stop to it. Some collectors place a value of about $300 on these, but most are uninterested because they were not produced by or under the auspices of W. Goebel Porzellanfabrik.

The Goebel Employee Service Plaque

This unique piece is quite similar to the Hum 187 display plaque but does not have the usual "Original Hummel Figures" inscription. On the occasion of an individual's 25th, 40th and 50th anniversary of employment with the company one of these plaques is presented, personalized with the employee's name and the date of the anniversary. A very small number of these pieces have surfaced in private collections. They are valued at $600-1000.

The Artist Display Plaque

The mold number for this display plaque is Hum 756. It was originally produced to commemorate the 1993 grand opening of the M.I. Hummel Museum in Texas, as you can see in the accompanying illustration. Subsequent to that event the plaque has been issued to commemorate at least two other events, one in 1994 and one in 1995, both in Germany.

The Goebel Employee Service Plaque.

Little Artist display plaque.

Special edition Puppy Love display plaque.

Special Edition Puppy Love Display Plaque

This display plaque bears the Hummel mold number 767 and a 1993 MID. It commemorates sixty years of Hummel figurine production.

The 1948 Christmas Plate

This plate was never put into production, but obviously a few managed to make their way into private hands. Perhaps this happened through samples given to sales representatives or inadvertent loss at trade shows. It measures 7-1/4" in diameter and the reverse side of the plate has three concentric raised circles, the center of which has the hand-inked words: "Entw. A. Moller Ausf. H. Sommer nach Hummel". Collector value range is in the mid five figure range.

MISCELLANEOUS

The Goebel Flying Bee

Goebel changed their trademark (backstamp) from the Crown Mark (TMK-1) to the Full Bee (TMK-2) in 1950. This large promotional display piece was made to depict

The 1948 Christmas plate.

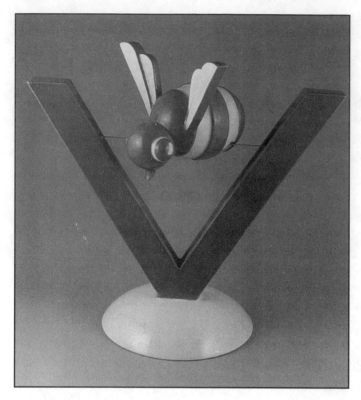

Goebel Flying Bee promotional piece.

Holy water font: unidentified except by incised M.I. Hummel signature.

the new mark. There are two sizes to be found. The one in the photo here is of the larger size. It is thought to be prototype for there are many more of the smaller size to be found. The secondary market value for any of them should be around $2000-$2500.

Unidentified Holy Water Font

This is a beautiful little font with an incised M.I. Hummel signature but no other apparent markings whatsoever. I have not been able to find it listed or illustrated in any references. The globe is colored a beautiful deep blue with white stars. The piece is unique and no there is no record of trading on the secondary market, therefore no valuation is attempted.

Unidentified Goebel Mold Number "Hs 1"

This piece is thought by some to be the forerunner to the Hum 88, Heavenly Protection. The two are quite similar, but the connection has not yet been proven. It could simply have been inspired by the Heavenly Protection fig-

Figure identified only as Goebel mold number HS 1, possibly related to Hum 88 (Heavenly Protection).

urine or the painting from which it was derived. The final conclusion must be made by the individual collector until some evidence is found to support or refute the theory.

Another possibility is that it is the Hum 108 prototype. The piece may have been a M.I. Hummel design that was not approved for production. See Heavenly Protection, Hum 88.

Goose Girl with Bowl

This mysterious piece was uncovered in Germany about 1989. It has an incised Crown mark. It is a 4-3/4" Goose Girl with an attached bowl. Upon close examination, it appears that they were joined before firing, lending legitimacy to the presumption that it was fashioned at the factory. The bowl is a Double Crown piece with an incised mold number "1."

There have been at least two more of these unusual pieces found. They are Hum 13, Meditation, and Hum 17, Congratulations. The attached pots are different from the one in the picture here. The pots are round, slightly tapered from bottom to a larger diameter at the top, and have four ridges around the main body. These are sample pieces that were not approved by the convent and never placed into production.

The collector value range is $6000-7000.

Limited Edition Little Fiddler

Little known in the U.S. is the limited production of a 7-1/2" Little Fiddler (Hum 2/I) with a gilded base. According to company promotional literature only fifty of these were made and they were part of a Goebel contest giveaway in Germany. This is probably one of the most severely limited production figures that Goebel has ever produced. The collector value is about $1700-$2000. Please see Chimney Sweep (Hum 12) for another gilded base figurine. Photo on page 96.

The unique Goose Girl with Bowl, discovered in 1989.

The limited edition gold gilt base Little Fiddler, Hum 2/1.

The underside of the base of the gold base Hum 2/1, showing the trademark and the German-language Golden Jubilee backstamp. It reads: "50 JAHRE M.I. HUMMEL-FIGUREN 1935-1985."

A piece of German promotional material for this figure.

English/Beswick pieces. Left to right with their incised mold numbers: Meditation (910); Trumpet Boy (903); Puppy Love (909).

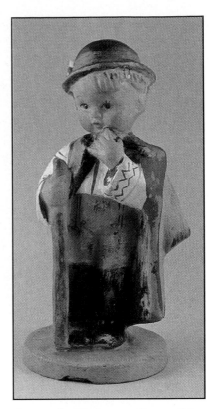

Left: Two examples of Shrine by Janet Robson. Each bears the Three Line (TMK-4) mark and the mold number ROB 422 incised and inked in, indicating there are Mother Mold Pieces. Both have the incised 1961 MID and measure 5¼".

A one-of-a-kind copy of one of the Internationals, Hum 851, in Hungarian dress. It was handmade for personal enjoyment by a talented artist many years ago.

The unique Goose Girl with Bowl, discovered in 1989.

Left: LITTLE FIDDLER, Hum 4. The left piece is the doll face. Note the very pale face and hands, the completely different head position and the lack of a neck kerchief. Each has the decimal point mold number designation 4. and the Crown mark and measures 5⅛".

Rear view of Hum 6 showing the "H" and "X" suspenders configuration discussed in the text.

BOOK WORM, Hum 8. A comparison between the normal skin coloration (left) and the pale coloration on the doll face piece. Both measure 4¼". The left bears a Stylized Bee mark. The one on the right is a doll face piece with a double Crown mark.

Left: GLOBE TROTTER, Hum 79. Rear view showing the different basket weave patterns discussed in text. Older figure is on the left.

COME BACK SOON, Hum 291. The Final Edition (1995) of the twenty-five plate series that started in 1971.

Left: LITTLE GARDENER, Hum 74. Left: 74., incised Crown Mark, split base, 4⅜". Note the height of the flower. Right: Missing Bee trademark, 4½".

HAPPY TRAVELER, Hum 109/0. Left: a Full Bee piece with black "Germany," donut base and the normal green color coat. Right: This is a doll face Hum 109/0 with a blue plaid coat. It has no apparent base markings. Both measure 5".

Right: CONCENTRATION, Hum 302, PFE.

Left: WHITSUNTIDE, Hum 163. Left: Incised Crown Mark, red candle in angel's hand. Right: Last Bee trademark (TMK-5), no candle. Both measure 6¾".

Right: MADONNA, Plaque, Hum 222. No apparent mark other than mold number. Measures 4" x 5". The wire frame is detachable.

Left: Special edition of AUF WIEDERSEHEN on wood base with the porcelain Airlift Memorial replica piece. Both have a special back-stamp and the edition is limited to 25,000. Wall: 7½". Figurine: Hum 153/0, 5½".

THE PROFESSOR, Hum 320. This is a master model. Note the red line around the base.

THE ART CRITIC, Hum 318. Demonstration piece with only the flesh tones and brown base color on the coat painted. Current-use trademark (TMK-7), First Issue backstamp, incised 1955 MID, 5¼". Valued at about $400.

SUNNY MORNING, Hum 313. Inked in incised 313 mold number, Full Bee trademark in an incised circle, 1955 MID, "© by W. Goebel, 1956," 4¼".

ARITHMETIC LESSON, Hum 303, PFE.

BIRTHDAY PRESENT, Hum 341. The figure on the left is an early factory sample model measuring 5¼" and bearing the Stylized Bee (TMK-3) trademark. The one on the right is the smaller (4") current production piece. The MID is 1989.

At left from top to bottom: RELAXATION, Hum 316, PFE, HELPING MOTHER, Hum 325, PFE. and AT THE FENCE, Hum 324, PFE.

DOLL BATH, Hum 319. Both figures bear the Three Line mark (TMK-5). The one on the left has an incised 1956 MID and the other has an MID of 197?. It was impossible to discern the fourth digit.

THE ARTIST, Hum 304. Left: Missing Bee trademark (TMK-6), incised 1955 MID. Right: Inked-in incised mold number indicating that this is a master model. It bears a stamped Full Bee trademark and "© by W. Goebel, 1955." Note the paint drip on the base. This feature has never made it to the production piece.

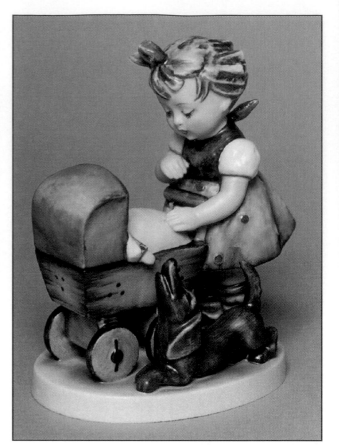

LUCKY BOY, Hum 335/0. The special limited edition. It measures 2½", bears an incised MID of 1989 and the sixtieth anniversary backstamp.

Factory sample of LUCKY BOY, Hum 335. It has a 1956 MID and measures 5¾".

MORNING STROLL, Hum 375. This is an early factory sample piece.

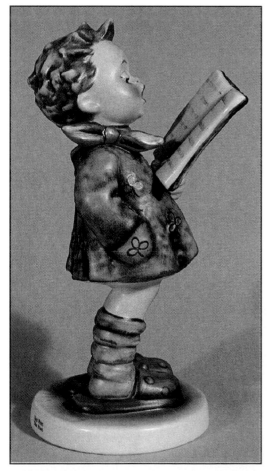

LUCKY FELLOW, Hum 560. An M.I. Hummel Club members-only exclusive offering. It is 3⅝" tall, bears the current use trademark (TMK-7), the special club backstamp and an incised 1989 MID.

THE POET, Hum 397.

Factory "Sample" of BEHAVE!, Hum 339.

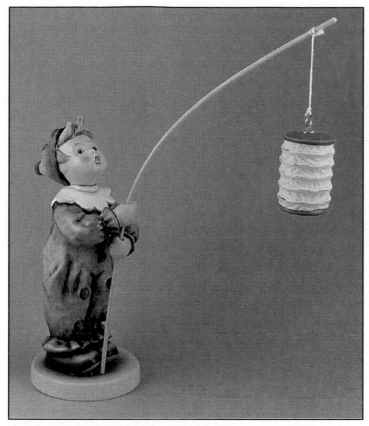

PARADE OF LIGHTS, Hum 616. Hummel mark (TMK-7), 6".

COME BACK SOON, Hum 545. Left: The regular production figure with TMK-6. Right: The 1995 "First Issue" version with TMK-7.

ROCK-A-BYE, Hum 574.

SHEPHERD BOY, Hum 395.

Above left:
NIMBLE FINGERS,
Hum 758. 4¾" high, 1993
incised MID,
First Issue 1995.
Above right: TO KEEP
YOU WARM Hum 759.
5" high, 1993 incised
MID, First Issue 1995.

Top right:
A STORY FROM
GRANDMA, Hum 620.

Middle right:
AT GRANDPA'S,
Hum 621.

Below right:
MAKING NEW
FRIENDS, Hum 2002.

Left: WELCOME
SPRING, Hum 635.
Hummel mark (TMK-7),
12¼", 1993 Century
Collection piece.

Left to Right: **MOTHER'S DARLING**, Hum 175. *Far Left:* Crown Mark, the bag in the right hand is pinkish and the upper part of her dress very light; Hum 175, Stylized Bee trademark, bag in right hand is blue and the upper part of the dress very dark.
SOLDIER BOY, Hum 332. Both of these bear the Three Line Mark. The one on the far right has the red medallion found on the earlier, more desirable pieces for collectors.

Left to Right: **WEARY WANDERER**, Hum 204. Both of these bear the Full Bee. The one on the left is probably the older of the two (the Full Bee is incised) and is referred to as the Blue eye variation. **LOST SHEEP**, Hum 68. Bears an incised Full Bee mark. It is the brown pants variation found on the older pieces. *Far Right:* Last Bee trademark figurine illustrating the normal clothing colors.

Left to Right: **KISS ME**, Hum 311. Bears the Three Line Mark, this is the older "socks on the doll variation"; Missing Bee mark with the regular no socks version. **HAPPY BIRTHDAY**, Hum 176. Both are Crown Marked pieces with the decimal designator 176., but the one on the far right also has a Full Bee mark. You can see that they are from different molds.

Left to Right: **HELLO**, Hum 124. The Figure on the far left is the green pants, pink vest variation found on the older pieces. The Last Bee marked figure to the right of the first one right is the norm for later releases. Next is **WAITER**, Hum 154, the older of the two Waiters, has an incised Crown Mark. It has gray pants. The far right figurine has the brown pants found on the newer releases.

1990 CHRISTMAS BELLS, Hum 776. The bell on the right is the normal color. The one on the left is the greenish yellow version made in limited edition for Christmas gift to company sales representatives.

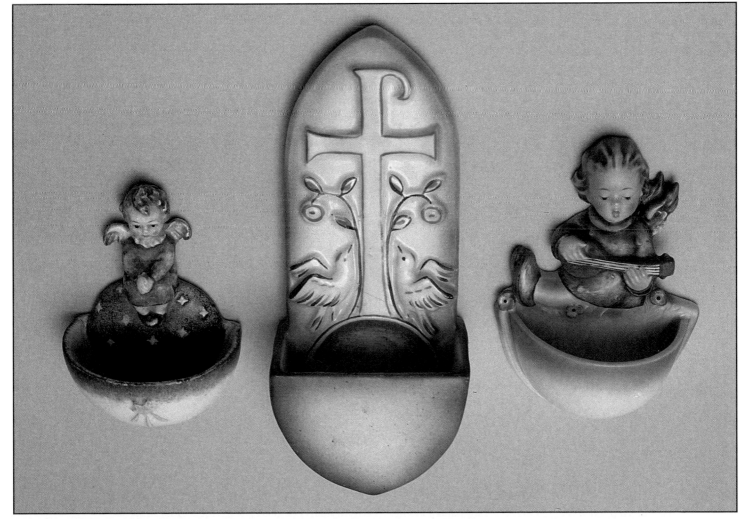

Holy Water Fonts. The *left* font bears the *M.I. Hummel* incised signature, but has no other apparent markings whatever.
The *center* one is the **Cross With Doves** font, Hum 77. It has the Crown (TMK-1) Mark and the incised signature on the back.
The font on the *right* is Hum 241, **Angel With Lute** that was never placed into regular production.

MADONNA HOLDING CHILD. *Left to Right:* Blue clock, Hum 151, Full Bee; Brown clock, Hum 151, Crown and Full Bee marks; White overglaze, Hum 151, double Full Bee mark.

FLOWER MADONNA. *Left to Right:* Normal color, Hum 10/III, Stylized Bee mark; Beige robe with orange piping, Hum 10/3, Stylized Bee mark; White overglaze, Hum 10/III, Stylized Bee mark.

SPRING CHEER, Hum 72. *Left to Right* there is a Full Bee piece, a small Stylized and a large Stylized Bee piece, a small Stylized and a large Stylized Bee piece. These three represent the major variations found in the older releases. The dress colors and the lack of flowers in the right hand are significant.

SENSITIVE HUNTER, Hum 6. The left, mold number 6, is a Crown Mark piece with the orange rabbit and "H" shaped suspenders on the back. The newer one on the right, 6/0 and missing Bee trademark, has the now common brown rabbit and "X" configuration of the suspenders.

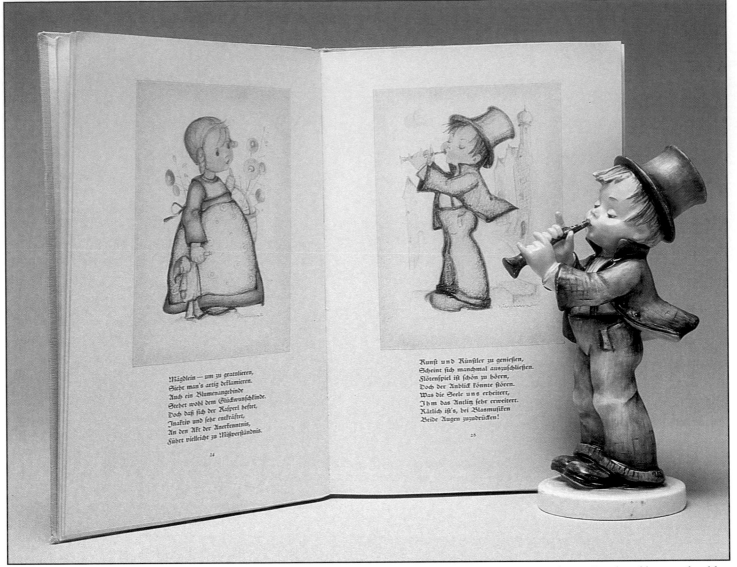

SERENADE, Hum 85 in all blue clothing. It measures 7½" high and has a donut base. No apparent markings. Displayed here with a like illustration from a German book illustrating Hummel drawings. It is likely a prototype that never made it into routine production.

RIDE INTO CHRISTMAS. An interesting five piece set from the Goebel factory illustrating an abbreviated version of painting process.

Internationals. *Left to Right:* **HUNGARIAN**, Hum 853, Crown Mark; **HUNGARIAN**, Hum 852, Crown Mark; **SWEDISH**, Hum 824; **SWEDISH**, Hum 824; **SWEDISH**, Hum 824. Note the blue eyes.

Internationals. *Left to Right:* **CZECHOSLOVAKIAN**, Hum 842, Full Bee mark; **CZECHOSLOVAKIAN**, Hum 842, Crown Mark; Country unknown, Crown Mark; **SERBIAN**, Hum 913; **SERBIAN**, Hum 913, "(R)".

Internationals. *Left to Right:* **SERBIAN**, Hum 947/0, Crown Mark; **SERBIAN**, Hum 947/0, double Crown Mark; **BULGARIAN**, Hum 810, double Crown Mark; **BULGARIAN**, Hum 810, Crown Mark.

Internationals. *Left to Right:* **BULGARIAN**, Mel. 9, double Crown Mark; **BULGARIAN**, Bul.2, Crown Mark; **SERBIAN**, Hum 904, Full Bee mark; **BULGARIAN**, Hum 811, double Crown Mark.

Internationals. *Left to Right:* Country unknown, no apparent markings; **SLOVAK** dress, there is an incised 82 or 89, but known to be Hum 831; Probably **SERBIAN**, Hum 806.

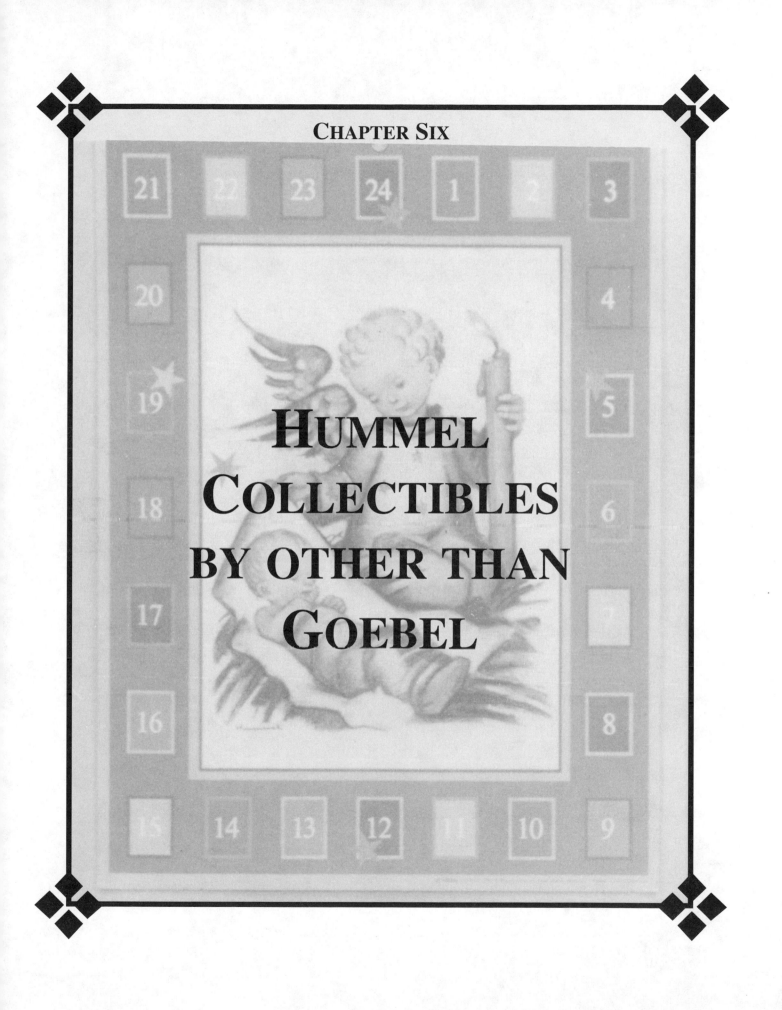

CHAPTER SIX

HUMMEL COLLECTIBLES BY OTHER THAN GOEBEL

HUMMEL COLLECTIBLES BY OTHER THAN GOEBEL

THE ARS EDITION, INC. / ARS AG COLLECTIBLES

The company Ars Sacra Josef Muller, Munich, Germany (now ars Edition GmbH) has had a long association with M.I. Hummel art.

In March of 1933 the company received a letter from the Siessen Convent that said: "Enclosed please find three proof sheets of the newest sketches of our young artist B. Hummel. We beg to inquire whether and under what conditions an edition of devout pictures in black and white, and later on in color, would be possible."

This modest beginning gave rise to many years of fruitful collaboration, and up to now the publishing house has printed more than three hundred Hummel motifs in the form of pictures for wall decoration, prayer books, postcards and books. Over the years it was possible for the publisher to procure most of these originals from the convent.

During the years 1981 to 1983 there have been put a number of products on the market under the name of Ars Edition, Inc. In 1983 ARS AG, Zug/Switzerland has been founded and obtained from the convent exclusive rights for the two-dimensional reproduction of original artworks and figurines on various products, such as limited editions for commemorative spoons and bells, stained glass, thimbles, note card assortments, candles, books, clocks, boxes and so on.

While most of the items you will see listed and illustrated here are no longer produced, the company is still in business. There is another company, Emil Fink Verlag in Stuttgart, Germany, that also has also published prints and is still in business today publishing prints, postcards and greeting cards.

The reason for listing the various products is to inform the collector about what is out there. Few of these products are assigned a collector value because there is no organized secondary market trading in most of them. Where possible, the original price and year will be given. As the years go by an organized secondary market will likely

Twelve different matted and framed prints. Size: 3-3/4" x 4-1/2".

evolve. It is you, the collector, who will dictate values as activity in the market expands.

There may be more products than are listed here. The catalogs and other material I researched did not provide as much detail and dating as I would have liked, so keep your eyes open.

The Prints

They range in size from postcards at about 2-3/4" x 4-1/4" to approximately 10" x 14". They were not all available in all sizes. Some were sold framed.

There are also some limited edition prints, larger in size. The company cataloged all of the pictures by title or subject, assigning "H" numbers beginning with H 101 for Hello There! and ending with H 626, A Gift for Jesus, as far as I could determine. There are several groups of consecutive numbers not used, and a couple of single numbers not used. There is no explanation. Perhaps the numbers are assigned to drawings or paintings not published or were meant to be assigned elsewhere. In many of the catalogs, these numbers are referenced no matter what the product.

H 101 Hello There!   H 102 Blessed Event   H 103 Good Morning   H 104 What's New?   H 105 Loves Laughing

H 106 My Baby Bumblebee   H 107 Nature's Child   H 108 Sunflower Shade   H 109 Baby and the Spider   H 110 Baby and the Bee

H 111 Innocence   H 112 The Unexpected Guest   H 113 Friend of the Flowers   H 114 Sleepy Time   H 116 Honey Lovers

H 118 The Song Birds   H 120 Slumber Time   H 121 Wishing Time   H 122 Morning Light   H 123 Daisy Duet

H124 Sunrise Shepherd H 125 Springtime Joys H 128 Daisy H 132 Dandelion H 133 My Wish Is Small

H 134 Heidi H 135 First Portrait H 136 Portrait of a Little Girl H 137 Curiosity H 138 Discovery

H 139 Spring Basket H 140 The Flower Girl H 141 Out of Tune H 142 Child of the Heart/I H 143 Young Crawler

H 144 Meeting in the Meadow (In Tune) H 145 Meeting on the Mountain (Whistler's Duet) H 178 The Opinion/II (Sing Along) H 147 Tit-for-Tat H 150 Carefree

  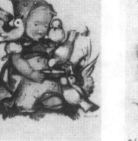  

H 151 Grandma's Story | H 152 Grandpa's Helper | H 153 On the Other Side | H 154 Cinderella | H 156 Hold Your Head High and Swallow Hard

H 157 Feathered Friends | H 158 Retreat to Safety | H 159 On Tiptoes | H 160 Behind the Fence | H 162 Summertime

H 163 Little Thrifty | H 164 Doll Mother | H 165 Prayer Before Battle | H 166 The Golden Rule | H 167 Let's Sing/I

H 191 School Girl | H 192 Little Scholar | H 193 Little Brother's Lesson | H 194 School Chums | H 195 Knit One, Purl Two

H 197 School Girls

H 198 School Boys

H 200 Captive

H 201 Mother's Helper

H 202 Little Bookkeeper

H 203 The Mountaineer

H 204 Ring Around the Rosie

H 205 The Goat Girl (Good Friends)

H 206 Vacation Time

H 207 Rosebud

H 208 The Flower Vendor

H 209 Blue Belle

H 210 Bye-Bye!

H 214 Adventure Bound

H 216 The Globetrotter

H 217 Hansel and Gretel

H 218 The Runaway

H 231 Kiss Me

H 232 Washday

H 234 The Little Sweeper

H 235 The Little Goat Herder

H 236 Feeding Time

H 237 The Fisherman (Just Fishing)

H 238 Good Hunting

H 239 The Boss (Hello)

H 240 The Professor

H 241 Little Pharmacist

H 242 The Stargazer

H 243 The Baker

H 244 The Waiter

H 245 Latest News

H 246 The Postman

H 237 Too Short to Read

H 248 The Conductor/I

H 249 The End of the Song

H 250 Little Cellist

H 251 The Artist

H 252 The Art Critic

H 253 The Poet

H 254 Confidentially

H 255 Little Boots

H 256 The Doctor

H 257 The Toothache (Boy with Toothache)

H 258 The Little Tailor

H 260 The Photographer

H 261 Chimney Sweep

H 262 The Draftsman (The Little Architect)

H 271 Just For You

H 273 Mountain's Peace (Forest Shrine)

H 276 Prayer Time

H 278 Resting

H 282 Spring's Return

H 283 The Birthday Gifts (We Wish You the Best)

H 284 Quartet

H 287 Sunny Weather

H 288 Stormy Weather

H 289 Wayside Harmony

H 290 Just Resting

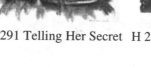

H 291 Telling Her Secret

H 292 Not for You!

H 297 Apple Tree Boy | H 298 Apple Tree Girl | H 299 Girl on Fence/I | H 300 Boy on a Fence | H 301 For Mother

H 302 For Father | H 303 Off to Town | H 304 Looks Like Rain | H 305 His Happy Pastime | H 306 Her Happy Pastime

H 307 Happy John | H 308 Coquettes | H 310 Farewell | H 311 Evening Tide | H 312 Twilight Tune

H 313 The Work Is Done | H 314 Homeward Bound | H 316 Winter Fun (Ride Into Christmas) | H 317 March Winds | H 333 This Heart Is Mine

H 334 Catch My Heart	H 335 I Like You Boy (Valentine Gift)	H 336 I Like You Girl (Valentine Joy)	H 337 Take Me Along	H 338 The Strummers

H 339 To Market, to Market	H 342 Serenade	H 346 Boys Ensemble	H 347 Girls Ensemble	H 348 Special Gift

H 349 Special Delivery	H 350 Bashful	H 352 Max and Moritz	H 354 A Smile is Your Umbrella	H 355 Begging His Share

H 371 Chick Girl	H 372 Playmates	H 374 A Little Hare	H 375 Favorite Pet	H 376 Chicken-Licken

H 377 Children on the Church Road

H 378 The Shepherd's Tune

H 379 Easter Playmates

H 380 Easter Basket

H 381 And One Makes a Dozen

H 382 Return to the Fold

H 383 In Full Harmony (Eventide)

H 384 Praise to God

H 385 Alleluja

H 386 The Easter Lamb

H 401 In Guardian Arms

H 402 Deliver Us from Evil

H 404 The Guardian Angel

H 405 Guardian Angel Preserve Us

H 406 The Renewal

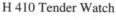

H 407 Boy's Communion

H 408 Girl's Communion

H 409 Angel/Trumpet

H 410 Tender Watch

H 411 Angel Duet

H 412 Candle Light   H 435 Angel/Horn   H 436 Angelic Care   H 437 Light of the World (Merry Christmas, Plaque)   H 438 Guiding Angel

H 441 Celestial Musician   H 442 Bearing Christmas Gifts (Christmas Angel)   H 444 The Littlest Candle   H 448 Angel/Harp (Song of Praise)   H 449 Angel/Mandolin

H 451 Watchful Angel   H 453 Guiding Light   H 454 Angel and Birds   H 471 Trinity   H 475 Alleluja Angel

H 477 Silent Night, Holy Night (Whitsuntide)   H 479 Joyous Christmas   H 480 Flying Angel   H 481 Jubilation   H 482 Prince of Peace

H 483 Merry Christmas and Happy New Year

H 484 Love and Luck

H 485 Glory to God in the Highest

H 486 Bless Your Soul on Christmas

H 487 Joyous Holidays

H 488 Good Luck in the New Year

*H 490 For All Men

*H 492 God Is Born5

*H 494 May You Sing

*H 496 We Wish the Very Best

H 497 Town Crier (Hear Ye, Hear Ye)

H 500 The Good Shepherd

H 520 Queen of May

H 521 Mary; Queen of May

H 522 Fruit of the Vine

H 523 Mother of God

H 524 Mary Mother, Queen Maid

H 525 Immaculata

H 526 Mother at the Window

H 527 Mother of Christ

H 528 Queen of the Rosary

H 529 Nativity

H 530 At Mary's Knee

H 531 Mary Take Us into Your Care

H 532 Madonna in Green

H 533 Loving Mother and Child

H 537 Born in Bethlehem

H 538 Blessings

H 539 Virgin Mother

H 540 Christ Child Sleeping

H 543 Christ is Born

H 615 Crossroads

H 616 Teach Me to Fly

H 617 Mail Is Here

H 619 Sunrise

H 620 Sing to the Mountains

H 622 Hard Letters

H 623 Easy Letters (With Loving Greetings)

H 624 Gift Bearers   H 625 Angel's Music   H 626 A Gift for Jesus

In 1982 Ars Edition, Inc. published a full color book-let/catalog, *The Hummel Collection,* copyright 1981, Ars Edition, Inc. That publication illustrated 292 M.I. Hummel artworks along with illustrations of details of twenty-four of them. It is with the kind permission of ARS AG that we reproduce them for you here, that you may finally have a reference of much of the artwork that is the basis for the many figurines and other collectibles.

Note: All photos are reproductions of postcards. The inscription in the four photos marked with an * is in the original art in German.

Limited Edition Prints

There are at least two prints identified as limited editions by ARS AG. They are from what is called the "Hummel Gallery" and are limited to 799 hand-numbered prints.

Carefree. Limited to 799 hand-numbered copies, this print is 27" x 24-1/2".

Alleluia. Limited to 799 hand-numbered copies, this print is 24-3/8" x 21-3/8".

This is the old style Advent Calendar.

Note Cards

There are at least twelve different bi-fold note cards available. There was no size given: they are listed only as "slightly oversized." Included were colored envelopes with lining featuring the Hummel signature. They were sold in boxes of twenty.

Calendars

There are four types of calendars that were produced by the company, two of which are the traditional month by month. Another is the Advent calendar. The fourth is a linen wall hanging type.

The company has produced a couple of large calendars annually for many years. The older ones are 10-1/2" x 16" at first, then approximately 12" x 16" for a time and spiral bound. They can be found in French, English and German. It is unclear in which years the French language version was published. There were format changes in 1984 and a significant change in 1989 to a larger 13" x 12" format. In 1984 they began producing the calendar for Goebel. There is also a small postcard calendar at 4-1/2" x 9-1/2" that features prints that can be easily detached for framing, etc.

Advent Calendars

The Advent calendars are a tradition. They have windows for each of the twenty-four days before Christmas and are a traditional part of European children's and many American children's Christmas. Each day one window is opened, revealing a piece of Hummel art with a religious theme. Each year the central Hummel picture is different. In 1986 the format was changed and from that year on four different designs were offered. The picture was a depiction of a winter scene utilizing actual M.I. Hummel figurines. The size of these new calendars was given as 15" x 11".

For at least two years Ars Edition produced a 16" x 21"(16" x 22-3/4" including wood) "Collector's Limited Edition Calendar" printed on linen and fitted with a wooden bar across the top and bottom. The first edition was released

The small Post Card Calendar and the M. I. Hummel-Figurine-Calendar 1987

The 1985 linen calendar by Ars Edition.

in 1981 and the theme was Sunny Weather (H 287), a drawing much like Stormy Weather except the children face right and there is no rain in the picture. For the second edition, the 1982 calendar, the theme was "Not for You". The next catalog available for study was from 1985 and there was no such calendar listed, but, as you can see from the illustration, the 1985 calendar was produced. The limit of the edition was 15,000 individually numbered calendars.

Wall Plaques

Wall plaques are available in several sizes and styles. The prints are mounted on wood and a hard finish is applied, making them very durable and attractive. They are square, rectangular and round and there are twenty-seven of them to be found. There are many others made by other companies as the prints have been readily available and easy to apply to many types of objects.

This is a double lid music box measuring
5-3/4" x 8-1/4".

Musical Wall Plaques

There are twelve designs of these. Six of them have red ribbon hangers and the others have a hanger on their back. They are 4" round wooden framed prints mounted with a music box movement. The music box is activated by pulling a round wooden knob on a string mounted at the bottom.

Music Boxes

Several different styles and sizes of music boxes have been available from Ars Edition, Inc. Today a licensee from ARS AG, Zug/Switzerland, the Art Decor Company (now Ercolano s.r.l.) in Sorrento, Italy, is producing the music boxes marketed by H & G Studios. There were about

Six Hummel jewelry music boxes featuring original art.

Four Hummel jewelry music boxes featuring scenes with Hummel figurines.

Another style of jewelry music boxes featuring original art. It measures 7-1/4" x 6".

twenty-five different motifs, five sizes and two basic styles at the time. See the section below on current production music boxes.

The boxes are made of furniture-grade wood with a fine finish and turned brass feet on each corner. You can barely see the feet in the accompanying photograph of four. These sold for $55 in 1986. A slightly larger size in this style that has a lock and key sold for $79 in 1986.

The rest of the music boxes were simple rectangular boxes and ranged in price from about $30 to $40 in the mid-1980s. A list of the sizes found follows:

10-1/4" x 8-1/4"
8-1/4" x 5-3/4"
7-1/4" x 6"
6" x 4-1/2"
5" x 4-5/8"

Jigsaw Puzzles

There are at least eight of these to be found. The four older puzzles can be identified by their yellow boxes with red printing. The newer ones have the art printed in full color on the boxes. See below for more information regarding puzzles.

Books

Ars Edition has published at least ten small books in English and possibly a few earlier in German. Most are

Examples of Hummel books produced by Ars Edition.

very small, about 4" x 6". One not illustrated here is *Ride into Christmas,* a book of pictures of figurines and hints for celebrating the Christmas season. It is 8" x 8-1/2". Also there are the six assorted little 3" x 4" address books and the book *The Hummel*.

Placemats and Coasters

These are found in sets of six coasters and sets of four placemats. The coasters are 4" squares with rounded corners. The placemats are rectangular and are made in two sizes: 12" x 9" and 15-3/4" x 11-7/8". The illustrations are photographs of actual Goebel M.I. Hummel figurines in models of life-like settings.

Wall Clocks

In all there are nine wall clocks in the Ars Edition, Inc. catalogs, in two styles. There are three quartz movement square clocks with a round print in the center. The designs are Umbrella Boy, Telling Her Secret and Meeting in the Meadow. The other style is a small, pendulum movement clock found in at least twelve different designs:

Mother's Helper
Follow the Leader
Umbrella Girl
Coquettes
Resting
Little Bookkeeper
Sunny Weather
School Girl
School Boys
School Chums
Globe Trotter
School Girls

Silk Carpets

A 1988 ARS AG catalog offered a "First Edition" silk carpet, limited to ninety-nine carpets worldwide. The carpet was described as having been made by hand-knotting 120 knots per square inch. The design was Celestial Musician and the size was listed as 31-1/2" x 42". In the spring 1990 issue of *Insights,* the M.I. Hummel Club newsletter, another of these was offered in a worldwide limited edition of fifty. It was similarly described and offered at $1,800. No mention of Ars Edition was made, but it can probably be safely assumed that it was a subsequent edition. The design of this tap-

The Ars Edition "First Edition" silk carpet.

estry was Umbrella Girl and the size was 35-1/4" x 26-1/2". See the description below of the tapestry.

Candles

There is a wide variety of candles in two sizes in the catalogs. They are a high quality candle. One catalog listing describes their cream-colored paraffin as the ideal color for placing the art on. Please turn to the Berta Hummel Museum product listing for more on candles.

Gift Wrap and Gift Cards

There are 18 designs of the gift card. They are 2-1/4" x 2-1/4" and come with envelopes. Gift tags have also been offered. One gift wrap illustrates a variety of M.I. Hummel artworks, all separated by bright red borders. (More on gift wrap below.)

Note Cards

A 1982 edition of an Ars Edition, Inc. catalog is the only one in which I found any mention of note cards. Only three were illustrated but the text accompanying stated that the "...notes featured many of the illustrations found in this booklet." There were at least three hundred illustrations so there are probably several dozen different designs out there.

Candles with Hummel designs.

A display of Hummel cards offered
by Ars Edition.

A leaded glass panel painted with the Hummel design Ring Around the Rosie.

Leaded Glass Panels

At least three of these painted leaded glass panels were available through ARS AG. The three known designs are Ring Around the Rosie (1986), Postman (1987), and Sunny Weather (much like Stormy Weather) (1988).

The size of these is 6-1/4" x 8-1/4". They were limited to 2500 pieces worldwide and are individually numbered. The release price in 1986 was $65. Others have been produced by a different company. They may or may not be from the same source. Please see page 178 for other glass panels.

Metal Trays

Two metal trays were offered in the early 1980s. The designs were Apple Tree Boy and Apple Tree Girl. They were oval in shape and measure 12" x 16".

Place Mats and Coasters

There are a total of fourteen pieces to be found. They consist of two sizes of four placemats, 12" x 9" and 15-3/4" x 11-7/8". There are six coaster designs measuring 4" square. They are made in England and cork-backed hard board with a heat resistant acrylic finish. The designs consist of photographs of figurines in realistic settings.

Christmas Ornaments

About thirty to forty different ornaments have been offered by Ars Edition, Inc./ARS AG over the years. The styles are widely varied. In 1982 they introduced a gold satin ball as a First Edition. Apparently they decided to change this to a more traditional glass ball, for in 1983 the First Edition was rendered in glass.

This is the fourth edition glass Christmas ornament, Merry Christmas (Hum 323).

Pill Boxes

There are four motifs to be found on the tops of these little 1-5/8" x 1-1/2" oval metal pill boxes: Wayside Harmony, Chick Girl, Easy Letters (With Loving Greetings, Hum 309) and Playmates.

They were no longer in the catalog in 1988. They sold for about $18 in the mid-1980s.

Pill boxes decorated with Hummel motifs.

Collector Spoons

In 1982, Ars Edition, Inc. began an annual collector spoon series with a twelve-piece set of silver plate 5" spoons with shield-like enamel finials each bearing a different M.I. Hummel design. The backs of the spoons bear the company name, the year of the edition and the M.I. Hummel signature. The series ended with the third set. Through many circumstances the sets may have been broken up so they may be found singly. The following is a list of the designs in each set.

Six silver collector spoons from Ars Edition, Inc.

First Edition	Second Edition	Third Edition
Sunny Weather	Hello	The Renewal
School Girl	Rosebud	Innocence
Farewell	On the Other Side	Just Resting
Wayside Harmony	Blessed Event	Behind the Fence
Chick Girl	Little Bookkeeper	My Dolly
Stormy Weather	Feeding Time	Star Gazer
School Boy	Slumber Time	Boy's
Not for You	Little Sweeper	Communion
Girl on Fence	Little Cellist	Postman
Playmates	Mother's Helper	Confidentially
	Little Goat Herder	Serenade
	Springtime Joys	Baker
		Goat Girl
		(Good Friends)

In 1986 a set of six 4-3/8" spoons began a new annual series. The finial shape had changed to round. These were also issued for three years and are listed here by edition in case the sets were broken up, to aid the collector in identifying them. They each bear the company name, the year of issue and the M.I. Hummel signature.

First Edition	Second Edition	Third Edition
His Happy Pastime	Sleepy Time	She Loves Me,
Her Happy Pastime	My Wish is Small	She Loves Me Not
Discovery	School Girl	He Loves Me, He
Tit-for-Tat	Little Scholar	Loves Me Not
Sunny Weather	Off to Town	We Wish You
Stormy Weather	Looks Like Rain	the Best
		Special Gift
		Harmony in Four Parts
		Special Delivery

There are as many as seven Mother's Day Spoons to be found beginning in 1982. They are 25K gold plate and have an enamel finial with the design on it. The length is 4-3/8" and each of them has "For Mother" engraved in the bowl. The missing years had no catalog listing.

1982 Special Gift
1983 ---
1984 ---
1985 ---
1986 ---
1987 First Outing
1988 For Mother

There was also an Annual Christmas Spoon, Thimble and Bell Series. These began in 1981. They are all engraved with the year and "Christmas" in the bowl of the spoon and on the body of the bell. Those missing from the list were not found in the catalogs of the corresponding year.

Christmas Spoon, Bell and Thimble

1981	Christmas Angel
1982	Guiding Angel
1983	Prayer of Adoration
1984	Heavenly Duo
1985	Guiding Light
1986	Celestial Musician
1987	Candle Light
1988	Angelic Guide

This is the 1986 Christmas Spoon and Bell (Celestial Musician) and the 1986 Annual Bell (Apple Tree Boy).

Annual Bells

The Annual Bell Series wasn't begun until 1983. They are silver plate and are 3-1/2" high. Each had the year and design engraved on the body of the bell. When they were first issued they cost about $20.

1983	Ring Around the Rosie
1984	Telling Her Secret
1985	Quartet (Harmony in Four Parts)
1986	Apple Tree Boy
1987	Follow the Leader
1988	Max and Moritz

Pendants

At one time the finial portion of the bells was made into pendants. It is not known how many different designs there were. The only one I have seen is of Sunny Weather and it is on a 24" chain. They came with a rope chain, but may be found with any other or no chain at all. They cost $10 in the early 1980s.

Thimbles

The series of six annual editions of six assorted thimbles each began in 1983. These thimbles are silver plate and are 1" high.

Little Bookkeeper, from the Annual Thimble Assortment, third edition.

Sunny Weather, from the Annual Thimble Assortment, third edition.

Special Gift, from the Annual Thimble Assortment, third edition.

Helping Mother, from the Annual Thimble Assortment, third edition.

Stormy Weather, from the Annual Thimble Assortment, third edition.

Special Delivery, from the Annual Thimble Assortment, third edition.

First Edition	*Second Edition*	*Third Edition*	*Fourth Edition*	*Fifth Edition*
Book Worm	Hello There!	Helping Mother	Apple Tree Girl	Chick Girl
Doll Mother	Baby and Spider	Little Bookkeeper	Little Goat Herder	Playmates
Prayer Before Battle	His Happy Pastime	Sunny Weather	Off to Town	Ring Around the Rosie
Knit One, Purl One	Her Happy Pastime	Stormy Weather	Apple Tree Boy	Harmony in Four Parts
Umbrella Boy	Discovery	Special Gift	Goat Girl (Friends)	Wayside Harmony
Umbrella Girl	Tit-for-Tat	Special Delivery	Happy John	Coquettes

Above: Annual Christmas Plates, 1987-1990.

Annual Christmas Plates

This is a four-plate series beginning in 1987. The beautiful porcelain plates are in full color and decorated with 24k gold. Made by Goebel and marketed by ARS AG, they are 7-1/2" in diameter and limited worldwide to 20,000 sequentially numbered plates.

Miniature Annual Plates

This is a series of six miniature plates (1") that are replicas of the first six plates in the Goebel Annual Plate Series, 1971 through 1976. The total production is 15,000 sets worldwide. The complete set, released in 1986, was offered at $150 including a wooden oval display frame designed for the set.

There is a second set depicting the 1977 through the 1982 plates. The series was planned but never produced.

Miniature Annual Plates. Miniature replicas of the 1971-76 plates in an oval wooden frame. Edition limited to 15,000.

THE REUTTER COLLECTION

M.W. Reutter Porzellanfabrik GmbH, a German porcelain firm, has been licensed to produce several items for the consumer and collector. Their market is primarily Europe, but some of their products have been found in American mail-order gift catalogs. The products are primarily tea or coffee services, but they also make a few other items. A list of their products follows:

Money Bank
Vase
Pill Box, approx. 1-1/2" x 2-1/4"
Box, 3-3/4" round with lid
Dish, 4" x 7" oval with pierced work border
Dish, 3" round with pierced work border
Dish, 5" round with pierced work border
Coffee Set for two
Coffee Set for four
Miniature Coffee Set, 2" high teapot
Doll Coffee Set

They furnished some information and photographs, but none illustrated the bank, vase or the Doll Coffee Set. The difference between the miniature and the doll size is not clear, but presumably the doll size is the larger of the two sets. The price list sent was in German marks, but the difference in price was not significant. It may be that after shipping costs and import duties are paid the U.S. retail is considerably different. One gift catalog listed the set at $44.95 plus S&H, but it was not clear whether it was the doll size or miniature. It was probably the doll size, as the illustration is of a set larger and more ornate than the miniature set in the accompanying photo.

Presently they make all these items in each of three Hummel designs: He Loves Me, He Loves Me Not (H 127), Lily of the Valley (H 130) and Hansel and Gretel (H 217). Their letter stated that they expected to add three more designs in 1997, but did not say which.

THE DANBURY MINT COLLECTION

This well-known division of the Norwalk, Connecticut company MBI has been in the business of offering fine collectibles for many years. Their Hummel products are either made by the Goebel company or licensed by ARS AG, Zug, Switzerland to have items bearing M.I. Hummel artwork made for them. ARS AG has very exacting standards and monitors the process to insure the highest quality. The collection is extensive and some items are appearing on the secondary market. There is not yet sufficient trade data, however, to establish realistic collector values for them except where noted. All Danbury Mint products are sold by mail-order subscription only. The collector is never obligated to purchase the entire series and is given the right to cancel the subscription at any time. It is possible that not all of the editions of the following collectible are sold out, especially some of the later

The Reutter
Coffee Set for
two.

The Miniature Coffee Set by Reutter.

Left to right: 3" bowl, 5" bowl, 4" x 7" oval bowl, pillbox and 3-3/4" box.

ones. To find out what may still be available call them at 1-800-243-4664.

Where possible the year of release and release price including shipping and handling will be quoted. The following is a list of known items produced by the Danbury Mint and/or related divisions of MBI.

Books, The Bible (Easton Press)
Books, Diary
Christmas Ornaments, porcelain
Christmas Ornaments, gold
 (The Christmas Ornament Collectors Club)
Clocks
Cookie Jars
Cup and Saucer collection
Eggs, porcelain
First Day Covers
Kitchen Canisters
Music Boxes
Plates, Collector
Salt and Pepper Shakers
Spice Jars
Stamps, postage (Postal Commemorative Society)
Tea Sets
Thimbles (Thimble Collectors Club)

Spice Jars

A collection of twenty-four porcelain spice jars bearing reproduction of original artwork and 23k decoration was offered by subscription beginning in January 1993. They were delivered to the collector at the rate of two every other month for $19.75 plus $1 shipping for each piece, for a total cost of $498. A wooden spice rack was also included for displaying the jars.

Kitchen Canisters

A set of four canisters was offered in 1993. They were decorated with pictures of M.I. Hummel figurines with an appropriate Bavarian scene for a background. They were offered for $239.40 including shipping in six monthly installments. They came in four different sizes as listed below:

Size	Volume	Design
5"	12 oz.	Timid Little Sister, Hum 394
6-1/2"	24 oz.	Barnyard Hero, Hum 195
7-1/2"	48 oz.	In Tune, Hum 414
8-1/2"	60 oz.	Little Goat Herder, Hum 200

The First Hummel Gold Christmas Ornament Collection

In 1988 Danbury offered a set of double-sided Hummel prints laminated in round form and surrounded by matching 24k gold finished decorative filigreed elements. There are thirty-six different designs measuring 2-3/4" in diameter. The ornaments were available by subscription at $18 each, including S&H. You could cancel your subscription at any time, but if you completed the collection the total would be $648.

The Hummel "School Children" Collector Thimbles

The Thimble Collectors club offered this series in 1993. It is a series of twenty-eight 24k gold electroplate thimbles, each bearing a Hummel artwork depicting a child connected in some way to school. They measure 1" high. With the series came a very nice wooden wall display with a brass identification plaque in the center. The thimbles cost $17 each with $1.50 S&H. The completed collection amounted to a total of $518.

Plates

Calendar Plate Collection

Hummel company literature from 1993 calls this plate a double first. It is the first time the Hummel calendar scene "Maypole" appears on a plate and it "...is also the first issue in the M.I. Hummel Calendar Plate Collection!" The collection is to consist of twelve plates. The plate is 8-1/4" in diameter. The design consists of the figurine Maypole in a realistic setting. A flyer promoting the plate states that "'Maypole is forever limited to an edition size of 75 firing days." The price was $29.95 plus $2.95 S&H, for a total of $32.90.

Playmates Collector Plate

In 1993 Danbury offered this 8-1/4" plate for $29.50 plus $2.95 S&H, for a total of $32.45. It was limited in edition number to those produced in twenty-five firing days. The design is the figurine placed on the cobblestone stoop in front of the door to a Bavarian home.

Land in Sight Collector Plate

This plate was issued in 1992. It is a large plate, 10-1/2" in diameter, and came with a handsome polished mahogany display base with identifying brass plaque. The design is surrounded with a 3/4" wide band of 24k gold. The design is the figurine Land in Sight in an extremely well rendered realistic sea setting. The number in the edition was not revealed but limited to the number produced in seventy-five firing days. The cost was $87 plus $2.85 shipping and handling, for a total of $89.85.

We Wish You the Best Century Plate

This plate was issued in 1993. It was a large plate, 10-1/2" in diameter, and came with a handsome polished mahogany display stand with a brass identifying plaque. The design in the center is surrounded by a 3/4" wide band of 24k gold. The design feature is the Hummel figurine "We Wish You the Best" Century Collection piece placed in a realistic setting. The number in the edition was not revealed, but limited to the number produced in a seventy-five firing day period. The cost was $87 plus $2.85 S&H, for a total of $89.85.

Little Companions Limited Edition Plate Series

In 1989-1990 Danbury issued a series of limited production collector plates. The plate designs are figurines photographed in realistic settings and applied to an 8-1/2" porcelain plate rimmed in 23k gold. The edition size was not revealed, but literature promoting the series states that the edition sized will be "...forever limited to the production capacity of fourteen full firing days." Available by mail order, the release price was $32.45 including shipping and handling costs. This makes the total price $389.40 for the completed series. This included a nice display rack. They are listed below:

Number	Design Theme	Hummel Mold
1	Apple Tree Boy and Apple Tree Girl	Hum 141, Hum 142
2	Stormy Weather	Hum 71
3	Tender Loving Care	Hum 376, Little Nurse
4	Squeaky Clean	Hum 412, Bath Time
5	Little Explorers	Hum 16, Little Hiker and Hum 49, To Market (girl only)
6	Surprise	Hum 94
7	Little Musicians	Hum 150, Happy Days
8	Budding Scholars	Hum 415, Thoughtful and Hum 418, What's New?
9	Hello Down There	Hum 394, Timid Little Sister
10	Come Back Soon	Hum 545
11	Country Crossroads	Unknown
12	Private Parade	Hum 86, Happiness and Hum 240, Little Drummer

Gentle Friends Limited Edition Plate Series

In 1991-92 Danbury issue a series of limited edition production plates. The designs are photographs of Hummel figurines in realistic settings applied to an 8-1/2" porcelain plate rimmed in 23k gold. The number in the edition is not revealed, but literature promoting the series states the edition size will be "...forever limited to the production capacity of fourteen full firing days". Available by mail-order subscription, the price for each including S&H was $32.45 for the first five in the series and $32.73 for the last seven (apparently S&H costs went up), for a total of $391.36 for the completed series. This included a nice display rack. Plates in the series are as follows

Number	Theme	Hummel Mold
1	Favorite Pet	Hum 361
2	Feathered Friends	Hum 344
3	Let's Sing	Hum 110
4	Playmates	Hum 58
5	Farm Boy	Hum 66
6	Lost Sheep	Hum 68
7	Feeding Time	Hum 199
8	Cinderella	Hum 337
9	Friends	Hum 136
10	Goose Girl	Hum 47
11	Strolling Along	Hum 5
12	Little Goat Herder	Hum 200

Porcelain Egg Collection

This collection of twelve eggs was offered in 1995. Each egg depicts a Hummel figurine in a realistic vignette and is approximately 3-3/8" high by 2-1/2" wide and came with an attractive hardwood base. They sold for $19.95 each plus $2.95 S&H, for a total of $22.90 each.

Porcelain Cup and Saucer Collection

This collection was offered in 1995 or 1996. It consists of twelve demitasse cups and saucers. M.I. Hummel figurines were depicted on the 2" high cups and saucers were decorated with a thematic border to match the figurine somehow or a design element on the figure itself. For example, apples were used to match Apple Tree Boy and raindrops to match Umbrella Girl. They were offered for $39.50 plus $1.75 S&H for a total of $41.25 each. The cost for the completed collection would be $495. A nice display fixture is included at no extra charge. The designs are listed following:

Apple Tree Girl	Little Fiddler
Apple Tree Boy	Stormy Weather
Postman	Goose Girl
Umbrella Girl	Happy Pastime
Umbrella Boy	Merry Wanderer
Blessed Event	Kiss Me

The Holy Bible

The Easton Press division of MBI made this beautiful leather-bound, gold-tooled Bible available to the collector in 1996. It is profusely illustrated using full color M.I. Hummel artwork and it is the first time her art has been used to illustrate a Bible. It is available in two versions, the New King James version for Protestants and the New American Bible, the official version recognized by the Roman Catholic church. The cost is $49 plus $5 S&H, for a total of $54.

Needlework

If you are handy with cross-stitch, crewelwork, embroidery, etc., you may benefit from the treasure trove of M.I. Hummel designs available in needlework. Some of the designs that are listed have been discontinued, but I have seen them, still in kit form, from time to time in antique shops and the like. I have also seen finished kits in the same places and at garage and estate sales. I am acquainted with someone who has had one in her "To Do Someday" bag for fifteen years, so you never know where you might turn one up, partially finished, finished or still in the kit form.

At least three companies have produced the kits: JCA Inc., 35 Scales Lane, Townsend, MA 01469; Jenson Designs from Denmark; and Paragon Needlecraft from the National Paragon Corporation of New York. JCA is still very much in business and producing dozens of kits for the aficionado. All mail to the last address available for Paragon has been returned by the U.S. Postal Service and a thorough search turned up no current address for Jenson Designs.

There are round, oval and square shapes and they are also made up for bell pulls and pillows. If you are really talented you are limited only by your imagination. If you make your own from a Hummel design, it's perfectly all right as long as it is for your own private use.

School Mates pair of cross-stitch projects.

JCA, INC.

Following are JCA's Hummel needlecraft products on the market as of October 1996.

Cross-stitch Leaflets.

84022	The Hikers (pair): Off to Town and Little Hiker
84023	Carefree Days (pair): Meeting in the Meadow and Meeting on the Mountain
84024	Little Friends (pair): Chick Girl and Playmates
84025	School Mates (pair): School Girl, Little Scholar
84034	Land in Sight: Hum 530
84035	Blessed Event: Hum 333
84036	The Apple Tree (pair): Apple Tree Girl, Apple Tree Boy
84037	Playtime (pair): Knit One, Purl One, Book Worm
84038	Ready for Rain (pair): Umbrella Boy and Umbrella Girl
84039	Alpine Afternoon (pair): Bashful, Globe Trotter
84042	The Birthday Gifts: We Wish You the Best
84043	Wee Three: Three standing girls in front of fence

Needle Treasures Kits (cross-stitch kits).

02607	Sunny Weather (original art for Wash Day)
02606	Ring Around the Rosie
02609	Not for You
02610	Telling Her Secret
02633	Wash Day
02634	Postman
02641	Stormy Weather
02642	Hansel and Gretel (girl and boy hiking)
02649	Sunny Weather (afghan)
04217	Blessed Event (baby quilt)
02662	Follow the Leader
02672	Max and Moritz
02675	Bashful: (banner)
02676	The Globetrotter (banner)
02677	Feeding Time
02678	Little Goat Herder
02687	The Strummers
02688	He Loves Me, He Loves Me Not (pillow)
02689	She Loves Me, She Loves Me Not (pillow)
06613	The Doctor (needlepoint)

Quartet cross-stitch project.

What's New? counted cross-stitch.

Christmas Kits (counted cross-stitch).

02864	Christmas Angel
02865	Candle Light
02874	Letter to Santa Claus
02882	Silent Night: Hum 54
02891	Celestial Musician: Hum 188
02897	Skier (Christmas stocking)
02927	Angel Duet

Weekenders (mini-needlecraft, 5"x7").

00750	Chicken-Licken (stitchery)
02755	Cinderella
02762	Sleepy Time
02775	Looks Like Rain
02802	What's New?
03513	Little Sweeper

Cross-stitch Greeting Cards.

02410	Off to Town
02411	Little Hiker
02412	Wash Day
02413	School Girl
02414	Little Scholar
02415	Not for You
02416	Postman
02417	The Doctor
02418	Looks Like Rain
02501	Celestial Musician
02502	Candlelight
02503	Letter to Santa
02504	Angel with Trumpet

Toy Truck

What will we find next? Yes, as you can see by the accompanying photograph, this is a M.I. Hummel truck. It was authorized by ARS AG and marketed through a toy company. It is a high quality, highly detailed model about 6" long. Everybody needs a Hummel eighteen-wheeler for their collection. Not everybody will get one, however, because although the number manufactured is not presently known, it is small. They were selling for about $35 for a few years, but when word got around recently that a dealer had a few in stock, they disappeared from the shelves rapidly.

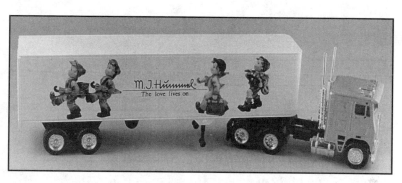

M.I. Hummel toy truck.

Cigar Bands (Unauthorized product)

Believe it or not, there are cigar bands. Many of them. One collector suggests that they might be gum or candy wrappers. They may very well be, but they look for all the world like cigar bands to me.

A few years ago an antique dealer sent me a set of fifteen mint condition bands, asking if I knew anything about them. I did not, of course, but arranged to buy the set of fifteen. When they arrived I couldn't believe how beautiful they were. They were high quality, full-color photographic reproductions of Hummel figurines in realistic settings. One is reproduced here for you to see the style. Each band has the notation "T.S.H. HIPPO."

The one on the upper left on page 174 is part of the first set I received. I have since uncovered similar bands, also in a set of fifteen. The one on the upper right is the same style as the first, but this time the illustration is of original M.I. Hummel art, not the figurine. Each of the styles also has the word "Hummelbeelden" on the reverse side of each of the bands.

Since I found the first two sets I have found two more styles, apparently from a different company. As you can see, they are not nearly as elaborate as the first ones. They are black and white photo reproductions of the figurines. The smaller ones are framed in gold color ink and they are found in one of five colors: red, yellow, green, blue or white (no color). The small ones measure 2-1/2" (6.4 cm)

Examples of cigar bands using M.I. Hummel designs.

and come in sets of forty-eight. As you can see, each is clearly identified, even down to the mold number, although they got it wrong in a couple of instances. The larger one, on the right, measures 4" (10 cm). I have found only white and red in this style. They are found in sets of twelve. Both styles are clearly numbered so you may know when you have obtained a complete set.

These, at least some of them, have to be of fairly recent vintage as one of them depicts Hum 416, Jubilee, which was issued in 1985.

Umbrella Girl Tapestry

In the spring 1990 issue of *Insights,* the newsletter of the M.I. Hummel Club, a tapestry was offered. Only fifty were made worldwide. They were hand-knotted of pure silk with 120 lines of knots per foot. They were made in Beijing, China, and measure 25-1/4"x 26-1/2". The initial offering was for $1,800. Although the newsletter entry did not mention Ars Edition, it is very likely that they were behind its production. There was another, very similar item offered by them in their last catalog. The descriptions are strikingly alike. See page 134 of the Ars Edition, Inc./ARS AG section.

Books

The reason this book is not listed with all the others is that it is not about collecting nor is it about M.I. Hummel exclusively. The reason for its being listed here is for your interest. The serious collector may want to find a copy of it.

The Unsung Heroes: Unheralded People Who Invented Famous Products

Nathan Aaseng

1989, Lerner Publications Company

There are eight people included in this book for young readers. Among them are the inventors of Coca Cola, McDonald's hamburgers and vacuum cleaners. "Sister Maria Innocentia's Gift, M.I. Hummel Figurines" is the chapter we are interested in.

Postage Stamps and First Day Covers

Stamps

A number of first day covers and foreign stamps depict Hummel art. They are not all covered here as it is difficult to ascertain just what and how many have been produced.

The first were released in 1990 by the island country of St. Vincent in the Caribbean. From then until 1992 six more countries joined them by issuing stamps. The stamps are all full color and similar in design. Each features a photograph of a different Hummel figurine as the central design. There are at least 100 to be collected. I was only able to identify 86 of them by manuscript deadline. Perhaps I will be able to uncover the rest by the time I am ready for the twelfth edition. Those I have identified are listed following:

Antigua & Barbuda.
Crossroads (Hum 331)
Flower Vendor (Hum 381)
Globe Trotter (Hum 79)
Good Hunting (Hum 307)
Homeward Bound (Hum 334)
Just Resting (Hum 112)
Little Hiker (Hum 16)
Mountaineer (Hum 315)

Cambodia.
Adventure Bound (Hum 347)
Doll Bath (Hum 319)
Doll Mother (Hum 67)
Pleasant Journey (Hum 406)
Prayer Before Battle (Hum 20)
Ring Around the Rosie (Hum 348)
Volunteers (Hum 50)
Kiss Me! (Hum 311)

Commonwealth of Dominica.
Celestial Musician (Hum 188)
Festival Harmony with Flute (Hum 173)
Festival Harmony with Mandolin (Hum 172)
Flying High Christmas Ornament (Hum 452)
Heavenly Angel (Hum 21)
Joyous News (Hum 27)
Merry Christmas - wall plaque (Hum 323)
Searching Angel- wall plaque (Hum 310)

Gambia.
Auf Wiedersehen (Hum 153)
Coquettes (Hum 179)
Daddy's Girls (Hum 371)
Going Home (Hum 383)
Max and Moritz (Hum 123)
Stormy Weather (Hum 71)
Telling Her Secret (Hum 196)
VacationTime plaque (Hum 125)

Ghana.
Autumn Harvest (Hum 355)
Bashful,(Hum 377)
Chick Girl (Hum 57)
Easter Greetings (Hum 378)
Farewell (Hum 65)
Favorite Pet (Hum 361)
Playmates (Hum 58)
The Run-A-Way (Hum 327)

Grenada and the Grenadines (Christmas Stamps).
Angel Duet - candleholder (Hum 193)
Christmas Angel (Hum 301)
Christmas Song (Hum 343)
Good Shepherd (Hum 42)
Hosanna (Hum 480)
Heavenly Lullaby (Hum 262)
Silent Night (Hum 54)
Watchful Angel (Hum 194)

Guyana.
Baker (Hum 128)
Begging His Share (Hum 9)
Congratulations (Hum 17)
Follow the Leader (Hum 369)
My Wish is Small (Hum 463)
Valentine Gift (Hum 387)
Valentine Joy (Hum 399)
We Wish You the Best (Hum 600)

Maldives.
Thoughtful (Hum 415)
Little Bookkeeper (Hum 306)
Little Scholar (Hum 80)
School Boys (Hum 170)
School Girl (Hum 81)
School Girls (Hum 177)
Smart Little Sister (Hum 346)
With Loving Greetings (Hum 309)

Saint Kitts and Nevis.
Apple Tree Boy (Hum 142)
Apple Tree Girl (Hum 141)
The Botanist (Hum 351)
For Father (Hum 87)
March Winds (Hum 43)
Ride into Christmas (Hum 396)
Umbrella Boy (Hum 152A)
Umbrella Girl (Hum 152B)

Saint Vincent.
The Artist (Hum 304)
Boots (Hum 143)
Chimney Sweep (Hum 12)
Hello (Hum 124)
Little Pharmacist (Hum 322)
Postman (Hum 119)
The Photographer (Hum 178)
Waiter (Hum 154)

Tanzania.
Close Harmony (Hum 336)
Happiness (Hum 86)
Happy Days (Hum 150)
In D Major (Hum 430)
Serenade (Hum 85)
Whitsuntide (Hum 163)

Uganda.
Big Housecleaning (Hum 363)
Happy Pastime (Hum 69)
Harmony in Four Parts (Hum 471)
Hear Ye, Hear Ye (Hum 15)
Little Celllist (Hum 89)
Little Sweeper (Hum 171)
Little Tailor (Hum 308)
Let's Sing (Hum 110)
Mischief Maker (Hum 342)
Mother's Helper (Hum 133)
Singing Lesson (Hum 63)
Star Gazer (Hum 132)
Tuba Player (Hum 437)
Wash Day (Hum 321)

Some or all of the stamps are also known to have been issued in commemorative blocks of one and four.

A few examples of Hummel postage stamps.

Example of a First Day Cover, created for the M.I. Hummel Museum in New Braunfels, Texas.

First Day Covers

For you non-philatelists a First Day Cover is an envelope with a new stamp that is postmarked the first day of issue of that stamp. Many countries will create a special postmark to be used on that particular First Day Cover on that day alone. Often there is a special privately printed envelope bearing some art or other decoration commemorating whatever the stamp design was intended to honor.

The First Day cover depicted on page 151 is not strictly a Hummel First Day Cover, but is interesting because of the special postmark created for it. As you can see by the return address it was a special event post office branch set up at the museum.

The Postal Commemorative Society of Norwalk, Connecticut (their address is the same as the Danbury Mint) is likely to have had an important role in the issuance of all the foreign country M.I. Hummel postage stamps discussed above. In 1991 they issued a series of First Day Covers utilizing the same stamps. They produced one hundred covers. Each bore a stamp depicting a figurine and a full color reproduction of the original Hummel art from which the figurine was modelled. They were issued by subscription at $7.75 per cover. Included was a very nice loose-leaf display album.

Research turned up a Swiss company that has produced first day covers. The company is known as Verlag Groth AG. I was unable to find an address for them, but it is likely there is a connection between them and the Postal Commemorative Society (Danbury Mint) because the stamps and first day covers all utilize the exactly same design layout and format.

Since 1989 there has been a First Day Cover issued from Rodental, Bavaria, Germany each year. These each bear a different Hummel design and a Hummel design cancellation mark. Sponsored by Goebel, commemorating the change from the old name "Oeslau" to Rodental where W. Goebel Porzellanfabrik is located. The stamps are not designs from M.I. Hummel artwork. The first seven designs were:

1989	Postman
1990	The Mail is Here
1991	Chimney Sweep
1992	Hear Ye, Hear Ye
1993	Baker
1994	Boots
1995	The Artist
1996	The Photographer
1997	Waiter

Stationery, Memo Pads, Note Cards, Christmas Cards, Gift Wrap, Calendars, Etc.

Several companies are licensed to produce these items. More information on cards, gift wrap, etc. is listed on the following pages. Those companies I have found so far:

Case Stationery Company, Yonkers, NY

Deluxe Corporation, Shoreview, MN

Goebel, Pennington, NJ

CPS Corporation, Franklin, TN

Emil Fink Verlag, Stuttgart, Germany

Ars sacra, now arsEdition, GmbH, Munich, Germany

The Case Stationery Company Products

Case apparently created their Hummel paper line based on the following eleven different M.I. Hummel figurines:

> Adventure Bound (Seven Swabians)
>
> Apple Tree Girl
>
> Happy Pastime
>
> Hello
>
> Merry Wanderer
>
> Postman
>
> School Boys
>
> Telling Her Secret
>
> Umbrella Girl
>
> We Congratulate
>
> Worship

These designs are used on the following products:
Desk caddy - 150 decorated sheets

Memo cube (desk item) - 700 decorated sheets

Memo book (desk item)

Stationery (6" x 8") eleven designs

Matching decorated envelopes

Folded note cards (6" x 8", unfolded)

Matching envelopes

Magnetic memo pads - decorated and ruled
    sheets, 3-1/4" x 6-1/2"

Case also produced some decorated metal storage tins. Four of them are filled with a packet of the stationery and envelopes listed above. The boxes measure 9-1/8" x 6-7/8" x 2-1/4". The designs are Adventure Bound (Seven Swabi-

Note cards from the Case Stationary Company.

Decorated storage tin and stationary from the Case Stationary Company.

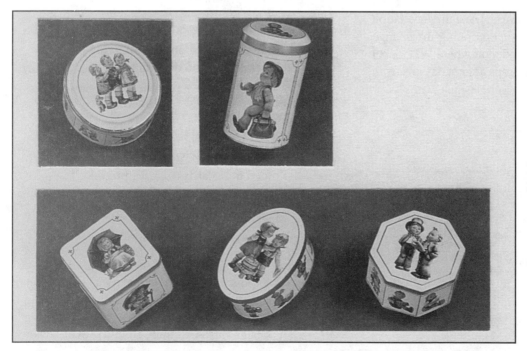

More decorated tins from the Case Stationary Company.

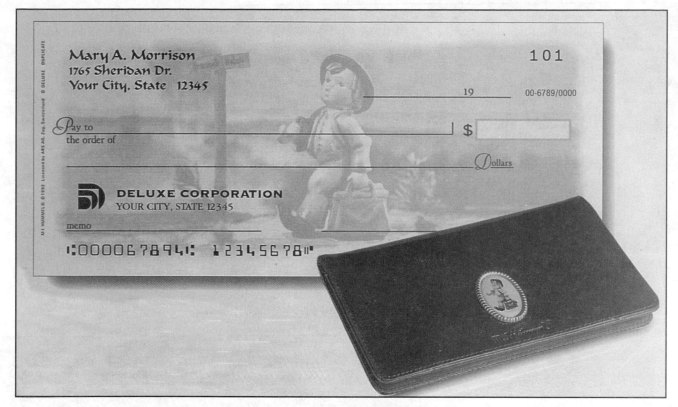

M.I. Hummel® check and checkbook from the Deluxe Corporation.

ans), Apple Tree Girl, School Boys and We Congratulate. All of these were photographed in realistic vignettes. They produced another decorated box the same size, but without decorated stationery. The design is oriented horizontally and utilizes the Angel Duet candleholder flanked by Festival Harmony with Flute and Festival Harmony with Mandolin. This design is called Power of Faith There is a stained glass window behind them.

Case also made five smaller tins. The color is white with gold trim. Each is decorated with color photographs of several figurines according to a theme.

Come Out and Play	5-1/8" dia. x 2-5/8"	Round
Special Editions	3-1/2" dia. x 5-1/2"	Round
Seasons	4-1/4" x 4-1/4" x 3-1/2"	Square
Home Sweet Home	3-3/4" x 5-3/4" x 2-3/8"	Oval
Merry Sounds of Music	4-1/4" x 4-1/4" x 3-1/4"	Octagonal

The Deluxe Corporation Products

Checks (four M.I. Hummel scenes represented)

Checkbook cover (burnished leather decorated with a medallion with the Merry Wanderer motif)

Checkbook cover (has facsimile of an M.I. Hummel signature)

Personalized note cards (figurines in realistic vignettes)

Personalized stationery (four lines of personalization with a Hummel decoration in the lower left corner)

Peel-and-stick address labels (up to three lines of personalization. Comes with a dispenser.)

CPS Corporation Products

CPS offers gift wrap in three different designs and colors, gift tags, Christmas cards, note cards, and a two-year planner.

A detail of one of the gift wrap designs from CPS Corporation.

A gift tag from CPS Corporation.

To: From:

Emil Fink Calendars

This company, also a publisher of prints and postcards, publishes four styles of calendars each year for the German-speaking public. How many have been published over the years is not presently known. They are all fairly small, about the size of a postcard or slightly larger. Three of the four are typically decorated with very familiar M.I. Hummel drawings and paintings. The other utilizes watercolor paintings that are much less familiar.

Ars Edition (now arsEdition) Calendars

Produced each year, these calendars are printed in German, English and several other languages. See the section on Ars Edition for further discussions of these particular calendars, page 129-130.

Display of three-dimensional greeting cards from Rococo.

Greeting Cards

Rococo is a line of everyday and Christmas Pop-Up cards made in England and distributed in the U.S. by Marian Heath Greeting Cards, Wareham, MA. They are ingenious cards that are mailed flat, but when you open them up they become three-dimensional. There are twenty different designs, of which two are religious and nine Christmas cards. The designs are:

Everyday or Special Occasion

Card Name	Mold No.	Hummel Name
Barnyard Hero	Hum 195	
Feeding Time	Hum 199	
Birthday Serenade	Hum 218	
Little Bookkeeper	Hum 306	
Kiss Me	Hum 311	
Our Secret	Hum 317	Not for You
	Hum 459	In the Meadow
Wash Day	Hum 321	
Blessed Event	Hum 333	
Sweet Greetings	Hum 352	

Religious or Christmas

Card Name	Mold No.	Hummel Name
Christmas Choir	Hum 2	Little Fiddler
	Hum 85	Serenade
	Hum 336	Close Harmony
	Hum 471	Harmony in Four Parts
Hear Ye, Hear Ye	Hum 15	
Holy Children	Hum 18	Christ Child
	Hum 83	Angel Serenade with Lamb
	Hum 238C	Angel with Trumpet
	Hum 359	Tuneful Angel
Christmas Blessing	Hum 42	Good Shepherd
	Hum 54	Silent Night
	Hum 454	Song of Praise
Bird Duet	Hum 169	
Little Angels	Hum 194	Watchful Angel
	Hum 357	Guiding Angel
	Hum 438	Sounds of the Mandolin
	Hum 571	Angelic Guide
The Mail is Here	Hum 226	
Angel Duet	Hum 261	
Merry Christmas	Hum 323	
Letter to Santa Claus	Hum 340	
Ride into Christmas	Hum 396	

Christmas Cards

The M. I. Hummel Club offered five different Christmas cards through their newsletter mailings in 1993 and 1994. The company producing these was Brett Forer. They came in boxes of 18 with envelopes. The themes were:

1993

A Gift for Jesus	H 626
Celestial Musician	H 441, Hum 188
Candle Light	H 412, Hum 192

1994

A Gift for Jesus	H 626
Tender Watch	H 410
Quartet	Hum 134

Postcards

Over the years a number of companies have produced postcards of M.I. Hummel art. The first of these were published in 1933 by Ars Sacra, Josef Muller in Munich. The company is now known as arsEdition. These first cards are the ones that inspired the idea of creating figurines from the art.

Telling Her Secret. Postcard #62.1291 by Ars Edition.

A 1991 promotional postcard from Goebel.

The Photographer. Postcard #4767
by Verlag Joseph Mueller.

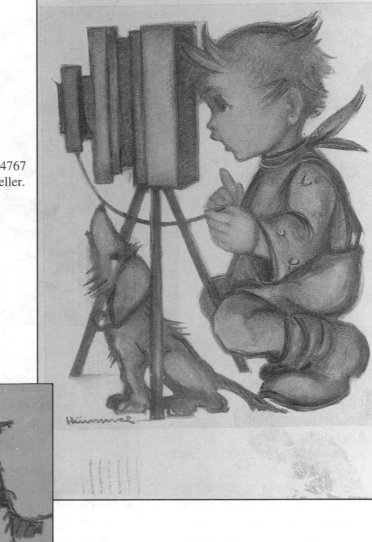

Perched on a Fence. Postcard #815
by Emil Fink Verlag.

Happy Pastime, Joyful and Book Worm. Postcard #156-514 by Classico.

Of interest to collectors of the postcards are the following publishers:

Ars sacra Josef Müller
Ars Edition
arsEdition GmbH, Munich, Germany

The cards are of two basic types: A photo of a figurine(s), usually in a realistic vignette, or a reproduction of M.I. Hummel art. There is a third type, produced by Goebel for promotional purposes. The card is usually a color photo of one or more figurines in an arrangement of related material or decorations suitable to the promotion.

A few postcards were published by other companies about twenty years ago, before the Convent, Goebel and their agents tightened the reins on rights. Many larger gift shops and similar operations had their own cards made for promotional purposes.

Tins Filled with Lebkuchen

These are produced by E. Otto Schmidt GmbH & Co. KG, Nuremberg, Germany. They are very attractive, approximately 11" x 7" x 4" deep metal containers decorated with M.I. Hummel art (vignettes of children). The box comes filled with traditional German cookies and gingerbread and is reusable.

Refrigerator Magnets (Unauthorized product)

About 1994 a gift shop offered what was described in their mail-order catalog as "NEW! GOLDTONE FRAMED 'HUMMEL PICTURES'."

Hummel refrigerator magnets.

The entry went on to say you could hang them as pictures or use them as magnets. They are 2-1/2" in diameter and the designs are M.I. Hummel art. There are at least eight different designs, four of which are depicted in the accompanying illustration. They were offered at about $15 for a set of four. The catalog entry states they are imported from Germany.

Jigsaw Puzzles

The F.X. Shmid Company, Salem, New Hampshire, offers at least eight M.I. Hummel jigsaw puzzles. Two of them have 1000 pieces and measure 29" x 23" when completed. The designs consist of figurines placed in realistic surroundings. One is called Springtime contains Coquettes and Easter Time. The other is called Good Friends and contains Friends and Playmates. They sell for about $20. They also offer a selection of at least six Mini Puzzles. They have 100 pieces and measure 7" x 7" when completed. The designs are the figurines: School Boys, Ring Around the Rosie, Blessed Event, Playmates, In Tune and Feathered Friends.

Snack Trays

A mail-order gift catalog has listed these as available off and on from around 1993. They are illustrated by figurines photographed in realistic settings. Three designs are illustrated: Home from Market, Hansel and Gretel and Be Patient. They are made of Melamine, measure 5-3/4" x 9-1/4" and have small holes should you wish to hang them as decoration. They sell for about $20 for a set of three.

"Moments To Remember" Pocket Watches

Gruen Watches, Exeter, Pennsylvania, produces a series of six different watches on 28" watch chains. The purchase includes a display dome on a wooden base. I have seen two different styles of watch case: a plain smooth case and one with a scalloped rim around the back and a fancy twisted rope style loop at the winder. The watches are 1-1/2" in diameter and are 23k gold-plated. They sell for about $65. The back features a photo of a figurine, and the watch face has the name of the figurine

and a facsimile M.I. Hummel signature. The movement is quartz. There are six different designs:

Hum 152/B	Umbrella Girl
Hum 315	Mountaineer
Hum 348	Ring Around the Rosie
Hum 353	Spring Dance
Hum 369	Follow the Leader
Hum 459	In the Meadow

Wooden Music Boxes

Made by Ercolano s.r.l., Sorrento, Italy for H & G Studios, Inc, West Palm Beach, Florida, these are high-quality handmade boxes with a print of a figurine in a realistic setting applied to the top. The prints are covered with a high-grade protective coating, making it appear as part of the top. There is a Swiss musical movement inside each, chosen to compliment the image on the box.

The boxes are made in two sizes. Large (7-1/2" x 6-1/2") sells for $139; Small (5-1/4" x 4-3/4") sells for $99. Each size is 2-7/8" deep. The following designs and sizes are available:

Design	Size	Tune
Doll Mother	Small	Rock-A-Bye Baby
Stormy Weather	Small & Large	Raindrops Keep Falling on my Head
Serenade	Small	The Sound of Music
For Mother	Small	Always
Ride into Christmas	Small & Large	Jingle Bells
Apple Tree Boy and Apple Tree Girl	Large	It's a Small World
Little Fiddler	Large	If I Were a Rich Man
Eventide	Large	A Whole New World
Merry Wanderer	Large	Take Me Home, Country Roads
Feathered Friends	Large	Swan Lake
Ring Around the Rosie	Large	Alouette
School Boys	Small	That's What Friends Are For
Skier	Small	Edelweiss

MBH514
Feathered Friends
7 1/2"x 6 1/2"x 2 7/8"
Tune: *Swan Lake*

MBH516
Ring Around The Rosie
7 1/2"x 6 1/2"x 2 7/8"
Tune: *Alouette*

MBH535
Strolling Along
5 1/4"x 4 3/4"x 2 7/8"
Tune: *My What A Happy Day*

MBH534
Happiness
5 1/4"x 4 3/4"x 2 7/8"
Tune: *Hi Lili, Hi Lo*

MBH531
School Boys
5 1/4"x 4 3/4"x 2 7/8"
Tune: *That's What Friends Are For*

MBH532
The Skier
5 1/4"x 4 3/4"x 2 7/8"
Tune: *Edelweiss*

MBH533
Coquettes
5 1/4"x 4 3/4"x 2 7/8"
Tune: *I Love You Truly*

Wooden music boxes made by Ercolano s.r.l. in Sorrento, Italy.

Five buildings from the Bavarian Village collection.

Design	Size	Tune
Coquettes	Small	I Love You Truly
Happiness	Small	Hi Lili, Hi Lo
Strolling Along	Small	My What a Happy Day
Farewell	Large	Auf Wiedersehen
The Mail Is Here	Large	Chariots of Fire

See also page 131-132.

Bavarian Village

Housed in Niles, Illinois, the Hawthorne collection is a unique series of miniature Bavarian Village structures made of ceramic. Each is electrically lit from the inside. Each represents a different structure and in the windows or doors of these structures is an M.I. Hummel design backlit by the interior light. Each bears an M.I. Hummel facsimile signature. There are eight designs presently available. They are listed below.

Name	Design Motif	Height
Angels Duet	Angel Duet & Candlelight	8"
Village Bakery	Baker	5-1/2"
Company's Coming	Little Sweeper	5-1/2"
Winter Comfort	Waiter	5-1/2"
Christmas Mail	Postman	5-3/8"
Off for the Holidays	Kindergartner	6"
Shoemaker Shop	Boots	5-1/4"
All Aboard Train Station	Merry Wanderer	5-3/4"

The prices range from about $50 to $60 each. There are a number of non-Hummel design accessories that you can buy to set up a little winter village

Metal canisters from the Olive Can Company.

Canisters

At least seven different sizes and designs of metal canisters are made by the Olive Can Company of Elgin, Illinois. Olive supplied me with the accompanying photograph of their line, but failed to include information on sizes and whether the designs of each can varied. The information came too late for any further inquiries.

THE SCHMID/BERTA HUMMEL COLLECTION

The history of the Schmid company's association with the art of M.I. Hummel goes all the way back to when the first figurines were put on the market in Germany in 1935. The Schmid company noticed them, arranged to buy a few and ended up being the Goebel company's U.S. distributor. Their association with the Goebel company first ended in 1968. About the same time Schmid began offering a selection of Hummel collectibles of their own manufacture or from other sources and in 1971 they offered a Christmas Plate utilizing the same original Hummel art as the Goebel 1971 first annual Christmas plate. As you might expect the companies ended up in court.

Berta Hummel, as she was known before taking her vows as a Franciscan nun, had created a large amount of work before taking entering the convent. All that work had become the property of the family, her mother Viktoria Hummel in particular, after her death. Schmid made an agreement with Mrs. Hummel allowing them to produce decorative items and other collectibles inspired by or using this early work of the artist.

Over the years Schmid produced a number of Berta Hummel collectibles, as they called them. At one point Goebel and Schmid entered into another agreement whereby Schmid once again became the U.S. distributor. In 1994 distribution was again taken over by Goebel of North America. As of this date the Schmid company is no longer operating. This section enumerates the *Schmid Berta Hummel Collection,* illustrating many of the pieces. There are no secondary market values (Collector Value) given for most of the items, as there has not yet been a market established for most. Many collectors are not even aware of them or, if aware, pay little attention to them. This will change over the years because none of the items are or have been in production for many years.

Limited Edition Prints and Berta Hummel Art

There have been roughly 130 small framed lithographic prints (reproductions) offered over the years. Schmid took these existing prints and had them framed in quantities sufficient to wholesale to the trade.

By far the most important of the prints by Schmid are the following described and illustrated limited edition issues.

Hummel's sensitive self-portrait, rendered in sepia tone, was released in 1981 in a limited edition of 525. Each print is sequentially numbered and signed by the artist's brother, Adolph Hummel. The print was issued at $125 and is valued at about $300 on the secondary market today.

A Self-Portrait. Image size 9-5/8" x 13-1/4".

The print of flowers was issued in 1980-81. The colors are rich earth tones with a cheerful red-orange poppy. The edition was limited to 450 and each was signed by the artist's brother, Adolph Hummel. The release price was $125 and it is presently valued at $650 on the secondary market.

A Time to Remember was issued in 1980-81 in an edition limited to 900. It is a color print depicting a boy with three children on a sled. There is a snow-covered fir tree in the background. Each of the prints is signed by Adolph Hummel, brother of the artist. There is penciled inscription in German around the border on 180 of the prints. The inscription translates: "Seasons Greetings from the Hummel family home in Massing, Bavaria, West Germany. The Hummel family wishes you and yours a Merry Christmas and a very happy and prosperous New Year." The picture depicts a Hummel family Christmas tradition of going into the woods to pick out a tree. The regular prints were released originally at $150 and are now

Poppies. Image size
11-1/2" x 14 -1/2".

valued at $300. The 180 copies with the Christmas inscription are worth about $1200.

Moonlight Return is a pastel Berta Hummel did to depict an incident in her brother Adolf's boyhood. The limited edition issue of this print is signed by him. The edition issue quantity was 900 and the release price was $150. It is now valued at $850-$1000 on the secondary market.

The Angelic Messenger print was issued in an edition of 600 and each print was signed by the artist's brother, Adolph Hummel. Two hundred of the prints are numbered as usual but the other 400 were given inscriptions in German. The inscriptions began on the left border and went over the top and down the right border. They are translated: "May the angel of Christmas abide with you, at Advent, and all year through." This edition is valued at $450 and

the one with the 75th anniversary inscription is valued at about $700. The regular edition is about $300.

The Birthday Bouquet print is thought to be the only self-portrait Berta Hummel ever did of herself as a young child. It seems that the Hummel children always picked flowers from their garden for their mother on her birthday. The story goes that Berta Hummel was away at art school and unable to come home for her mother's birthday, she painted this portrait and sent it home to her mother. It was issued in 1985 in three editions for a total quantity of 520. The Birthday Greeting Edition was limited to 195 signed and numbered prints. They were signed and inscribed by Adolf Hummel as follows: "The Hummel family of Massing, Germany wishes you a very happy birthday." This edition was issued at $450. The Heirloom Edition is lim-

A Time to Remember.

PROOF

A. Hummel

Moonlight Return. Image size 10-3/4" x 16-1/2".

Angelic Messenger.
Image size 12-1/2" x 16".

Birthday Bouquet.

ited to 225 and bears the written inscription by Adolf Hummel: "A child's loving gift is a remembrance, that lives like a bouquet in our hearts." It was originally issued at $375. The Regular Edition was limited to 100 prints that were signed and numbered by Adolf Hummel. This edition was issued at $195.

Paperweight

This was called the "Sister Berta Hummel Visage Paperweight" in promotional literature. It is a beautiful French sulfide crystal paperweight measuring 2-1/4" in diameter and 1-7/8" high. It was limited in production to 4000. Each is individually etched with the number on the bottom of the piece.

Pieces from Schmid's Hummel-inspired coffee service.

Side view of the Schmid Berta Hummel paperweight.

Top view of the Schmid Berta Hummel crystal paperweight.

Coffee Service

In approximately 1970 Schmid released a twenty-one-piece coffee service for six. It consisted of six cups and saucers, six cake plates, a sugar, creamer and coffeepot, each with a different Berta Hummel design. They were apparently short-lived and disappeared from the market soon after. The assorted designs used on the pieces in the set are all artwork accomplished after Berta Hummel joined the convent. This could be part or all of the reason they were removed from the market.

There is no way of knowing how many sets were produced and sold, but they are in short supply. The photos accompanying were furnished by a collector. As you can see, the cake plates are missing so I have no idea what the designs were. The production of the set was authorized by the Hummel family and is so noted on the backstamp. Please turn to page 143 for more on coffee and tea services.

Tranquility. Limited edition of 15,000.

Serenity. Limited edition of 15,000.

Plates and Cups

"Tranquility" and "Serenity" Plate Series

The first of this two-plate series was Tranquility, released in 1978. The second, Serenity, was issued in 1982. Each of these is about 10" in diameter. The edition quantities were limited to 15,000 for each plate. The plate is hand-painted museum-quality porcelain with an application of 24k gold. The resulting soft glowing finish was achieved by a unique technique that required six separate kiln firings.

Annual Christmas Plate Series

Matching mini-plates, bells, cups and ornaments.

Year	Plate Design	Plate Value ($)	Bell	Cup	Ornament
1971	Angel with Candle	20-25			
1972	Angel with Flute	15-20	X		
1973	Nativity	75-95	X		
1974	Guardian Angel	10-15	X		X

Year	Plate Design	Plate Value ($)	Bell	Cup	Ornament
1975	Christmas Child	15-20	X	X	X
1976	Sacred Journey	10-15	X		X
1977	Herald Angel	10-15	X		X
1978	Heavenly Trio	10-15	X		X
1979	Starlight Angel	10-15	X		X
1980	Parade into Toyland	15-20	X	X	X
1981	A Time to Remember	25-30	X		X
1982	Angelic Procession	30-35	X		X
1983	Angelic Message	25-30	X		X
1984	A Gift From Heaven	35-40	X		X
1985	Heavenly Light	30-35	X		X
1986	Tell the Heavens	40-45	X		X
1987	Angelic Gifts	35-40	X		X
1988	Cheerful Cherubs	65-70	X		X
1989	Angelic Musician	45-50	X		X
1990	Angel's Light	40-45	X		X

Angel with Candle, 1971 Christmas Plate from Schmid.

Angel with Flute, 1972 Christmas Plate from Schmid.

Nativity, 1973 Christmas Plate from Schmid.

The Guardian Angel, 1974 Christmas Plate from Schmid.

Christmas Child, 1975 Christmas Plate from Schmid.

Sacred Journey, 1976 Christmas Plate from Schmid.

Herald Angel, 1977 Christmas Plate from Schmid.

Heavenly Trio, 1978 Christmas Plate from Schmid.

Starlight Angel, 1979 Christmas Plate from Schmid.

A Time To Remember, 1981
Christmas Plate from Schmid.

Nativity, 1973 Christmas Bell from
Schmid.

Angel with
Flute, 1972
Christmas Bell
from Schmid.

Nativity, 1973
Christmas Bell
from Schmid.

The Guardian
Angel, 1974
Christmas Bell
from Schmid.

Christmas
Child, 1975
Christmas Bell
from Schmid.

Sacred Journey,
1976 Christmas
Bell from
Schmid.

Herald Angel,
1977 Christmas
Bell from
Schmid.

Heavenly Trio,
1978 Christmas
Bell from
Schmid.

Starlight Angel,
1979 Christmas
Bell from
Schmid.

Parade Into
Toyland, 1980
Christmas Bell
from Schmid.

God's Little Messenger Series: Silent Wonder. Plate: 7-1/2"
diameter, limited edition of 15,000. Miniature Plate: 4-3/4"
diameter. Thimble (not shown): 1" high. Ornament (not
shown): 3-1/2" diameter. Bell: 4-1/2" high, limited edition
of 5,000. Cup: 2-1/2" high.

God's Little Messenger Series: Heavenly Melody. Plate: 7-1/2"
diameter, limited edition of 15,000. Miniature Plate: 4-3/4"
diameter. Thimble (not shown): 1" high. Ornament (not shown):
3-1/2" diameter. Bell: 4-1/2" high, limited edition of 5,000. Cup:
2-1/2" high.

177-157

Cheerful Cherubs, 1988 Christmas Plate, 7-1/2" diameter,
Eighteenth Edition.

God's Little Messenger Series:
Sweet Blessings. Plate: 7-1/2"
diameter, limited edition of
15,000. Miniature Plate: 4-1/4"
diameter. Thimble: 1" high.
Ornament: 3-1/4" diameter. Bell:
4-1/2" high, limited edition of
5,000. Cup: 2-1/2" high.

God's Little Messenger Series: A Message From Above. Plate: 7-1/2" diameter, limited edition of 15,000. Miniature Plate: 4-3/4" diameter. Thimble: 1" high. Ornament: 3-1/4" diameter. Bell: 4-1/2" high, limited edition of 5,000. Cup: 2-1/2" high.

Heavenly Melody, 1994 Ornament.

Silent Wonder, 1993 Ornament.

Angelic Procession, 1982 Christmas Bell, 6-1/4", Eleventh Edition.

1982 Mother's Day Bell, 6-1/4" high. Seventh Edition.

1982 Christmas Ornament, 3-1/4" diameter, Eleventh Edition.

1982 Annual Cup, 2-1/2" diameter, 2-1/2" high. Tenth Edition.

1982 Christmas Plate, 7-1/2" diameter, Eleventh Edition.

Playing Hooky, 1972 Mother's Day Plate from Schmid.

The Little Fisherman, 1973 Mother's Day Plate from Schmid.

The Bumblebee, 1974 Mother's Day Plate from Schmid.

Message of Love, 1975 Mother's Day Plate from Schmid.

Devotion for Mothers, 1976 Mother's Day Plate from Schmid.

Moonlight Return, 1977 Mother's Day Plate from Schmid.

Afternoon Stroll, 1978 Mother's Day Plate from Schmid.

Cherubs Gift, 1979 Mother's Day Plate from Schmid.

Mother's Helpers, 1980 Mother's Day Plate from Schmid.

Playtime, 1981 Mother's Day Plate from Schmid.

Schmid Mother's Day Bell, 1976.

Schmid Mother's Day Bell, 1977.

Schmid Mother's Day Bell, 1978.

Schmid Mother's Day Bell, 1979.

Schmid Mother's Day Bell, 1980.

Untitled, 1972 Annual Cup from Schmid.

The Bumblebee, 1974 Annual Cup from Schmid.

Christmas Child, 1975 Annual Cup from Schmid.

Devotion for Mothers, 1976 Annual Cup from Schmid.

Moonlight Return, 1977 Annual Cup from Schmid.

Afternoon Stroll, 1978 Annual Cup from Schmid.

Cherub's Gift, 1979 Annual Cup from Schmid.

Parade Into Toyland, 1980 Annual Cup from Schmid.

1982 Mother's Day Plate, 7-1/2" diameter. Eleventh Edition.

1988 Mother's Day Plate, Young Reader. 7-1/2" diameter. Seventeenth Edition.

God's Littlest Messenger Series

This is a four-year series that began in 1991. The plates had a release price of $60 and the production was limited to 15,000 pieces. The matching bells were limited to 5000 and the original price was $58. There were also a miniature plate, thimble, cup and ornament in the series. See illustrations for sizes. The designs for each year are as follows:

1991: A Message from Above
1992: Sweet Blessings
1993: Silent Wonder
1994: Heavenly Melody

Annual Mother's Day Plates, Bells and Cups

Beginning in 1972 Schmid produced a series of 7-1/2" plates. In 1976 they began producing matching bells at 6-1/2" high and cups at 2-1/2" high. Inexplicably there is also a matching cup to be found for the year 1974. The series ended with the 1990 plate. In the years 1981 through 1984 other matching pieces were made. Intermittently these were eggs, thimbles and trinket boxes. These will be covered later.

Year	Plate Design	Plate Value ($)	Bell	Cup
1972	Playing Hooky	20		
1973	The Little Fisherman	40		
1974	The Bumblebee	30		X
1975	Message of Love	25		
1976	Devotion for Mothers	20	X	X
1977	Moonlight Return	30	X	X
1978	Afternoon Stroll	20	X	X
1979	Cherub's Gift	30	X	X
1980	Mother's Helpers	30	X	
1981	Playtime	25	X	X
1982	The Flower Basket	45	X	X
1983	Spring Bouquet	35	X	X
1984	A Joy to Share	30	X	
1985	A Mother's Journey	40	X	
1986	Home from School	40	X	
1987	Mother's Little Learner	60		X
1988	Young Reader	85	X	
1989	Pretty as a Picture	80	X	
1990	Mother's Little Athlete	80	X	

Annual Cups

The Annual Cup Series (12 in the series) was introduced in 1973 with an untitled design. The art was of a baby in a basket with a bird and flowers. This cup was not a match to any other piece in the collection. The next year the design matched the 1974 Mother's Day plate and the year following, 1975, the cup design matched that of the same year's Christmas Plate. The cup design reverted to match the Mother's Day plate in 1976 for four more years when in 1980 it once again was made matching the Christmas plate. This was the last time, for after this the cups matched the Mother's Day design until the Annual Cup Series ended with the twelfth edition in 1984. See charts below.

Stained Glass

For three years Schmid issued a 6" diameter round stained glass decoration. The design was applied to the glass. It is framed in lead in the traditional manner of stained glass and a chain hanger is provided. Six were found cataloged, two each year matching the Christmas and the Mother's Day motifs. (See page 136.)

Year	Christmas Design	Mother's Day Design
1976	Sacred Journey	Devotion for Mothers
1977	Herald Angel	Moonlight Return
1978	Heavenly Trio	Afternoon Stroll

Thimbles

The original series of three porcelain thimbles began in 1982. They are 1" high and the designs matched the corresponding designs for the Mother's Day plates. They were originally issued at $10. Designs were The Flower Basket (1982), Spring Bouquet (1983) and A Joy to Share (1984).

Trinket Boxes

At the same time the collector porcelain egg was introduced a three-piece series of porcelain trinket boxes with lids was started. These are 2-1/2" in diameter and sold for $20 at release. Designs were the same as the thimbles: The Flower Basket (1982), Spring Bouquet (1983) and A Joy to Share (1984).

Schmid stained glass decoration, 1976.

Schmid stained glass decoration, 1977.

The Flower Basket, 1982 egg, 3" high with base. Second edition.

Schmid stained glass decoration, 1978.

Collector Eggs

The original series of four porcelain eggs began in 1981. They are 3" high when placed on the base that came with them. Each design was the same as the corresponding year of the Mother's Day plate: Playtime (1981), The Flower Basket (1982), Spring Bouquet (1983) and A Joy to Share (1984). They were issued at $35 retail price.

Statuette Ornaments

In 1983 Schmid released the first in a series of what were called statuette ornaments. These were little 4-1/2" figures with bases for standing up and provisions for hanging on the Christmas tree. The first edition (1983) was called Hark the Herald and was a boy with a trumpet tucked under his right arm and his left hand stuck in his pocket. The second edition, 1984, was called Sweetheart

Hark the Herald statuette-theme collection.

Alpine Boy statuette ornament. Third edition, 1985.

and is similar to the figurine Little Shopper (Hum 96). No more were found in the catalogs and literature studied, but it is known that a third edition, Alpine Boy, was released. See accompanying photographs. The retail price at the time was about $18.

"Hark the Herald" Statuette-Theme Collection

In 1984 Schmid introduced this group of items to commemorate the seventy-fifth year since Berta Hummel's birth. Apparently inspired by the 1984 statuette ornament Sweetheart, each of these items consisted of either a three-

Base of Hark the Herald.

Hark the Herald statuette ornament. First edition, 1983.

Sweetheart statuette ornament.
Second edition, 1984.

dimensional figure or a bas-relief incorporated into its design. The following is a list of the items and their 1984 retail price:

Type of Piece	Size	Issue Price
Plate	7" diameter	$40
Medallion Ornament	2-7/8" diameter	$10
Bell	5-1/4" high	$20
Mug	3-1/4" high	$15
Thimble	1" high	$10
Music Box	5-1/4" high	$30
Trinket Box	3-1/2" diameter	$15

Music Boxes and Other Musical Items

At least 70 different music boxes have been offered by Schmid over the years. A few other musical items can be found, such as round wall music boxes, musical jewelry boxes, musical key chains, musical bookends and even a musical cube with designs on all four sides and the top.

Schmid
limited
edition music
box,
introduced in
1981.

Limited Edition Music Box

In 1981 Schmid introduced what their brochure described as a: "...first limited edition inlaid Sorrento wooden music box..." The motif for the box is Devotion. The edition was limited to 5000 sequentially numbered music boxes at $150. There may be more boxes in this issue, but they are not found in the catalogs and other literature available for study. The catalog collection was incomplete.

Annual Music Boxes

Although seldom cataloged, there were annual, year-dated music boxes made in the same design as the annual releases of the Christmas and Mother's Day plates beginning in 1974. Although I could only find them referenced in 1976 and 1977 in catalogs and other promotional literature, they were presumably offered every year. The ones found referenced were 4" x 5-1/4" x 2" high. They sold for $20-$25 in the 1970s.

Other Music Boxes

There are at least 42 Berta Hummel design music boxes in varying shapes and sizes. All are made of wood. The shapes and sizes are listed here:

Number of Different Designs	Shape	Size
42	Rectangular	4-1/4" x 3" x 2-1/4" high
12	Rectangular	5-3/4" x 3-7/8" x 2" high
3	Heart-shaped	5-1/4" x 6-1/4" x 1-3/4" high
4	Oval-shaped	4-1/4" x 6-1/4" x 1-3/4" high

Musical Wall Pictures (round)

There are six of these to be found. They are round, wooden, 5-1/4" in diameter and are activated by a pull cord on the bottom.

Musical Wall Pictures (Shadow Box)

At one point Schmid offered these in four sizes. There were actually only two sizes of shadow box pictures. They were available with or without musical movements. If you look at the accompanying photograph of five shadow box pictures you will see three of them with what appears to be drawers at the bottom. This concealed the movement and made the pictures larger as a result.

Musical Jewelry Boxes

Fifteen of these can be found, in two sizes and shapes. They are footed metal boxes with a satin top bearing the Berta Hummel artwork.

There six different designs found on two sizes of rectangular boxes: 3" x 2-1/2" x 2-1/4" high and 3-3/4" and 4-3/4 x 2" high. The other three are heart-shaped and their size is 4-1/2" x 6-1/4" x 2" high.

Assorted Hummel items from a Schmid catalog.

Miscellaneous Other Musical and Non-musical Items

Six different musical key chains, 1-1/2" x 1-1/4"
One pair of musical bookends, 6-1/4" wide x 7-1/4" high
One pair of bookends with assorted prints, 3-7/8" wide x 6" high
Musical cube with 5 different prints, 4" square
Wall-mount key rack with print
1975 linen calendar, 17-1/2" x 30". The design matches the Mother's Day plate of the same year.
Needlepoint kit of the same design as above. 18" x 18".

Candles

Some dated candles were made to match the various limited annual plates, cups, bells etc. There are otherwise dozens of candles in various sizes bearing Berta Hummel art. The company also offered a wide variety of candle stands made of metal and wood, some of which were even musical. None of these had any Berta Hummel designs on them.

NEW ENGLAND COLLECTORS SOCIETY

A little 4" diameter plate was illustrated at the end of the Schmid section and reported as something of an enigma in the previous edition of this book. It was produced under Schmid's auspices for the New England Collectors Society (NECS). I found it in a family member's home and assumed that Schmid could fill me in with the necessary details. Alas, they could find no record of it nor could they find anyone in the company that knew anything of it and by this writing the company is no longer doing business. I contacted the Bradford Exchange and they had no information regarding the plate. I also met with a dead end trying to find any information about the New England Collectors Society.

I asked in that last edition if anyone could help with any further information about the plate. A number of collectors sent much interesting and valuable information.

Apparently the NECS was established at some time in the late 1970s or very early 1980s and came under the ownership of Reed and Barton Silversmiths soon thereafter. The first product was probably a collector spoon produced in 1981. Then came a bell and a pendant in 1982. Each of these three were made by Reed and Barton and rendered in Damascene, which they describe as "...a rich blend of pure gold, silver, copper and bronze." The NECS advertising flyers all named Reed and Barton Silversmiths as the maker of these items. The following is what is hoped to be a complete listing of all of the NECS products with as much detail as is available. All items listed following were available by mail-order subscription only.

Christmas Spoons

For two years Christmas spoons were issued in silver plate and Damascene. They measure 6-1/8" long.

Year	Design	Release Price
1981	Herald Angel	$14.50 + 1.50 S&H
1982	Joyful Trumpeter	$14.50 + 1.75 S&H

The Herald Angel Christmas Spoon.

Spoons

In 1982 NECS issued a set of twelve spoons. The artwork was rendered in Damascene and the remainder of the spoon in silver plate. Each was sold for $14.50 plus $1.50 shipping and handling. That totals $192 total outlay at release price, for the completed collection. This included a nice display rack. The designs are in the following list.

Lighting the Way	Heavenly Child
A Child's Gift	Moonlight Journey
Starlight Angel	Baker's Helper
Evening Walk	Spring Delight
Cherubs Gift	A Child's Treasures
Christmas Morning	Barefoot Boy

The Starlight Angel pendant.

The Heavenly Gifts silver/ Damascene Christmas Bell.

Pendants

There are two 24k gold-plated and Damascene pendants and neck chains, both issued in 1982.

Occasion	Design Theme	Release Price
Mother's Day	Devotion to Mother	$19.50 + 1.75 S&H
Christmas	Starlight Angel	19.50 + 1.75 S&H

Angelic Procession porcelain Christmas Bell.

Christmas Bells

There were two Christmas bells released by the NECS. The 1982 bell is 5" tall and the 1983 is 4" tall.

Plates

Year	Design Theme	Medium	Release Price
1982	Heavenly Gifts	Silver plate/ Damascene	$19.50 + 1.75 S&H
1983	Angelic Procession	Porcelain	$14.50 + 1.75 S&H

The New England Collectors Society issue two sets of 12 mini-plates each. Each plate measures 4" in diameter. The first set corresponded with Schmid's full-size Mother's Day or Christmas plates. The mini-plates were produced under Schmid's auspices. Each plate in each set was sold for $12.50 plus $1.75 shipping and handling. This totals $171 for each set of 12.

Plate Set Number One

No.	Design Theme	Corresponding Schmid Plate
1	Cherub's Gift	1979 Mother's Day
2	Starlight Angel	1979 Christmas
3	Parade into Toyland	1980 Christmas
4	A Time to Remember	1981 Christmas
5	Afternoon Stroll	1978 Mother's Day
6	Playtime	1981 Mother's Day
7	Heavenly Trio	1978 Christmas
8	Mother's Helpers	1980 Mother's Day
9	Herald Angel	1977 Christmas
10	Christmas Child	1975 Christmas
11	Devotion for Mothers	1976 Mother's Day
12	Sacred Journey	1976 Christmas

The 4" plates and 2-1/2" boxes with lids.

New England Collectors Society's Christmas Plate, backstamp.

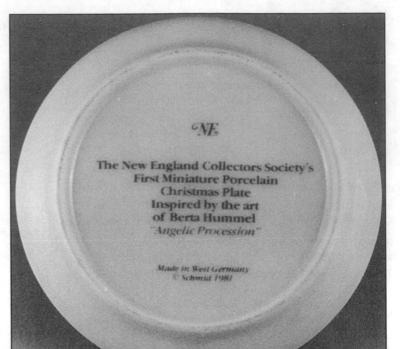

New England Collectors Society mini-plates.

Plate Set Number Two

1	Angelic Messenger
2	Flower Basket (Schmid 1982 Mother's Day)
3	Spring Bouquet
4	Story Time
5	Tidings from on High
6	Evening Serenade
7	Unknown
8	Angelic Caroler
9	Heavenly Caroler
10	Radiant Gifts
11	Heaven's Offerings
12	Guardian Angels

BERTA-HUMMEL-MUSEUM COLLECTION

In German this museum is called "Das Berta Hummel Museum Im Hummel Haus." Translated this means "The Berta Hummel Museum in the Hummel House." The museum is located in Massing, Germany, in the home where Berta Hummel was born. (See chapter 1 for a description of the museum and its contents, a photograph of the entry and some interior photographs of the museum.) Berta's nephew Albert Hummel, son of her brother Adolf, is the director of the museum. He provided photographs of the museum and some of its offerings. They own the rights to all Hummel artwork done prior to her entering the convent and license others to use it on collectibles from time to time. One example is the collection of mini-plates produced by the Schmid Brothers company for the New England Collectors Society. The museum offers a similar set of these plates. There are six of them, along with matching pill boxes. They also offer a large array of candles in three sizes, postcards of pre-convent M.I. Hummel art and eight beautiful full color posters.

Three sizes of candles available from the Berta Hummel Museum.

Berta Hummel Throw

This is a 66" x 48" 100% cotton blanket with fringe around the perimeter. It is colored in mute greens, blues, reds and yellows. The theme is Joyous Celebration, a manger scene.

The label sometimes found on older Berta Hummel Museum collectibles.

Poster No. 5, Poster No. 2.

Poster No. 3, Poster No. 4.

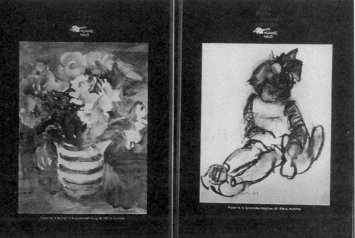

Poster No. 6, Poster No. 8.

Poster No. 9, Poster No. 7

W. Goebel Collection Products From Danbury Mint and Others

Porcelain Dolls

Danbury introduced a doll series in 1988 with the Umbrella Girl. The doll's heads, arms and legs were cast and hand-painted in the traditional manner by the artisans at W. Goebel Porzellanfabrik, maker of the M.I. Hummel figurines. They bear the signature and the Goebel trademarks on the back of the neck. Although they are cataloged at Goebel by mold number, the dolls do not bear the number. The dolls were released at $250. The dolls in the series are listed following:

Mold Number	Design
512	Umbrella Girl
513	Little Fiddler
514	Friend or Foe?
515	Unknown
516	Merry Wanderer
517	Goose Girl
518	Umbrella Boy
519	Ride into Christmas

There has been another released since the last edition of this book: School Girl. The Hummel mold number for the porcelain parts is not known but is probably the "Unknown" mold number 515 in the list above.

Kitchen Molds

Six of these were offered by subscription beginning in 1991. Danbury shipped them to the collector one every three months at $103.50 each, including shipping and handling, for a total of $621. These were made by Goebel and they are cataloged by a Goebel mold number, but the pieces do not bear the number. They do bear the incised signature. The six are listed below:

Mold Number	Size	Design
669	7-1/2" diameter	Baking Day, Hum 301
670	7-1/2" diameter	A Fair Measure, Hum 345
671	7-1/2" diameter	Sweet As Can Be, Hum 541
672	2-5/8" x 8"	For Father
673	2-5/8" x 8"	Girl Holding a Dish
674	2-5/8" x 8"	Baker, Hum 128

Angels of Christmas Ornament Series

This is a series of full color decorated Christmas ornaments made by Goebel for Danbury for subscription distribution beginning in 1990. They were issued one every other month. They were released at $42 each, including $2.50 shipping and handling, for a total of $420. Goebel cataloged them according to mold number but did not place this number on the figures. Goebel also utilized the same molds to release another series of ornaments. (See Angels of Christmas listing.) The designs for the Danbury Mint ornaments follow:

Mold Number	Size	Design
575	3"	Heavenly Angel, Hum 21
576	3"	Festival Harmony w/ Mandolin, Hum 172
577	3"	Festival Harmony with Flute, Hum 173
578	3"	Celestial Musician, Hum 188
579	2-1/2	Song of Praise, Hum 454
580	2-1/2"	Angel with Lute, Hum 238/A
581	3"	Prayer of Thanks
582	3"	Gentle Song
585	2-1/2"	Angel in Cloud
586	2-1/2"	Angel with Trumpet, Hum 238/C

Candleholders

The Danbury Mint issued four candleholders made for them by Goebel. The first two were released three months apart in 1989 and the next two were released likewise in 1990. They each cost $145.50 including shipping and handling. Goebel catalogs the molds with mold numbers, but the pieces do not bear those numbers. They are listed below:

Mold Number	Size	Year	Design
676	6-1/2"	1988	Apple Tree Boy, Hum 141
677	6-1/2"	1988	Apple Tree Girl, Hum 142
678	6-1/2"	1989	She Loves Me, She Loves Me Not
679	6-1/2"	1989	Good Friends, Hum 182

Goose Girl Figurine

In 1995 or 1996 Danbury released this famous figurine in white overglaze with just the eyes, eyebrows and lips of the girl and the eyes of the geese painted. These are made by Goebel from the Hummel mold Hum 47/II, 7-1/2" size for the Danbury Mint. It should be noted here that Goebel announced its Expressions of Youth series in the summer 1992 issue of *Insights*, the M.I. Hummel Club newsletter. There were six figurines in the series including this one. The cost of the Danbury Mint Goose Girl was $199 plus $6 shipping and handling, for a total of $205.

Goebel Products

The M.I. Hummel Club (Goebel Collectors Club at that time) gave members a box of Note Paper and Envelopes with round gold seals as a renewal premium in the 1984-85 club year. There were two designs: Coffee Break and What Now?. Folded, they measure 5" x 3-3/4".

Paperweight

This consists of a delicate lacework by Abbey Lace of Bath, England in a design reminiscent of Umbrella Girl set against a velour background and placed in a clear glass paperweight. It is 3-1/2" in diameter. Assembled in England. The collector value is about $25.

The Glass Goose Girl

Many collectors are familiar with this interesting piece, but before Lawrence Wonsch's guide *Hummel Copycats* few, if any, knew the history behind them. Wonsch goes into great detail about the historical background and the company. L.E. Smith Glass Company originated the piece in 1937 and is still producing it. Inspired by the M.I. Hummel Goose Girl, this hollow figure can be found

Note paper issued by the Goebel Collectors Club (previously M.I. Hummel Club).

The Glass Goose Girl, created by the L.E. Smith company.

in thirty-three distinct variations according to color, size, base variations and some other characteristics detailed in Wonsch's book. I will tell you that those with a plain glass base are pre-1970 vintage and those with the textured wheat straw base, as in the accompanying photograph, were produced from 1970 on. Some of the colors are amber, blue, and green, and there are others. The collector value ranges from $25 to $75.

The Avon Collectibles

All of you have heard of the Avon Lady, and recently she has been able to bring you some new M.I. Hummel collectibles. Avon began a series of crystal collector's pieces in 1994. Each is a Christmas item made of 24% lead crystal and features a figurine as the theme. The first one has gained some recognition on the secondary market, so there is the possibility that the others will also. The four in the series to date are listed below.

Avon crystal bell with Hummel design.

1993	Trinket Box (4"x4" high)	Hum 239A	Girl with Nosegay
1994	Bell (5-3/4" high)	Hum 135	Soloist
1995	Candleholders (3-1/2")	Hum 454	Song of Praise
1996	Plate (8-1/2" dia.)	Hum 194	Watchful Angel

The Trinket Box sold for $39.95 in 1994 and is presently bringing about $100 among Avon collectors.

Avon crystal trinket box with Hummel design.

Avon crystal plate with Hummel design.

THE
W. GOEBEL
COLLECTION

CHAPTER SEVEN

THE W. GOEBEL COLLECTION

GOEBEL INDEX
(ENGLISH NAME AND MOLD NUMBER)

The names of a few of the M.I. Hummel pieces have been changed by the factory over the years, resulting in some confusion. Some pieces are known by two or even three names due to these changes and to differing translations from the original German. As many names as possible have been included in this listing to facilitate location of these figures.

Use this index to look up the name of the figure and ascertain its appropriate mold number. You can then find the figure in the Hummel collection listings, which are arranged by mold number.

Name	Hummel Mold Number
The Accompanist	453
Accordion Boy	185
Adoration	23
Adoration (with Eventide) (bookends)	90B (90A)
Adoration with Bird (Bird Lovers)	105
Advent Group (Girl with Nosegay, Girl with Fir Tree, Boy with Horse) (candleholders)	115, 116 & 117
Advent Group with candle	31
Adventure Bound (Seven Swabians)	347
Angel at Prayer (font) (facing left)	91/A
Angel at Prayer (font) (facing right)	91/B
Angel Cloud (font)	206
Angel Duet	261
Angel Duet (candleholder)	193
Angel Duet (font)	164
Angel in Cloud (ornament)	585
Angel Lights (candleholder)	241
Angel Serenade with Lamb	83
Angel Sitting (see Angel with Bird)	22
Angel Trio (Christmas Angels): Angel with Lute	238/A
Angel Trio (Christmas Angels): Angel with Accordion	238/B
Angel Trio (Christmas Angels): Angel with Trumpet	238/C

Name	Hummel Mold Number
Angel Trio (candleholders): Joyous News, Angel with Lute	38
Angel Trio (candleholders): Joyous News, Angel with Accordion	39
Angel Trio (candleholders): Joyous News, Angel with Trumpet	40
Angel with Bird (font)	22, 167, 354/C
Angel with Lute (ornament)	580
Angel with Trumpet (ornament)	586
Angelic Care (Watchful Angel)	194
Angelic Sleep (candleholder)	25
Angelic Song	144
The Angler	566
Anniversary Bell (never released)	730
Anniversary Clock	750
Anniversary Display Plaque (Sixty Year)	767
Anniversary Plate 1975, Stormy Weather	280
Anniversary Plate 1980, Spring Dance	281
Anniversary Plate 1985, Auf Wiedersehen	282
Annual Bell 1978, Let's Sing	700
Annual Bell 1979, Farewell	701
Annual Bell 1980, Thoughtful	702
Annual Bell 1981, In Tune	703
Annual Bell 1982, She Loves Me, She Loves Me Not	704
Annual Bell 1983, Knit One, Purl One	705
Annual Bell 1984, Mountaineer	706
Annual Bell 1985, Girl with Sheet Music	707
Annual Bell 1986, Sing Along	708
Annual Bell 1987, With Loving Greetings	709
Annual Bell 1988, Busy Student	710
Annual Bell 1989, Latest News	711
Annual Bell 1990, What's New?	712
Annual Bell 1991, Favorite Pet	713
Annual Bell 1992, Whistler's Duet	714
Annual Plate 1971, Heavenly Angel	264
Annual Plate 1972, Hear Ye, Hear Ye	265
Annual Plate 1973, Globe Trotter	266

Name	Hummel Mold Number
Annual Plate 1974, Goose Girl	267
Annual Plate 1975, Ride into Christmas	268
Annual Plate 1976, Apple Tree Girl	269
Annual Plate 1977, Apple Tree Boy	270
Annual Plate 1978, Happy Pastime	271
Annual Plate 1979, Singing Lesson	272
Annual Plate 1980, School Girl	273
Annual Plate 1981, Umbrella Boy	274
Annual Plate 1982, Umbrella Girl	275
Annual Plate 1983, Postman	276
Annual Plate 1984, Little Helper	277
Annual Plate 1985, Chick Girl	278
Annual Plate 1986, Playmates	279
Annual Plate 1987, Feeding Time	283
Annual Plate 1988, Little Goat Herder	284
Annual Plate 1989, Farm Boy	285
Annual Plate 1990, Shepherd's Boy	286
Annual Plate 1991, Just Resting	287
Annual Plate 1992, Wayside Harmony	288
Annual Plate 1993, Doll Bath	289
Annual Plate 1994, Doctor	290
Annual Plate 1995, Come Back Soon (Final in series)	291
An Apple a Day	403
Apple Tree Boy (with Apple Tree Girl) (bookends)	252/A (252/B)
Apple Tree Boy (Fall)	142
Apple Tree Boy (lamp)	230
Apple Tree Girl (with Apple Tree Boy) (bookends)	252/B (252/A)
Apple Tree Girl (Spring)	141
Apple Tree Girl (table lamp)	229
Arithmetic Lesson	303
Art Critic	318
The Artist	304
The Artist (display plaque)	756
At Grandpa's	621

Name	Hummel Mold Number
At the Fence	324
Auf Wiedersehen	153
Autumn Harvest	355
Ba-Bee Rings	30 A&B
Baker	128
Band Leader	129
Band Leader (plate)	742
Banjo Betty (Joyful)	53
Barnyard Hero	195
Bashful	377
Bath Time	412
Be Patient	197
Begging His Share	9
Behave	339
Being Punished (plaque)	326
Big Housecleaning	363
Bird Duet	169
Bird Lovers (Adoration with Bird)	105
Bird Watcher	300
Birthday Candle	440
Birthday Present	341
Birthday Serenade	218
Birthday Serenade (table lamp)	231
Birthday Serenade (table lamp)	234
Birthday Wish	338
Blessed Child (Infant of Krumbad)	78
Blessed Event	333
Blessed Mother	372
Blossom Time	608
Blue Cloak Madonna (Madonna)	151
Book Worm	3
Book Worm	8
Book Worms (bookends)	14A&B
Boots	143

Name	Hummel Mold Number
The Botanist	351
Boy with Accordion (part of Little Band)	390
Boy with Horse (see Advent Group, Children Trio)	239/C
Boy with Toothache	217
Brother (Our Hero)	95
A Budding Maestro	477
The Builder	305
Busy Student	367
Call to Glory	739
Call to Worship (clock)	441
Candlelight	192
Carefree	490
Carnival	328
Celebrate with Song	790
Celestial Musician	188
Celestial Musician (bell)	779
Celestial Musician (ornament)	578,646
Chapel Time (clock)	442
Cheeky Fellow	554
Chef, Hello (Hello)	124
Chick Girl	57
Chick Girl (with Playmates) (bookends)	61/B (61/A)
Chick Girl (candy box)	111/57
Chicken-Licken	385
Child in Bed (plaque)	137
Child Jesus (font)	26
Child with Flowers (font)	36
Children Trio: Girl with Nosegay	239/A
Children Trio: Girl with Doll	239/B
Children Trio: Boy with Horse	239/C
Children's Prayer	448
Chimney Sweep (Smokey)	12
Christ Child	18
Christmas Angels (Angel Trio)	238/A,B&C

Name	Hummel Mold Number
Christmas Bell 1988, Ride into Christmas	775
Christmas Bell 1990, Letter to Santa Claus	776
Christmas Bell 1991, Hear Ye, Hear Ye	777
Christmas Bell 1992, Harmony in Four Parts	778
Christmas Bell 1993, Celestial Musician	779
Christmas Bell 1994, Festival Harmony with Lute	780
Christmas Bell 1995, Festival Harmony with Flute	781
Christmas Bell 1996, Heavenly News	
Christmas Ornament 1990, Peace on Earth	484
Christmas Ornament 1991, Angelic Guide	571
Christmas Ornament 1992, Light Up the Night	622
Christmas Ornament 1993, Herald on High	623
Christmas Ornament 1994, Celestial Musician	646
Christmas Ornament 1995, Fest Harmony w/ Mandolin	647
Christmas Ornament 1996, Fest Harmony w/ Flute	648
Christmas Ornament 1997	596
Christmas Plate, 1995 (Figural), Fest Harm Flute	693
Christmas Plate, 1996 (Figural), Fest Harm Mando	694
Christmas Plate, 1997 (Figural), Christmas Song	343
Cinderella	337
Clock, Anniversary	750
Close Harmony	336
Coffee Break	409
Come Back Soon	545
Companions	370
Concentration	302
Confidentially	314
Congratulations	17
Coquettes	179
Country Song (clock)	443
Country Suitor	760
Cradle Song (Lullaby) (candleholder)	24
Cross with Doves (font)	77
Crossroads	331

Name	Hummel Mold Number
Culprits	56/A
Culprits (table lamp)	44/A
Daddy's Girls	371
Daisies Don't Tell	380
Daisies Don't Tell (6" plate)	736
Delicious	435
Delivery Angel	301
Devotion (font)	147
Display Plaque (The Artist)	756
Display Plaque (Little Visitor)	
Display Plaque (Puppy Love)	767
Display Plaque (Tally)	460
Display Plaque (Valentine Gift)	717
Do I Dare?	411
Doctor	127
Doll Bath	319
Doll Mother	67
Doll Mother (with Prayer Before Battle) (bookends)*	76/A (76B)
Don't Be Shy	379
Dove (font)	393
Drummer (Little Drummer)	240
Duet	130
Easter Greetings	378
Easter Playmates (Easter Time)	384
Easter Time (Easter Playmates)	384
An Emergency	436
Errand Girl (Little Shopper)	96
Evening Prayer	495
Eventide	99
Eventide (with Adoration) (bookends)	90A (90B)
Eventide (table lamp)	104
A Fair Measure	345
Fall (Apple Tree Boy)	142
Farewell (Goodbye)	65

Name	Hummel Mold Number
Farewell (table lamp)*	103
Farm Boy (Three Pals)	66
Farm Boy (with Goose Girl) (bookends)	60/A (60B)
Fascination	649
Father's Joy (For Father)	87
Favorite Pet	361
Feathered Friends	344
Feeding Time	199
Feeding Time (with Little Goat Herder (bookends)	250/B (250/A)
Festival Harmony with Flute	173
Festival Harmony with Flute (ornament)	577
Festival Harmony with Madonna	172
Festival Harmony with Madonna (ornament)	576
The Fisherman (see Just Fishing)	373
Flitting Butterfly (plaque)	139
Florist	349
Flower Girl	548
Flower Madonna	10
Flower Vendor	381
Flowers for Mother (plate)	500
Flute Song	407
Flying Angel	366
Flying High	452
Follow the Leader	369
Fond Goodbye (miniature Mail Coach w/ clock tower)	660
For Father (Father's Joy)	87
For Father (7-1/8" plate)	293
For Keeps	630
For Mother	257
Forest Shrine	183
Forever Yours	793
Forty Winks	401
Four Seasons Plate Series (see below)	
Four Seasons: Winter Melody	296

Name	Hummel Mold Number
Four Seasons: Summertime Stroll	297
Four Seasons: Autumn Glory	298
Four Seasons: Springtime Serenade	299
A Free Flight	569
Free Spirit	564
Friend or Foe	434
Friends	136
Friends Forever Plate Series (7-1/8" diameter) see following	
Friends Forever: Meditation	292
Friends Forever: For Father	293
Friends Forever: Sweet Greetings	294
Friends Forever: Surprise (final in the series of four)	295
From Me to You	629
From My Garden	795
From the Heart	761
Gay Adventure (Joyful Adventure)	356
Gentle Fellowship	628
A Gentle Glow	439
Gentle Song (ornament)	586
A Gift from a Friend	485
Girl with Accordion	259
Girl with Doll (see Children Trio)	239 A, 239 B, 239 C
Girl with Fir Tree (see Advent Group)	116
Girl with Frog (Little Velma)	219
Girl with Horn (part of Little Band)	391
Girl with Nosegay (see Advent Group, Children Trio)	115
Girl with Sheet Music (part of Little Band)	389
Globe Trotter	79
Going Home	383
Going to Grandma's	52
Good Friends	182
Good Friends (with She Loves Me, She Loves Me Not) (bookends)	251/A (251B)
Good Friends (table lamp)	228
Good Hunting	307

Name	Hummel Mold Number
Good Luck	419
Good Night	214C
Good Shepherd	42
Good Shepherd (font)	35
Goodbye (Farewell)	65
Goose Girl	47
Goose Girl (with Farm Boy) (bookends)	60B (60A)
Grandma's Girl	561
Grandpa's Boy	562
The Guardian	455
Guardian Angel (font)	29
Guardian Angel (font)	248
Guiding Angel	357
Happiness	86
Happy Birthday	176
Happy Bugler (Tuneful Goodnight) (plaque)	180
Happy Days (Happy Little Troubadours)	150
Happy Days (table lamp)	232
Happy Days (table lamp)	235
Happy Little Troubadours (Happy Days)	150
Happy New Year (Whitsuntide)	163
Happy Pastime	69
Happy Pastime (ashtray)	62
Happy Pastime (candy box)	111/69
Happy Traveler	109
Harmony in Four Parts	471
Hear Ye, Hear Ye	15
Heart and Soul	559
Heavenly Angel	21
Heavenly Angel (font)	207
Heavenly Angel (ornament)	575
Heavenly Angel (Christmas tree topper)	755
Heavenly Lullaby	262
Heavenly Protection	88

Name	Hummel Mold Number
Heavenly Song**	113
Hello (Chef, Hello)	124
Hello (perpetual calendar)	788A
Hello World	429
Helping Mother	325
Herald Angels (candleholder)	37
Herald on High (ornament)	623
High Tenor (see Soloist)	135
The Holy Child	70
Holy Family (font)	246
Home from Market	198
Homeward Bound	334
Honey Lover	312
Horse Trainer	423
Hosanna	480
I Brought You a Gift	479
I Didn't Do It	626
I Forgot	362
I'll Protect Him	438
I'm Carefree	633
I'm Here	478
I Wonder	486
I Won't Hurt You	428
In D Major	430
In the Meadow	459
In Tune	414
Infant of Krumbad (Blessed Child)	78
Is It Raining?	420
It's Cold	421
It's Cold (6" plate)	735
Joyful (Betty Banjo)	53
Joyful (ashtray)	33
Joyful (candy box)	111/53
Joyful and Let's Sing (double figure on a wooden base)***	120

Name	Hummel Mold Number
Joyful Adventure (Gay Adventure)	356
Joyous News	27
Jubilee	416
Just Dozing	451
Just Fishing (The Fisherman)	373
Just Resting	112
Just Resting with Wayside Harmony (double figure)	121
Just Resting (table lamp)	225
The Kindergartner	467
Kiss Me	311
Knit One, Purl One	432
Knitting Lesson	256
Land in Sight	530
Latest News	184
Let's Sing	110
Let's Sing (ashtray)	114
Let's Sing (candy box)	111/110
Let's Tell the World	487
Letter to Santa Claus	340
Little Architect (Truant)	410
Little Band (Girl with Sheet Music, Boy with Accordion, Girl with Horn)	389, 390, 391
Little Band	392
Little Band (candleholder)	388
Little Band (candleholder/music box)	388/M
Little Band (music box)	392/M
Little Bookkeeper	306
Little Cellist	89
Little Drummer (Drummer)	240
Little Fiddler (Violinist)	2
Little Fiddler (Violinist)	4
Little Fiddler (plaque)	93
Little Fiddler (plaque)	107
Little Gabriel	32
Little Gardener	74

Name	Hummel Mold Number
Little Goat Herder	200
Little Goat Herder(with Feeding Time) (bookends)	250/A (250/B)
Little Guardian	145
Little Helper	73
Little Hiker	16
Little Homemakers (mini-plates)	745-748
Little Music Makers (mini-plates)	741-744
Little Nurse	376
The Little Pair	449
Little Pharmacist	322
Little Scholar	80
Little Shopper (Errand Girl)	96
Little Sweeper	171
Little Tailor	308
Little Thrifty	118
Little Troubadour	558
Little Velma (Girl with Frog)	219
Little Visitor	563
Littlest Angel	365
Lost Sheep	68
Lost Stocking	374
Love from Above (ornament)	481
Love's Bounty	751
Lucky Boy	335
Lucky Fellow	560
Lullaby (Cradle Song) (candleholder)	24
Lute Song	368
Madonna (plaque)	48
Madonna (plaque with metal frame)	222
Madonna and Child (font)	243
Madonna and Child (plaque in relief)	249
Madonna Holding Child (Blue Cloak Madonna)	151
Madonna Holding Child	155
Madonna with Halo	45

Name	Hummel Mold Number
Madonna without Halo	46
The Mail is Here (Mail Coach)	226
The Mail is Here (Mail Coach) (plaque)	140
Make a Wish	475
Making New Friends	2002
The Mamas and the Papas (Old People)	181, 189, 190, 191, 202
March Winds	43
Max and Moritz	123
Meditation	13
Meditation (7-1/8" plate)	292
Merry Wanderer	7
Merry Wanderer	11
Merry Wanderer (plaque)	92
Merry Wanderer (plaque)	106
Merry Wanderer (plaque)	263
Mischief Maker	342
Morning Concert	447
Morning Stroll	375
Mother's Aid (see Helping Mother)	
Mother's Darling	175
Mother's Day Plate (Flowers for Mother)	500
Mother's Helper	133
Mountaineer	315
My Wish is Small	463
A Nap	534
Nativity Set	214/A, B, C, D, E, F, G, H, J, K, M, N, O
Nativity Set (large)	260/A, B, C, D, E, F, G, H, J, M, N, O, P, R
Naughty Boy (see Being Punished)	326
Nimble Fingers	758
No Thank You	535
Not for You	317
Off to School	329

Name	Hummel Mold Number
Old People (see The Mamas and the Papas)	
On Holiday	350
On Our Way	472
On Secret Path	386
One for You, One for Me	482
One Plus One	556
One, Two, Three	555
Our Hero (see Brother)	
Out of Danger	56B
Out of Danger (table lamp)	44/B
Parade of Lights	616
Pay Attention	426
Perpetual Calendar: Hello	788A
Perpetual Calendar: Surprise	788B
A Personal Message	446
The Photographer	178
Pixie	768
Playmates	58
Playmates (candy box)	111/58
Playmates (with Chick Girl) (bookends)	61/A (61/B)
Pleasant Journey	406
Pleasant Moment	425
The Poet	397
Postman	119
Practice Makes Perfect	771
Prayer Before Battle	20
Prayer Before Battle (with Doll Mother) (bookends)	76B (76A)
Prayer of Thanks (ornament)	581
Pretty Please	489
The Professor	320
Puppy Love	1
Puppy Love (display plaque)	767
Puppy Love & Serenade (double figure)***	122
Quartet (plaque)	134

Name	Hummel Mold Number
Relaxation	316
Retreat to Safety	201
Retreat to Safety (plaque)	126
Ride into Christmas	396
Ring Around The Rosie	348
Rock-A-Bye	574
The Run-A-Way	327
Sad Song	404
Saint George	55
Scamp	553
School Boy (School Days)	82
School Boys	170
School Days (School Boy)	82
School Girl	81
School Girls	177
School's Out	538
Seated Angel (see Angel with Bird)	167
Sensitive Hunter	6
Serenade	85
Serenade & Puppy Love(double figure)***	122
Seven Swabians (see Adventure Bound)	347
She Loves Me, She Loves Me Not	174
She Loves Me, She Loves Me Not (with Good Friends) (bookends)	251B (251A)
She Loves Me, She Loves Me Not (table lamp)	227
Shepherd Boy	395
Shepherd's Boy	64
Shining Light	358
Shrine (table lamp)	127
Signs of Spring	203
Silent Night (candleholder)	54
Sing Along	433
Sing with Me	405
Singing Lesson (ashtray)	34
Singing Lesson	63

Name	Hummel Mold Number
Singing Lesson (candy box)	111/63
Sister	98
Skier	59
Sleep Tight	424
Smart Little Sister	346
Smiling Through	408
Smiling Through (plaque)	690
Smokey (Chimney Sweep)	12
Soldier Boy	332
Soloist (High Tenor)	135
Song of Praise	454
Song of Praise (ornament)	579
Sound the Trumpet	457
Sounds of the Mandolin	438
Spring (Apple Tree Boy)	141
Spring Bouquet	398
Spring Cheer	72
Spring Dance	353
Standing Boy (plaque)	168
Standing Madonna with Child	274
Star Gazer	132
Star Gazer (plaque)	237
A Stitch in Time	255
Store Plaque (English)	187
Store Plaque (English) (Schmid Brothers)	210
Store Plaque (English)	211
Store Plaque (French)	208
Store Plaque (German)	205
Store Plaque (Spanish)	213
Store Plaque (Swedish)	209
Store Plaque, Tally (English, new in 1986)	460
Stormy Weather (Under One Roof)	71
A Story from Grandma	620
Story Time (see Storybook Time)	

Name	Hummel Mold Number
Storybook Time (Story Time)	458
Street Singer	131
Strike Up the Band	668
Strolling Along	5
Strum Along	557
Sunny Morning	313
Supreme Protection	364
Surprise	94
Surprise (perpetual calendar)	788B
Surprise (7-1/8" plate)	295
The Surprise	431
Swaying Lullaby	165
Sweet As Can Be	541
Sweet Greetings	352
Sweet Greetings (7-1/8" plate)	294
Sweet Music	186
A Sweet Offering	549
Tally (display plaque)	460
Telling Her Secret	196
Thanksgiving Prayer	641
Thanksgiving Prayer (ornament)	596
Thanksgiving Prayer (Christmas plate)	694
Thanksgiving Prayer (bell)	783
That's That	488
Thoughtful	415
Three Pals (Farm Boy)	66
Timid Little Sister	394
To Keep You Warm	759
To Market	49
To Market (table lamp)	101
To Market (table lamp)	223
Town Children	157-162
Traveling Trio (see A Trio of Wishes)	721
A Trio of Wishes	721

Name	Hummel Mold Number
Truant (see Little Architect)	410
True Friendship	402
Trumpet Boy	97
Tuba Player	437
Tuneful Angel	359
Tuneful Goodnight (Happy Bugler) (plaque)	180
Tuneful Trio	757
Two Hands, One Treat	493
Umbrella Boy	152/A
Umbrella Girl	152/B
Under One Roof (Stormy Weather)	71
Vacation Time (plaque)	125
Valentine Gift	387
Valentine Gift (6" plate)	738
Valentine Gift (display plaque)	717
Valentine Joy	399
Valentine Joy (6" plate)	737
Village Boy	51
Violinist (Little Fiddler)	2
Visiting an Invalid	382
Volunteers	50
Volunteers (table lamp)	102
Waiter	154
Wall Vase: Boy and Girl	360/A
Wall Vase: Boy	360/B
Wall Vase: Girl	360/C
Wash Day	321
Watchful Angel (Angelic Care)	194
Wayside Devotion	28
Wayside Harmony	111
Wayside Harmony and Just Resting (double figure on a wooden base)***	121
Wayside Harmony (table lamp)	II/111, II/112, 224
Weary Wanderer	204
We Come in Peace	754

Name	Hummel Mold Number
We Congratulate	214E
We Congratulate (with base)	220
We Wish You the Best	600
Welcome Spring	635
Well Done!	400
What Now?	422
What's New?	418
Where Are You?	427
Where Did You Get That?	417
Which Hand?	258
Whistler's Duet	413
White Angel (font)	75
Whitsuntide (Happy New Year)	163
Will It Sting?	450
Winter Melody	296
Winter Song	476
With Loving Greetings	309
Worship	84
Worship (font)	164

Key: *Not known to exist in any collector's hands
    **Removed by Goebel from "Open Edition" status in mid-1981
    ***Existence unsubstantiated outside factory archives

HUMMEL COLLECTION LISTING

The following list of Hummel pieces is arranged by the appropriate Hummel mold number in ascending order. To fully understand all of the notations you must read and study the first two chapters of this book very carefully.

You will find the price listings almost complete, but it is impossible to conscientiously assign a value to each and every model that exists today. (Please refer to the introduction and to the beginning of chapter 2 for a discussion of value determination). I have tried to count the possible number of pieces according to size: there are approximately 1500 in this list. This number does not take into consideration variations due to mold size variation, color variation and model design differences. When it was impossible to obtain pricing information on a particular figure size or variation, the appropriate space is left blank or the listing is omitted altogether. In the latter case, it was not possible to ascertain and document all existing models. From time to time it is possible to establish the existence of a piece but without sure information as to size or trademark. In these cases the corresponding space is left blank.

As evidenced by this eleventh edition, this book is periodically updated and improved, and these values and other information will be incorporated in subsequent editions.

As stated earlier, the sizes are approximate but as accurate as possible. Almost all lists are contradictory, but in most cases within reasonable agreement. The sizes listed are those most frequently encountered in those listings and notated as the "Basic Size." (See definition in glossary). Most of the time this is the smallest size for each figure. Frequently, however, there would be one smaller size listed, but the preponderance of other listings would indicate a 1/4" or 1/2" larger size. In these cases the larger size was assumed the more representative. Any sizes given in captions are actual hands-on measurements.

For purposes of simplification the various trademarks have been abbreviated in the list. You will notice two different abbreviations for each trademark symbol: both systems of identification are used regularly throughout collector literature. Should you encounter any trouble interpreting the abbreviations, refer to the list below or to the glossary.

Trademark	Abbreviations	Dates
Crown	CM, TMK-1	1934-1950
Full Bee	FB, TMK-2	1940-1959
Stylized Bee	Sty Bee, TMK-3	1958-1972
Three Line Mark	3-line, TMK-4	1964-1972
Last Bee Mark	LB, TMK-5	1970-1980
Missing Bee Mark	MB, TMK-6	1979-1991
Hummel Mark (Current)	HM, TMK-7	1991-Present

HUM 1: PUPPY LOVE

PUPPY LOVE, Hum 1. Left: Decimal designator in the mold number, "1.", incised Crown Mark (TMK-1), donut base, black "Germany," 5" tall. Center: Full Bee Mark (TMK-2) in an incised circle, black "Germany," 5-1/2" tall. Right: Last Bee (TMK-5), donut base, 4-7/8" tall.

Part of the original 46 pieces offered in 1935, Puppy Love was first known as the "Little Violinist." It can be found in Crown Mark (TMK-1) through the Missing Bee (TMK-6). It was retired in 1988, never to be produced again. Many of the original group of 46 have been found rendered in terra cotta and Puppy Love is no exception, although so far only one is known to exist in any private collection.

The most significant variation occurs in Crown pieces only. In this variation the head is tilted slightly to the right instead of the typical left, he wears a black hat and there is no neck tie. This very rare variation can bring $4,500 on the collector market.

It is possible, though unlikely, that you may encounter a mold number variation of this piece. It seems that in the initial stages of planning and modeling the figurines there was no formal designation of the mold number, and Puppy Love has been found with the mold number FF15.

Hum No.	Basic Size	Trademark	Current Value
1	5"	TMK-1, CM	450-700
1	5"	TMK-2, FB	300-350
1	5"	TMK-3, Sty. Bee	235-275
1	5"	TMK-4, 3-line mark	200-225
1	5"	TMK-5, LB	180-190
1	5"	TMK-6, MB	170-180

HUM 2: LITTLE FIDDLER

Originally known as the "Violinist," this little fellow is almost always wearing a brown derby with an orange hat band. The figure has been made in five sizes since its initial introduction as part of the original 46. The two largest sizes were temporarily withdrawn from production in 1989. The smallest, Hum 2/4/0, was introduced into the line in 1984 and will remain as an open edition. It was the first of a new series of very small figurines issued as matching pieces to a series of mini-plates introduced at the same time. A few Little Fiddlers with the Crown Mark (TMK-1) have been found in faience finish. These are valued at about 20% more than the regular Crown pieces.

LITTLE FIDDLER, Hum 2. Left: 2/II. This figure has an incised Crown Mark (TMK-1) that is colored in green. Note the unusually pale face. This black and white photo doesn't show it well, but this is an example of what collectors refer to as a "doll face" or faience piece (see color section and chapter 5). It has a donut base and measures 10-15/16". Right: Has mold number 2/II, Last Bee (TMK-5) trademark, incised 1972 MID and measures 11".

LITTLE FIDDLER, Hum 2/0. The left figure has a small Stylized Bee (TMK-3) trademark, a brown color derby hat with an orange hat band and measures 5-3/4". The figure on the right is of the older vintage Full Bee (TMK-2) trademark era. It has a black hat, a black "Germany" beneath the base and is 5-1/4" tall. Both figures have a donut base.

The limited edition gold gilt base Little Fiddler, Hum 2/I. See chapter 5.

The underside of the base of the gold base Hum 2/I showing the trademark and the German language Golden Jubilee backstamp. It reads: "50 JAHRE M.I. HUMMEL-FIGUREN 1935-1985."

Doll Face LITTLE FIDDLER, Hum 2. This unusual example of the Little Fiddler bears an incised Crown mark (TMK-1) that is colored in green. It has a donut base and measures 10-15/16".

A mold number variation has been found with the mold number FF 16. In the days before the figurines were given the official "Hum" designation the "FF" was used (on the first three models). It is possible, but not likely, that you will encounter this variation.

Hum No.	Basic Size	Trademark	Current Value ($)
2/4/0	3-1/2"	TMK-6, MB	90
2/0	6"	TMK-1, CM	400-500
2/0	6"	TMK-2, FB	290-325
2/0	6"	TMK-3, Sty. Bcc	225-250
2/0	6"	TMK-4, 3-line	205-225
2/0	6"	TMK-5, LB	205
2/0	6"	TMK-6, MB	205
2/I	7-1/2"	TMK-1, CM	520-650
2/I	7-1/2"	TMK-2, FB	375-400

Hum No.	Basic Size	Trademark	Current Value ($)
2/I	7-1/2"	TMK-3, Sty. Bee	300-325
2/I	7-1/2"	TMK-4, 3-line	280-300
2/I	7-1/2"	TMK-5, LB	260
2/I	7-1/2"	TMK-6, MB	260
2/II	11"	TMK-1, CM	1700-2150
2/II	11"	TMK-2, FB	1200-1400
2/II	11"	TMK-3, Sty. Bee	1000-1100
2/II	11"	TMK-4, 3-line	925-950
2/II	11"	TMK-5, LB	850-900
2/II	11"	TMK-6, MB	850
2/III	12-1/4"	TMK-1, CM	2000-2500
2/III	12-1/4"	TMK-2, FB	1400-1600
2/III	12-1/4"	TMK-3, Sty. Bee	1200-1300
2/III	12-1/4"	TMK-4, 3-line	1100
2/III	12-1/4"	TMK-5, LB	1000-1100
2/III	12-1/4"	TMK-6, MB	1000

HUM 3: BOOK WORM

One of the original 46 released in 1935, this figure (a girl reading a book) appears more than once in the collection. It is also found in a smaller size as Hum 8 and in the Hum 14A and B bookends (Book Worms) with a companion figure of a boy reading. The larger Hum 3/II and Hum 3/III have been out of current production for some time. The Hum 3/III with older trademarks is avidly sought by collectors. The numbers 3/II and 3/III are occasionally found with the Arabic number size designator (3/2 and

BOOKWORM, Hum 3. Left: Crown Mark, 5-1/2". Right: 3/I, Missing Bee mark, 5-1/2".

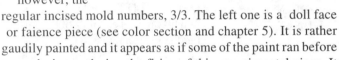

BOOKWORM, Hum 3. There is no apparent trademark on either of these. There are, however, the regular incised mold numbers, 3/3. The left one is a doll face or faience piece (see color section and chapter 5). It is rather gaudily painted and it appears as if some of the paint ran before drying or during the firing of this experimental piece. It measures 9-1/2". The white overglaze piece measures 10".

3/3 respectively). The two larger sizes have been temporarily withdrawn from current production.

There is a mold number variation. Before the figurines were given "Hum" mold numbers this figure was given the incised mold number FF 17. It is possible, but not likely, that you will encounter this variation.

Hum No.	Basic Size	Trademark	Current Value ($)
3/I	5-1/2"	TMK-1, CM	525-550
3/I	5-1/2"	TMK-2, FB	400-420
3/I	5-1/2"	TMK-3, Sty. Bee	330-355
3/I	5-1/2"	TMK-4, 3-line	290-310
3/I	5-1/2"	TMK-5, LB	270-280
3/I	5-1/2"	TMK-6, MB	270
3/II	8"	TMK-1, CM	1350-1690
3/II	8"	TMK-2, FB	1000-1200
3/II	8"	TMK-3, Sty. Bee	800-850
3/II	8"	TMK-5, LB	675-700
3/II	8"	TMK-6, MB	675
3/III	9-1/2"	TMK-1, CM	2000-2500
3/III	9-1/2"	TMK-2, FB	1400-1600
3/III	9-1/2"	TMK-3, Sty. Bee	1200-1400
3/III	9-1/2"	TMK-5, LB	1000-1200
3/III	9-1/2"	TMK-6, MB	1000

HUM 4: LITTLE FIDDLER

This is the same design as the Hum 2, Little Fiddler. The difference is of course, that this is a smaller size than any of the original three sizes of the Hum 2. One wonders why they used two different mold numbers for the same basic piece in the original 46 released in 1935. Another difference is that Little Fiddler, Hum 4, wears a black hat. There is a significant variation found in some of the Crown Mark (TMK-1) pieces. The head is tilted to his right instead of the usual tilt to his left and he wears no tie. This variation can fetch $4,500 on the collector market. Refer to the color section to see a photo of a Hum 4 with this variation that is also in the faience finish. The mold number is sometimes found with the decimal point (4.) designator, which can increase its value by up to 10%.

Hum No.	Basic Size	Trademark	Current Value ($)
4	4-3/4"	TMK-1, CM	370-460
4	4-3/4"	TMK-2, FB	265-285
4	4-3/4"	TMK-3, Sty. Bee	220-240
4	4-3/4"	TMK-4, 3-line	200-210
4	4-3/4"	TMK-5, LB	185-195
4	4-3/4"	TMK-6, MB	185

LITTLE FIDDLER, Hum 4. The left piece is the doll face. Note the very pale face and hands, the completely different head position and the lack of a neck kerchief. Each has the decimal point mold number designation 4. and the Crown mark and measures 5-1/8".

HUM 5: STROLLING ALONG

One of the first 46 figures released in 1935, Hum 5 appears in only one basic size, 4-3/4". This figure similar to Hum 7, Merry Wanderer. The most notable variation found in Hum 5 is that the latest figures have the boy looking straight ahead while the older ones have him looking to the side. Strolling Along was removed from production at the end of 1989.

STROLLING ALONG, Hum 5. Left: Mold number is 5., has a Double Crown mark, a black "Germany" and measures 5". Right: Last Bee mark, 4-7/8".

Hum No.	Basic Size	Trademark	Current Value ($)
5	4-3/4"	TMK-1, CM	450-700
5	4-3/4"	TMK-2, FB	300-350
5	4-3/4"	TMK-3, Sty. Bee	235-275
5	4-3/4"	TMK-4, 3-line	200-225
5	4-3/4"	TMK-5, LB	180-190
5	4-3/4"	TMK-6, MB	170-180

HUM 6: SENSITIVE HUNTER

Called "The Timid Hunter" when first released among the original 46, this figure has remained in production ever since.

The most notable variation is the "H" shape of the suspenders used with the lederhosen. This variation is associated with all of the Crown Mark figures and most of those with the Full Bee. The "H" variation will generally bring about 30% more than the value for the "X" pieces. The later models have an "X" shape configuration. Crown Mark pieces have been found having the "X" shape suspenders. The color of the rabbit was usually orange until 1981 when the company changed it to brown for all newly produced pieces. Sensitive Hunter can also be found with the decimal (6.) designator. This can add up to 10% to its collector value.

The smallest of the sizes listed here, Hum 6/2/0, was added in 1985 as the second in a series of new smaller figurines matching mini-plates of the same design.

SENSITIVE HUNTER, Hum 6. Left: Decimal point designator in the mold number 6., double Crown mark (TMK-1), donut base, black "Germany," red rabbit, 4-3/4". Center: 6/0, Full Bee (TMK-2) mark, donut base, black "Germany," red rabbit, 4-3/4". Right: 6/0, Missing Bee (TMK-6), brown rabbit, 4-11/16".

Rear view of Hum 6 showing the "H" and "X" suspenders configuration discussed in the text.

Effective December 31, 1984, Goebel announced that the new production piece in the 7-1/2" size (Hum 6/II) was placed on a "temporary withdrawn from production" status.

Hum No.	Basic Size	Trademark	Current Value ($)
6/2/0	4"	TMK-6, MB	90-135
6	4-3/4"	TMK-1, CM	500+
6/0	4-3/4"	TMK-1, CM	350-440
6/0	4-3/4"	TMK-2, FB	250-270
6/0	4-3/4"	TMK-3, Sty. Bee	225-250
6/0	4-3/4"	TMK-4, 3-line	190-200
6/0	43/4"	TMK-5, LB	175-185
6/0	4-3/4"	TMK-6, MB	175

Hum No.	Basic Size	Trademark	Current Value ($)
6/I	5-1/2"	TMK-1, CM	450-575
6/I	5-1/2"	TMK-2, FB	335-350
6/I	5-1/2"	TMK-3, Sty. Bee	280-300
6/I	5-1/2"	TMK-4, 3-line	250-260
6/I	5-1/2"	TMK-5, LB	230-240
6/I	5-1/2"	TMK-6, MB	230
6/II	7-1/2"	TMK-1, CM	800-1000
6/II	7-1/2"	TMK-2, FB	575-625
6/II	7-1/2"	TMK-3, Sty. Bee	480-515
6/II	7-1/2"	TMK-4, 3-line	425-450
6/II	7-1/2"	TMK-4, 3-line	425-450
6/II	7-1/2"	TMK-5, LB	400-425
6/II	7-1/2"	TMK-6, MB	400

HUM 7: MERRY WANDERER

One of the original 46 figurines released in 1935 the same design also appears as Hum 11. The Merry Wanderer is probably found in more sizes and variations than any other single figure in the collection. There are at least 12 different sizes known to exist. There is even a huge six-foot concrete replica of the figure on the factory grounds in Germany. An eight-foot-high Merry Wanderer was displayed on the grounds of the former location of the M.I. Hummel Club in Tarrytown, New York, and subsequently was placed in storage for several years. It was retrieved for display at the Donald E. Stephens Museum in Rosemont, Illinois, and will eventually be displayed at the Goebel Gallery and M.I. Hummel Museum in Rosemont when the construction of those buildings is finished. It is also part of every dealer and collector's display plaque made prior to the 1986 introduction of the Tally display plaque, Hum 460. In 1990 the Merry Wanderer display plaque was reintroduced.

The rarest of sizes is the Hum 7/III, which was temporarily withdrawn from production in 1991. Any reinstatement date has yet to be revealed.

The rarest of the base variations is illustrated in the accompanying photograph. Collectors refer to it variously as the "double base," "stepped up base" or the "stair step" base. It is found on the Hum 7/I size of all the Crown Mark (TMK-1) and Full Bee (TMK-2) 7/I's, but only on the older Stylized Bee (TMK-3) pieces.

The 7/III size has been found in the faience finish. These can bring up to 20%-50% more than the top value for the Crown Mark pieces. The 1996 Goebel suggested retail price list places a $24,000 value on the 30" "Jumbo" Merry Wanderer. The few "Jumbo" figures in private collectors' hands are generally used as promotional figures in showrooms and shops. They rarely bring full retail price. Few, if any, paid the full recommended retail price. The dealers purchase at wholesale and often will sell at little or no profit after a period of time to put the money back into their business.

MERRY WANDERER, Hum 7/I. This Stylized Bee marked figurine shows the rare stepped-up base.

Hum No.	Basic Size	Trademark	Current Value ($)
7/0	6-1/4"	TMK-1, CM	480-520
7/0	6-1/4"	TMK-2, FB	365-380
7/0	6-1/4"	TMK-3, Sty. Bee	300-335
7/0	6-1/4"	TMK-4, 3-line	275-285
7/0	6-1/4"	TMK-5, LB	245-260
7/0	6-1/4"	TMK-6, MB	245
7/I (double step base)	7"	TMK-1, CM	1200-1500
7/I (double step base)	7"	TMK-2, FB	900-1000
7/I (double step base)	7"	TMK-3, Sty. Bee	750-850
7/I (plain base)	7"	TMK-3, Sty. Bee	320-360
7/I	7"	TMK-4, 3-line	265-280
7/I	7"	TMK-5, LB	250-260
7/I	7"	TMK-6, MB	250
7/II	9-1/2"	TMK-1, CM	1700-2200
7/II	9-1/2"	TMK-2, FB	1300-1600
7/II	9-1/2"	TMK-3, Sty. Bee	1050-1100
7/II	9-1/2"	TMK-4, 3-line	935-970
7/II	9-1/2"	TMK-5, LB	850-900
7/II	9-1/2"	TMK-6, MB	850-900
7/III	11-1/4"	TMK-1, CM	1850-2250
7/III	11-1/4"	TMK-2, FB	1375-1425
7/III	11-1/4"	TMK-3, Sty. Bee	1200-1300
7/III	11-1/4"	TMK-4, 3-line	1000-1200
7/III	11-1/4"	TMK-5, LB	925-950
7/III	11-1/4"	TMK-6, MB	925
7/X	30"	TMK-5, LB	12,000-15,000

HUM 8: BOOK WORM

This figure is the same as Hum 3 except much smaller. It was one of the original 46 to be offered at the Leipzig Fair in 1935. It is found in only one size. One terra cotta Book Worm is known to be in collectors' hands, and if one exists, more may be out there.

Hum No.	Basic Size	Trademark	Current Value ($)
8	4"	TMK-1, CM	390-480
8	4"	TMK-2, FB	230-250
8	4"	TMK-3, Sty. Bee	215-225
8	4"	TMK-4, 3-line	205-215
8	4"	TMK-5, LB	195-205
8	4"	TMK-6, MB	195

BOOKWORM, Hum 8. A comparison between the normal skin coloration (left) and the pale coloration on the doll face piece. Both measure 4-1/4". The left bears a Stylized Bee mark. The one on the right is a doll face piece with a double Crown mark.

HUM 9: BEGGING HIS SHARE

There are two notable variations of this piece. Although originally designed to be a candleholder, until 1964 it can be found with and without the candle-holding hole in the cake. In 1964 the hole was eliminated when the figurine was remodeled. The Stylized Bee (TMK-3) pieces seem to be those found most often without the hole. The Crown Mark (TMK-1) is the rarest occurrence of the no-hole variation.

Although not a major variation in terms of value, the fact that the earliest of the TMK-1 pieces have brightly colored striped socks is worth mentioning. Also, the earliest of these are the ones more likely to be found without the hole in the cake.

A very rare variation is illustrated by the left figure in the photo below. This no-base, large-shoes figure may have been intended to be utilized as a bookend piece or it may have been simply an experiment. Whatever the case, if found it would command a low five-figure sum.

Hum No.	Basic Size	Trademark	Current Value ($)
9 (hole)	5-1/2"	TMK-1, CM	600
9 (w/o hole)	5-1/2"	TMK-1, CM	900-1000
9 (hole)	5-1/2"	TMK-2, FB	500
9 (w/o hole)	5-1/2"	TMK-2, FB	395
9 (hole)	5-1/2"	TMK-3, Sty. Bee	275-325
9 (w/o hole)	5-1/2"	TMK-3, Sty. Bee	225-240
9	5-1/2"	TMK-4, 3-line	220
9	5-1/2"	TMK-5, LB	220
9	5-1/2"	TMK-6, MB	220

BEGGING HIS SHARE candleholder, Hum 9. Left: Stamped Crown mark (TMK-1), 5-1/4". A very unusual piece. Note the lack of the traditional base. The oversize shoes are utilized as a base. Probably a prototype that never went into regular production. Right: Stylized Bee in the incised circle, black "Western Germany," 5-1/4".

BEGGING HIS SHARE, Hum 9. The doll face piece is on the left. Note the much more pale face. Both have the decimal point designator in the mold number, 9., double Crown marks, donut bases and measure 5-5/8".

HUM 10: FLOWER MADONNA

Several color and mold variations are known for this figure. In both sizes it appears in color and in white over-glaze. There have been reports of the figure occurring in tan, beige or brown, and in a royal blue, as well as in terra cotta in 10/III (13") and in 10/I size (9-1/2") with the Crown Mark.

The Crown Mark pieces all have the open style or "doughnut" type halo. The figure was remodeled in the mid-1950s, eliminating the hole in the halo (closed halo). Because this took place during a trademark transition from the Crown to the Full Bee marks, the Full Bee trademarked figures are the pieces in which both type halos are found.

FLOWER MADONNA, Hum 10. Left to right (A through D): A. The mold number has decimal designators as follows: 10./1.. Has an incised Crown Mark (TMK-1) and a stamped Crown Mark green in color. The overall color is beige and the robe has no piping. Measures 8-3/8". B. Mold number is the regular 10/1. It has a large Stylized Bee (TMK-3) in an incised circle, is beige with orange piping, measures 8" and has a green "Western Germany" beneath. C. The mold number is rendered in pencil, 10/1/11 and incised as 10. There is a green "Germany" stamped beneath. There are no other apparent markings. The color is blue cloak over a green gown. D. 10/1, white overglaze, large Stylized Bee (TMK-3), measures 9-3/8".

Base of a special edition white overglaze FLOWER MADONNA and wood display stand.

The Full Bee pieces with open halo bring about 20% more than those with closed halos. This variation has no significant influence on the white overglaze pieces.

The values of the significantly early color variations are $1,500 to $2,200 for the 10/I size and $2,000 to $2,800 for the 10/III size.

In 1996, the 50th anniversary of M.I. Hummel's death, Goebel issued a special edition of this piece in the 8-1/4" size for $225. The figure was on a hardwood base with a brass plaque (see photo below left).

Hum No.	Basic Size	Trademark	Current Value ($)
10/I (white)	9-1/2"	TMK-1, CM	330-420
10/I (white)	9-1/2"	TMK-2, FB	230-250
10/I (white)	9-1/2"	TMK-3, Sty. Bee	195-215
10/I (white)	8-1/4"	TMK-5, LB	165
10/I (color)	9-1/2"	TMK-1, CM	775-970
10/I (color)	9-1/2"	TMK-2, FB	575-600
10/I (color)	8-1/4"	TMK-3, Sty. Bee	480-500
10/I (color)	8-1/4"	TMK-5, LB	390-400
10/I (color)	8-1/4"	TMK-6, MB	390
10/III (white)	13"	TMK-1, CM	600-750
10/III (white) - open halo	13"	TMK-2, FB	470-500
10/III (white) - closed halo	13"	TMK-2, FB	420-460
10/III (white)	13"	TMK-3, Sty. Bee	370-390
10/III (white)	11-1/2"	TMK-5, LB	300
10/III (white)	11-1/2"	TMK-6, MB	1000-1300
10/III (color) open halo	13"	TMK-2, FB	775-825
10/III (color) closed halo	13"	TMK-2, FB	725-775
10/III (color)	13"	TMK-3, Sty. Bee	600-625
10/III (color)	11-1/2"	TMK-5, LB	500
10/III (color)	11-1/2"	TMK-6, MB	500

Open and closed halo variations of the Flower Madonna.

HUM 11: MERRY WANDERER

This is the same design as the Hum 7, Merry Wanderer. Although most of the Hum 7's have five buttons on their vest, there are six- and seven-button versions of the 11/2/0 size. These bring a bit more than the five-button version of the 11/2/0 size, but it is not significant (about 10%).

The Hum 11 model of the Merry Wanderer has been found with faience finish.

In 1993, as part of a special Disneyland and Disney World promotion, an unknown number of the small Merry Wanderers were given a special decal transfer mark beneath the base to commemorate the occasion. The piece was supposed to be sold along with a similar-size limited edition Mickey Mouse. The Mickey Mouse has an incised mold number of 17322, a limited edition indicator and TMK-7. The Merry Wanderer is a regular production 11/2/0. The problem is that the Merry Wanderers did not make it to the theme parks in time for the promotion. The edition for the pair on a wooden base was 1500. The first sales of them on the secondary market apparently took place at the site of the M.I. Hummel Club Member Convention in Milwaukee, Wisconsin, in May 1993. Some private individuals were selling the figures out of their hotel room for $650 a set. They have been advertised for as high as $1,000 since then.

Hum No.	Basic Size	Trademark	Current Value ($)
11/2/0	4-1/4"	TMK-1, CM	250-315
11/2/0	4-1/4"	TMK-2 *FB	180-200
11/2/0	4-1/4"	TMK-3, Sty. Bee	150-160
11/2/0	4-1/4"	TMK-4, 3-line	135-145
11/2/0	4-1/4"	TMK-5, LB	125-135
11/2/0	4-1/4"	TMK-6, MB	125
11/0	4-3/4"	TMK-1, CM	350-435
11/0	4-3/4"	TMK-2, FB	250-275
11/0	4-3/4"	TMK-3, Sty. Bee	215-225
11/0	4-3/4"	TMK-4, 3-line	190-200
11/0	4-3/4"	TMK-5, LB	175-185
11/0	4-3/4"	TMK-6, MB	175

*The 6 and 7 button variation of this one will bring $200-225

MERRY WANDERER, Hum 11. Left: Double Crown mark, split base (quartered), 4-7/8". Right: 11., Crown mark, "Made in U.S. ZONE," black "Germany," split base

MERRY WANDERER, Hum 11. Left: 11 2/0, Full Bee in an incised circle, black "Germany," 7 buttons on vest, 4-3/8". Right: 11/0, Stylized Bee mark, 5 buttons, 4-5/8".

MERRY WANDERER. Bears the decimal mold number designator 11., a double Crown mark and a split (quartered) base. Valued at about $500. It is not likely to be a demonstration piece due to its age. It is placed here because of its similarity to the others, which are known to be demonstration pieces.

HUM 12: CHIMNEY SWEEP

When first introduced in 1935 as part of the original group displayed at the Leipzig Fair, this figure was called "Smokey." The small 4" size was not added to the line until well into the 1950s, and consequently no Crown

CHIMNEY SWEEP, Hum 12. Left 12/1, Full Bee mark, donut base 6-3/8". Right: 12/I, Stylized Bee, donut base 5-3/4".

Mark (TMK-1) pieces are found in that size. There are many variations in size, but none are significant. Examples found in sales lists are 4", 5-1/2", 6-1/4" and 6-3/8".

There was a surprise in store for those who bought the 1992 Sampler (a Hummel introductory kit). In it was the usual club membership discount and that year's figurine, Chimney Sweep. Along with the figure came a special display base of a roof top and chimney. In 1995 Goebel produced for German retail promotion a special edition of the Chimney Sweep with a gilded base. The edition was limited to 500 pieces. Two Hummel pieces can now be found with this base: the Chimney Sweep and the 2/I Little Fiddler.

Hum No.	Basic Size	Trademark	Current Value ($)
12/2/0	4"	TMK-2, FB	155-175
12/2/0	4"	TMK-3, Sty. Bee	135-145
12/2/0	4"	TMK-4, 3-line	120-125
12/2/0	4"	TMK-5, LB	110-120
12/2/0	4"	TMK-6, MB	110
12	5-1/2"	TMK-1, CM	400-460
12	5-1/2"	TMK-2, FB	300-365
12/I	5-1/2"	TMK-1, CM	380-405
12/I	5-1/2"	TMK-2, FB	290-315
12/I	5-1/2"	TMK-3, Sty. Bee	240-260
12/I	5-1/2"	TMK-4, 3-line	210-225
12/I	5-1/2"	TMK-5, LB	195-205
12/I	5-1/2"	TMK-6, MB	195

HUM 13: MEDITATION

The Hum 13/0 and the Hum 13/II sizes were the first to be released in 1935. The most significant variations are with regard to the flowers in the baskets. When first released the 13/II had flowers in the basket, but sometime in the Last Bee mark (TMK-5) era it was restyled to reflect no flowers in the basket and the style remains so today.

Variations in the Hum 13/0 are with regard to the pigtails. The first models of the figure in the Crown Mark (TMK-1) era sported short pigtails with a painted red ribbon. By the time the Full Bee (TMK-2) mark was being utilized the ribbon had disappeared and the pigtails had grown longer.

The larger Hum 13/V was copyrighted in 1957 and has a basket filled with flowers. It is scarce in the older trademarks and hardly ever found for sale. It was temporarily withdrawn from production as of December 31, 1989, with no announced date for reinstatement.

There is a very unusual and probably unique Meditation that has a bowl attached to its side. There have been

three different figurines found with bowls attached. The other two are Goose Girl and Congratulations.

Hum No.	Basic Size	Trademark	Current Value ($)
13/2/0	4-1/4"	TMK-2, FB	260-325
13/2/0	4-1/4"	TMK-3, Sty. Bee	160-175
13/2/0	4-1/4"	TMK-4, 3-line	140-155
13/2/0	4-1/4"	TMK-5, LB	130-140
13/2/0	4-1/4"	TMK-6, MB	130
13/0	5-1/4"	TMK-1, CM	410-500
13/0	6"	TMK-2, FB	295-325
13/0	5-1/4"	TMK-3, Sty. Bee	245-265
13/0	5"	TMK-4, 3-line	215-230
13/0	5"	TMK-5, LB	205-210
13/0	5"	TMK-6, MB	205
13/II (13/2) (w/flowers)	7"	TMK-1, CM	3000-4500
13/II (13/2) (w/flowers)	7"	TMK-2, FB	2500-4000

Hum No.	Basic Size	Trademark	Current Value ($)
13/II (13/2) (w/flowers)	7"	TMK-3, Sty. Bee	2250
13/II	7"	TMK-5, LB	400-450
13/II	7"	TMK-6, MB	400
13/V	13-3/4"	TMK-2, FB	4000-5000
13/V	13-3/4"	TMK-3, Sty. Bee	1800-2500
13/V	13-3/4"	TMK-4, 3-line	1200-1500
13/V	13-3/4"	TMK-5, LB	1000-1200
13/V	13-3/4"	TMK-6, MB	1000-1200

MEDITATION, Hum 13. Left: the old style 13/2, 7" size with flowers in the basket. Double Crown mark and "Made in Germany" beneath the base. Right: The newer style 13/II, 7" size without any flowers in the basket. The latter has the Missing Bee trademark.

HUM 14A and HUM 14B: BOOK WORMS (Bookends)

These are two figures, a boy and a girl (see Hum 3 and Hum 8). As far as is known to date, there is no other occurrence of the Boy Book Worm anywhere else in the collection. It occurs only in conjunction with the bookends (Hum 14A and Hum 14B) in only one size. These bookends do not have wooden bases. (Other bookends in the collection typically do have wooden bases.) There are holes provided where the figures are weighted with sand, etc., and usually sealed with a factory sticker, gold in color. These are listed as "temporarily withdrawn" on current Goebel lists.

BOOKWORMS bookends, Hum 14 A and Hum 14 B. Both have the Stylized Bee mark (TMK-3) in an incised circle, black "Western Germany" and measure 5-3/4".

Hum No.	Basic Size	Trademark	Current Value ($)
14/A&B	5-1/2"	TMK-1, CM	1000-12000
14/A&B	5-1/2"	TMK-2, FB	550-650
14/A&B	5-1/2"	TMK-3, Sty. Bee	500-550
14/A&B	5-1/2"	TMK-4, 3-line	450-500
14/A&B	5-1/2"	TMK-5, LB	400-450
14/A&B	5-1/2"	TMK-6, MB	400-450

HUM 15: HEAR YE, HEAR YE

Among the first 46 to be released by Goebel at the Leipzig Fair, this figure was first called "Night Watchman" and remained so until around 1950. Serious collectors seek out the larger 7-1/2" size with the Arabic size designator 15/2, for it represents the oldest of Crown Mark (TMK-1) figures

Hum No.	Basic Size	Trademark	Current Value ($)
15/2/0	4"	TMK-5, LB	135-145
15/2/0	4"	TMK-6, MB	135
15/0	5"	TMK-1, CM	375-500
15/0	5"	TMK-2, FB	265-285
15/0	5"	TMK-3, Sty. Bee	225-245
15/0	5"	TMK-4, 3-line	195-220
15/0	5"	TMK-5, LB	180-190
15/0	5"	TMK-6, MB	180
15/I	6"	TMK-1, CM	450-600
15/I	6"	TMK-2, FB	330-350
15/I	6"	TMK-3, Sty. Bee	275-290

Hum No.	Basic Size	Trademark	Current Value ($)
15/I	6"	TMK-4, 3-line	245-260
15/I	6"	TMK-5, LB	225-240
15/I	6"	TMK-6, MB	225
15/II	7-1/2"	TMK-1, CM	900-1500
15/II	7-1/2"	TMK-1, CM	800-1100
15/II	7-1/2"	TMK-2, FB	440-600
15/II	7-1/2"	TMK-3, Sty. Bee	410-440
15/II	7-1/2"	TMK-4, 3-line	410-440
15/II	7-1/2"	TMK-5, LB	375-390
15/II	7-1/2"	TMK-6, MB	375

HEAR YE, HEAR YE, Hum 15. Left 15/0, stamped Crown Mark (TMK-1), donut base, 5-3/8". Right: 15/0, Full Bee (TMK-2), donut base, black "Germany," 5-5/8".

HUM 16: LITTLE HIKER

One of the original 46 released in 1934 in the 16/I and 16/2/0 sizes. The only significant variation is with the mold number. The mold number is sometimes found with only the 16 and sometimes with the decimal designator "16." in the 5-1/2" to 6" size. These are found with the Crown (TMK-1) and the Full Bee (TMK-2) trademark and will bring about 15% more than comparably trademarked 16/I's.

Hum No.	Basic Size	Trademark	Current Value ($)
16/2/0	4-1/4"	TMK-1, CM	220-280
16/2/0	4-1/4"	TMK-2, FB	150-175
16/2/0	4-1/4"	TMK-3, Sty. Bee	125-145
16/2/0	4-1/4"	TMK-4, 3-line	120-125
16/2/0	4-1/4"	TMK-5, LB	110-120
16/2/0	4-1/4"	TMK-6, MB	110
16/I	5-1/2"	TMK-1, CM	400-500
16/I	5-1/2"	TMK-2, FB	280-320
16/I	5-1/2"	TMK-3, Sty. Bee	225-240
16/I	5-1/2"	TMK-4, 3-line	215-225
16/I	5-1/2"	TMK-5, LB	200-210
16/I	5-1/2"	TMK-6, MB	200

LITTLE HIKER, Hum 16. Left is a Double Crown Marked (TMK-1) piece measuring 5-1/2" with black "Made in Germany" beneath the base. The one on the right has an incised Full Bee (TMK-2) and a stamped Full Bee mark as well. It measures 5-7/8" and has a black "Germany" beneath the base.

HUM 17: CONGRATULATIONS

One of the original 1935 releases, there is a very unusual, perhaps unique, version of this piece where a bowl is attached to the figure's right rear. The figure in this version does not have the normal base.

When first modeled the figure had no socks. Later versions (after 1970) have a new hairstyle that appears to be a little longer. The flowers in the pot are larger and she wears socks. This change was made during the Three Line Mark (TMK-4) and Stylized Bee (TMK-5) era so you can find either version with these marks. Obviously the no-socks piece would be the more desirable one.

Hum No.	Basic Size	Trademark	Current Value ($)
17/0 (no socks)	6"	TMK-1, CM	360-450
17/0 (no socks)	6"	TMK-2, FB	260-285
17/0 (no socks)	6"	TMK-3, Sty. Bee	240-260
17/0 (socks)	6"	TMK-3, Sty. Bee	215-235
17/0 (no socks)	6"	TMK-4, 3-line	210-225
17/0 (socks)	6"	TMK-4, 3-line	190-210
17/0 (socks)	6"	TMK-5, LB	180-190
17/0 (socks)	6"	TMK-6, MB	180
17/2 or 17/II	8-1/4"	TMK-1, CM	5000-7500
17/2 or 17/II	8-1/4"	TMK-2, FB	4000-5000
17/2 or 17/II	8-1/4"	TMK-3, Sty. Bee	3000-4000

CONGRATULATIONS, Hum 17. Left: 17/0, Double Crown Mark (TMK-1), 3-3/4". Right: 17/0, Small Stylized Bee (TMK-3), 3-3/4".

HUM 18: CHRIST CHILD

This figure is very similar to the Christ Child figure used in the Nativity Sets, Hum 214 and 260. It is known to have been produced in a solid white overglaze. The white piece is rare. Christ Child has been temporarily withdrawn from production.

Hum No.	Basic Size	Trademark	Current Value ($)
18	2"x6"	TMK-1, CM	260-325
18	2"x6"	TMK-2, FB	185-200
18	2"x6"	TMK-3, Sty. Bee	155-170
18	2"x6"	TMK-4, 3-line	135-145
18	2"x6"	TMK-5, LB	130-135
18	2"x6"	TMK-6, MB	130

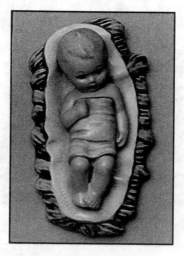

CHRIST CHILD, Hum 18. Stylized Bee mark, 3-1/4" x 5-7/8".

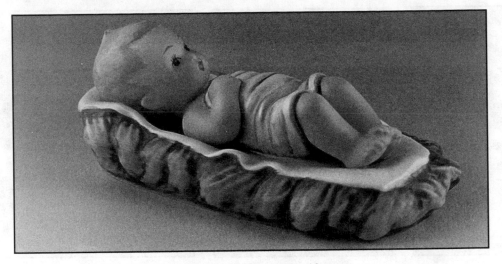

CHRIST CHILD, Hum 18.

HUM 19: PRAYER BEFORE BATTLE (Ashtray, Closed Number)

Until 1986, when one of these surfaced in the United States, it was thought this was a closed number and the piece never produced. Even though one was found (temporarily) it may well be the only one ever made. The reason I noted "temporarily" found follows: It seems that a lady brought the piece to the Goebel Collectors' Club in Tarrytown, New York, for identification. The paint finish was badly damaged as a result of her having put it in a dishwasher to clean it. Goebel Master Sculptor Gerhard Skrobek coincidentally was there. He speculated that the reason the paint was damaged was because it was probably a sample piece, painted but never fired so that the paint had not bonded to the figurine. Subsequent investigation

of Goebel records revealed that the design was rejected by the Siessen Convent, and therefore never placed in production. Furthermore there is no example in the company archives. How it got out of the factory and to the U.S. remains a mystery. It seems the lady left, taking her piece with her, and no one present could remember her name or where she was from. A realistic value cannot be placed on this unique piece.

The most recent footnote to this story: a noted and very serious collector pursued the search until he finally did find the ashtray and its owner. His attempt to purchase it was rebuffed due to a sentimental attachment to the piece.

HUM 20: PRAYER BEFORE BATTLE

Few changes of any significance have affected the collector value of this piece since its initial release in 1935. It has been listed at 4" and 4-1/2" in the price lists over the years, but is presently 4-1/4".

There has been one most unusual figure uncovered, which exhibits peculiar color variations (see accompanying photograph). The horse is gray, black and white instead of the normal tan, the wagon is a dark green with red wheels, the socks are the same green color and his clothes are dark green and brown. The horn is a shiny gold. This may be a one-of-a-kind experimental piece that somehow

made it out of the factory, but who knows? It is from the late Ed Wunner's collection and the photo is courtesy of Rue Dee Marker.

Hum No.	Basic Size	Trademark	Current Value ($)
20	4-1/4"	TMK-1, CM	310-390
20	4-1/4"	TMK-2, FB	220-240
20	4-1/4"	TMK-3, Sty. Bee	190-210
20	4-1/4"	TMK-5, LB	155-165
20	4-1/4"	TMK-6, MB	155

PRAYER BEFORE BATTLE, Hum 20, with peculiar color variations.

Another view of the PRAYER BEFORE BATTLE with the unusual paint colors.

PRAYER BEFORE BATTLE, Hum 20. Left: Full Bee (TMK-2) mark, black "Germany," 4-1/2". Right: Last Bee (TMK-5) mark, 4-1/8".

HUM 21: HEAVENLY ANGEL

First known as the Little Guardian and later Advent Angel, this figure was among the 46 original releases in 1935. This is the same motif used on the famous 1971 annual plate by Goebel and the Schmid company. The 21/0 size was the first to be introduced. It was followed by the larger sizes soon after.

The only variation of any significance in terms of value is the white overglaze model. It has not been found, but factory records indicate that it was produced.

Hum No.	Basic Size	Trademark	Current Value ($)
21/I	6-3/4"	TMK-6, MB	230
21/II	8-3/4"	TMK-1, CM	825-1025
21/II	8-3/4"	TMK-2, FB	600-625
21/II	8-3/4"	TMK-3, Sty. Bee	500-525
21/II	8-3/4"	TMK-4, 3-line	450-465
21/II	8-3/4"	TMK-5, LB	415-425
21/II	8-3/4"	TMK-6, MB	415

*One of the only two pieces in the Goebel collection where this "1/2" designator is used. The other is Blessed Child, Hum 78.

Hum No.	Basic Size	Trademark	Current Value ($)
21/0	4-1/4"	TMK-1, CM	220-275
21/I	4-1/4"	TMK-2, FB	150-170
21/0	4-1/4"	TMK-3, Sty. Bee	135-145
21/0	4-1/4"	TMK-4, 3-line	115-125
21/0	4-1/4"	TMK-5, LB	110-120
21/0	4-1/4"	TMK-6, MB	110
*21/0/1/2	6"	TMK-1, CM	400-500
*21/0/1/2	6"	TMK-2, FB	265-285
*21/0/1/2	6"	TMK-3, Sty. Bee	230-250
*21/0/1/2	6"	TMK-4, 3-line	205-220
*21/0/1/2	6"	TMK-5, LB	190-200
*21/0/1/2	6"	TMK-6, MB	190
21/I	6-3/4"	TMK-1, CM	450-585
21/I	6-3/4"	TMK-2, FB	330-355
21/I	6-3/4"	TMK-3, Sty. Bee	280-300
21/I	6-3/4"	TMK-4, 3-line	245-260
21/I	6-3/4"	TMK-5, LB	230-240

HEAVENLY ANGEL, Hum 21. Left: Small Stylized Bee (TMK-3) mark, 5-3/4". Right: Last Bee (TMK-5) mark, 5-3/4". Both have the mold number rendered thus: 21/0.

HUM 22: ANGEL WITH BIRD or ANGEL SITTING (Holy Water Font)

A figure sometimes known as Seated or Sitting Angel with birds. This font has variations in bowl design and appears in two basic sizes. The mold number 22 has been known to appear with the decimal point size designator "22." The latter will bring about 15% more than the 22/0 counterpart in the Crown Mark. The 22/I size is a closed edition.

Hum No.	Basic Size	Trademark	Current Value ($)
22/0	2-3/4"x3-1/2"	TMK-1, CM	85-100
22/0	2-3/4"x3-1/2"	TMK-2, FB	55-65
22/0	2-3/4"x3-1/2"	TMK-3, Sty. Bee	45-55
22/0	2-3/4"x3-1/2"	TMK-4, 3-line	40-45
22/0	2-3/4"x3-1/2"	TMK-5, LB	40
22/0	2-3/4"x3-1/2"	TMK-6, MB	40
22/I	3-1/4"x4"	TMK-1, CM	400-500
22/I	3-1/4"x4"	TMK-2, FB	350-400
22/I	3-1/4"x4"	TMK-3, Sty. Bee	300-350

ANGEL WITH BIRD Font, Hum 22/0. Stylized Bee, 3-7/8".

HUM 23: ADORATION

Known in the early years as "Ave Maria" and "At the Shrine," this member of the 1935 group was originally released in the smaller size. Soon after came the 23/III.

Both sizes have been produced in white overglaze, but they are quite scarce. When found for sale they usually go for about $3,500-3,800.

Hum No.	Basic Size	Trademark	Current Value ($)
23/I	6-1/4"	TMK-1, CM	650-810
23/I	6-1/4"	TMK-2, FB	470-500
23/I	6-1/4"	TMK-3, Sty. Bee	395-415
23/I	6-1/4"	TMK-4, 3-line	350-370
23/I	6-1/4"	TMK-5, LB	325-340
23/I	6-1/4"	TMK-6, MB	325
23/III	9"	TMK-1, CM	1000-1300
23/III	9"	TMK-2, FB	720-760
23/III	9"	TMK-3, Sty. Bee	625-650
23/III	9"	TMK-4, 3-line	545-570
23/III	9"	TMK-5, LB	510-530
23/III	9"	TMK-6, MB	510

ADORATION, Hum 23. Left: 23/1, Stylized Bee mark (TMK-3) in an incised circle, black "Western Germany," 6-1/2". Right: 23/III, Last Bee mark (TMK-5), split base (diagonally), 9".

HUM 24: LULLABY (Candleholder)

This piece is quite similar to Hum 262, except that this one is a candleholder.

The larger 24/III was withdrawn from production for some time and reinstated in the early 1980s. It disappeared once again, however, from the Goebel price lists and has remained so for several years. The other size, 24/I, was listed as temporarily withdrawn at the end of 1989. By 1995, it was back on the suggested retail price list.

The larger (24/III) was out of production for some time, but has recently been reissued. The 24/III bearing older marks commands premium prices. The 24/III is sometimes found as 24/3. It was not listed in the 1995 suggested retail price list.

Back in 1992 I received a letter from a collector describing a "Lullabye" candleholder with a "music box attached." It was purchased in 1951 in Hawaii. I was unable to confirm this and have no photo, but it may be out there.

LULLABY (candleholder), Hum 24. Left: Bears the mold number 24/1 and a small Stylized Bee (TMK-3) mark. Right: Bears the mold number 24/I and the Last Bee (TMK-5). Both measure 3-3/8". Note the candle hole variation. The older one is molded in so that the hole is not obvious without the candle in it.

Hum No.	Basic Size	Trademark	Current Value ($)
24/I	3-1/4"x5"	TMK-1, CM	385-460
24/I	3-1/4"x5"	TMK-2, FB	250-275
24/I	3-1/4"x5"	TMK-3, Sty. Bee	215-235
24/I	3-1/4"x5"	TMK-4, 3-line	180-195
24/I	3-1/4"x5"	TMK-5, LB	175
24/I	3-1/4"x5"	TMK-6, MB	175
24/III	6"x8"	TMK-1, CM	1400-1700
24/III	6"x8"	TMK-2, FB	500-700
24/III	6"x8"	TMK-3, Sty. Bee	310-400
24/III	6"x8"	TMK-5, LB	250-300
24/III	6"x8"	TMK-6, MB	250-300

HUM 25: ANGELIC SLEEP (Candleholder)

One of the original 46 figures displayed at the Leipzig Fair in 1935. It was made in white overglaze for a short period, but not for export to the U.S. The white overglazed pieces are considered rare and can bring up to $2,500 when sold.

ANGELIC SLEEP, Hum 25. Left: Full Bee (TMK-2) trademark, 3-7/8", black "Germany." Right: Small Stylized Bee (TMK-3), 3-1/2".

Hum No.	Basic Size	Trademark	Current Value ($)
25	3-1/2"x5"	TMK-1, CM	325-410
25	3-1/2"x5"	TMK-2, FB	225-250
25	3-1/2"x5"	TMK-3, Sty. Bee	190-215
25	3-1/2"x5"	TMK-4, 3-line	170-185
25	3-1/2"x5"	TMK-5, LB	160-170
25	3-1/2"x5"	TMK-6, MB	160

ANGELIC SLEEP, Hum 25. Rear view of the above showing the hole variations between the two.

HUM 26: CHILD JESUS (Holy Water Font)

One of the original 1935 releases. The color of the robe is normally a deep orange-red. A very significant variation has appeared in the Stylized Bee (TMK-3) mark, 26/0 size.

The font has been produced in two sizes all along, although the larger size has not appeared in the Goebel price list for some years.

Hum No.	Basic Size	Trademark	Current Value ($)
26/0	1-1/2"x5"	TMK-1, CM	85-100
26/0	1-1/2"x5"	TMK-2, FB	55-65
26/0	1-1/2"x5"	TMK-3, Sty. Bee	45-55
26/0	1-1/2"x5"	TMK-4, 3-line	25-45
26/0	1-1/2"x5"	TMK-5, LB	40
26/0	1-1/2"x5"	TMK-6, MB	40
26/I	2-1/2"x6"	TMK-1, CM	350-500
26/I	2-1/2"x6"	TMK-2, FB	300-350
26/I	2-1/2"x6"	TMK-3, Sty. Bee	250-300

CHILD JESUS Font, Hum 26/0. Stylized Bee mark, 5-1/8".

HUM 27: JOYOUS NEWS

This piece is considered to be fairly scarce in the first three trademarks. As far as is presently known, there are probably less than 100 in collectors' hands. The 27/III is sometimes found as 27/3. It was out of production for several years, but has been back in production for some time now. Older marked figures command a premium price. There is a smaller size (27/I) but it is rare. This 2-3/4" version is a candleholder. There are only a few presently known to exist. The Crown Mark 27/I's are valued at $350-500. The Full Bee 27/I's are valued at $250-350.

JOYOUS NEWS, Hum 27/3. Large Stylized Bee (TMK-3) in an incised circle, black "Western Germany," 4-1/2".

Hum No.	Basic Size	Trademark	Current Value ($)
27/III	4-1/4"x4-3/4"	TMK-1, CM	1200-1800
27/III	4-1/4"x4-3/4"	TMK-2, FB	750-1000
27/III	4-1/4"x4-3/4"	TMK-3, Sty. Bee	500-750
27/III (27/3)	4-1/4"x4-3/4"	TMK-5, LB	160-185
27/III	4-1/4"x4-3/4"	TMK-6, MB	195

HUM 28: WAYSIDE DEVOTION

This figurine is one of the initial 1935 designs displayed at the Leipzig Fair.

Both sizes have been found with the Arabic size designator 28/2 and 28/3. The larger, 8-1/2" size also appears without the designator on all on the Crown Mark (TMK-1)

figurines. These are valued at roughly 20% above the regularly marked counterpart.

The figure was produced for a short time in white overglaze. These are considered rare and are valued at about $2,500.

WAYSIDE DEVOTION, Hum 28/II. Left: Stylized Bee, 6-7/8". Right: Last Bee (TMK-5), 7-1/2".

Hum No.	Basic Size	Trademark	Current Value ($)
28/II	7-1/2"	TMK-1, CM	790-990
28/II	7-1/2"	TMK-2, FB	585-615
28/II	7-1/2"	TMK-3, Sty. Bee	480-505
28/II	7-1/2"	TMK-4, 3-line	425-450
28/II	7-1/2"	TMK-5, LB	395-410
28/II	7-1/2"	TMK-6, MB	395
28	8-3/4"	TMK-1, CM	1300-1600
28/III	8-1/2"	TMK-1, CM	1000-1300
28/III	8-1/2"	TMK-2, FB	750-780
28/III	8-1/2"	TMK-3, Sty. Bee	625-670
28/III	8-1/2"	TMK-4, 3-line	550-585
28/III	8-1/2"	TMK-5, LB	520-535
28/III	8-1/2"	TMK-6, MB	520

HUM 29: GUARDIAN ANGEL (Holy Water Font)

This figure is not in current production and is highly sought by collectors. A similar piece (Hum 248) exists and is considered to be a redesign of Hum 29. Hum 29 is, therefore, unlikely to ever be reissued. It has been found with the decimal point designator.

GUARDIAN ANGEL Font, Hum 29. Incised Crown Mark, 5-3/4".

Hum No.	Basic Size	Trademark	Current Value ($)
29.	2-3/4"x6"	TMK-1, CM	1100-1350
29/0	2-1/2"x5-5/8"	TMK-1, CM	1100-1350
29/0	2-1/2"x5-5/8"	TMK-2, FB	1000-1200
29/0	2-1/2"x5-5/8"	TMK-3, Sty. Bee	900-1000
29/I	3"x6-3/8"	TMK-1, CM	1500-1800
29/I	3"x6-3/8"	TMK-2, FB	1300-1500

HUM 30A and HUM 30B: BA-BEE RINGS (Wall Plaques)

BA-BEE RINGS. Left: 30/0 B., Crown Mark, red in color, 4-5/8". Right 30/1., double Crown Mark, red in color, 5-3/8".

Part of the original collection released in 1935, these figures are found in two basic sizes.

Figures with the rings painted red in the Crown (TMK-1) era are found in both sizes and there has been at least one reported in bisque finish in the 30/0 size. Both of these are considered rare. They are also possibly found in the white overglaze finish. Value in red rings: $4,000-5,000.

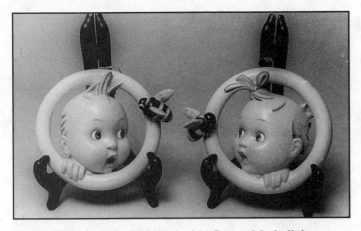

BA-BEE RINGS. Left 30/1., double Crown Mark, light tan color, 5-3/8". Right: 30/1 B, incised Crown Mark, light tan.

The figure remains in production in a buff color (rings) in the 5" size only.

Hum No.	Basic Size	Trademark	Current Value ($)
30/A&B	5" diam.	TMK-1, CM	325-425
30/A&B	5" diam.	TMK-2, FB	250-300
30/0 A&B	5" diam.	TMK-3, Sty. Bee	200-220
30/0 A&B	5" diam.	TMK-4, 3-line	180-200
30/0 A&B	5" diam.	TMK-5, LB	170-180
30/0 A&B	5" diam.	TMK-6, MB	170
30/I A&B	6" diam.	TMK-1, CM	2500-3000

HUM 31: ADVENT GROUP (Candleholder)

This was often called Advent Group or Silent Night "with Black Child" until several of the same mold numbers began showing up with a white child where the black child was ordinarily. It is thought by some that, in fact, the white child version may bc the more rare of the two. Whatever thc case, both are quite rare. Very similar to Hum 54, Silent Night, Hum 31 was produced first in 1935 with the other original 45. Both versions have been found in the Crown Mark (TMK-1) only. See Hum 54, Hum 113 and Hum 754.

Collector value for the Hum 31 with black child: $6,000-8,000

Collector value for the Hum 31 with white child: $6,000-8,000

ADVENT GROUP, Hum 31. Both measure 3-1/2" and bear the incised Crown Mark (TMK-1).

HUM 32: LITTLE GABRIEL

When first released in 1935 this figure was called "Joyous News." It continues to be produced today, but only in the 5" size (Hum 32 without the "/I" designator).

Little Gabriel has been redesigned. Thc older pieces have the arms that are attached to each other up to the hands. The new design has the arms separated.

LITTLE GABRIEL, Hum 32. Left: figure is a Hum 32/0 with a Full Bee (TMK-2) mark. It measures 5-1/8". On the right is a Missing Bee (TMK-6) mold number 32 measuring 5" tall.

Hum No.	Basic Size	Trademark	Current Value ($)
32/0	5"	TMK-1, CM	250-315
32/0	5"	TMK-2, FB	180-195
32/0	5"	TMK-3, Sty. Bee	150-160
32/0	5"	TMK-4, 3-line	130-140
32/0	5"	TMK-5, LB	125-130
32/0	5"	TMK-6, MB	125
32	5"	TMK-6, MB	125
32	6"	TMK-1, CM	2200-3000
32	6"	TMK-2, FB	1800-2000
32/I	6"	TMK-1, CM	2200-3000
32/I	6"	TMK-2, FB	1800-2000
32/I	6"	TMK-3, Sty. Bee	1500-1700

HUM 33: JOYFUL (Ashtray)

An ashtray utilizing a figure very similar to Hum 53, with the addition of a small bird on the edge of the tray next to the figure. This piece was temporarily removed from production effective December 31, 1984, with no date for reinstatement given.

The piece has been found in the faience finish. This will bring a mid to high five-figure amount when found.

JOYFUL ashtray, Hum 33. Both bear the Crown Mark (TMK-1) and measure 3-3/4". The one on the left is an example of the faience pieces. This one is rather poorly and gaudily painted. See color section and chapter 5.

Hum No.	Basic Size	Trademark	Current Value ($)
33	3-1/2"x6"	TMK-1, CM	300-400
33	3-1/2"x6"	TMK-2, FB	200-250
33	3-1/2"x6"	TMK-3, Sty. Bee	160-180
33	3-1/2"x6"	TMK-4, 3-line	130-150
33	3-1/2"x6"	TMK-5, LB	100-125
33	3-1/2"x6"	TMK-6, MB	100-125

HUM 34: SINGING LESSON (Ashtray)

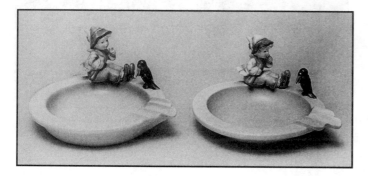

SINGING LESSON ashtray, Hum 34. Left: Full Bee mark (TMK-2). This is an oversize ashtray measuring 4" x 6-1/2". Right: Stylized Bee mark (TMK-3), 3-7/8" x 6-3/16".

An ashtray utilizing a figure very similar to Hum 64, with a small bird perched on the edge of the tray instead of the boy's shoes.

This ashtray was listed as temporarily withdrawn from production at the end of 1989 with no date of reinstatement given.

Hum No.	Basic Size	Trademark	Current Value ($)
33	3-1/2"x6"	TMK-1, CM	285-350
33	3-1/2"x6"	TMK-2, FB	195-220
33	3-1/2"x6"	TMK-3, Sty. Bee	165-185
33	3-1/2"x6"	TMK-4, 3-line	130-150
33	3-1/2"x6"	TMK-5, LB	100-140
33	3-1/2"x6"	TMK-6, MB	100-125

HUM 35: GOOD SHEPHERD (Holy Water Font)

Part of the original collection released in 1935, this figurine has had only minor modifications over the years. It remains in production today with no significant variations affecting collector value.

THE GOOD SHEPHERD Font, Hum 35. Left: Double Crown mark, 5-1/2". Right: No apparent mark other than the mold number, 4-5/8".

Hum No.	Basic Size	Trademark	Current Value ($)
35/0	2-1/4"x4-3/4"	TMK-1, CM	80-100
35/0	2-1/4"x4-3/4"	TMK-2, FB	55-60
35/0	2-1/4"x4-3/4"	TMK-3, Sty. Bee	45-55
35/0	2-1/4"x4-3/4"	TMK-4, 3-line	45
35/0	2-1/4"x4-3/4"	TMK-5, LB	40
35/0	2-1/4"x4-3/4"	TMK-6, MB	40
35	2-1/4"x4-3/4"	TMK-1, CM	275-325
35/I	2-3/4"x5-3/4"	TMK-1, CM	250-300
35/I	2-3/4"x5-3/4"	TMK-2, FB	200-250
35/I	2-3/4"x5-3/4"	TMK-3, Sty. Bee	150-200

GOOD SHEPHERD Font, 35/0 Stylized Bee mark, 4-13/16".

HUM 36: CHILD WITH FLOWERS (Holy Water Font)

CHILD WITH FLOWERS Font, Hum 36/0. Last Bee mark, 4-1/4".

One of the original 46 released in 1935 there have been only minor modifications over the years. It remains in production today.

Has been found with the decimal point designator, "36." in the Crown Mark, 36/I size.

Hum No.	Basic Size	Trademark	Current Value ($)
36/0	2-3/4"x4"	TMK-1, CM	80-100
36/0	2-3/4"x4"	TMK-2, FB	55-65
36/0	2-3/4"x4"	TMK-3, Sty. Bee	45-55
36/0	2-3/4"x4"	TMK-4, 3-line	45
36/0	2-3/4"x4"	TMK-5, LB	40
36/0	2-3/4"x4"	TMK-6, MB	40
36.	3-1/2"x4-1/2"	TMK-1, CM	350-400
36/I	3-1/2"x4-1/2"	TMK-1, CM	300-350
36/I	3-1/2"x4-1/2"	TMK-2, FB	150-250
36/I	3-1/2"x4-1/2"	TMK-3, Sty. Bee	100-150

HUM 37: HERALD ANGELS (Candleholder)

This is a group of figures very similar to Hum 38, 39 and 40, placed together on a common round base with a candle receptacle in the center. There are two versions, one with a low and one with a higher candleholder. The higher holder is found on the older pieces. This candleholder has been temporarily withdrawn from current production.

Hum No.	Basic Size	Trademark	Current Value ($)
37	2-1/4"x4"	TMK-1, CM	320-400
37	2-1/4"x4"	TMK-2, FB	230-250
37	2-1/4"x4"	TMK-3, Sty. Bee	180-210
37	2-1/4"x4"	TMK-4, 3-line	170-180
37	2-1/4"x4"	TMK-5, LB	160
37	2-1/4"x4"	TMK-6, MB	160

HERALD ANGELS candleholder, Hum 37. Small Stylized Bee (TMK-3), 2-7/8" x 4-5/8".

HUM 38, HUM 39, HUM 40: ANGEL TRIO (Candleholders)

These three figures are presented as a set of three and are usually sold as a set. They each come in three versions according to size and candle size. For some unknown reason they are not in the current price list.

Hum 38: Joyous News, Angel with Lute
Hum 39: Joyous News, Angel with Accordion
Hum 40: Joyous News, Angel with Horn

ANGEL TRIO candleholders. Left: Angel with Lute, Hum 38, Full Bee mark, black "Germany," 2-3/4". Center: Angel with Accordian, Hum 39, Full Bee mark black "Germany," 2-5/8". Right: Angel with Horn, Hum 40, Full Bee mark, black "Germany," 2-5/8".

Hum No.	Basic Size
I/38/0, 1/39/0, I/40/0	2", 0.6-cm candle diameter
III/38/0, III/39/0, III/40/0	2", 1.0-cm candle diameter
III/38/I, III/39/I, III/40/I	2-3/4", 1.0-cm candle diameter

HUM 41: SINGING LESSON (Closed Number)

This figure had been listed as a closed number but the existence of the piece is now substantiated. Details are not known but the piece is said to be similar to Hum 63, Singing Lesson, without the base. There are no known examples, but samples in this category have turned up from time to time.

HUM 42: GOOD SHEPHERD

The 42 mold number has been found with the decimal point designator. There are two very rare variations: a blue gown rather than the normal brownish color and a white gown with blue stars. This is found on the 42/0 size in the Crown (TMK-1) and Full Bee (TMK-2) figures.

No longer produced in the 7-1/2" size.

Hum No.	Basic Size	Trademark	Current Value ($)
42.	6-1/4"	TMK-1, CM	500-600
42/0	6-1/4"	TMK-1, CM	440-550
42/0	6-1/4"	TMK-2, FB	310-340
42/0	6-1/4"	TMK-3, Sty. Bee	265-285
42/0	6-1/4"	TMK-4, 3-line	235-250
42/0	6-1/4"	TMK-5, LB	220
42/0	6-1/4"	TMK-6, MB	220
42/I	7-1/2"	TMK-1, CM	6500-7500
42/I	7-1/2"	TMK-2, FB	5500-6500

GOOD SHEPHERD, Hum 42. Left: Incised Crown Mark (TMK-1) colored blue, 7-5/8". Right: 42/0, Full Bee (TMK-2) trademark, black "Germany," 6-1/2".

HUM 43: MARCH WINDS

This is one of the original 46 released in 1935.

There appear to be two slightly different designs. In the earlier pieces the boy looks more toward the rear than in the newer ones, but there are no significant variations to be found. It is still in production today. A smaller size has recently been added.

Hum No.	Basic Size	Trademark	Current Value ($)
43/5/0	2-3/4"	TMK-7, HM	55
43	5"	TMK-1, CM	290-360
43	5"	TMK-2, FB	200-225
43	5"	TMK-3, Sty. Bee	170-190
43	5"	TMK-4, 3-line	150-160

Hum No.	Basic Size	Trademark	Current Value ($)
43	5"	TMK-5, LB	145-150
43	5"	TMK-6, MB	145

MARCH WINDS, Hum 43. The left figure bears the Full Bee (TMK-2) trademark, is 5-1/2" and bears a black "Germany" beneath the base. The one on the right has a small Stylized Bee (TMK-3) trademark and is 4-7/8" tall.

HUM 44/A: CULPRITS (Table Lamp)

HUM 44/B: OUT OF DANGER (Table Lamp)

Both of these lamps were part of the original 46 designs that were released in 1935. Both are about 9" tall and were temporarily withdrawn from production at the end of 1989. No date for reinstatement was given.

There are no significant variations that would affect the collector value of either one, only minor changes such as the location of the switch.

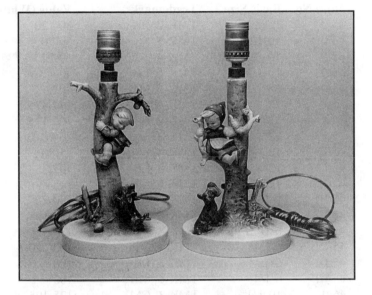

Hum No.	Basic Size	Trademark	Current Value ($)
44/A	9-1/2"	TMK-1, CM	450-600
44/A	9-1/2"	TMK-2, FB	350-400
44/A	9-1/2"	TMK-3, Sty. Bee	275-320
44/A	9-1/2"	TMK-4, 3-line	225-260
44/A	9-1/2"	TMK-5, LB	225-260
44/A	9-1/2"	TMK-6, MB	225-260
44/B	9-1/2"	TMK-1, CM	450-600
44/B	9-1/2"	TMK-2, FB	350-400
44/B	9-1/2"	TMK-3, Sty. Bee	275-320
44/B	9-1/2"	TMK-4, 3-line	225-260
44/B	9-1/2"	TMK-5, LB	225-260
44/B	9-1/2"	TMK-6, MB	225-260

Left: CULPRIT table lamp, Hum 44/A. Double Full Bee mark (TMK-2) incised and stamped, black "Germany," W. Goebel, 9-1/4". Right: OUT OF DANGER table lamp, Hum 44/B. Full Bee mark (TMK-2), black "Germany," W. Goebel, 8-3/8".

HUM 45: MADONNA WITH HALO

MADONNA WITH HALO, Hum 45/0. Left: White overglaze, small Stylized Bee (TMK-3), 10-3/4". Right: Full Bee (TMK-2) trademark in an incised circle, red stars in the halo, 10-1/2". The halo has blue stars in the Last Bee (TMK-5) era.

HUM 46: MADONNA WITHOUT HALO

These Madonnas were part of the original 46 figures that were released in 1935 at the Leipzig Fair. They are often confusing to collectors because of their similarity. Apparently they are also occasionally confused with each other at the factory. Sometimes the mold number appears on the wrong piece, possibly explained in some cases by the fact that the two pieces are identical without the halo, which is an add-on piece during assembly. The fact that they are sometimes found with both mold numbers incised on one piece lends evidence to the theory that the body is from the same mold and the mold number is impressed after assembly, but before firing.

At least nine legitimate variations have been found. The chief differences are in size, color and glaze treatment. They are found in color and white overglaze. The known color variations are beige, rose, light blue, royal blue and ivory. They have also been found in terra cotta.

In 1982 both the 45/III and the 46/III were temporarily withdrawn from production, and in 1984 the 45/0 and 46/0 were also withdrawn temporarily. Also the 46/I was temporarily withdrawn in 1989, apparently leaving only the 45/I, Madonna with Halo, available to collectors. By the 1995 price list they were again available in the 45/I size. They are listed as available in either the regular color or the white overglaze.

While variations are rampant, only the appearance in terra cotta and one other has any significant effect on value. There is a variation where there are red-painted stars on the underside of the halo. This variation can as much as triple the value for its counterpart without the stars. The terra cotta Madonnas are valued at about $1,500-2,500.

Hum No.	Basic Size	Trademark	Value (White)	Value (Color)
45/0	10-1/2"	TMK-2, FB	80-120	100-170
45/0	10-1/2"	TMK-3, Sty. Bee	50-70	85-100
45/0	10-1/2"	TMK-4, 3-line	40-50	70-85
45/0	10-1/2"	TMK-5, LB	40	60-70
45/0	10-1/2"	TMK-6, MB	40	60
45/I	12"	TMK-1, CM	140-175	225-300
45/I	12"	TMK-2, FB	100-115	165-185
45/I	12"	TMK-3, Sty. Bee	80-90	140-150
45/I	12"	TMK-4, 3-line	75-80	125-130
45/I	12"	TMK-5, LB	70	115
45/I	12"	TMK-6, MB	70	115
45/III	6-1/4"	TMK-1, CM	190-220	300-400
45/III	6-1/4"	TMK-2, FB	140-165	200-225
45/III	6-1/4"	TMK-3, Sty. Bee	120-130	170-185
45/III	6-1/4"	TMK-4, 3-line	100-120	150-165
45/III	6-1/4"	TMK-5, LB	100	140
45/III	6-1/4"	TMK-6, MB	100	140
46/0	10-1/4"	TMK-1, CM	125-195	200-250
46/0	10-1/4"	TMK-2, FB	80-120	100-170
46/0	10-1/4"	TMK-3, Sty. Bee	50-70	85-100
46/0	10-1/4"	TMK-4, 3-line	40-50	70-85
46/0	10-1/4"	TMK-5, LB	40	60-70
46/0	10-1/4"	TMK-6, MB	40	60
46/I	11-1/4"	TMK-1, CM	140-175	225-300
46/I	11-1/4"	TMK-2, FB	100-115	165-185
46/I	11-1/4"	TMK-3, Sty. Bee	80-90	140-150
46/I	11-1/4"	TMK-4, 3-line	75-80	125-130
46/I	11-1/4"	TMK-5, LB	70	115
46/I	11-1/4"	TMK-6, MB	70	115
46/III	16"	TMK-1, CM	190-220	300-400
46/III	16"	TMK-2, FB	140-165	200-225
46/III	16"	TMK-3, Sty. Bee	120-130	170-185
46/III	16"	TMK-4, 3-line	100-120	150-165
46/III	16"	TMK-5, LB	100	140
46/III	16"	TMK-6, MB	100	140

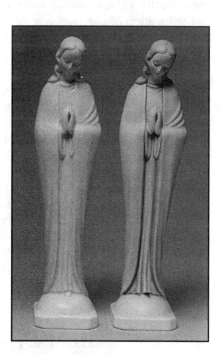

MADONNA WITHOUT HALO, Hum 46/0. Left is white overglaze and right is painted. Both are small Stylized Bee (TMK-3) pieces measuring 10-1/2".

HUM 47: GOOSE GIRL

GOOSE GIRL Bowl. This exceedingly rare piece was found in Germany in 1989. It measures 4-7/8" and has an incised Crown mark. Upon examining it closely, it appears that the bowl was attached to the figurine before firing, lending legitimacy to the speculation that it was fashioned by Goebel. The bowl is a double Crown mark piece and has an incised mold number "1". Two other bowl pieces have shown up with a different style of bowl: Meditation (Hum 13) and Congratulations (Hum 17).

GOOSE GIRL, Hum 47. Left: 47/0, Full Bee mark, black "Germany," 5-1/4". Center: 47/0, Stylized Bee mark, 4-3/4". Right: 47 3/0, Full Bee mark, black "Germany," 4-1/4".

A very popular piece, probably the most famous among collectors and non-collectors alike. Interestingly, for a model that dates back practically to day one and in three sizes, there are no variations significant enough to have an effect on collector value. The occurrence of the decimal designator might have a slight influence with some collectors, but not a great degree of significance.

There is, of course, the Goose Girl with a bowl attached. This piece is thought to be unique; a sample that somehow found its way into the collector market. I photographed this one in a home in Germany. No others have turned up. There are two similar pieces: Congratulations, Hum 17, and Meditation, Hum 13.

Hum No.	Basic Size	Trademark	Current Value ($)
47/3/0	4"	TMK-1, CM	310-390
47/3/0	4"	TMK-2, FB	220-245
47/3/0	4"	TMK-3, Sty Bee	190-215
47/3/0	4"	TMK-4, 3-line	165-180
47/3/0	4"	TMK-5, LB	155-160
47/3/0	4"	TMK-6, MB	155
47	5"	TMK-1, CM	410-515
47/0	4-3/4"	TMK-1, CM	410-515
47/0	4-3/4"	TMK-2, FB	290-320
47/0	4-3/4"	TMK-3, Sty. Bee	245-265
47/0	4-3/4"	TMK-4, 3-line	215-235
47/0	4-3/4"	TMK-5, LB	205-210
47/0	4-3/4"	TMK-6, MB	205
47/II	7-1/2"	TMK-1, CM	800-1000
47/II	7-1/2"	TMK-2, FB	575-625
47/II	7-1/2"	TMK-3, Sty. Bee	485-520
47/II	7-1/2"	TMK-4, 3-line	425-450
47/II	7-1/2"	TMK-5, LB	400-420
47/II	7-1/2"	TMK-6, MB	400

HUM 48: MADONNA (Wall Plaque)

This plaque has been known to appear in a white overglaze in the 48/0 and the 48/II sizes in a bisque finish. The 48/II can sometimes be found as 48/2. There are two variations of the 48/II in the Crown Mark. The 48/II size in current-use trademark has been temporarily withdrawn from production. The effective date was December 31, 1984, with no reinstatement date given.

The white overglaze pieces appear in the Crown Mark (TMK-1) and are very rare.

Hum No.	Basic Size	Trademark	Current Value ($)
48/0	3"x4"	TMK-1, CM	250-300
48/0	3"x4"	TMK-2, FB	115-130
48/0	3"x4"	TMK-3, Sty. Bee	95-115
48/0	3"x4"	TMK-4, 3-line	90-95
48/0	3"x4"	TMK-5, LB	80-85
48/0	3"x4"	TMK-6, MB	80
48	4-3/4"x6"	TMK-1, CM	450-570
48/II	4-3/4"x6"	TMK-1, CM	400-520
48/II	4-3/4"x6"	TMK-2, FB	200-220

Hum No.	Basic Size	Trademark	Current Value ($)
48/II	4-3/4"x6"	TMK-3, Sty. Bee	145-160
48/II	4-3/4"x6"	TMK-5, LB	135-145
48/II	4-3/4"x6"	TMK-6, MB	135
48/V	8-1/4"x10-1/2"	TMK-1, CM	1500-1800
48/V	8-1/4"x10-1/2"	TMK-2, FB	1300-1400
48/V	8-1/4"x10-1/2"	TMK-3, Sty. Bee	1000-1200

MADONNA Plaque, Hum 48/2. Left: Stylized Bee mark, 4-5/8" x 5-3/4", white overglaze. Right: Full Bee mark, 4-5/8" x 5-5/8".

HUM 49: TO MARKET

The 49/I size was out of current production for at least 20 years and then reinstated in the early 1980s. Goebel placed it on a temporarily withdrawn from production status on December 31, 1984, and it remains so today. The 49 mold number has occasionally been found with the decimal point size designator. Some 49/0's have surfaced with no bottle in the basket. The 49/3/0 size is routinely produced with no bottle in the basket.

TO MARKET, Hum 49. Left: 49./0., double Crown Mark, donut base, 5-7/16". Right: 49/0, Last Bee mark, 5-3/8".

Hum No.	Basic Size	Trademark	Current Value ($)
49/3/0	4"	TMK-1, CM	300-375
49/3/0	4"	TMK-2, FB	215-240
49/3/0	4"	TMK-3, Sty. Bee	180-200
49/3/0	4"	TMK-4, 3-line	160-175
49/3/0	4"	TMK-5, LB	150-160
49/3/0	4"	TMK-6, MB	150
49/0	5-1/2"	TMK-1, CM	500-650
49/0	5-1/2"	TMK-2, FB	330-400
49/0	5-1/4"	TMK-3, Sty. Bee	300-320
49/0	5-1/2"	TMK-4, 3-line	265-295
49/0	5-1/2"	TMK-5, LB	250-265
49/0	5-1/2"	TMK-6, MB	250
49.	6-1/4"	TMK-1, CM	1100-1300
49.	6-1/4"	TMK-2, FB	750-900
49/I	6-1/4"	TMK-1, CM	800-1100
49/I	6-1/4"	TMK-2, FB	600-700
49/I	6-1/4"	TMK-3, Sty. Bee	500-600
49/I	6-1/4"	TMK-4, 3-line	440-450
49/I	6-1/4"	TMK-5, LB	400-440
49	6-1/4"	TMK-6, MB	400

HUM 50: VOLUNTEERS

The 50/0 and 50/I sizes were out of production for some years and difficult to find with the older trademarks. Both were reinstated in 1979. The new pieces have the Last Bee (TMK-5). The 50/I has once again been withdrawn from current production with no published reinstatement date.

The small Hum 50/2/0, Volunteers, was released with a special backstamp commemorating the allied victory in Operation Desert Storm. Reportedly limited to 10,000 pieces worldwide, it was to be sold only through military post and base exchanges. This particular variation has already risen to a range of $275-350 on the collector market.

Hum No.	Basic Size	Trademark	Current Value ($)
50/2/0	5"	TMK-1, CM	400-500
50/2/0	5"	TMK-2, FB	305-415
50/2/0	5"	TMK-3, Sty. Bee	245-270
50/2/0	5"	TMK-4, 3-line	220-235

Hum No.	Basic Size	Trademark	Current Value ($)
50/2/0	5"	TMK-5, LB	205-215
50/2/0	5"	TMK-6, MB	205
50/0	5-1/2"	TMK-1, CM	540-600
50/0	5-1/2"	TMK-2, FB	375-425
50/0	5-1/2"	TMK-3, Sty. Bee	325-375
50/0	5-1/2"	TMK-5, LB	270
50/0	5-1/2"	TMK-6, MB	270
50.	6-1/2"	TMK-1, CM	1000-1500
50/I	6-1/2"	TMK-1, CM	900-1400
50/I	6-1/2"	TMK-2, FB	600-700
50/I	6-1/2"	TMK-3, Sty. Bee	470-485
50/I	6-1/2"	TMK-5, LB	430-450
50/I	6-1/2"	TMK-6, MB	430

Photo showing the Desert Shield/Desert Storm backstamp on the base of the Volunteers figurine. The normal month and day date found with the backstamp is February 28. There is a rare version where it reads February 24. The number of these is not known, but a few of them have been found.

VOLUNTEERS, Hum 50. Left: 50/0, incised Crown Mark, black "Germany," 5-7/8". Center: 50/0, Full Bee in an incised circle, black "Western Germany," 6-1/16". Right: 50 2/0, Missing Bee mark, 4-7/8", white overglaze.

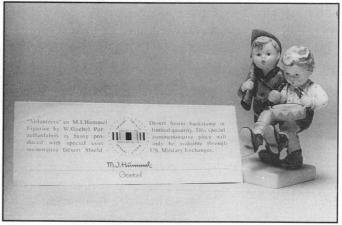

VOLUNTEERS, Hum 50. 50 2/0, Hummel Mark current use mark or (TMK-7), 4-3/4". This is the Volunteers with the special Desert Shield/Desert Storm backstamp.

HUM 51: VILLAGE BOY

Placed in production around 1934-35, this figure is still being produced. The 51/I was taken out of production sometime in the 1960s and the early figures are considered rare. Out of production for some 20 years, the 51/I was placed back in production for a short time and was once again place on temporarily withdrawn status, effective December 31, 1984. It remains so today. In the mid-1990s Goebel introduced a new, smaller size: 51/5/0

There were many minor variations over the years, but the one most important to collectors occurs in the Crown Mark (TMK-1) 51/3/0 size. The boy wears a blue jacket and a yellow kerchief instead of the normal green jacket and red kerchief. When found, this variation is valued at about $2,500.

Hum No.	Basic Size	Trademark	Current Value ($)
51/5/0	2-3/4"	TMK-7, HM	55
51/3/0	4"	TMK-1, CM	225-265
51/3/0	4"	TMK-2, FB	150-175
51/3/0	4"	TMK-3, Sty. Bee	135-150
51/3/0	4"	TMK-4, 3-line	120
51/3/0	4"	TMK-5, LB	110
51/3/0	4"	TMK-6, MB	110
51/2/0	5"	TMK-1, CM	250-315
51/2/0	5"	TMK-2, FB	185-200
51/2/0	5"	TMK-3, Sty. Bee	155-170
51/2/0	5"	TMK-4, 3-line	135-150
51/2/0	5"	TMK-5, LB	125-135
51/2/0	5"	TMK-6, MB	125
51/0	6"	TMK-1, CM	440-550

Hum No.	Basic Size	Trademark	Current Value ($)
51/0	6"	TMK-2, FB	320-350
51/0	6"	TMK-3, Sty. Bee	260-290
51/0	6"	TMK-4, 3-line	235-250
51/0	6"	TMK-5, LB	220-235
51/0	6"	TMK-6, MB	220
51	7-1/4"	TMK-1, CM	500-650
51/I	7-1/4"	TMK-1, CM	450-600
51/I	7-1/4"	TMK-2, FB	300-375
51/I	7-1/4"	TMK-3, Sty. Bee	250-300
51/I	7-1/4"	TMK-5, LB	225-240
51/I	7-1/4"	TMK-6, MB	225

VILLAGE BOY, Hum 51, Left: 51./0., double Crown mark, donut base, 6-1/2". Right: 51/0, Last Bee mark, 6-3/8".

HUM 52: GOING TO GRANDMA'S

A very early figurine in the line. All of the older pieces in both sizes are found in the square base. A redesign and a new oval base were part of the transition to the Last Bee (TMK-5) era. You can, therefore, find TMK-5 pieces with either base, but the older, square base is the most desirable.

The figure has been found with the decimal designator in the Crown Mark (TMK-1).

Hum No.	Basic Size	Trademark	Current Value ($)
52/0	4-3/4"	TMK-1, CM	500-600
52/0	4-3/4"	TMK-2, FB	350-400
52/0	4-3/4"	TMK-3, Sty. Bee	325-350

Hum No.	Basic Size	Trademark	Current Value ($)
52/0	4-3/4"	TMK-4, 3-line	275-325
52/0 (square base)	4-3/4"	TMK-5, LB	275-300
52/0 (oval base)	4-3/4"	TMK-5, LB	250-270
52/0	4-3/4"	TMK-6, MB	250
52.	6"	TMK-1, CM	900-1200
52/I	6"	TMK-1, CM	700-1000
52/I	6"	TMK-2, FB	520-550
52/I	6"	TMK-3, Sty. Bee	425-470
52/I	6"	TMK-5, LB	350-400
52/I	6"	TMK-6, MB	350

GOING TO GRANDMA'S, Hum 52. Shows the appearance of the cone when it holds candies and the later model oval base.

GOING TO GRANDMA'S, Hum 52. Left: Decimal designator in the mold number 52., incised Crown Mark (TMK-1), black "Made in Germany" stamped on and lacquered over, 6". Right: 52/I, Stylized Bee (TMK-3) mark in an incised circle, black "Western Germany," 6-1/4".

HUM 53: JOYFUL

This figure was once known as "Banjo Betty." There are major size variations. As the figure emerged from the Crown Mark (TMK-1) era and transitioned into the Full

JOYFUL, Hum 53. Left: Full Bee (TMK-2) mark in an incised circle, black "Germany," 3-3/4". Right: Missing Bee (TMK-5), 3-3/4".

Bee (TMK-2) period, it began to grow larger. Both the normal sizes and the larger variations appeared during the Full Bee (TMK-2) period and by the time the transition to the Stylized Bee (TMK-3) was finished, it was back to the normal 4" basic size. The oversize pieces consistently bring a higher price than the normal size pieces. They are valued at about 20%-25% more than the normal size.

A much more rare variation is the orange dress (instead of the normal blue) found on some very early Crown Mark (TMK-1) "Joyfuls." Collector value $3,000-3,500.

Hum No.	Basic Size	Trademark	Current Value ($)
53	4"	TMK-1, CM	225-300
53	4"	TMK-2, FB	150-175
53	4"	TMK-3, Sty. Bee	130-150
53	4"	TMK-4, 3-line	115-130
53	4"	TMK-5, LB	110-115
53	4"	TMK-6, MB	110

HUM III/53: JOYFUL (Candy Box)

There are two styles of candy boxes. The transition from the old to the new took place in the Stylized Bee (TMK-3) period. There are, therefore, old and new styles to be found with the Stylized Bee trademark. The older style would, of course, be the more desirable to collectors.

Hum No.	Basic Size	Trademark	Current Value ($)
III/53	6-1/4"	TMK-1, CM	450-530
III/53	6-1/4"	TMK-2, FB	350-400
III/53 (old style)	6-1/4"	TMK-3, Sty. Bee	275-325
III/53 (new style)	6-1/4"	TMK-3, Sty. Bee	150-200
III/53	6-1/4"	TMK-4, 3-line	120-150
III/53	6-1/4"	TMK-5, LB	120-150
III/53	6-1/4"	TMK-6, MB	120-150

JOYFUL candy dish, Hum III/53. Old style bowl on left, new style on the right.

HUM 54: SILENT NIGHT (Candleholder)

This piece is almost identical to the Hum 31 (Advent Group) candleholder, except that most of the Hum 31's have a black child on the left, and most of the Hum 54's have a white child on the left.

There have been at least three distinctly different molds, including the current production model.

The significant variation to be found, and the most valuable, is that of the black child. These can be found in

the Crown Mark (TMK-1) and the Full Bee (TMK-2) trademarks only. They are valued at $6,000-8,000.

Hum No.	Basic Size	Trademark	Current Value ($)
54	4-3/4"x5-1/2"	TMK-1, CM	540-675
54	4-3/4"x5-1/2"	TMK-2, FB	380-420
54	4-3/4"x5-1/2"	TMK-3, Sty. Bee	340-365
54	4-3/4"x5-1/2"	TMK-4, 3-line	295-335

Hum No.	Basic Size	Trademark	Current Value ($)
54	4-3/4"x5-1/2"	TMK-5, LB	270-290
54	4-3/4"x5-1/2"	TMK-6, MB	270

SILENT NIGHT, Hum 54. Left: Full Bee (TMK-2), black "Germany," 3-3/4". Center: Double Full Bee (TMK-2), incised and stamped; black "Germany," 3-3/4". Right: Last Bee (TMK-6), 3-1/2".

HUM 55: SAINT GEORGE

This figure is substantially different in style from most others in the collection and is difficult to locate most of the time, even though it is listed as in current production. The following sizes have been encountered in various lists: 6-1/4", 6-5/8", 6-3/4". Some of the early (Crown Mark) pieces will have a bright red painted saddle. This is the rarest variation and brings $2,000-2,500. Has been reported to appear in white overglaze.

It is reportedly being restyled to make the sword blade less vulnerable to breakage.

SAINT GEORGE, Hum 55. The mold number is incised with the decimal designator on this particular example thus: "55.". It has an incised Crown Mark and stamped Full Bee mark and

Hum No.	Basic Size	Trademark	Current Value ($)
55	6-3/4"	TMK-1, CM	600-750
55	6-3/4"	TMK-2, FB	425-475
55	6-3/4"	TMK-3, Sty. Bee	360-395
55	6-3/4"	TMK-4, 3-line	325-350
55	6-3/4"	TMK-5, LB	300-325
55	6-3/4"	TMK-6, MB	300

HUM 56/A: CULPRITS

CULPRITS, Hum 56/A. Left: Stylized Bee mark, 6-3/8". Right: Last Bee mark, 6-3/4".

HUM 56/B: OUT OF DANGER

OUT OF DANGER, Hum 56/B. Left: Small Stylized Bee (TMK-3) piece measuring 6-1/4". Right: this figure has the Missing Bee (TMK-6) mark and is 6-1/8" tall.

Culprits was released in the mid-1930s. Out of Danger was not introduced until the early 1950s. There have been minor changes over the years, but none having any influence on normal collector values.

Hum No.	Basic Size	Trademark	Current Value ($)
56	6-1/4"	TMK-1, CM	425-525
56	6-1/4"	TMK-2, FB	375-400
56/A	6-1/4"	TMK-2, FB	375-400
56/A	6-1/4"	TMK-3, Sty. Bee	310-350
56/A	6-1/4"	TMK-4, 3-line	275-300
56/A	6-1/4"	TMK-5, LB	250-275
56/A	6-1/4"	TMK-6, MB	250
56/B	6-1/4"	TMK-2, FB	375-400
56/B	6-1/4"	TMK-3, Sty. Bee	310-350
56/B	6-1/4"	TMK-4, 3-line	275-300
56/B	6-1/4"	TMK-5, LB	250-275
56/B	6-1/4"	TMK-6, MB	250

HUM 57: CHICK GIRL

There are many mold types and sizes. The chief mold variation shows different numbers of chicks on the base. For instance, the 57/0 has two chicks and the larger, 57/I, has three. It has been found with mold number and no size designator in the 4-1/4" size, "57."

Hum No.	Basic Size	Trademark	Current Value ($)
57/2/0	3"	TMK-5, LB	135-140
57/2/0	3"	TMK-6, MB	135
57/0	3-1/2"	TMK-1, CM	310-400
57/0	3-1/2"	TMK-2, FB	225-250
57/0	3-1/2"	TMK-3, Sty. Bee	190-215
57/0	3-1/2"	TMK-4, 3-line	165-180
57/0	3-1/2"	TMK-5, LB	155-165
57/0	3-1/2"	TMK-6, MB	155
57	4-1/4"	TMK-1, CM	550-650
57/I	4-1/4"	TMK-1, CM	500-600
57	4-1/4"	TMK-2, FB	400-440
57/I	4-1/4"	TMK-2, FB	360-395
57/I	4-1/4"	TMK-3, Sty. Bee	300-325
57/I	4-1/4"	TMK-4, 3-line	260-285
57/I	4-1/4"	TMK-5, LB	250-260
57/I	4-1/4"	TMK-6, MB	250

CHICK GIRL, Hum 57. Left: Double Crown Mark (TMK-1), 4-1/8". Right: 57/I, Stylized Bee mark (TMK-3), 4-5/16".

HUM III/57: CHICK GIRL (Candy Box)

There are two styles of candy boxes. The transition from the old to the new took place in the Stylized Bee period, so both can be found with the Stylized Bee (TMK-3) mark. Naturally the old style is the more desirable.

Hum No.	Basic Size	Trademark	Current Value ($)
III/57	5-1/4"	TMK-1, CM	450-530
III/57	5-1/4"	TMK-2, FB	350-400
III/57 (old)	5-1/4"	TMK-3, Sty. Bee	275-325
III/57 (new)	5-1/4"	TMK-3, Sty. Bee	150-200
III/57	5-1/4"	TMK-4, 3-line	120-150
III/57	5-1/4"	TMK-5, LB	120-150
III/57	5-1/4"	TMK-6, MB	120-150

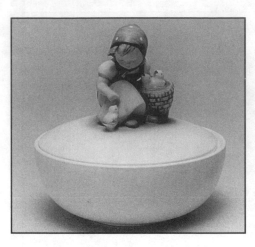

CHICK GIRL candy dish, Hum III 57. Stylized Bee mark (TMK-3). Old style bowl.

HUM 58: PLAYMATES

PLAYMATES, Hum 58/0. Left: Full Bee (TMK-2), black "Germany," 3-7/8". Right: Small Stylized Bee (TMK-3) mark, 3-7/8".

There are no variations in any trademark era that have any significant effect on value. A similar figure was used on bookend Hum 61/A and candy box Hum III/58.

Hum No.	Basic Size	Trademark	Current Value ($)
58/2/0	3-1/2"	TMK-5, LB	135-140
58/2/0	3-1/2"	TMK-6, MB	135
58/0	4"	TMK-1, CM	310-400
58/0	4"	TMK-2, FB	225-250
58/0	4"	TMK-3, Sty. Bee	190-215
58/0	4"	TMK-4, 3-line	165-180
58/0	4"	TMK-5, LB	155-165
58/0	4"	TMK-6, MB	155
58	4-1/2"	TMK-1, CM	550-650
58/I	4-1/2"	TMK-1, CM	500-600
58	4-1/2"	TMK-2, FB	385-420
58/I	4-1/2"	TMK-2, FB	360-395
58/I	4-1/2"	TMK-3, Sty. Bee	300-325
58/I	4-1/2"	TMK-4, 3-line	260-285
58/I	4-1/2"	TMK-5, LB	250-260
58/I	4-1/2"	TMK-6, MB	250

HUM III/58: PLAYMATES (Candy Box)

There are two styles of candy boxes. The transition from the old to the new took place during the Stylized Bee (TMK-3) period, therefore each may be found with that trademark. The older style is, of course, more desirable to collectors.

The figure was temporarily withdrawn from production at the end of 1989 with no reinstatement date given.

Hum No.	Basic Size	Trademark	Current Value ($)
III/58	5-1/4"	TMK-1, CM	450-530
III/58	5-1/4"	TMK-2, FB	350-400
III/58 (old)	5-1/4"	TMK-3, Sty. Bee	275-325
III/58 (new)	5-1/4"	TMK-3, Sty. Bee	150-200
III/58	5-1/4"	TMK-4, 3-line	120-150
III/58	5-1/4"	TMK-5, LB	120-150
III/58	5-1/4"	TMK-6, MB	120-150

PLAYMATES candy dish, Hum III/58. Old style bowl.

HUM 59: SKIER

Newer models have metal ski poles and older models have wooden poles. For a short time this figure was made with plastic poles. The poles are replaceable and are not

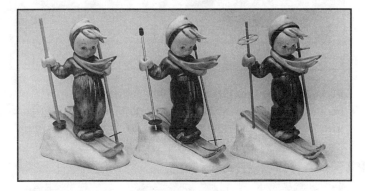

SKIER, Hum 59. Left: Stylized Bee mark (TMK-3), wooden poles. Center: Last Bee mark (TMK-5), metal poles. Right: Last Bee mark, plastic poles. All measure 5-1/4".

considered significant in the valuation of the piece in the case of wooden and metal poles. There is, however, some difficulty with the plastic ski poles found on most of the Stylized Bee (TMK-3) pieces. The small round discs at the bottom of the poles are molded integral with the pole. Some collectors and dealers feel that the intact plastic ski poles on the Stylized Bee pieces are a bit more valuable than those with wooden or metal replacements.

Hum No.	Basic Size	Trademark	Current Value ($)
59.	5-1/4"	TMK-1, CM	425-500
59	5-1/4"	TMK-1, CM	425-500
59	5-1/4"	TMK-2, FB	375-400
59	5-1/4"	TMK-3, Sty. Bee	245-270
59	5-1/4"	TMK-4, 3-line	210-235
59	5-1/4"	TMK-5, LB	195-210
59	5-1/4"	TMK-6, MB	195

HUM 60/A and HUM 60/B: FARM BOY and GOOSE GIRL (Bookends)

The overall height of the bookends is 6". The figurines themselves measure 4-3/4". Notice the lack of bases on the figurines. Most often the trademark is found stamped on the base and not on the figurines. Noted collector Robert Miller has confirmed, by removing the boy from a 60/A bookend, that some of the earliest production pieces are occasionally found with the mold number

incised on the bottom of feet. The mold number has also been observed on the back of the slippers on other early pieces.

There are no significant variations affecting value.

These bookends have been temporarily withdrawn from production status effective December 31, 1984, with no date for reinstatement given.

Hum No.	Basic Size	Trademark	Current Value ($)
60/A&B	6"	TMK-1, CM	500-575
60/A&B	6"	TMK-2, FB	400-450
60/A&B	6"	TMK-3, Sty. Bee	300-325
60/A&B	6"	TMK-5, LB	225-300
60/A&B	6"	TMK-6, MB	225-300

FARM BOY (Hum 60A) and GOOSE GIRL (Hum 60B) bookends. Left figure measures 3-3/8" and the other 4-7/8". Both bear the Stylized Bee mark (TMK-3).

HUM 61A and HUM 61/B: PLAYMATES and CHICK GIRL (Bookends)

Overall height of each bookend is 6". The figures are 4". Note that the figures used do not have the usual base. The trademark is usually marked on the wood portion. The trademark and mold number may or may not appear on the bottom of the figures if removed from the base. Some bookend pieces are marked so, especially the earliest.

The bookends were temporarily withdrawn from production status effective December 31, 1984, with no date for reinstatement given.

Hum No.	Basic Size	Trademark	Current Value ($)
60/A&B	6"	TMK-1, CM	500-575
60/A&B	6"	TMK-2, FB	400-450
60/A&B	6"	TMK-3, Sty. Bee	300-325
60/A&B	6"	TMK-5, LB	225-300
60/A&B	6"	TMK-6, MB	225-300

PLAYMATES (Hum 61A) and CHICK GIRL (Hum 61B) bookends. Both have Stylized Bee marks (TMK-3). Left figure measures 4-1/4" and right measures 4".

HUM 62: HAPPY PASTIME (Ashtray)

There are no significant variations affecting this figure's value. This piece, as all ashtrays, has been temporarily withdrawn from production with no published reinstatement date.

The figure used is similar to Hum 69 except that the bird is positioned on the edge of the tray rather than on the girl's leg as on the Hum 69.

HAPPY PASTIME ashtray, Hum 62. Last Bee mark (TMK-5), 3-1/2".

The Happy Pastime ashtray figure turned up in 1993 without its ashtray. This is an anomaly and has no significant value. It is interesting, but is likely to be a unique accident. It apparently got packed and shipped out of the factory unnoticed.

Hum No.	Basic Size	Trademark	Current Value ($)
62	3-1/2"x6-1/4"	TMK-1, CM	300-400
62	3-1/2"x6-1/4"	TMK-2, FB	200-250
62	3-1/2"x6-1/4"	TMK-3, Sty. Bee	160-180
62	3-1/2"x6-1/4"	TMK-4, 3-line	130-150
62	3-1/2"x6-1/4"	TMK-5, LB	100-125
62	3-1/2"x6-1/4"	TMK-6, MB	100-125

HUM 63: SINGING LESSON

First offered in the late 1930s, Singing Lesson has changed a little over the years but has no significant variations. Occasionally it has been found with the decimal designator on the Crown Mark (TMK-1). This is an indication that it is an early Crown piece, but it does not have a significant impact on value.

SINGING LESSON, Hum 63. Left: 63., incised Crown Mark (TMK-1), U.S. Zone Germany, 3". Center: 63., double Crown Mark, Made in Germany, 2-3/4". Right: Last Bee mark (TMK-5), 3".

Hum No.	Basic Size	Trademark	Current Value ($)
63	2-3/4"	TMK-1, CM	225-280
63	2-3/4"	TMK-2, FB	150-175
63	2-3/4"	TMK-3, Sty. Bee	130-145
63	2-3/4"	TMK-4, 3-line	115-135
63	2-3/4"	TMK-5, LB	110-115
63	2-3/4"	TMK-6, MB	110

HUM III/63: SINGING LESSON (Candy Box)

There are two styles of bowls. The transition from the old to the new took place in the Stylized Bee (TMK-3) period, therefore both are found with the Stylized Bee trademark. The old style with this mark is, of course, the more desirable to collectors.

Hum No.	Basic Size	Trademark	Current Value ($)
III-63	5-1/4"	TMK-1, CM	450-530
III-63	5-1/4"	TMK-2, FB	350-400
III-63 (old)	5-1/4"	TMK-3, Sty. Bee	275-325
III-63 (new)	5-1/4"	TMK-3, Sty. Bee	150-200
III-63	5-1/4"	TMK-4, 3-line	120-150
III-63	5-1/4"	TMK-5, LB	120-150
III-63	5-1/4"	TMK-6, MB	120-150

SINGING LESSON candy dish, Hum III/63. Left: Last Bee mark (TMK-5). Right: Stylized Bee mark (TMK-5), old style bowl.

HUM 64: SHEPHERD'S BOY

There are no significant variations that could affect the normal pricing of the various trademarked figurines. There seem to be a number of size variations to be found.

Hum No.	Basic Size	Trademark	Current Value ($)
64	5-1/2"	TMK-1, CM	400-500

Hum No.	Basic Size	Trademark	Current Value ($)
64	5-1/2"	TMK-2, FB	290-315
64	5-1/2"	TMK-3, Sty. Bee	250-275
64	5-1/2"	TMK-4, 3-line	210-240
64	5-1/2"	TMK-5, LB	200-210
64	5-1/2"	TMK-6, MB	200

SHEPHERD'S BOY, Hum 64. Left: Full Bee mark (TMK-2) with a registered trademark symbol associated, black "Germany," 5-3/4". Right: Last Bee (TMK-5), 5-1/2".

SHEPHERD'S BOY, Hum 64. Full Bee mark, black "Germany," 6-1/8".

HUM 65: FAREWELL

The first models of this figurine, the 65/0 size, in a small 4" basic size, are very rare and highly sought by serious collectors. Apparently a very limited number were made. They are found in the Crown Mark (TMK-1) and the Full Bee (TMK-2) only.

The 4-3/4" basic size carried the 65/I mold number for a while, but in the late 1970s it became 65 only. This size is also sometimes found with the decimal designator on the early Crown Mark and Full Bee mark pieces.

An interesting variation occured in the Missing Bee mark (TMK-6) era. It seems that a few of the baskets were attached wrong, resulting in a gap between the arm and the basket on the inside. The pieces with this variation are valued a bit above normal by some collectors. Mistakes such as this are not common, but do happen once in a while. For instance, sometimes a bottle is inadvertently left out of a basket during assembly. Most of the time it is only an interesting oddity, but enough of the incorrect-basket Farewell models were made that it is an attractive figure to some collectors.

Farewell is a retired figurine. The mold was scheduled to be broken up on December 31, 1993. All that were produced during 1993 bear a special "Final Issue" backstamp and were accompanied by a small medallion proclaiming it as a "Final Issue."

FAREWELL, Hum 65. Left: Incised Crown Mark and a stamped Full Bee mark, black "Germany," 4-7/8". Right: Full Bee mark in an incised circle, black "Germany," 4-7/8".

Hum No.	Basic Size	Trademark	Current Value ($)
65/0	4"	TMK-2, FB	6000-7500
65/0	4"	TMK-3, Sty. Bee	5000-6000
65.	4-3/4"	TMK-1, CM	450-500
65/I	4-3/4"	TMK-1, CM	450-500
65.	4-3/4"	TMK-2, FB	360-400
65/I	4-3/4"	TMK-2, FB	360-400
65/I	4-3/4"	TMK-3, Sty. Bee	300-350
65/I	4-3/4"	TMK-4, 3-line	265-300
65	4-3/4"	TMK-5, LB	240-265
65	4-3/4"	TMK-6, MB	240

HUM 66: FARM BOY

FARM BOY, Hum 66. Left: Decimal designator in mold number 66., double Crown Mark (TMK-1), donut base. "Made in Germany" stamped on base and lacquered over, 5-1/8". Right: Full Bee (TMK-2) in an incised circle, black "Germany," donut base, 6".

A figure similar to that used in bookend Hum 60/A. Older versions have larger shoes. In fact, in the older version the whole piece appears fatter overall. It has been known as Three Pals in the past and is occasionally found with the decimal point size designator.

Hum No.	Basic Size	Trademark	Current Value ($)
66	5-1/4"	TMK-1, CM	500-575
66	5-1/4"	TMK-1, CM	500-575
66	5-1/4"	TMK-2, FM	400-450
66	5-1/4"	TMK-3, Sty. Bee	300-325
66	5-1/4"	TMK-4, 3-line	275-300
66	5-1/4"	TMK-5, LB	225-275
66	5-1/4"	TMK-6, MB	225-275

HUM 67: DOLL MOTHER

Released in the late 1930s, Doll Mother was first known as Little Doll Mother.

There are no significant mold or paint variations in any trademark period that have any effect on value.

Hum No.	Basic Size	Trademark	Current Value ($)
67.	4-3/4"	TMK-1, CM	380-470
67	4-3/4"	TMK-1, CM	380-470
67	4-3/4"	TMK-2, FB	275-300
67	4-3/4"	TMK-3, Sty. Bee	230-250
67	4-3/4"	TMK-4, 3-line	200-225
67	4-3/4"	TMK-5, LB	190-200
67	4-3/4"	TMK-6, MB	190

DOLL MOTHER, Hum 67. Left: 67., double Crown Mark, "Made in Germany," 4-3/8". Right: Full Bee mark, black "Germany," 4-3/4".

HUM 68: LOST SHEEP

Sizes found referenced in lists are as follows: 4-1/4", 4-1/2", 5-1/2" and 6-1/2". This figure is found most commonly with green pants. A reference to a figure with orange pants (6-1/2") was found, but the color variation considered rarest is the one with brown pants. The collector value for the brown pants variation is about 25% above the value for the normal green pants piece.

There are four or five different color variations involving the coat, pants and shirt of the figure. Oversize pieces bring premium prices.

The decimal point designator has been found on some early Crown Mark (TMK-1) figures.

The 68/0 and 68/2/0 sizes were retired at the end of 1992. Each of them made in 1992 bear the special "Final Issue" backstamp indicating this. See the introductory pages for an explanation and illustration of this mark. In addition there is a "Final Issue" medallion accompanying the figurines.

Hum No.	Basic Size	Trademark	Current Value ($)
68/2/0	4-1/2"	TMK-2, FB	195-215
68/2/0	4-1/2"	TMK-3, Sty. Bee	170-195
68/2/0	4-1/2"	TMK-4, 3-line	145-170
68/2/0	4-1/2"	TMK-5, LB	130-145
68/2/0	4-1/2"	TMK-6, MB	130
68	5-1/2"	TMK-1, CM	415-505
68	5-1/2"	TMK-1, CM	415-505
68	5-1/2"	TMK-2, FB	340-365
68/0	5-1/2"	TMK-2, FB	310-335
68	5-1/2"	TMK-3, Sty. Bee	295-320

Hum No.	Basic Size	Trademark	Current Value ($)
68/0	5-1/2"	TMK-3, Sty. Bee	270-295
68/0	5-1/2"	TMK-4, 3-line	200-225
68/0	5-1/2"	TMK-5, LB	190-200
68/0	5-1/2"	TMK-6, MB	190

LOST SHEEP, Hum 68. Left: Incised Full Bee (TMK-2) trademark and a donut base with a black "Germany" beneath, 6". Right: 68/0 mold number with the Last Bee (TMK-5) trademark. Measures 5-1/2".

HUM 69: HAPPY PASTIME

This piece was in a group that was issued a short time after the initial 46 were released in 1935. There have been changes over the years, but nothing significant enough to influence the normal pricing in any trademark era. Happy Pastime was retired on December 31, 1996. All figures produced in 1996 bear the "Final Issue" backstamp and the medallion.

HAPPY PASTIME, Hum 69. Left: Small Stylized Bee (TMK-3), 3-3/8". Right: Missing Bee (TMK-6), 3-3/8".

Hum No.	Basic Size	Trademark	Current Value ($)
69	3-1/4"	TMK-1, CM	300-360
69	3-1/4"	TMK-2, FB	215-235
69	3-1/4"	TMK-3, Sty. Bee	175-200
69	3-1/4"	TMK-4, 3-line	150-170
69	3-1/4"	TMK-5, LB	145-150
69	3-1/4"	TMK-6, MB	145

HUM III/69: HAPPY PASTIME (Candy Box)

There are two styles of candy boxes. The transition from the old to the new took place during the Stylized Bee (TMK-3) period, so both the old and new can be found bearing the Stylized Bee (TMK-3) trademark.

There have been no other significant changes.

Hum No.	Basic Size	Trademark	Current Value ($)
III/69	6"	TMK-1, CM	450-530
III/69	6"	TMK-2, FB	350-400
III/69 (old)	6"	TMK-3, Sty. Bee	275-325
III/69 (new)	6"	TMK-3, Sty. Bee	150-200
III/69	6"	TMK-4, 3-line	120-150
III/69	6"	TMK-5, LB	120-150
III/69	6"	TMK-6, MB	120-150

HAPPY PASTIME candy dish, Hum III/69. Last Bee mark (TMK-5).

HUM 70: THE HOLY CHILD

THE HOLY CHILD, Hum 70. Left: Full Bee (TMK-2), black "Germany," 7-3/8". Right: Last Bee (TMK-5), 6-7/8".

There have been no paint and finish variations significant enough to affect the value of any trademark era piece. There was a general restyling of the whole collection over the years, to the more textured finish of the clothing of today's figures.

There are some much sought-after oversize pieces, generally valued at about 20% above the normal value listed.

Hum No.	Basic Size	Trademark	Current Value ($)
70	6-3/4"	TMK-1, CM	320-400
70	6-3/4"	TMK-2, FB	225-250
70	6-3/4"	TMK-3, Sty. Bee	190-215
70	6-3/4"	TMK-4, 3-line	170-180
70	6-3/4"	TMK-5, LB	160-170
70	6-3/4"	TMK-6, MB	160

HUM 71: STORMY WEATHER

This figure has been known as Under One Roof. Some earlier models were produced with a split base underneath. The split base model with the Full Bee mark shows that the split is laterally oriented. The new models also have the split base, but it is oriented longitudinally.

A Crown Mark Stormy Weather has been found that differs from the norm. Among other things the boy figure in the piece has no kerchief. It is most likely a prototype, inasmuch as it is not signed. Other than the oddity described above, there were no significant variations over the years until the small 71/2/0 (5") was introduced. After a period of time it became obvious that the method of painting the underside of the umbrella had changed. The first models released exhibit the brush strokes of hand-painting, and the later ones had been airbrushed. Serious collectors seek out this variation. It is valued at about $500-600.

The 71 mold number was changed to 71/I during the Missing Bee (TMK-6) period. The mold number can be found rendered either way on those pieces.

Hum No.	Basic Size	Trademark	Current Value ($)
71/2/0	5"	TMK-6, MB	270
71	6-1/4"	TMK-1, CM	825-930
71	6-1/4"	TMK-2, FB	600-640
71	6-1/4"	TMK-3, Sty. Bee	500-525
71	6-1/4"	TMK-4, 3-line	445-470
71	6-1/4"	TMK-5, LB	415-440
71	6-1/4"	TMK-6, MB	415
71/I	6-1/4"	TMK-6, MB	415

STORMY WEATHER, Hum 71. Left: Crown Mark, split base, 6". Right: Stylized Bee mark in an incised circle, black "Western Germany," split base, 6".

HUM 72: SPRING CHEER

Released soon after the initial issue of 46, this figurine was originally called It's Spring. It is modeled from the Hummel art called Just for You, H 271. Goebel announced that another piece modeled from the same art work will be the renewal premium for M.I. Hummel Club members who renew for their twentieth year of membership. It is called Forever Yours and is numbered Hum 793.

There have been some significant variations in Spring Cheer over its years of production. It was initially released in a yellow dress and with no flowers in the right hand. These can be found in the Crown Mark (TMK-1), the Full Bee (TMK-2) and the Stylized Bee (TMK-3). During the Stylized Bee (TMK-3), the figure was produced with a green dress and flowers in the right hand. Current pieces are configured in the latter way. However, some of the old (no flowers in right hand) models were left over, and these were painted with a green dress to match the new model. This is the rarest of the two green dress models.

The company lists the figurine as temporarily withdrawn from production as of December 31, 1984, with no reinstatement date.

Value of the green dress, no flowers in right hand: $1,200-1,500.

Hum No.	Basic Size	Trademark	Current Value ($)
72	5"	TMK-1, CM	400-500
72	5"	TMK-2, FB	275-300
72	5"	TMK-3, Sty. Bee	225-250
72	5"	TMK-4, 3-Line	200-225
72	5"	TMK-5, LB	165-185
72	5"	TMK-6, MB	165-185

SPRING CHEER, Hum 72. Left: Full Bee (TMK-2), black "Germany," 5-1/2". Note there are no flowers in the right hand. The dress is yellow. Center: Stylized Bee (TMK-1) mark, no flowers in right hand, green dress, 5-1/4". All newer versions have flowers in the right hand as in the right figurine in the photo.

HUM 73: LITTLE HELPER

LITTLE HELPER, Hum 73. The older is on the right. It has an incised Full Bee trademark (TMK-2) and measures 4-3/8". The one on the left is a 4" Stylized Bee (TMK-3) piece.

There are no significant variations from any of the trademark eras affecting the normal values for this figurine.

Hum No.	Basic Size	Trademark	Current Value ($)
73	4-1/4"	TMK-1, CM	220-280
73	4-1/4"	TMK-2, FB	150-175
73	4-1/4"	TMK-3, Sty. Bee	125-145
73	4-1/4"	TMK-4, 3-line	120-125
73	4-1/4"	TMK-5, LB	110-120
73	4-1/4"	TMK-6, MB	110

HUM 74: LITTLE GARDENER

This figure was found in several lists with the following sizes: 4", 4-1/4", 4-1/2". Earlier versions are found on an oval base, and more recent or current pieces are on the round base. The major variation encountered is a dark green dress rather than the present lighter-colored dress. Some of the earliest models have a very light green or yellowish dress.

Some other variations make it easy to spot the older pieces. On the Crown Mark (TMK-1) and Full Bee (TMK-2) figures, the flower at the base is tall and almost egg-shaped. On the Stylized Bee (TMK-3) figures, the flower is about one-half the height of the earlier flowers, and from the Last Bee (TMK-5) on, they are rather flattened in comparison.

These variations, however, have no effect on the normal value of the piece for their respective trademarks. They represent normal changes through the years.

There is one variation that bears watching. In the spring of 1992, Goebel took this figurine out of normal production for two years, resuming normal production in

LITTLE GARDENER, Hum 74. Last Bee (TMK-5), 4-1/4".

LITTLE GARDENER, Hum 74. Left: 74., incised Crown Mark, split base, 4-3/8". Note the height of the flower. Right: Missing Bee trademark, 4-1/2".

1994. From the spring of 1992 until the end of the year, Little Gardener was used as a district managers' special promotional piece and each piece bears a special promotion back-stamp. The only place they were available was at authorized M.I. Hummel dealers conducting district manager special promotions and in Canada at artist's promotions. Each of these pieces bears the appropriate backstamp identifying it as such. The figurines were available on a first-come, first-served basis.

Hum No.	Basic Size	Trademark	Current Value ($)
74	4-1/4"	TMK-1, CM	220-280
74	4-1/4"	TMK-2, FB	150-175
74	4-1/4"	TMK-3, Sty. Bee	125-145
74	4-1/4"	TMK-4, 3-line	120-125
74	4-1/4"	TMK-5, LB	110-120
74	4-1/4"	TMK-6, MB	110

HUM 75: WHITE ANGEL (Holy Water Font)

WHITE ANGEL Font, Hum 75. Stylized Bee mark, 4-3/8".

Although this piece is also known as the Angelic Prayer or White Angel Font, it is not white, but painted with color. It has been produced in two sizes, 1-3/4" x 3-1/2" and 3" x 4-1/4", but only the larger is still produced. It is the older and smaller one that is usually called the White Angel Font.

Hum No.	Basic Size	Trademark	Current Value ($)
75	1-3/4"x3-1/2"	TMK-1, CM	75-100
75	1-3/4"x3-1/2"	TMK-2, FB	55-70
75	1-3/4"x3-1/2"	TMK-3, Sty. Bee	45-55
75	1-3/4"x3-1/2"	TMK-4, 3-line	45
75	1-3/4"x3-1/2"	TMK-5, LB	40-45
75	1-3/4"x3-1/2"	TMK-6, MB	40

HUM 76/A and HUM 76/B: DOLL MOTHER and PRAYER BEFORE BATTLE (Bookends)

These bookends are unique. It is possible, but not likely, that they might be found in a collector's possession. There are no known examples in private hands, only in factory archives.

HUM 77: CROSS WITH DOVES (Holy Water Font)

In past editions of this book it was reported that there was only one example of this piece and it was in the factory archives. At least nine now reside in private collections. The one in the photo accompanying is an incised Crown Mark piece with the M.I. Hummel signature on the back. It has been reported in white. If sold, this font would likely bring $5,000-10,000, in color or white.

CROSS WITH DOVES Font, Hum 77.

Back side of the Hum 77. Font showing the Crown mark and the M.I. Hummel incised signature.

CROSS WITH DOVES Font, Hum 77. The same piece after professional restoration.

HUM 78: BLESSED CHILD

Known in the past as In the Crib and Infant of Krumbad, this piece can be found in seven different sizes and three finishes. All sizes except one have been either retired or temporarily withdrawn from production, with no stated reintroduction date.

The normal finish is a sepia-tone bisque. The figures were available painted in full color for a time, then withdrawn, reissued and finally discontinued. There was also a white overglaze finish reportedly produced for European market only. The color pieces are valued at two times the normal price listed for the size, and the white overglaze figures are valued at about two to three times the normal price, also depending on the size.

There are two pieces still available. One is the small 78/0, 2-1/4" size, which is difficult to get because this size was discontinued in the Stylized Bee (TMK-3) period. It has been redesigned and issued in the sepia-tone finish without the 78/0 incised mold number. It bears only the Missing Bee (TMK-6) or the Hummel Mark (TMK-7) and is sold in the Siessen Convent only. It is unavailable elsewhere. The other one is also available only at the convent. It is the 4-1/2" Hum 78/11 1/2" mold.

Hum No.	Basic Size	Trademark	Current Value ($)
78/0	1-3/4"	TMK-2, FB	200-250
78/0	1-3/4"	TMK-3, Sty. Bee	150-200
78/0	1-3/4"	TMK-6, MB	100
78/I	2-1/2"	TMK-3, Sty. Bee	35-55
78/I	2-1/2"	TMK-4, 3-line	30-40
78/I	2-1/2"	TMK-5, LB	30-40
78/I	2-1/2"	TMK-6, MB	30-40
78/II	3-1/2"	TMK-3, Sty. Bee	45-65
78/II	3-1/2"	TMK-4, 3-line	35-45
78/II	3-1/2"	TMK-5, LB	35-45
78/II	3-1/2"	TMK-6, MB	35-45
78/III	5-1/4"	TMK-1, CM	250-300
78/III	5-1/4"	TMK-2, FB	150-250
78/III	5-1/4"	TMK-3, Sty. Bee	50-60
78/III	5-1/4"	TMK-4, 3-line	40-55
78/III	5-1/4"	TMK-5, LB	40-55
78/III	5-1/4"	TMK-6, MB	40-55

Hum No.	Basic Size	Trademark	Current Value ($)
78/V	7-3/4"	TMK-3, Sty. Bee	75-125
78/V	7-3/4"	TMK-4, 3-line	75-100
78/V	7-3/4"	TMK-5, LB	50-100
78/V	7-3/4"	TMK-6, MB	50-75
78/VI	10"	TMK-1, CM	300-500
78/VI	10"	TMK-2, FB	200-300
78/VI	10"	TMK-3, Sty. Bee	150-200
78/VI	10"	TMK-4, 3-line	150-200
78/VI	10"	TMK-5, LB	100-150
78/VI	10"	TMK-6, MB	100-150
78/VIII	13-1/2"	TMK-1, CM	450-650
78/VIII	13-1/2"	TMK-2, FB	400-500
78/VIII	13-1/2"	TMK-3, Sty. Bee	250-400
78/VIII	13-1/2"	TMK-4, 3-line	250-350
78/VIII	13-1/2"	TMK-5, LB	250-300
78/VIII	13-1/2"	TMK-6, MB	200-300
*78/11 1/2"	4"	TMK-6, MB	100-150

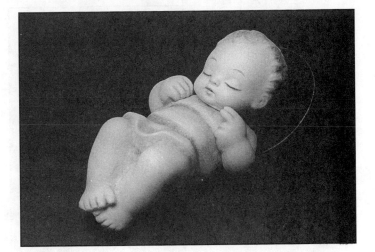

BLESSED CHILD, Hum 78. This one bears the Full Bee trademark, measures 4-3/4 in length and has the original wire halo.

*One of the two only pieces in the collection to use this "1/2" designator. The other is Hum 21, Heavenly Angel.

HUM 79: GLOBE TROTTER

One of the pre-WWII releases. There are no significant variations that directly affect the value of the pieces under the various trademarks, but there are some interesting variations that can help you spot the earlier figures without examining the marks. The Crown Mark (TMK-1) and Full Bee (TMK-2) exhibit a double weave in the baskets (see accompanying photos). The weaving changed from double weave to single weave during the Stylized Bee (TMK-3) era, so you may find them in either configuration in that trademark. A few of the older marked figures will also sport a dark green hat instead of the normal reddish brown color. This piece was permanently retired in 1991.

Hum No.	Basic Size	Trademark	Current Value ($)
79	5"	TMK-1, CM	500-650
79	5"	TMK-2, FB	350-350
79 (old style)	5"	TMK-3, Sty. Bee	250-300
79 (new style)	5"	TMK-3, Sty. Bee	220-240
79	5"	TMK-4, 3-line	200-210
79	5"	TMK-5, LB	180-190
79	5"	TMK-6, MB	180-190

GLOBE TROTTER, Hum 79. Left: Stamped Crown Mark (TMK-1), donut base, 4-7/8". Right: Incised Full Bee (TMK-2), black "Germany," donut base, 5-1/4".

GLOBE TROTTER, Hum 79. Rear shot showing the old style double weave basket.

GLOBE TROTTER, Hum 79. Rear view showing the different basket weave patterns discussed in text. Older figure is on the left.

GLOBE TROTTER, Hum 79. This photo shows the Final Issue Medallion and the new style single weave basket.

LITTLE SCHOLAR, Hum 80. Has the Full Bee (TMK-2) trademark, donut base, black "Germany" and measures 5-5/8".

HUM 80: LITTLE SCHOLAR

No figures were produced with variations that would affect their normal value. There is one variation, however, that may help you pick out the older pieces without examining the bases. The Crown Mark (TMK-1) and the Full Bee mark (TMK-2) pieces will have dark brown shoes instead of the lighter color of those produced later.

Hum No.	Basic Size	Trademark	Current Value ($)
80	5-1/2"	TMK-1, CM	390-480
80	5-1/2"	TMK-2, FB	280-315
80	5-1/2"	TMK-3, Sty. Bee	235-260
80	5-1/2"	TMK-4, 3-line	205-225
80	5-1/2"	TMK-5, LB	195-205
80	5-1/2"	TMK-6, MB	195

HUM 81: SCHOOL GIRL

There are no variations affecting the value of any of the models of this piece. There are, however, some worth noting. The smallest of the figures, the 81/2/0, 4" basic size, has flowers in the basket. All other sizes are devoid of flowers. The older figures have a black book bag and a pink blouse.

The figure has been found with the decimal point designator on the Crown Mark (TMK-1) larger 5-1/4" basic size.

Goebel issued a special edition of this figurine in the Hum 81/2/0 size in 1996 in commemoration of the 125th anniversary of the company. Each figure bears a special 125th anniversary backstamp. In addition, the inscription "International Collectible Exposition" is place around the base.

Hum No.	Basic Size	Trademark	Current Value ($)
81/2/0	4-1/4"	TMK-1, CM	270-335
81/2/0	4-1/4"	TMK-2, FB	195-225
81/2/0	4-1/4"	TMK-3, Sty. Bee	165-175
81/2/0	4-1/4"	TMK-4, 3-line	145-155
81/2/0	4-1/4"	TMK-5, LB	135-145
81/2/0	4-1/4"	TMK-6, MB	135
81.	5-1/4"	TMK-1, CM	400-485
81/0	5-1/4"	TMK-1, CM	350-435
81	5-1/4"	TMK-2, FB	300-325
81/0	5-1/4"	TMK-2, FB	250-270
81/0	5-1/4"	TMK-3, Sty. Bee	220-245
81/0	5-1/4"	TMK-4, 3-line	185-210
81/0	5-1/4"	TMK-5, LB	175-185
81/0	5-1/4"	TMK-6, MB	175

SCHOOL GIRL, Hum 81. Left: 81/0 Full Bee mark, black "Germany," donut base, 5-1/4". Right: 81/0, Last Bee mark, 4-7/8".

SCHOOL GIRL, Hum 81. Note the flowers in the basket. Stylized Bee trademark, 4-1/2".

HUM 82: SCHOOL BOY

Sizes found in various lists are 4", 4-3/4", 5-1/2" and 7-1/2". The figure has been known as School Days in the past. It is occasionally found having the decimal point size designator in the Crown Mark (TMK-1) pieces. There are no other significant variations.

SCHOOL BOY, Hum 82/0. Left: Double Crown mark, donut base, 4-7/8". Center: Full Bee mark in an incised circle, black "Germany," 5". Right: Full Bee mark, black "Germany," donut base, 5-3/4".

Hum No.	Basic Size	Trademark	Current Value ($)
82/2/0	4"	TMK-1, CM	270-335
82/2/0	4"	TMK-2, FB	195-225
82/2/0	4"	TMK-3, Sty. Bee	165-175
82/2/0	4"	TMK-4, 3-line	145-155
82/2/0	4"	TMK-5, LB	135-145
82/2/0	4"	TMK-6, MB	135
82.	5-1/2"	TMK-1, CM	400-485
82	5-1/2"	TMK-1, CM	350-435
82	5-1/2"	TMK-2, FB	300-325
82/0	5-1/2"	TMK-2, FB	250-270
82/0	5-1/2"	TMK-3, Sty. Bee	220-245
82/0	5-1/2"	TMK-4, 3-line	185-210
82/0	5-1/2"	TMK-5, LB	175-185
82/0	5-1/2"	TMK-6, MB	175
82/II	7-1/2"	TMK-1, CM	800-1000
82/II	7-1/2"	TMK-2, FB	575-650
82/II	7-1/2"	TMK-3, Sty. Bee	475-550
82/II	7-1/2"	TMK-5, LB	400-450
82/II	7-1/2"	TMK-6, MB	400

HUM 83: ANGEL SERENADE WITH LAMB

Another piece in the collection with a similar name (Angel Serenade) is part of the Nativity Set. They do not look alike, but the name may confuse you.

There are no significant variations, only minor changes over the years. Until recently these figures were apparently made in limited quantities (from the Stylized Bee (TMK-3) period to the Missing Bee (TMK-6) period), but now they seem to be readily available again.

Hum No.	Basic Size	Trademark	Current Value ($)
83	5"	TMK-1, CM	395-500
83	5"	TMK-2, FB	275-315
83	5"	TMK-3, Sty. Bee	240-260
83	5"	TMK-4, 3-line	210-230
83	5"	TMK-5, LB	195-210
83	5"	TMK-6, MB	195

ANGEL SERENADE WITH LAMB, Hum 83. Full Bee mark in an incised circle, black "Germany," 5-3/4".

HUM 84: WORSHIP

Sizes reported in various lists are 5", 6-3/4", and 14-1/2". The figure has been found with the decimal point size designator. The 84/V was temporarily withdrawn from production at the end of 1989 with no reinstatement date revealed.

The small piece, 84/0, has been found in white overglaze. These are valued at $400-500.

WORSHIP, Hum 84. Mold number is rendered as 84./5. and the figurine bears the large Stylized Bee mark (TMK-3). It measures 13-1/8".

Hum No.	Basic Size	Trademark	Current Value ($)
84.	5"	TMK-1, CM	340-400
84/0	5"	TMK-1, CM	290-360
84/0	5"	TMK-2, FB	210-240
84/0	5"	TMK-3, Sty. Bee	175-195
84/0	5"	TMK-4, 3-line	155-175
84/0	5"	TMK-5, LB	145-155
84/0	5"	TMK-6, MB	145
84/V	13"	TMK-1, CM	1800-2800
84/V, 84/5	13"	TMK-2, FB	1350-1800
84/V, 84/5	13"	TMK-3, Sty. Bee	1100-1350
84/V, 84/5	13"	TMK-4, 3-line	800-1100
84/V, 84/5	13"	TMK-5, LB	800-1100
84/V, 84/5	13"	TMK-6, MB	800-1100

HUM 85: SERENADE

Introduced in the late 1930s, this figurine has undergone normal changes of style, colors and finishes over the years, but none have had a significant impact on the collector value.

SERENADE, Hum 85/2. Full Bee mark, black "Germany," donut base, 7-5/8".

An interesting variation concerns the boy's fingers on the flute. You can find figures with some fingers extended (see color section for an example) while other versions have all fingers down. It seems, however, that there is no association with any particular mark or marks one way or the other.

The decimal designator can be found with the mold number on the older Crown Mark (TMK-1) pieces in both sizes.

There is a beautiful blue Hum 85 in the 7-1/2" size illustrated on the first page of the color section. It has no apparent markings. So far this is the only one in a blue suit to be found. It seems peculiar that the normal Serenades were not rendered in blue, as that is the color M.I. Hummel used in the original art work (H 342) on which the piece is modeled. There has also been a Serenade found with the incised mold number 85/0. This one is painted with an airbrush rather than the usual brush.

Both of these are most likely samples that did not obtain the approval of the convent.

Hum No.	Basic Size	Trademark	Current Value ($)
85/4/0	3-1/2"	TMK-5, LB	70-85
85/4/0	3-1/2"	TMK-6, MB	90
85/0	4-3/4"	TMK-1, CM	240-305
85/0	4-3/4"	TMK-2, FB	175-190
85/0	4-3/4"	TMK-3, Sty. Bee	145-165
85/0	4-3/4"	TMK-4, 3-line	130-145
85/0	4-3/4"	TMK-5, LB	120-130

Hum No.	Basic Size	Trademark	Current Value ($)
85/0	4-3/4"	TMK-6, MB	120
85.	7-1/2"	TMK-1, CM	875-1100
85/II	7-1/2"	TMK-1, CM	825-1025
85/II	7-1/2"	TMK-2, FB	585-635
85.	7-1/2"	TMK-2, FB	635-685
85/II	7-1/2"	TMK-3, Sty. Bee	490-525
85/II	7-1/2"	TMK-4, 3-line	440-465
85/II	7-1/2"	TMK-5, LB	410-430
85/II	7-1/2"	TMK-6, MB	410

HUM 86: HAPPINESS

HAPPINESS, Hum 86. Left: Full Bee (TMK-2), black "Germany," 5-1/8". Right: Last Bee (TMK-5) mark, 5-1/2".

Another late 1930s entry into the collection, with no changes or variations significant enough to affect value.

Sizes reported in various lists are 4-1/2", 4-1/4", 5" and 5-1/2".

Hum No.	Basic Size	Trademark	Current Value ($)
86	4-3/4"	TMK-1, CM	240-305
86	4-3/4"	TMK-2, FB	175-190
86	4-3/4"	TMK-3, Sty. Bee	145-165
86	4-3/4"	TMK-4, 3-line	130-145
86	4-3/4"	TMK-5, LB	120-130
86	4-3/4"	TMK-6, MB	120

HUM 87: FOR FATHER

For Father is yet another late 1930s release, formerly called Father's Joy. The significant variations have to do with the beer stein and the color of the radishes.

A few early Crown Mark (TMK-1) pieces have been found with the initials "HB" painted on the stein (see accompanying photograph). The radishes on these figures have a definite greenish cast. These pieces are rare and can be priced as high as $5,000.

The other important variation is found on Full Bee (TMK-2) and Stylized Bee (TMK-3) trademark figures,

FOR FATHER, Hum 87. Left: Full Bee mark (TMK-2), donut base, black "Germany," red radishes, 5-11/16". Right: Stamped Full Bee mark (TMK-2) in an incised circle, black "Western Germany," donut base, brown radishes, 5-3/4".

FOR FATHER, Hum 87. Mold number is rendered with the decimal designator 87., double Crown Mark, donut base. Note the "HB" on the stein standing for Hofbrau House in Munich. This is a very scarce item. Also there is a very distinct green highlighting on the radishes not appearing on any other variations.

where the radishes are colored orange. The collector value for this variation is $2,000-2,500.

In 1996 Goebel announced the Personal Touch figurines. There are four figurines in the line that lend themselves well to this application, one of which is For Father. Goebel will inscribe onto the figure a personalization of your choice. The other three figures used for personalization are Bird Duet (Hum 69), Latest News (Hum 184) and The Guardian (Hum 455).

Hum No.	Basic Size	Trademark	Current Value ($)
87.	5-1/2"	TMK-1, CM	395-500
87	5-1/2"	TMK-1, CM	395-500
87	5-1/2"	TMK-2, FB	275-315
87	5-1/2"	TMK-3, Sty. Bee	240-260
87	5-1/2"	TMK-4, 3-line	210-230
87	5-1/2"	TMK-5, LB	195-210
87	5-1/2"	TMK-6, MB	195

HUM 88: HEAVENLY PROTECTION

This figure was first introduced in the late 1930s in the 9-1/4" size with a decimal designator 88. or 88 without the decimal in the Crown Mark (TMK-1), the Full Bee (TMK-2) and the Stylized Bee (TMK-3) trademarks. The transition from the 88 to the 88/II mold number took quite some time. It began in the Full Bee era and was completed in the Stylized Bee era, so you can find the mold number rendered either way with either of those two trademarks.

The large size has been found in white overglaze in the Crown and Full Bee marks.

There is a similar piece in the Goebel line that some theorize may have either inspired Heavenly Protection or was inspired by it. It is mold number HS 1 and is illustrated in chapter 5. Also see Hum 108.

HEAVENLY PROTECTION, Hum 88. Left: Full Bee (TMK-2) mark, base split in quarters beneath, black "Germany," 9-3/8". Right: 88/II, small Stylized Bee (TMK-3), donut base, 8-5/8".

Hum No.	Basic Size	Trademark	Current Value ($)
88/I	6-3/4"	TMK-3, Sty. Bee	495-525
88/I	6-3/4"	TMK-4, 3-line	425-450
88/I	6-3/4"	TMK-5, LB	400-425
88/I	6-3/4"	TMK-6, MB	395
88. or 88	9-1/4"	TMK-1, CM	1200-1500
88. or 88	9-1/4"	TMK-2, FB	950-1050
88. or 88	9-1/4"	TMK-3, Sty. Bee	750-850
88/II	9-1/4"	TMK-2, FB	850-1000
88/II	9-1/4"	TMK-3, Sty. Bee	725-800
88/II	9-1/4"	TMK-4, 3-line	650-700
88/II	9-1/4"	TMK-5, LB	600-650
88/II	9-1/4"	TMK-6, MB	600

HUM 89: LITTLE CELLIST

There have been no major variations over the years that would have an impact on the collector value of this figurine.

There are some differences worth noting. The newer models have a base that has flattened corners (see accompanying photograph). The older models have squared-off corners. Also in the older models the boy's head is up and his eyes are wide open, whereas on the new models the head is down and his eyes are cast down as if concentrating on his steps. The transition from old to new style was during the Stylized Bee (TMK-3) era, so the old and the new can be found with this mark, the older obviously being the more desirable to collectors.

LITTLE CELLIST, Hum 89. Left: 89/1, double Crown Mark (TMK-1), 4-6/16". Right: 89/I, small Stylized Bee (TMK-3) mark, 5-5/16". Note the difference in the eyes and the bases of the old versus the newer piece.

Hum No.	Basic Size	Trademark	Current Value ($)
89/I	6"	TMK-1, CM	395-500
89/I	6"	TMK-2, FB	275-315
89/I	6"	TMK-3, Sty. Bee	240-260
89/I	6"	TMK-4, 3-line	210-230
89/I	6"	TMK-5, LB	195-210
89/I	6"	TMK-6, MB	195
89.	8"	TMK-1, CM	1400-1750
89	8"	TMK-1, CM	1200-1500
89/II	8"	TMK-2, FB	875-940
89/II	8"	TMK-3, Sty. Bee	700-800
89/II	8"	TMK-4, 3-line	650-675
89/II	8"	TMK-5, LB	600-650
89/II	8"	TMK-6, MB	600

LITTLE CELLIST, Hum 89. Left: 89/II, Stylized Bee (TMK-3) stamped in an incised circle, 7-7/8", black "Western Germany." Right: 89/II, Last Bee (TMK-5) trademark, 7-1/2". Note the textured hat and clothing on the newer of the two pieces and the different bases.

HUM 90/A and HUM 90/B: EVENTIDE and ADORATION (Bookends)

ADORATION, Hum 90/B, half of the bookends. No apparent markings. Measures 3-3/4" (figure only).

Up until late 1984 it was thought that these pieces were never produced except in sample form and never were released on the market. The Adoration half of the set has been found. It is not likely that these bookends were ever put into production, but more than one was obviously made as at least two of the Adoration halves have made it into private collections.

HUM 91: ANGEL AT PRAYER (Holy Water Font)

The only notable variation in these figures is that the older ones have no halo and the newer models do. The transition from no halo to halo took place in the Stylized Bee (TMK-3) era, and both types of figures may be found in that trademark.

Hum No.	Basic Size	Trademark	Current Value ($)
91/A&B	2"x4-3/4"	TMK-1, CM	250-350
91/A&B	2"x4-3/4"	TMK-2, FB	150-200
91/A&B	2"x4-3/4"	TMK-3, Sty. Bee	130-140
91/A&B	2"x4-3/4"	TMK-3, Sty. Bee	120-130
91/A&B	2"x4-3/4"	TMK-4, 3-line	100-110
91/A&B	2"x4-3/4"	TMK-5, LB	90-100
91/A&B	2"x4-3/4"	TMK-6, MB	90-100

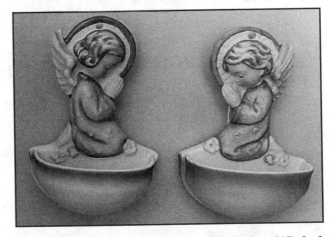

ANGEL AT PRAYER Font, Hum 91A and Hum 91B. Left: 91B, Last Bee mark, 5". Right: 91A, Stylized Bee mark, 4-7/8".

HUM 92: MERRY WANDERER (Wall Plaque)

MERRY WANDERER Plaque, Hum 92. Last Bee mark, 4-3/4" x 5".

There are two distinct sizes to be found in the Crown (TMK-1) and Full Bee (TMK-2) trademark pieces. The newer ones are all in the smaller size. There are also some differences with regard to the placement of the incised M.I. Hummel signature, but there are no variations having a significant impact on the collector value. Some of the older Crown Mark pieces have been found with the decimal designator.

Hum No.	Basic Size	Trademark	Current Value ($)
92.	4-3/4"x5-1/8"	TMK-1, CM	350-425
92	4-3/4"x5-1/8"	TMK-1, CM	300-375
92	4-3/4"x5-1/8"	TMK-2, FB	200-250
92	4-3/4"x5-1/8"	TMK-3, Sty. Bee	185-200
92	4-3/4"x5-1/8"	TMK-4, 3-line	160-175
92	4-3/4"x5-1/8"	TMK-5, LB	150-160
92	4-3/4"x5-1/8"	TMK-6, MB	150

HUM 93: LITTLE FIDDLER (Wall Plaque)

In current production, this plaque bears the Little Fiddler motif, which appears many times in the collection. The older models show less background detail.

The accompanying photograph shows both the old and the newer designs. The older one is valued at about $2,000-2,500.

The figure was temporarily withdrawn from production as of December 31, 1991.

Hum No.	Basic Size	Trademark	Current Value ($)
93	4-3/4"x5-1/8"	TMK-1, CM	300-375
93	4-3/4"x5-1/8"	TMK-2, FB	200-250
93	4-3/4"x5-1/8"	TMK-3, Sty. Bee	185-200
93	4-3/4"x5-1/8"	TMK-4, 3-line	160-175
93	4-3/4"x5-1/8"	TMK-5, LB	150-160
93	4-3/4"x5-1/8"	TMK-6, MB	150

LITTLE FIDDLER Plaque, Hum 93. Left: 93., double Crown Mark, 4-3/4" x 5-1/8". Right: Last Bee mark, 4-3/4" x 5-1/8".

HUM 94: SURPRISE

First placed in the line in the late 1930s in two basic sizes, this figurine continues in production in those sizes today.

The 94/I size has been found erroneously marked 94/II. The error was apparently caught early, for only a very few have shown up.

Older examples of the 94/I size have been found without the "/I".

Hum No.	Basic Size	Trademark	Current Value ($)
94/3/0	4-1/4"	TMK-1, CM	280-350
94/3/0	4-1/4"	TMK-2, FB	200-240
94/3/0	4-1/4"	TMK-3, Sty. Bee	170-190
94/3/0	4-1/4"	TMK-4, 3-line	150-170
94/3/0	4-1/4"	TMK-5, LB	140-150
94/3/0	4-1/4"	TMK-6, MB	149
94	5-1/2"	TMK-1, CM	575-700
94	5-1/2"	TMK-2, FB	400-440
94/I	5-1/2"	TMK-1, CM	520-650
94/I	5-1/2"	TMK-2, FB	375-415
94/I	5-1/2"	TMK-3, Sty. Bee	315-350

Hum No.	Basic Size	Trademark	Current Value ($)
94/I	5-1/2"	TMK-4, 3-line	275-300
94/I	5-1/2"	TMK-5, LB	260-275
94/I	5-1/2"	TMK-6, MB	260

SURPRISE, Hum 94. Left: Crown Mark, "U.S.-ZONE Germany," 5-3/4". Right: 94/1, Stylized Bee mark, 5-1/2".

HUM 95: BROTHER

The earliest Crown Mark (TMK-1) pieces can be found with the decimal point designator. There are no other variations of any great significance.

The figure has been known as Our Hero. The older mold style comes with a blue coat.

Hum No.	Basic Size	Trademark	Current Value ($)
95.	5-1/2"	TMK-1, CM	385-475
95	5-1/2"	TMK-1, CM	360-450
95	5-1/2"	TMK-2, FB	260-290
95	5-1/2"	TMK-3, Sty. Bee	225-250
95	5-1/2"	TMK-4, 3-line	190-225
95	5-1/2"	TMK-5, LB	180-190
95	5-1/2"	TMK-6, MB	180

BROTHER, Hum 95. Left: 95., no apparent trademark, but probably a Crown era piece, donut base, 5-1/2". Center: Stylized Bee mark (TMK-3), 5-5/8". Right: Missing Bee mark (TMK-6), 5-5/8".

HUM 96: LITTLE SHOPPER

Introduced in the late 1930s, this figurine has changed little over the years. There are no changes or variations that have any influence on the collector value.

LITTLE SHOPPER, Hum 96. Small Stylized Bee (TMK-3), 4-1/2".

Hum No.	Basic Size	Trademark	Current Value ($)
96	4-3/4"	TMK-1, CM	360-450
96	4-3/4"	TMK-2, FB	260-290
96	4-3/4"	TMK-3, Sty. Bee	225-250
96	4-3/4"	TMK-4, 3-line	190-225
96	4-3/4"	TMK-5, LB	180-190
96	4-3/4"	TMK-6, MB	180

HUM 97: TRUMPET BOY

The boy's coat is normally green. Some of the older models, particularly those produced during the post-war U.S. Occupation era, have a blue painted coat. Trumpet Boy in the Crown Mark (TMK-1) is fairly rare, but most assuredly exists. The Crown Mark era piece will have "Design Patent No. 116, 464" inscribed beneath (see accompanying photo).

A query with a photograph to Goebel regarding this anomaly brought the following response: "The Trumpet Boy shown in the photo seems to be a very old figurine dating back to pre-war years. The bottom of the piece allows the assumption that production date may go back as far as the late 1930s (possibly cast from the first model). The stamp Design Patent No. 116.464 indicates that the piece was originally shipped to England. All merchandise shipped at that time to that country was liable to be marked

with the respective design patent number ...". The collector value for a Trumpet Boy so marked is $800-1,200.

I have a photograph in my research files of what appears to be a stamped Crown Mark Trumpet Boy, but I have never examined the figurine personally. In the letter that accompanied the photos the collector wrote: "Other experts... have informed me that my figurine has a 'hand painted, red, Crown trademark.' The coat on my Trumpet Boy is green and (it) does not have any other markings you refer to in your description."

Hum No.	Basic Size	Trademark	Current Value ($)
97	4-3/4"	TMK-1, CM era	240-305
97	4-3/4"	TMK-2, FB	175-190
97	4-3/4"	TMK-3, Sty. Bee	145-165
97	4-3/4"	TMK-4, 3-line	130-145
97	4-3/4"	TMK-5, LB	120-130
97	4-3/4"	TMK-6, MB	120

TRUMPET BOY, Hum 97. Stylized Bee mark (TMK-3), 4-1/2".

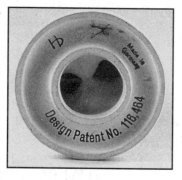

TRUMPET BOY, Hum 97. Shows the unique mold number rendering discussed in the accompanying text.

HUM 98: SISTER

This figure was introduced in the late 1930s in the 5-3/4" basic size, and a smaller size was introduced during the Stylized Bee (TMK-3) trademark period.

Some of the larger size pieces from the Crown Mark (TMK-1) era through the Stylized Bee (TMK-3) era are found with the 98 mold number with and without the decimal designator (see Hum 788B).

SISTER, Hum 98. Left: Full Bee mark (TMK-2), black "Germany," donut base, 5-3/4". Right: 98/2/0, Last Bee mark (TMK-5), 1962 MID, 4-3/4".

Hum No.	Basic Size	Trademark	Current Value ($)
98/5/0	2-3/4"	TMK-7	55
98/2/0	4-3/4"	TMK-3, Sty. Bee	160-180
98/2/0	4-3/4"	TMK-4, 3-line	140-155
98/2/0	4-3/4"	TMK-5, LB	130-140
98/2/0	4-3/4"	TMK-6, MB	130
98.	5-1/4"	TMK-1, CM	385-500
98.	5-3/4"	TMK-2, FB	285-340
98.	5-3/4"	TMK-3, Sty. Bee	250-300
98/0	5-3/4"	TMK-3, Sty. Bee	225-250
98/0	5-3/4"	TMK-4, 3-line	190-225
98/0	5-3/4"	TMK-5, LB	180-190
98/0	5-3/4"	TMK-6, MB	180

HUM 99: EVENTIDE

There are three versions of this figurine to be found. Apparently when first released in the late 1930s the lambs were placed toward the left side of the base. For whatever reason they were moved to the right side soon after and there they remain to this day. This piece has also been found without the sheep. The collector value range for both the left-side sheep and the no sheep versions is $2,300-2,800. There is also a rare white overglazed version valued at about the same amount.

Hum No.	Basic Size	Trademark	Current Value ($)
99	4-3/4"	TMK-1, CM	630-825
99	4-3/4"	TMK-2, FB	450-500
99	4-3/4"	TMK-3, Sty. Bee	380-410
99	4-3/4"	TMK-4, 3-line	335-360
99	4-3/4"	TMK-5, LB	315-335
99	4-3/4"	TMK-6, MB	315

EVENTIDE, Hum 99. Stylized Bee mark (TMK-3), 4-1/2".

HUM 100: SHRINE (Table Lamp)

Extremely rare 7-1/2" table lamp. As far as can be determined only three or four currently exist in collectors' hands. The lamps found so far bear the Crown or the Full Bee trademarks. There are two versions of the lamp post. The most common is the tree trunk post. The rarest is the fluted post, which is valued at about $4,000-5,000.

HUM 101: TO MARKET (Table Lamp)

There are two versions of this 7-1/2" lamp with regard to the lamp stem or post. Of the few that have been found, most exhibit the "tree trunk" base (see accompanying photograph). Rarer are the less elaborate fluted stem and plain stem examples. The "plain" description refers only to the paint finish: the CM fluted stem is painted white whereas the plain version is painted light beige. The plain version is found in both the Crown and the Full Bee trademarks.

Hum No.	Basic Size	Trademark	Current Value ($)
101 (fluted)	7-1/2"	TMK-1, CM	2000-3000
101 (plain)	7-1/2"	TMK-1, CM	2000-3000
101 (plain)	7-1/2"	TMK-2, FB	1500-2500
101 (tree trunk)	7-1/2"	TMK-1, CM	1200-1500
101	7-1/2"	TMK-2, FB	700-1000
101	7-1/2"	TMK-3, Sty. Bee	500-600

TO MARKET table lamp, Hum 101. Rear view showing the regular and the tree trunk style lamp stem.

TO MARKET table lamp, Hum 101. Left: Full Bee mark (TMK-2), 6-1/2". Right: Stylized Bee in an incised circle, 7-1/8".

HUM 102: VOLUNTEERS (Table Lamp)

There are only a few examples of this piece known to exist in private collections. The few found so far all bear the Crown trademark and have a plain white post. They are valued at $4,000-5,000.

HUM 103: FAREWELL (Table Lamp)

This is an extremely rare piece: very few are known to exist. If sold it could bring up to $5,000.

HUM 104: EVENTIDE (Table Lamp)

Very few examples of this table lamp are known to be in collectors' hands at present. If sold it could bring up to $5,000.

HUM 105: ADORATION WITH BIRD or BIRD LOVERS

BIRD LOVERS or ADORATION WITH BIRD, Hum 105. Double Crown Mark (TMK-1), split base, 4-13/16".

First discovered about 1977, this piece was not previously thought to exist. It bears the mold number 105. This number was a "Closed Number," a number supposedly never used and never intended for use on an original Hummel piece. There have been at least 10 to 15 pieces found since the initial discovery. As is customary, the collector who found the piece named it. Although named Bird Lovers, it is also sometimes known as Adoration with Bird because of its similarity to Hum 23, Adoration. The major variation in the figures is in the girl's pigtail. A Hum 105 in fine condition is valued at $5,000-6,000.

HUM 106: MERRY WANDERER (Wall Plaque in a Wooden Frame)

Limited examples have been found of this extremely rare plaque, which was apparently only made for a short time. Perhaps this is because the plaque is basically the same as Hum 92 except for the wooden frame. Of those that have been found, all have the Crown Mark (TMK-1). They are valued at about $3,000-4,000.

HUM 107: LITTLE FIDDLER (Wall Plaque in a Wooden Frame)

Limited examples of this extremely rare plaque have been found. It was apparently only made for a short time. Perhaps this is because the plaque is basically the same as Hum 93 except for the wooden frame. Those that have been found all have the Crown Mark (TMK-1). They are valued at about $4,000.

HUM 108: ANGEL WITH BOY AND GIRL AT FEET (Wall Plaque in Relief) (Closed Number)

It is unlikely that any of these will ever find their way into collectors' hands. It cannot be certain that it is even an angel with children as described in the name above. A 1950s Goebel catalog lists the plaque as described, but it is not listed as a Hummel design. The deduction is made because of the description similar to the name and the mold number designation of 108 listed in factory records.

HUM 109: HAPPY TRAVELER

HAPPY TRAVELER, Hum 109. Left is mold number 109/0 with Full Bee (TMK-2) mark, a donut base, 5-1/8", black "Germany." Right has mold number 109, Last Bee (TMK-5) trademark and measures 4-3/4".

This figurine was placed in production in the late 1930s in a 5" basic size. An 8" basic size was added in the Full Bee (TMK-2) era. The large size was retired in 1982.

There has been a curious variation to surface in the 109/0 size. The normal colors for the figurine are brown for the hat and green for the jacket. The variation has a green hat and a blue jacket. It has no trademark and is the only one known. It may be unique.

HAPPY TRAVELER, Hum 109/0. Left: a Full Bee piece with black "Germany," donut base and the normal green color coat. Right: This is a doll face Hum 109/0 with a blue plaid coat. It has no apparent base markings. Both measure 5".

Hum No.	Basic Size	Trademark	Current Value ($)
109/0	5"	TMK-1, CM	260-325
109/0	5"	TMK-2, FB	190-210
109/0 or 109	5"	TMK-3, Sty. Bee	100-180
109/0 or 109	5"	TMK-4, 3-line	140-155
109/0 or 109	5"	TMK-5, LB	130-140
109/0	5"	TMK-6, MB	130
109.	8"	TMK-1, CM	1000-1200
109/II	8"	TMK-2, FB	700-800
109/II	8"	TMK-3, Sty. Bee	400-500
109/II	8"	TMK-4, 3-line	350-400
109/II	8"	TMK-5, LB	325-350
109/II	8"	TMK-6, MB	325-350

HUM 110: LET'S SING

One of the group of new designs introduced in the late 1930s. There have been no variations significant enough to have any impact on the normal pricing structure for the various pieces.

Hum No.	Basic Size	Trademark	Current Value ($)
110	3-1/2"	TMK-1, CM	350-480
110	3-1/2"	TMK-2, FB	250-325
110/0	3-1/4"	TMK-1, CM	230-400
110/0	3-1/4"	TMK-2, FB	160-190
110/0	3-1/4"	TMK-3, Sty. Bee	140-160
110/0	3-1/4"	TMK-4, 3-line	125-140
110/0	3-1/4"	TMK-5, LB	115-125
110/0	3-1/4"	TMK-6, MB	115
110/I	3-7/8"	TMK-1, CM	310-400
110/I	3-7/8"	TMK-2, FB	220-250
110/I	3-7/8"	TMK-3, Sty. Bee	190-220
110/I	3-7/8"	TMK-4, 3-line	165-180
110/I	3-7/8"	TMK-5, LB	155-165
110/I	3-7/8"	TMK-6, MB	155

LET'S SING, Hum 110. Left: Bears no mold number, Full Bee (TMK-2) trademark, 3-1/2", black "Germany," "© W. Goebel." Center: Mold number 110/0, Three Line Mark (TMK-4), 1938 MID, 3". Right: Mold number 110/0, Last Bee (TMK-5), 3-1/4".

HUM III/110: LET'S SING (Candy Box)

There are two styles of candy boxes. The transition from the old to the new took place during the Stylized Bee (TMK-3) period. Therefore both the old and the new can be found in the Stylized Bee mark.

Temporarily removed from production in 1989 with no reinstatement date.

Hum No.	Basic Size	Trademark	Current Value ($)
III/110	6"	TMK-1, CM	450-530
III/110	6"	TMK-2, FB	350-400
III/110 (old)	6"	TMK-3, Sty. Bee	275-325
III/110 (new)	6"	TMK-3, Sty. Bee	150-200
III/110	6"	TMK-4, 3-line	120-150
III/110	6"	TMK-5, LB	120-150
III/110	6"	TMK-6, MB	120-150

LET'S SING candy dish, Hum III/110. Last Bee mark (TMK-5).

HUM 111: WAYSIDE HARMONY

This figure was introduced in the late 1930s. It has changed a bit over the years, but there are no variations that have any significant impact on the collector value.

There does exist a curious variation where the bird is missing. This is an aberration wherein the bird was probably inadvertently left off during assembly. This sometimes happens to small parts and is not considered a rare variation.

This piece has been known to appear with roman numeral size designators instead of the arabic number indicated.

WAYSIDE HARMONY, Hum 111. Left: 111/1, incised Full Bee mark, black "Germany," © W. Goebel, 5-1/2". Right: 111/I, Three Line Mark, incised 1938 MID, 5-1/8".

Hum No.	Basic Size	Trademark	Current Value ($)
111/3/0	3-3/4"	TMK-1, CM	270-335
111/3/0	3-3/4"	TMK-2, FB	195-220
111/3/0	3-3/4"	TMK-3, Sty. Bee	165-190
111/3/0	3-3/4"	TMK-4, 3-line	145-165
111/3/0	3-3/4"	TMK-5, LB	135-145
111/3/0	3-3/4"	TMK-6, MB	135
111.	5"	TMK-1, CM	535-650
111/1	5"	TMK-1, CM	490-610
111/1	5"	TMK-2, FB	350-390
111/1	5"	TMK-3, Sty. Bee	300-330
111/1	5"	TMK-4, 3-line	265-285
111/1	5"	TMK-5, LB	245-265
111/1	5"	TMK-6, MB	245

HUM II/111 or HUM II/112: WAYSIDE HARMONY (Table Lamp)

This lamp was made for a short period of time in the 1950s. Perhaps to avoid confusion and/or to conform with the mold numbering sytem, the lamp was slightly redesigned and assigned a new number, Hum 224. Whatever the reason, there are a few of these II/111 Wayside Harmony lamps around. They occur in the Crown, Full Bee and Stylized Bee trademarks. The figures are quite scarce, but for some reason are valued at only $300-450.

HUM II/112: JUST RESTING (Table Lamp)

This lamp was made for a short period of time in the 1950s. Perhaps to avoid confusion and/or conform the mold numbering system, the number was changed to 225 with a concurrent slight redesign. Whatever the reason, there are a few of these II/112 Just Resting lamps around. They occur in the Crown, Full Bee and Stylized Bee trademarks. Although quite rare, for some reason the figures are valued at only $300-450.

HUM 112: JUST RESTING

There have been no variations significant enough to influence the normal pricing structure of this piece. One example has been found of a curious variation on the 112/1 size: there is no basket present on the base. This was probably the result of an inadvertant omission while it was being assembled, and somehow it slipped by the quality control inspectors. This happens occasionally with small pieces such as bottles in baskets and birds. It is not usually considered important but merely a curiosity.

JUST RESTING, Hum 112/1. Left: Stamped and incised Full Bee (TMK-2) mark, black "Germany," W. Goebel, 5-1/8". Right: Three Line Mark (TMK-4), 1938 MID, 4-7/8".

Hum No.	Basic Size	Trademark	Current Value ($)
112/3/0	3-3/4"	TMK-1, CM	265-330
112/3/0	3-3/4"	TMK-2, FB	195-215
112/3/0	3-3/4"	TMK-3, Sty. Bee	165-185
112/3/0	3-3/4"	TMK-4, 3-line	145-160
112/3/0	3-3/4"	TMK-5, LB	135-145
112/3/0	3-3/4"	TMK-6, MB	135
112	5"	TMK-1, CM	545-665
112/I	5"	TMK-1, CM	500-625
112/I	5"	TMK-2, FB	360-400
112/I	5"	TMK-3, Sty. Bee	300-340
112/I	5"	TMK-4, 3-line	260-290
112/I	5"	TMK-5, LB	250-260
112/I	5"	TMK-6, MB	250

HUM 113: HEAVENLY SONG (Candleholder)

This four-figure piece is a candleholder. It is quite similar to Hum 54 and was produced in extremely small numbers. Only a few are known to reside in private collections. The actual number is not known, but less than 50 would be a reasonable estimate. They do pop up from time to time and have been found in the Crown, Full Bee, Stylized Bee and Last Bee trademarks. The Goebel company announced in 1981 that they were removing Heavenly Song from production permanently. It is considered extremely rare in any of the trademarks.

Hum No.	Basic Size	Trademark	Current Value ($)
113	3-1/2"x4-3/4"	TMK-1, CM	5000-6000
113	3-1/2"x4-3/4"	TMK-2, FB	4000-5000
113	3-1/2"x4-3/4"	TMK-3, Sty. Bee	3000-4000
113	3-1/2"x4-3/4"	TMK-5, LB	1000-2000

HEAVENLY SONG candleholder, Hum 113. Left: Double Crown Mark (TMK-1), 3-1/2". Note the shiny porcelain-like finish and atypical paint. Right: Large Stylized Bee (TMK-3) in an incised circle, black "Western Germany," 2-5/8".

HEAVENLY SONG candleholder, Hum 113. This is a rare porcelain-like figurine that may fall into the faience category. It is much like the left figurine in the previous photograph. The middle child's dress is dark green and the baby's gown is a very dark blue. This one has an incised Crown (TMK-1), but the incised M.I. Hummel signature is either too light to discern or absent.

HUM 114: LET'S SING (Ashtray)

This piece is an ashtray with a figure very like Hum 110 at the edge of the dish. It is found with the figure on either the right or left side of the tray. Viewed from the front, the older ones have the figure on the right side. There are very few of this variation known. It was changed during the Full Bee (TMK-2) so it can be found with either the Crown or Full Bee trademark.

As is the case with all the ashtrays in the line, this piece is listed as temporarily withdrawn from production with no reinstatement date given.

LET'S SING ashtray, Hum 114. Left: Last Bee Mark (TMK-5), 3-5/8". Right: Full Bee mark (TMK-2), 3-1/2".

Hum No.	Basic Size	Trademark	Current Value ($)
114 (on right)	3-1/2"x6-3/4"	TMK-1, CM	400-500
114 (on right)	3-1/2"x6-3/4"	TMK-2, FB	300-350
114	3-1/2"x6-3/4"	TMK-2, FB	200-225
114	3-1/2"x6-3/4"	TMK-3, Sty. Bee	150-175
114	3-1/2"x6-3/4"	TMK-4, 3-line	125-140
114	3-1/2"x6-3/4"	TMK-5, LB	100-110
114	3-1/2"x6-3/4"	TMK-6, MB	100-110

HUM 115 (Girl with Nosegay), HUM 116 (Girl with Fir Tree), HUM 117 (Boy with Horse): ADVENT GROUP (Candleholders)

This group of three figures has a Christmas theme, and each of the figures is provided with a candle receptacle. Hum 115 is a girl holding flowers, Hum 116 is a girl with a Christmas tree, and Hum 117 is a boy with a toy horse. The original models were made with the "Mel" prefix followed by 1, 2 and 3 for 115, 116 and 117 respectively. These were prototypes, but many apparently got into the market (see the section on "Mel" pieces in chapter 5).

ADVENT GROUP candleholders. Left: Hum 115, small Stylized Bee (TMK-3) mark, 3-1/2". Center: Hum 116, small Stylized Bee mark, 3-5/8". Right: Hum 117, small Stylized Bee, 3-1/2".

Hum No.	Basic Size	Trademark	Current Value ($)
115, 116, 117	3-1/2"	TMK-1, CM	400-480 (set)
115, 116, 117	3-1/2"	TMK-2, FB	185-200 (set)
115, 116, 117	3-1/2"	TMK-3, Sty. Bee	175-185 (set)
115, 116, 117	3-1/2"	TMK-4, 3-line	160-175 (set)
115, 116, 117	3-1/2"	TMK-5, LB	150-160 (set)
115, 116, 117	3-1/2"	TMK-6, MB	150 (set)

HUM 118: LITTLE THRIFTY

This figurine, introduced in the late 1930s, is also a coin bank. It is usually found with a key and lockable metal plug beneath the base, but these are sometimes lost over the years.

Although not terribly significant in terms of value, there is a difference in design between the older and the newer pieces. The most obvious is a less thick base on the new design. This design change took place during the Stylized Bee (TMK-3) trademark period, so the old and the new designs can be found with that mark.

Hum No.	Basic Size	Trademark	Current Value ($)
118	5"	TMK-1, CM	260-350
118	5"	TMK-2, FB	200-225
118	5"	TMK-3, Sty. Bee	160-180
118	5"	TMK-4, 3-line	140-155

Hum No.	Basic Size	Trademark	Current Value ($)
118	5"	TMK-5, LB	130-140
118	5"	TMK-6, MB	130

LITTLE THRIFTY, Hum 118. The one on the left represents the older design. It measures 5-1/2", has the large Stylized Bee (TMK-3) trademark and bears a black "Germany" beneath the base. The one on the right has the Last Bee (TMK-5) trademark and is 5-1/8" in height. Note the variation in the bases.

HUM 119: POSTMAN

Introduced about 1940, this figure has been released in several different sizes and distinct mold variations, but only one size was listed until 1989, when a smaller version (119/2/0) was released. With the release of the 119/2/0, the larger 119 became 119/0 beginning with the Missing Bee (TMK-6) trademark pieces.

There are no variations significant enough to influence normal values for the Postman.

POSTMAN, Hum 119. Left: Stylized Bee (TMK-3) mark, 4-7/8". Right: 119 2/0, Missing Bee (TMK-6) mark, 1985 MID, 4-1/2".

Hum No.	Basic Size	Trademark	Current Value ($)
119/2/0	4-1/2"	TMK-6, MB	115-120
119	5-1/4"	TMK-1, CM	250-315
119	5-1/4"	TMK-2, FB	180-200
119	4-3/4"	TMK-3, Sty. Bee	180-225
119	5-1/4"	TMK-3, Sty. Bee	150-170
119	5-1/4"	TMK-4, 3-line	135-150
119	5 1/4"	TMK-5, LB	125-135
119	5-1/4"	TMK-6, MB	125
119/0	5-1/4"	TMK-6, MB	125

HUM 120: JOYFUL and LET'S SING (Double Figure on a Wooden Base)

No examples known to be in private collections. Known from factory records only.

HUM 121: WAYSIDE HARMONY and JUST RESTING

No examples known to be in private collections. Exists in factory archives only. The figures on the wooden base are very similar to the Hum 111 and Hum 112, but have different incised mold numbers.

HUM 122: PUPPY LOVE and SERENADE

No examples known to be in private collections. Exists in factory archives only.

HUM 123: MAX AND MORITZ

Released about 1940, this figurine was once known as Good Friends. An important variation has been found in a few Crown Mark (TMK-1) examples, where the figure has black hair rather than the lighter, blonde hair. In fact,

these figures appear to be painted in darker colors overall. When found, these pieces are valued at about $1,500. (See Hum 788A).

MAX AND MORITZ, Hum 123. The one on the right is the older, bearing the Full Bee Mark (TMK-2). It has a donut base and an incised 1939 MID, is 5-3/8" tall and has W. Goebel inscribed in script. The left figure has the 3-line mark (TMK-4), measures 5" and has a donut base.

Hum No.	Basic Size	Trademark	Current Value ($)
123	5-1/4"	TMK-1, CM	420-525
123	5-1/4"	TMK-2, FB	305-325
123	5-1/4"	TMK-3, Sty. Bee	245-275
123	5-1/4"	TMK-4, 3-line	215-245
123	5-1/4"	TMK-5, LB	205-215
123	5-1/4"	TMK-6, MB	205

HUM 124: HELLO

Introduced around 1940, this figurine was once known as Chef, Hello. When first released it had grey pants and coat and a pink vest. This changed to green pants, brown coat and pink vest and then finally to the brown coat and pants with white vest used on the pieces from some time in the Stylized Bee (TMK-3) trademark period to the present. The variation in shortest supply is the green pants version.

The figure has been found with the decimal designator in the Crown and Full Bee trademarks. The 124/I size has been temporarily removed from production with no reinstatement date given.

HELLO, Hum 124. Right: 124/0, Full Bee (TMK-2) in an incised circle, donut base, black "Germany" beneath the base, five buttons on vest (only four of which are painted), green pants, brown jacket, red hair, 6-1/4".

Right: 124/I, Missing Bee (TMK-5) mark, donut base, five painted buttons, brown pants, purple jacket, brown hair, 6-3/8".

Hum No.	Basic Size	Trademark	Current Value ($)
124.	6-1/2"	TMK-1, CM	650-750
124.	6-1/2"	TMK-2, FB	400-500
124/0	6-1/4"	TMK-2, FB	275-315
124/0	6-1/4"	TMK-3, Sty. Bee	240-260
124/0	6-1/4"	TMK-4, 3-line	210-230
124/0	6-1/4"	TMK-5, LB	195-210
124/0	6-1/4"	TMK-6, MB	195
124/I	7"	TMK-1, CM	550-650
124/I	7"	TMK-2, FB	350-450
124/I	7"	TMK-3, Sty. Bee	275-325
124/I	7"	TMK-4, 3-line	240-250
124/I	7"	TMK-5, LB	220-230
124/I	7"	TMK-6, MB	220-230

HUM 125: VACATION TIME (Wall Plaque)

There are two distinctly different designs of this figure. The transition from the old to the new took place in the Stylized Bee (TMK-3) period, so you can find the old and the new styles in that trademark. The newest style has now lost one fence picket for a count of five. The old has six.

Hum No.	Basic Size	Trademark	Current Value ($)
125	4-3/8"x5-1/4"	TMK-1, CM	500-600
125	4-3/8"x5-1/4"	TMK-2, FB	250-325
125	4"x 4-3/4"	TMK-3, Sty. Bee	185-195
125	4"x 4-3/4"	TMK-4, 3-line	180
125	4"x 4-1/4"	TMK-5, LB	175
125	4"x 4-1/4"	TMK-6, MB	175

VACATION TIME Plaque, Hum 125. Left: Full Bee mark, 6 pickets in the fence, 4-3/8" x 5-3/8". Right: Last Bee mark, 5 pickets in the fence, 4" x 4-7/8".

HUM 126: RETREAT TO SAFETY (Wall Plaque)

This plaque was released around 1940 and was in continuous production until 1989, when it was temporarily withdrawn from production. No reinstatement date has been given.

RETREAT TO SAFETY Plaque, Hum 126.

Hum No.	Basic Size	Trademark	Current Value ($)
126	4-3/4"x4-3/4"	TMK-1, CM	500-600
126	4-3/4"x4-3/4"	TMK-2, FB	250-325
126	4-3/4"x4-3/4"	TMK-3, Sty. Bee	185-195
126	4-3/4"x4-3/4"	TMK-4, 3-line	180-185
126	4-3/4"x4-3/4"	TMK-5, LB	175-185
126	4-3/4"x4-3/4"	TMK-6, MB	175

HUM 127: DOCTOR

DOCTOR, Hum 127. Full Bee mark, black "Germany," donut base, 5-1/4".

Doctor joined the line about 1940. On the Crown Mark (TMK-1) and Full Bee (TMK-2) figures the doll's feet extend slightly beyond the edge of the base. They must have proved vulnerable to breakage because the feet were restyled so they no longer extended over the base. The sizes in various lists range from 4-3/4" to 5-1/4". The larger sizes are generally the older pieces.

Hum No.	Basic Size	Trademark	Current Value ($)
127	4-3/4"	TMK-1, CM	290-360
127	4-3/4"	TMK-2, FB	200-250
127	4-3/4"	TMK-3, Sty. Bee	175-200
127	4-3/4"	TMK-4, 3-line	150-175
127	4-3/4"	TMK-5, LB	145-150
127	4-3/4"	TMK-6, MB	145

HUM 128: BAKER

Although this figure, like most, underwent changes over the years, none are important enough to influence the normal values of the pieces.

Hum No.	Basic Size	Trademark	Current Value ($)
128	4-3/4"	TMK-1, CM	350-445
128	4-3/4"	TMK-2, FB	250-285
128	4-3/4"	TMK-3, Sty. Bee	220-245
128	4-3/4"	TMK-4, 3-line	185-220
128	4-3/4"	TMK-5, LB	175-185
128	4-3/4"	TMK-6, MB	175

BAKER, Hum 128. Left: Full Bee mark, black "Germany," donut base, 5-1/8". Center: Stylized Bee mark, 4-3/4". Right: Missing Bee mark, 4-7/8".

HUM 129: BAND LEADER

Another circa 1940 release. This figure has not been found with any significant mold variations.

A new, smaller size without the music stand was introduced in 1987 as the fourth in a four-part series of small figurines intended to match four mini-plates in the same motif.

Hum No.	Basic Size	Trademark	Current Value ($)
129/4/0	3-1/2"	TMK-5, LB	90-100
129/4/0	3-1/2"	TMK-6, MB	90
129	5-1/4"	TMK-1, CM	360-450
129	5-1/4"	TMK-2, FB	260-290
129	5-1/4"	TMK-3, Sty. Bee	230-260
129	5-1/4"	TMK-4, 3-line	190-215
129	5-1/4"	TMK-5, LB	180-190
129	5-1/4"	TMK-6, MB	180

BAND LEADER, Hum 129. Left: Full Bee mark in an incised circle, black Germany, split base in quarters, 6". Right: Last Bee mark, 5-1/8".

HUM 130: DUET

Some older figures with the Crown trademark have a very small lip on the front of the base, sort of a mini-version of the stepped or double base variation found on the Merry Wanderer. These lip base Duets also have incised musical notes on the sheet music and are valued at about $800-$1,000.

Another variation is the absence of the kerchief on the figure wearing the top hat. This is found on some Full Bee (TMK-2) and Stylized Bee (TMK-3) pieces. If found, they are valued at about $2,000-3,500.

Duet was permanently retired on December 31, 1995. The mold was destroyed.

Hum No.	Basic Size	Trademark	Current Value ($)
130	5-1/4"	TMK-1, CM	500-625
130	5-1/4"	TMK-2, FB	350-400
130	5-1/4"	TMK-3, Sty. Bee	300-330
130	5-1/4"	TMK-4, 3-line	260-290
130	5-1/4"	TMK-5, LB	250-260
130	5-1/4"	TMK-6, MB	250

DUET, Hum 130. Left: 130., double incised Crown Marks (one of which is colored blue), 5-1/4". Right: Full Bee mark, black "Germany," 5-5/8".

HUM 131: STREET SINGER

This figure was introduced about 1940 in one size and has remained in one size to current production. There are no significant mold variations to be found.

STREET SINGER, Hum 131. Left: The mold number is 131., but there is no trademark apparent. The underlined word "Originalmuster" on the side of the base is partially visible in the photo here. This indicates that this was at one time a master model. Right: Stylized Bee mark, 5".

Hum No.	Basic Size	Trademark	Current Value ($)
131	5"	TMK-1, CM	340-410
131	5"	TMK-2, FB	240-275
131	5"	TMK-3, Sty. Bee	200-240
131	5"	TMK-4, 3-line	180-200
131	5"	TMK-5, LB	170-180
131	5"	TMK-6, MB	170

HUM 132: STAR GAZER

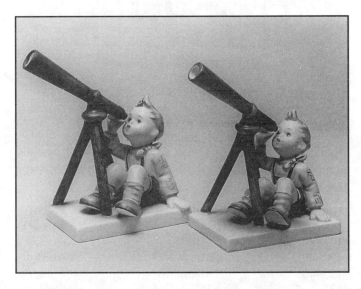

A few of the older Crown Mark (TMK-1) pieces have a darker blue or purple shirt, but the normal color on later pieces is a lighter blue or purple.

The straps on the boy's lederhosen are normally crossed in the back. If there are no straps the value is increased, valued at about 20% above the normal value.

Hum No.	Basic Size	Trademark	Current Value ($)
132	4-3/4"	TMK-1, CM	395-500
132	4-3/4"	TMK-2, FB	275-315
132	4-3/4"	TMK-3, Sty. Bee	240-260
132	4-3/4"	TMK-4, 3-line	210-230
132	4-3/4"	TMK-5, LB	195-210
132	4-3/4"	TMK-6, MB	195

STARGAZER, Hum 132. Left: Full Bee mark in an incised circle, black "Germany," 4-7/8". Right: Stylized Bee mark, split base, 4-7/8".

HUM 133: MOTHER'S HELPER

MOTHER'S HELPER, Hum 133. The original 1939 design is represented by the figure on the left. It bears the small Stylized Bee (TMK-3) trademark in an incised circle and measures 5". The right figure in the photo is a Last Bee (TMK-5) piece. It has a donut base and is 4-3/4" tall.

Released about 1939-1940 in a 5" basic size, this figurine has but one major variation to look for. Several Crown-era pieces have surfaced with the stool reversed and only one leg of the stool showing when viewed from the rear. The norm has two legs visible from the rear. The basic size of 5" has remained the same, although older versions are generally larger than the newer models.

Hum No.	Basic Size	Trademark	Current Value ($)
133	5"	TMK-1, CM	350-420
133	5"	TMK-2, FB	250-290
133	5"	TMK-3, Sty. Bee	205-250
133	5"	TMK-4, 3-line	185-205
133	5"	TMK-5, LB	175-185
133	5"	TMK-6, MB	175

HUM 134: QUARTET (Wall Plaque)

Another of the circa 1940 releases, this plaque has remained in the line in the same basic size. There are no significant mold variations influencing the normal pricing structure. It has been temporarily removed from production without a reinstatement date.

Hum No.	Basic Size	Trademark	Current Value ($)
134	6"x6"	TMK-1, CM	600-725
134	6"x6"	TMK-2, FB	360-400
134	6"x6"	TMK-3, Sty. Bee	300-350
134	6"x6"	TMK-4, 3-line	265-285
134	6"x6"	TMK-5, LB	250-265
134	6"x6"	TMK-6, MB	250

QUARTET, Plaque, Hum 134.
Stylized Bee mark, 5-1/2" x 6-1/4".

HUM 135: SOLOIST

Released in the early 1940s as High Tenor, this piece has remained in continuous production since. It has no significant mold variations influencing price.

In 1986 a new smaller version, 135/4/0, was released as the third in a series of four small figurines and matching mini-plates. Because of the new size designator in the smaller model, the larger model is now incised with the mold number 135/0. This change was instigated in the Missing Bee mark (TMK-6) era.

SOLOIST, Hum 135. 4-7/8", Stylized Bee (TMK-3) trademark, black "Western Germany."

Hum No.	Basic Size	Trademark	Current Value ($)
135/5/0	2-3/4"	TMK-7	55
135/4/0	3-1/2"	TMK-5, MB	90-100
135/4/0	3-1/2"	TMK-6, LB	90
135	4-3/4"	TMK-1, CM	240-310
135	4-3/4"	TMK-2, FB	175-200
135	4-3/4"	TMK-3, Sty. Bee	150-175
135	4-3/4"	TMK-4, 3-line	130-150
135	4-3/4"	TMK-5, LB	120-150
135	4-3/4"	TMK-6, MB	120
135	4-3/4"	TMK-6, MB	120

HUM 136: FRIENDS

Sizes found in various lists were 5", 10-3/4", and 11-1/2". There have been at least two examples of this piece found that are made of a terra cotta. These are in the 136/V size. The terra cotta pieces are valued at about $7500-8000.

Released circa 1940 in two sizes, it was originally known as Good Friends.

Also found in white overglaze in the Crown Mark (TMK-1), this very rare variation is valued at $3,500-4,000.

FRIENDS, Hum 136. Left: 136., Crown Mark, white overglaze, 11-1/4". Center: 136., Crown Mark, terra cotta finish, 10-1/4". Right: 136., Crown Mark, "U.S. ZONE Germany," 10-3/4".

Hum No.	Basic Size	Trademark	Current Value ($)
136/I	5"	TMK-1, CM	400-500
136/I	5"	TMK-2, FB	275-325
136/I	5"	TMK-3, Sty. Bee	250-275
136/I	5"	TMK-4, 3-line	210-250
136/I	5"	TMK-5, LB	195-210
136/I	5"	TMK-6, MB	195
136	10-3/4"	TMK-1, CM	3000-3300
136	10-3/4"	TMK-2, FB	2000-2200
136/V	10-3/4"	TMK-1, CM	2000-2300
136/V	10-3/4"	TMK-2, FB	1500-1700
136/V	10-3/4"	TMK-3, Sty. Bee	1300-1400
136/V	10-3/4"	TMK-4, 3-line	1100-1300
136/V	10-3/4"	TMK-5, LB	1080-1100
136/V	10-3/4"	TMK-6, MB	1080

HUM 137/A and HUM 137/B: CHILD IN BED (Wall Plaques)

The mold number is found as 137/B until the Last Bee (TMK-5) era, when the B was dropped. Until recently it was speculated that there might have been a matching piece with the mold number 137/A. A few of these have now surfaced. Apparently they were never produced in any quantity and are valued at $5,000-7,500.

CHILD IN BED Plaque, Hum 137/B. Stylized Bee mark, 3".

Hum No.	Basic Size	Trademark	Current Value ($)
137/B	2-3/4"x2-3/4" (round)	TMK-1, CM	300-400
137/B	2-3/4"x2-3/4" (round)	TMK-2, FB	150-175
137/B	2-3/4"x2-3/4" (round)	TMK-3, Sty. Bee	100-125
137/B	2-3/4"x2-3/4" (round)	TMK-4, 3-line	65-70
137	2-3/4"x2-3/4" (round)	TMK-5, LB	60-65
137	2-3/4"x2-3/4" (round)	TMK-6, MB	60

HUM 138: BABY IN CRIB (Wall Plaque)

Although all factory records indicate that this piece was never released for sale to the consumer and only prototypes were produced, at least six are known to reside in private collections. It dates from around 1940.

These figures have only been found with the Full Bee (TMK-2) trademark. They are valued at $4,000-5,500.

HUM 139: FLITTING BUTTERFLY (Wall Plaque)

Released circa 1940, this figure has not undergone any significant mold variation that would affect the normal value for the various trademarked pieces.

This figure was out of production for some time. It has been reissued in a new mold design with the same number.

Hum No.	Basic Size	Trademark	Current Value ($)
139	2-1/2"x2-1/2"	TMK-1, CM	120-175
139	2-1/2"x2-1/2"	TMK-2, FB	85-100
139	2-1/2"x2-1/2"	TMK-3, Sty. Bee	70-85
139	2-1/2"x2-1/2"	TMK-4, 3-line	65-70
139	2-1/2"x2-1/2"	TMK-5, LB	60-65
139	2-1/2"x2-1/2"	TMK-6, MB	60

FLITTING BUTTERFLY Plaque, Hum 139. Full Bee mark in an incised circle, 2-3/8" square.

HUM 140: THE MAIL IS HERE or MAIL COACH (Wall Plaque)

MAIL COACH Plaque, Hum 140. Last Bee trademark, 6-3/4" x 4-1/2".

This plaque predates the figurine by the same name and design. It was introduced into the line around 1940.

While there are no significant mold variations, there is a finish variation of importance. Some of the early plaques were produced in white overglaze for the European market. These are found bearing the Crown Mark (TMK-1) and are valued at $1,000-1,500.

Hum No.	Basic Size	Trademark	Current Value ($)
140	4-1/2"x6-1/4"	TMK-1, CM	500-600
140	4-1/2"x6-1/4"	TMK-2, FB	250-350
140	4-1/2"x6-1/4"	TMK-3, Sty. Bee	185-200
140	4-1/2"x6-1/4"	TMK-4, 3-line	180-185
140	4-1/2"x6-1/4"	TMK-5, LB	175-180
140	4-1/2"x6-1/4"	TMK-6, MB	175

HUM 141: APPLE TREE GIRL

This figure has also been known as Spring. The following sizes are found in various lists: 4", 4-1/4", 6", 6-3/4", 10", 10-1/2", 29". In one list references were made to a "rare old base" and a "brown base." These are apparently references to the "tree trunk base" variation. This variation will bring about 30% more than the value given in the chart below. The 4" size has no bird perched on the branch, in contrast to all the larger sizes (although there has been at least one, a 141/I, reported to have no bird: perhaps a factory worker's inadvertant omission).

Hum No.	Basic Size	Trademark	Current Value ($)
141/3/0	4"	TMK-1, CM	260-325
141/3/0	4"	TMK-2, FB	200-220
141/3/0	4"	TMK-3, Sty. Bee	160-190

Hum No.	Basic Size	Trademark	Current Value ($)
141/3/0	4"	TMK-4, 3-line	140-160
141/3/0	4"	TMK-5, LB	130-140
141/3/0	4"	TMK-6, MB	130
141	6"	TMK-1, CM	600-750
141	6"	TMK-2, FB	400-450
141/I	6"	TMK-1, CM	500-650
141/I	6"	TMK-2, FB	350-400
141/I	4"	TMK-3, Sty. Bee	300-350
141/I	6"	TMK-4, 3-line	260-300
141/I	6"	TMK-5, LB	245-260
141/I	6"	TMK-6, MB	245
141/V	10-1/2"	TMK-3, Sty. Bee	1350-1400
141/V	10-1/2"	TMK-5, LB	1080-1200
141/V	10-1/2"	TMK-6, MB	1080
141/X	33"	TMK-5, LB	*24,000

*There are a few of these "Jumbo" figures in collectors' hands. They are generally used as promotional figures in showrooms and shops. Rarely do they bring full retail price.

APPLE TREE GIRL, Hum 141. Left: 141 3/0, Full Bee mark, black "Germany," painted brown base, 4-5/16". Right: 141 3/0, Full Bee mark, black "Germany," 4-1/4".

HUM 142: APPLE TREE BOY

This figure has also been known as Fall. Sizes found in various lists are as follows: 3-3/4", 4", 4-1/2", 6", 6-1/2", 10", 10-1/2" and 29". In one list references were made to a "rare old base" and a "brown base." These are apparently references to the "tree trunk base" variation. This variation will bring about 30% more than the figure in the value chart below. The 4" size has no bird perched on the branch, in contrast to all the larger sizes.

APPLE TREE BOY, Hum 142. Left: 142 3/0, double Full Bee mark (incised and stamped), black "Germany," old style rounded, brown color base, 4". Right: 142 3/0, Stylized Bee mark in an incised circle, newer style base, 3-15/16".

Hum No.	Basic Size	Trademark	Current Value ($)
142/3/0	4"	TMK-1, CM	260-325
142/3/0	4"	TMK-2, FB	200-220
142/3/0	4"	TMK-3, Sty. Bee	160-190
142/3/0	4"	TMK-4, 3-line	140-160
142/3/0	4"	TMK-5, LB	130-140
142/3/0	4"	TMK-6, MB	130
142	6"	TMK-1, CM	600-750
142	6"	TMK-2, FB	400-450
142/I	6"	TMK-1, CM	500-650
142/I	6"	TMK-2, FB	350-400
142/I	6"	TMK-3, Sty. Bee	300-350
142/I	6"	TMK-4, 3-line	260-300
142/I	6"	TMK-5, LB	245-260
142/I	6"	TMK-6, MB	245
142/V	10-1/4"	TMK-3, Sty. Bee	1350-1400
142/V	10-1/4"	TMK-5, LB	1080-1200
142/V	10-1/4"	TMK-6, MB	1080
142/X	33"	TMK-5, LB	*24,000

*There are a few of these "Jumbo" figures in collectors' hands. They are generally used as promotional figures in showrooms and shops. Rarely do they bring full retail price.

HUM 143: BOOTS

This figure was first released around 1940 in two basic sizes. Although many size variations have been found, none is significant in terms of affecting value.

Hum No.	Basic Size	Trademark	Current Value ($)
143/0	5-1/4"	TMK-1, CM	360-450
143/0	5-1/4"	TMK-2, FB	260-290
143/0	5-1/4"	TMK-3, Sty. Bee	225-250
143/0	5-1/4"	TMK-4, 3-line	190-225
143/0	5-1/4"	TMK-5, LB	180-190
143/0	5-1/4"	TMK-6, MB	180
143/I	6-3/4"	TMK-1, CM	600-750
143/I	6-3/4"	TMK-2, FB	400-500
143/I	6-3/4"	TMK-3, Sty. Bee	350-400
143/I	6-3/4"	TMK-4, LB	300-350
143/I	6-3/4"	TMK-5, MB	300

BOOTS, Hum 143. Left: Full Bee mark, black "Germany," donut base 6-13/16". Right: 143/1, Stylized Bee mark, donut base, 6-3/4".

HUM 144: ANGELIC SONG

There are no significant variations of Angelic Song affecting the normal value of the pieces. The figure was first released about 1940.

ANGELIC SONG, Hum 144. Last Bee mark, 4-1/8".

Hum No.	Basic Size	Trademark	Current Value ($)
144	4-1/4"	TMK-1, CM	270-335
144	4-1/4"	TMK-2, FB	200-225
144	4-1/4"	TMK-3, Sty. Bee	165-185
144	4-1/4"	TMK-4, 3-line	145-160
144	4-1/4"	TMK-5, LB	135-145
144	4-1/4"	TMK-6, MB	135

HUM 145: LITTLE GUARDIAN

Released in the early 1940s, this figurine is still in production today. There are no variations significant enough to impact collector values.

Hum No.	Basic Size	Trademark	Current Value ($)
145	3-3/4"	TMK-1, CM	270-335
145	3-3/4"	TMK-2, FB	200-225
145	3-3/4"	TMK-3, Sty. Bee	165-185
145	3-3/4"	TMK-4, 3-line	145-165
145	3-3/4"	TMK-5, LB	135-145
145	3-3/4"	TMK-6, MB	135

LITTLE GUARDIAN, Hum 145. Measures 3-5/8" tall and has the Last Bee (TMK-5)

HUM 146: ANGEL DUET (Holy Water Font)

There have been many variations with regard to the shapes and positions of the heads and wings of this figure, but none significant. This font has been in continuous production since its introduction in the early 1940s.

Hum No.	Basic Size	Trademark	Current Value ($)
146	2"x4-3/4"	TMK-1, CM	395-500
146	2"x4-3/4"	TMK-2, FB	275-315
146	2"x4-3/4"	TMK-3, Sty. Bee	240-260
146	2"x4-3/4"	TMK-4, 3-line	210-230
146	2"x4-3/4"	TMK-5, LB	195-210
146	2"x4-3/4"	TMK-6, MB	195

ANGEL DUET Font, Hum 146.
Stylized Bee mark, 4-5/8".

HUM 147: ANGEL SHRINE (Holy Water Font)

This figure has been in continuous production since its release in the early 1940s. There are no important mold or finish variations affecting its value.

DEVOTION Font, Hum 147. Stylized Bee mark, 5-1/4".

Hum No.	Basic Size	Trademark	Current Value ($)
147	3"x5"	TMK-1, CM	100-150
147	3"x5"	TMK-2, FB	75-90
147	3"x5"	TMK-3, Sty. Bee	60-75
147	3"x5"	TMK-4, 3-line	55-60
147	3"x5"	TMK-5, LB	50-55
147	3"x5"	TMK-6, MB	50

HUM 148: UNKNOWN (Closed Number)

Records indicate that this piece could be a Farm Boy (Hum 66) with no base. No examples have even been found. You can remove the figure from the bookend Hum 60/A and have the same figure, but the mold number will not be present.

HUM 149: UNKNOWN (Closed Number)

Records indicate that this could be a Goose Girl (Hum 47) with no base. No known examples in collectors' hands. You can remove the figure from the bookend Hum 60/B and have the same piece, but the mold number will not be present.

HUM 150: HAPPY DAYS

Sizes referenced in price lists were: 4-1/4", 5-1/4", 6", and 6-1/4". This figure has been known in the past as Happy Little Troubadours. It has been found with the decimal point designator.

There are no mold or finish variations significant enough to influence values.

Hum No.	Basic Size	Trademark	Current Value ($)
150/2/0	4-1/4"	TMK-2, FB	225-260
150/2/0	4-1/4"	TMK-3, Sty. Bee	200-225
150/2/0	4-1/4"	TMK-4, 3-line	170-200
150/2/0	4-1/4"	TMK-5, LB	160-170
150/2/0	4-1/4"	TMK-6, MB	160
150/0	5-1/4"	TMK-2, FB	375-425
150/0	5-1/4"	TMK-3, Sty. Bee	325-375
150/0	5-1/4"	TMK-4, LB	270

Hum No.	Basic Size	Trademark	Current Value ($)
150/0	5-1/4"	TMK-5, MB	270
150	6"	TMK-1, CM	1000-1500
150	6"	TMK-2, FB	700-800
150/I	6"	TMK-1, CM	900-1400
150/I	6"	TMK-2, FB	600-700
150/I	6"	TMK-3, Sty. Bee	470-485
150/I	6"	TMK-5, LB	430-450
150/I	6"	TMK-6, MB	430

HAPPY DAYS, Hum 150. Left: 150/0. Full Bee (TMK-2) mark, black "Germany," split base, 5-1/4". Right: 150/0, Last Bee (TMK-5) mark, 5-1/8".

HUM 151: MADONNA HOLDING CHILD

Sometimes called the Blue Cloak Madonna because of the most commonly found painted finish, this figure was temporarily withdrawn from production in 1989. It was back in production in a blue and white overglaze as per the 1993 Goebel price listing, but in 1995 was listed once again as temporarily withdrawn from production.

The figure has appeared in other finishes. The rarest three finishes are those with the rich dark brown cloak, the dark blue cloak and the ivory cloak. Always occurring in the Crown Mark (TMK-1), these are valued at $6,500-7,500 depending on condition.

Sizes ranging from 12" to 14" have been referenced, and the figure has appeared with the Crown, Full Bee and Stylized Bee marks. It has appeared in blue cloak, white overglaze, and in a brown cloak. The brown cloak is the rarest.

MADONNA HOLDING CHILD, Hum 151. Left: The Brown Cloak Madonna with decimal designator

mold number "151.". It has an incised Crown Mark (TMK-1), a stamped Full Bee (TMK-2) mark, a black "Germany" and measures 12-1/2". Center: Double Full Bee (TMK-2), one incised and one stamped. White overglaze measuring 12-7/8". Right: Blue cloak, Full Bee mark, 12-3/4".

Hum No.	Basic Size	Trademark	Current Value ($) (color)	Current Value ($) (white)
151	12"	TMK-1, CM	1350-1750	600-700
151	12"	TMK-2, FB	800-1100	460-500
151	12"	TMK-4, LB	675-725	320-375
151	12"	TMK-5, MB	675	320

HUM 152/A: UMBRELLA BOY

Introduced in one size in the early 1940s. A second, smaller size was introduced in the Full Bee (TMK-2) period. There are no mold or finish variations that influence value.

The earliest Crown Mark (TMK-1) examples were produced with the incised mold number 152.

Left: UMBRELLA BOY, Hum 152/A. 152 0 A, Three Line Mark (TMK-4), incised 1957 MID, 4-5/8" Right: UMBRELLA GIRL, Hum 152/B. 152/0 B, Three Line Mark, incised 1957 MID, 4-3/4".

Hum No.	Basic Size	Trademark	Current Value ($)
152/0 A	5"	TMK-2, FB	775-825
152/0 A	5"	TMK-3, Sty. Bee	650-680
152/0 A	5"	TMK-4, 3-line	550-600
152/0 A	5"	TMK-5, LB	530-550
152/0 A	5"	TMK-6, MB	530
152	8"	TMK-1, CM	3000-5000
152/A	8"	TMK-2, FB	2000-2500
152/A	8"	TMK-3, Sty. Bee	1500-1700
152/A	8"	TMK-4, 3-line	1400-1450
152/A	8"	TMK-5, LB	1300-1400
152/A	8"	TMK-6, MB	1300

HUM 152/B: UMBRELLA GIRL

Obviously created to match the Umbrella Boy, one wonders why this figure was introduced at the end of the 1940s, several years after Umbrella Boy. In any case, it may be found in two sizes, the smaller appearing in the Full Bee trademark period. There are no significant variations influencing values.

Hum No.	Basic Size	Trademark	Current Value ($)
152/0 B	4-3/4"	TMK-2, FB	775-825
152/0 B	4-3/4"	TMK-3, Sty. Bee	650-680

Hum No.	Basic Size	Trademark	Current Value ($)
152/0 B	4-3/4"	TMK-4, 3-line	550-600
152/0 B	4-3/4"	TMK-5, LB	530-550
152/0 B	4-3/4"	TMK-6, MB	530
152/B	8"	TMK-1, CM	3000-5000
152/B	8"	TMK-2, FB	2000-2500
152/B	8"	TMK-3, Sty. Bee	1500-1700
152/B	8"	TMK-4, 3-line	1400-1450
152/B	8"	TMK-5, LB	1300-1400
152/B	8"	TMK-6, MB	1300

HUM 153: AUF WIEDERSEHEN

This figure was first released in the mid-1940s in the 7" basic size (the name means "goodbye" in English). A smaller size was introduced during the Full Bee (TMK-2) era.

In a rare version of this double figure piece the little boy wears a Tyrolean cap. This variation is found only in the 153/0 size. In most examples of these pieces he wears no hat but is waving a handkerchief, as is the girl. The rare version is valued at about $1,800-2,500. Sizes found in various lists are as follows: 5-1/2", 5-7/8". The 153/I size is listed as reinstated. (See color section.)

AUF WIEDERSEHEN, Hum 153. Left: 153/0, Full Bee mark, black "Germany," 5-1/4". Right: 153/0 Stylized Bee, 5-3/8".

In 1993 Goebel issued a special edition of this figurine along with a replica of the Berlin Airlift Memorial at Templehof Airport in Berlin. This was to commemorate the Berlin Airlift at the end of WWII. Both pieces bear a special backstamp containing the flags of Germany, France, England and the United States. The edition was limited to 25,000. The original issue was priced at $330 and is still valued at about the same.

Hum No.	Basic Size	Trademark	Current Value ($)
153/0	5-1/4"	TMK-1, CM	440-550
153/0	5-1/4"	TMK-2, FB	315-350
153/0	5-1/4"	TMK-3, Sty. Bee	260-290
153/0	5-1/4"	TMK-4, 3-line	230-260
153/0	5-1/4"	TMK-5, LB	220-230
153/0	5-1/4"	TMK-6, MB	220
153/0	5-1/4"	TMK-1, CM	540-725
153/0	5-1/4"	TMK-2, FB	375-425
153/0	5-1/4"	TMK-3, Sty. Bee	285-320
153/0	5-1/4"	TMK-5, LB	270-285
153/0	5-1/4"	TMK-6, MB	270

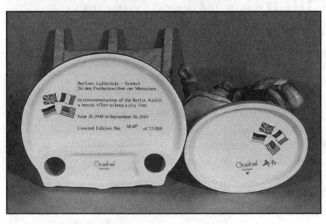

Bases of the memorial replica and Hum 153/0 respectively, showing the special markings.

Special edition of AUF WIEDERSEHEN on wood base with the porcelain Airlift Memorial replica piece. Both have a special backstamp and the edition is limited to 25,000. Wall: 7-1/2". Figurine: Hum 153/0, 5-1/2".

HUM 154: WAITER

First released in the 1940s in two sizes, this figure has appeared with several different labels on the wine bottle. All are now produced with a "Rhine Wine" label. Earlier versions have much darker pants than those in current production. The variation in which the label on the bottle reads "Whiskey" is from the Full Bee (TMK-2) era and is valued at $2,000.

WAITER, Hum 154. Left to right (A through D): A. 154., Crown mark, donut base, "U.S. ZONE Germany," 6-1/2". B. 154., Crown mark, donut base, black "Germany," 6-1/2". C. 154/0, Full bee mark, Donut base, Black "Germany," 6-1/8". D. 154/1 Stylized Bee mark, donut base, 6-13/16".

Hum No.	Basic Size	Trademark	Current Value ($)
154/0	6"	TMK-1, CM	395-500
154/0	6"	TMK-2, FB	275-325
154/0	6"	TMK-3, Sty. Bee	240-260
154/0	6"	TMK-4, 3-line	210-230
154/0	6"	TMK-5, LB	195-210
154/0	6"	TMK-6, MB	195
154	7"	TMK-1, CM	750-850
154	7"	TMK-2, FB	400-450
154	7"	TMK-1, CM	520-650
154	7"	TMK-2, FB	375-425
154	7"	TMK-3, Sty. Bee	300-350
154	7"	TMK-5, LB	260-300
154	7"	TMK-6, MB	260

MADONNA HOLDING CHILD, Hum 155, plaque. 13" high, incised Hummel signature, mold number, Crown trademark and W. Goebel.

HUM 155: MADONNA HOLDING CHILD (Closed Number)

Records indicate this figure may be a Madonna holding child. The photograph shown here is of the Madonna plaque It is large, measuring 13" high. It has the incised M.I. Hummel signature and mold number, a Crown trademark and W. Goebel on the back. Because it is unique and there is no trade data, no realistic collector value can be determined.

HUM 156: UNKNOWN (Closed Number)

Records indicate this figure may be a wall plaque of a mother and child. No known examples.

HUM 157 through HUM 162: "TOWN CHILDREN" (Closed Numbers)

These are 1940s sample figurines where the children are dressed much more formally than in typical figurines. There are sample models of some of them in the Goebel archives and they are atypical of M.I. Hummel figurines. They do not wear the traditional costumes, but rather appear to be dressed in more modern clothes. Sister Maria Innocentia is known to have asked on at least one occasion, "How shall I draw for the Americans?" One can speculate that these pieces, never approved, were an attempt to produce a few for the American market.

Until recently these numbers have been listed as unknown. Records indicate that the figurines were modeled and considered for production but never released.

None are known outside the archives. (See photo accompanying, Hum 157 and Hum 158.)

Referred to as "Town Children," this boy and girl were never named or produced. As you'll recognize immediately, the subjects are slimmer and more citified than the rural look that is typical of M.I. Hummel children. These samples were sculpted in 1943.

HUM 163: WHITSUNTIDE

WHITSUNTIDE, Hum 163.
Left: Incised Crown Mark,
red candle in angel's hand.
Right: Last Bee trademark
(TMK-5), no candle. Both
measure 6-3/4".

WHITSUNTIDE, Hum
163. Full Bee mark in an
incised circle, black
"Western Germany,"
split base (in quarters), 7".

This figure is sometimes known as Happy New Year. It is one of the early (mid-1940) releases and was removed from production about 1960, then reinstated in 1977. The older pieces are very scarce and highly sought by collectors. In older versions the angel appears holding a red or a yellow candle and is without the candle in newer models.

Hum No.	Basic Size	Trademark	Current Value ($)
163	7-1/4"	TMK-1, CM	1000-1200
163	7-1/4"	TMK-1, CM	800-1000
163	7-1/4"	TMK-2, FB	600-750
163	7-1/4"	TMK-3, Sty. Bee	350-335
163	7-1/4"	TMK-4, 3-line	305-335
163	7-1/4"	TMK-5, LB	290-305
163	7-1/4"	TMK-6, MB	290

HUM 164: WORSHIP (Holy Water Font)

From its introduction to the line in the mid-1940s to current production models there have been no significant variations that have any impact on value.

Hum No.	Basic Size	Trademark	Current Value ($)
164	2-3/4"x4-3/4"	TMK-1, CM	100-150
164	2-3/4"x4-3/4"	TMK-2, FB	70-80
164	2-3/4"x4-3/4"	TMK-3, Sty. Bee	60-70
164	2-3/4"x4-3/4"	TMK-4, 3-line	55-60
164	2-3/4"x4-3/4"	TMK-5, LB	50-55
164	2-3/4"x4-3/4"	TMK-6, MB	50

WORSHIP Font, Hum 164, Crown
Mark, black "Germany," 4-13/16".
Right: Stylized Bee mark, 4-7/8".

HUM 165: SWAYING LULLABY (Wall Plaque)

Introduced in the 1940s, this plaque was apparently made in limited quantities and then at some point was removed from production. It does occur in all trademarks, however, and was reinstated in 1978, only to be withdrawn from production again in 1989 with no specific date given for reinstatement.

SWAYING LULLABY
Plaque, Hum 165. Full Bee
mark, 4-1/2" x 5-1/4".

Hum No.	Basic Size	Trademark	Current Value ($)
165	4-1/2"x5-1/4"	TMK-1, CM	600-750
165	4-1/2"x5-1/4"	TMK-2, FB	400-500
165	4-1/2"x5-1/4"	TMK-3, Sty. Bee	300
165	4-1/2"x5-1/4"	TMK-5, LB	200
165	4-1/2"x5-1/4"	TMK-6, MB	200

HUM 166: BOY WITH BIRD (Ashtray)

Introduced into the collection in the mid-1940s, this figure was in continuous production until 1989, when it was listed as temporarily withdrawn with no reinstatement date. There are no significant mold or finish variations.

BOY WITH BIRD Ashtray, Hum 166. Last Bee mark (TM-5), 3-1/4" x 6".

Hum No.	Basic Size	Trademark	Current Value ($)
166	3-1/4"x6-1/4"	TMK-1, CM	300-400
166	3-1/4"x6-1/4"	TMK-2, FB	200-250
166	3-1/4"x6-1/4"	TMK-3, Sty. Bee	160-180
166	3-1/4"x6-1/4"	TMK-4, 3-line	130-150
166	3-1/4"x6-1/4"	TMK-5, LB	100-125
166	3-1/4"x6-1/4"	TMK-6, MB	100-125

HUM 167: ANGEL WITH BIRD (Holy Water Font)

Sometimes called Angel Sitting, this font was first produced in the 1940s. There have been changes over the years but none that have any effect on the normal values. Still in production today.

Hum No.	Basic Size	Trademark	Current Value ($)
167	3-1/4"x4-1/4"	TMK-1, CM	100-125
167	3-1/4"x4-1/4"	TMK-2, FB	75-85
167	3-1/4"x4-1/4"	TMK-3, Sty. Bee	60-70
167	3-1/4"x4-1/4"	TMK-4, 3-line	55-60
167	3-1/4"x4-1/4"	TMK-5, LB	50-55
167	3-1/4"x4-1/4"	TMK-6, MB	50

ANGEL WITH BIRD Font, Hum 167. Stylized Bee mark, 4-1/4".

HUM 168: STANDING BOY (Wall Plaque)

Introduced in the mid-1940s, this figure must have been produced in limited numbers for the first 20 years because examples in the first three trademarks have never been available in any but small quantities. It was taken out of production in the Stylized Bee (TMK-3) period, reinstated in 1978 and taken out of production yet again in 1989 with no published reinstatement date.

Hum No.	Basic Size	Trademark	Current Value ($)
168	4-1/8"x5-1/2"	TMK-1, CM	500-600
168	4-1/8"x5-1/2"	TMK-2, FB	300-400
168	4-1/8"x5-1/2"	TMK-3, Sty. Bee	200-250
168	4-1/8"x5-1/2"	TMK-5, LB	125-150
168	4-1/8"x5-1/2"	TMK-6, MB	125-150

STANDING BOY Plaque, Hum 168. Full Bee mark in an incised circle, 4" x 5-1/2".

HUM 169: BIRD DUET

There are many variations in this figure, but none that have any impact on the normal values of the pieces. It was introduced in the 1940s and has been in continuous production since.

Goebel announced the production of Personal Touch figurines in 1996. Four figurines in the line lend themselves well to this application: Bird Duet is one of these. The other three are Latest News (Hum 184), The Guardian (Hum 455) and For Father (Hum 87). Goebel fire a permanent personalization of your choice onto the figure.

BIRD DUET, Hum 169. Left: Crown Mark, 4". Right: Last Bee mark, 4".

Hum No.	Basic Size	Trademark	Current Value ($)
169	4"	TMK-1, CM	260-325
169	4"	TMK-2, FB	185-220
169	4"	TMK-3, Sty. Bee	160-185
169	4"	TMK-4, 3-line	140-160
169	4"	TMK-5, LB	130-140
169	4"	TMK-6, MB	130

HUM 170: SCHOOL BOYS

Originally released in only one size in the 1940s, this figure was introduced in a new smaller size in the Stylized Bee (TMK-3) period. The larger size, 180/III, was permanently retired by Goebel in 1982. It is now considered a closed edition.

There are no variations important enough to affect values.

SCHOOL BOYS, Hum 170/I. Last Bee trademark, 1961 MID, 7-3/4".

Hum No.	Basic Size	Trademark	Current Value ($)
170/I	7-1/2"	TMK-3, Sty. Bee	1350-1450
170/I	7-1/2"	TMK-4, 3-line	1150-1250
170/I	7-1/2"	TMK-5, LB	1100-1150
170/I	7-1/2"	TMK-6, MB	1100
170	10"	TMK-1, CM	4000-4500
170	10"	TMK-2, FB	3000-3500
170	10"	TMK-3, Sty. Bee	1800-2200
170/III	10"	TMK-3, Sty. Bee	1600-1800
170/III	10"	TMK-4, 3-line	1500
170/III	10"	TMK-5, LB	1500
170/III	10"	TMK-6, MB	1500

HUM 171: LITTLE SWEEPER

First released in the mid-1940s in one size, 171. A smaller size, 171/4/0, was introduced in 1988 as part of a four-piece series with matching mini-plates. As a result of this new mold number, the old 171 was changed to 171/0. There are no variations significant enough to have an impact on collector values.

Hum No.	Basic Size	Trademark	Current Value ($)
171/4/0	3"	TMK-5, LB	90-100
171/4/0	3"	TMK-6, MB	90
171	4-1/2"	TMK-1, CM	240-305
171	4-1/2"	TMK-2, FB	175-200

Hum No.	Basic Size	Trademark	Current Value ($)
171	4-1/2"	TMK-3, Sty. Bee	150-175
171	4-1/2"	TMK-4, 3-line	130-150
171	4-1/2"	TMK-5, LB	120-130
171	4-1/2"	TMK-6, MB	120
171/0	4-1/2"	TMK-6, MB	120

LITTLE SWEEPER, Hum 171. Left: Full bee (TMK-2), 4-3/4", black "Germany." Right: Last Bee (TMK-5), 4-1/4".

HUM 172: FESTIVAL HARMONY (Angel with Mandolin)

The major variations of this figure are found in the Crown and Full Bee marks. The earliest CM and some FB (very rare) have flowers extending from the base well up onto the gown and the bird is perched on top of the flowers (rather than on the mandolin as in later models).

This variation of the piece is valued at $3,000-3,500.

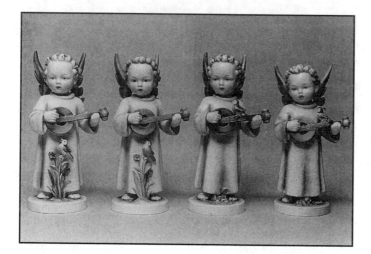

FESTIVAL HARMONY, Hum 172. Left to right (A through D): A. Incised Crown Mark (TMK-1) and a stamped Full Bee (TMK-2) trademark. Donut base, 10-3/4", stamped with "© W. Goebel" beneath the base. B. Same as the previous except for a different bird and a black "Germany." C. A Full Bee piece exhibiting the same characteristics listed for the previous figure except for the now very small flowers and the bird moved to the mandolin. The bird is colored brown. D. This one has a small Stylized Bee trademark. Note the textured gown and the altered flowers. The bird is now colored blue. It measures 10-1/8".

The majority of the Full Bee pieces show the flowers just barely extending up over the bottom edge of the gown and the bird situated on the mandolin. The above variations invariably are found on pieces marked with the plain incised mold number 172.

The 172/II size was temporarily withdrawn from production effective December 31, 1984, with no reinstatement date given.

There is one example in existence where the bird is perched on the arm rather than on the mandolin. This was probably an error in assembly that somehow made it past the quality control inspection. There are several instances of this type of error among other figures with small pieces (such as bottles in baskets), and it usually does not influence value.

Hum No.	Basic Size	Trademark	Current Value ($)
172/4/0	3-1/8"	TMK-7, HM	105
172/0	8"	TMK-4, 3-line	300-350
172/0	8"	TMK-5, LB	280-300
172/0	8"	TMK-6, MB	280
172 (bird on flowers)	10-3/4"	TMK-1, CM	2700-3200
172 (bird on flowers)	10-3/4"	TMK-2, FB	2200-2500
172 (bird on mandolin)	10-3/4"	TMK-2, FB	1000-1300
172 (bird on mandolin)	10-3/4"	TMK-3, Sty. Bee	700-1000
172/II	10-3/4"	TMK-3, Sty. Bee	600-700
172/II	10-3/4"	TMK-4, 3-line	500-550
172/II	10-3/4"	TMK-5, LB	400-425
172/II	10-3/4"	TMK-6, MB	400-425

HUM 173: FESTIVAL HARMONY (Angel with Flute)

The major variations of this figure are to be found with the Crown and Full Bee marks. The Crown and some (very rare) Full Bee pieces have the flowers extending from the base well up onto the gown front. This variation of the piece is valued at $3,000-3,500. Most of the Full Bee pieces have the flowers barely extending from the base up over the bottom edge of the gown.

These variations are always found on the pieces marked with the plain incised 173 with no size designator.

The Hum 173 Crown and Full Bee trademarked figures seem to be in shorter supply than those same pieces in the 172 mold number. Probably they were not sold in the same quantities because of the flutes' vulnerability to breakage.

The 173/II size was temporarily withdrawn from production effective December 31, 1984, and no reinstatement date was given.

FESTIVAL HARMONY, Hum 173. Left to right (A through D): A. Bears the mold number with decimal size designator, 172., an incised Crown Mark (TMK-1) and stamped Full Bee (TMK-2). It measures 1-1/4", has a donut base and a black "Germany."
B. Exhibits the same characteristics as the previous one except it measures 11". C. The mold number on this one is a plain 173. It has a Full Bee trademark, donut base, measures 11" and has a black "Germany." Note the bird is much smaller and the very small flowers. D. This mold number is 173/II, it bears the Missing Bee (TMK-6) trademark and measures 10-7/8". Note the absence of flowers and the textured gown.

Hum No.	Basic Size	Trademark	Current Value ($)
173/0	8"	TMK-3, Sty. Bee	350-375
173/0	8"	TMK-4, 3-line	300-350
173/0	8"	TMK-5, LB	280-300
173/0	8"	TMK-6, MB	280
173 (high flowers)	11"	TMK-1, CM	2900-3400
173 (high flowers)	11"	TMK-2, FB	2400-2700
173 (medium flowers)	11"	TMK-2, FB	1200-1500
173 (low flowers)	11"	TMK-3, Sty. Bee	700-1000
173/II	11"	TMK-3, Sty. Bee	600-700
173/II	11"	TMK-4, 3-line	500-550
173/II	11"	TMK-5, LB	400-425
173/II	11"	TMK-6, MB	400-425

HUM 174: SHE LOVES ME, SHE LOVES ME NOT

Released in the 1940s and in continuous production in one size since then.

The earliest models were produced with eyes open and a very small feather in the hat. A flower was added to the left fence post and the feather grew larger on the Full Bee (TMK-2) pieces, although some are found in the older style. The third change was manifest by the time the Three Line mark (TMK-4) was in use, where the fence post flower is missing and the boy's eyes are downcast. There are transition pieces for each of these changes, so you may encounter the changes associated with more than one trademark. The current production pieces have the eyes down.

Hum No.	Basic Size	Trademark	Current Value ($)
174	4-1/4"	TMK-1, CM	450-550
174	4-1/4"	TMK-2, FB	350-400
174 (eyes up)	4-1/4"	TMK-3, Sty. Bee	250-300
174 (eyes down)	4-1/4"	TMK-3, Sty. Bee	200-225
174	4-1/4"	TMK-4, 3-line	180-190
174	4-1/4"	TMK-5, LB	170
174	4-1/4"	TMK-6, MB	170

SHE LOVES ME, SHE LOVES ME NOT, Hum 174. Left: Full Bee mark in an incised circle, black "Western Germany," 4-3/8". Center: Three Line Mark, incised 1955 MID, 4-3/8". Right: Stylized Bee mark, 4-1/4".

HUM 175: MOTHER'S DARLING

MOTHER'S DARLING, Hum 175. The left figure is older, with an incised Crown Mark (TMK-1) and a black Full Bee (TMK-2) trademark. The one on the right has the Stylized Bee (TMK-3) trademark. They both measure 5-1/2".

The most significant variation of this figure is found in the color of the bags. The older versions have bags colored light pink and yellow-green. The newer ones are blue and red. These variations are insignificant except they allow the collector to spot older pieces without examining the bases. Differences in value are based on earlier trademarks rather than color variation. This figurine will be permanently retired in 1997. During the year all those produced will bear the "Final Issue" backstamp and medallion.

Hum No.	Basic Size	Trademark	Current Value ($)
175	5-1/2"	TMK-1, CM	395-500
175	5-1/2"	TMK-2, FB	275-315
175	5-1/2"	TMK-3, Sty. Bee	240-260
175	5-1/2"	TMK-4, 3-line	210-330
175	5-1/2"	TMK-5, LB	195-210
175	5-1/2"	TMK-6, MB	195

HUM 176: HAPPY BIRTHDAY

The 176/0 has been written "176" (without using the "slash 0" designator) in the Crown and Full Bee marks. In the 5-1/3" size it utilizes the decimal point designator ("176.") in the Crown and Full Bee marks.

The figure was released in the 1940s and is still in production today. There are no mold or finish variations that influence current value.

Hum No.	Basic Size	Trademark	Current Value ($)
176.	5-1/3"	TMK-1, CM	390-500
176.	5-1/3"	TMK-2, FB	300-340
176/0	5-1/2"	TMK-2, FB	275-315

Hum No.	Basic Size	Trademark	Current Value ($)
176/0	5-1/2"	TMK-3, Sty. Bee	240-260
176/0	5-1/2"	TMK-4, 3-line	210-230
176/0	5-1/2"	TMK-5, LB	195-210
176/0	5-1/2"	TMK-6, MB	195
176	6-1/2"-7"	TMK-1, CM	565-700
176	6-1/2"-7"	TMK-2, FB	400-450
176/I	6"	TMK-1, CM	540-675
176/I	6"	TMK-2, FB	385-430
176/I	6"	TMK-3, Sty. Bee	320-360
176/I	6"	TMK-5, LB	270-300
176/I	6"	TMK-6, MB	270

HAPPY BIRTHDAY, Hum 176. Left: Decimal designator in the mold number 176., incised Crown Mark (TMK-1), black "Germany," 5-5/8". Right: Decimal designator in the mold number 176., incised Crown Mark (TMK-1) and Full Bee (TMK-2), donut base, black "Germany," 5-1/2".

HUM 177: SCHOOL GIRLS

First produced in the 1940s, this figure remains in the line today in a smaller size. No mold or finish variations have an influence on value, outside the normal evolutionary changes on the various trademarked figures.

The 177/III was permanently retired in 1989. It is now a closed edition.

SCHOOL GIRLS, Hum 177/I. Last Bee trademark, 1961 MID, 7-1/2".

Hum No.	Basic Size	Trademark	Current Value ($)
177/I	7-1/2"	TMK-3, Sty. Bee	1350-1450
177/I	7-1/2"	TMK-4, 3-line	1150-1250
177/I	7-1/2"	TMK-5, LB	1100-1150
177/I	7-1/2"	TMK-6, MB	1100
177	9-1/2"	TMK-1, CM	4000-4500
177	9-1/2"	TMK-2, FB	3000-3500
177	9-1/2"	TMK-3, Sty. Bee	1800-2200
177/III	9-1/2"	TMK-3, Sty. Bee	1600-1800
177/III	9-1/2"	TMK-4, 3-line	1500
177/III	9-1/2"	TMK-5, LB	1500
177/III	9-1/2"	TMK-6, MB	1500

HUM 178: THE PHOTOGRAPHER

THE PHOTOGRAPHER, Hum 178. Left: Three Line Mark (TMK-4), incised copyright symbol ©, 1948 MID, 4-3/4". Right: Missing Bee (TMK-6), 1948 MID, 4-5/8".

This figure was released about 1950 in only one size and is still produced in the same size.

Color and mold variations exist, but outside of the value differences due to trademark changes the variations have no influence on the value of the pieces.

Hum No.	Basic Size	Trademark	Current Value ($)
178	4-3/4"	TMK-1, CM	520-650
178	4-3/4"	TMK-3, Sty. Bee	300-350
178	4-3/4"	TMK-4, 3-line	275-300
178	4-3/4"	TMK-5, LB	260-275
178	4-3/4"	TMK-6, MB	260

HUM 179: COQUETTES

Older versions of this figure have a blue dress and yellow flowers on the back of the fence posts. The girls are a bit chubbier and the hairstyle of the girl with the red kerchief is swept back.

COQUETTES, Hum 179. Stylized Bee mark (TMK-3), 5".

First released around 1950, this figure was not produced with any mold or finish variations that significantly impact its price.

Hum No.	Basic Size	Trademark	Current Value ($)
179	5-1/4"	TMK-1, CM	520-650
179	5-1/4"	TMK-2, FB	375-425
179	5-1/4"	TMK-3, Sty. Bee	300-350
179	5-1/4"	TMK-4, 3-line	275-300
179	5-1/4"	TMK-5, LB	260-275
179	5-1/4"	TMK-6, MB	260

HUM 180: TUNEFUL GOODNIGHT (Wall Plaque)

This plaque is rare in the older marks. It is sometimes called Happy Bugler, is 5" x 4-3/4" in size and was redesigned toward the end of the Last Bee trademark era. The newer design has the bugle in a more forward position, making it very vulnerable to breakage.

The piece was originally released about 1950. There are no important variations affecting value.

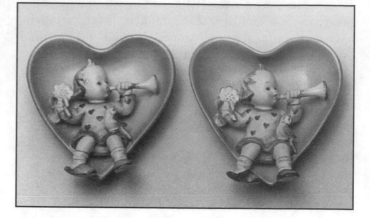

Hum No.	Basic Size	Trademark	Current Value ($)
180	4"x4-3/4"	TMK-1, CM	500-600
180	4"x4-3/4"	TMK-2, FB	350-450
180	4"x4-3/4"	TMK-3, Sty. Bee	250-300
180	4"x4-3/4"	TMK-4, 3-line	200-225
180	4"x4-3/4"	TMK-5, LB	200
180 (new style)	4"x4-3/4"	TMK-6, LB	200

TUNEFUL GOOD NIGHT Plaque, Hum 180. Left: Incised Crown Mark, 4-3/4" x 5". Right: Stylized Bee in an incised circle, black "West Germany," 4-3/4" x 5".

HUM 181, 189, 190, 191 and 202: OLD PEOPLE "THE MAMAS AND THE PAPAS" (Closed Numbers)

These are the only known M.I. Hummel figurines to feature old people as their subject. They are more like caricatures than realistic renderings. The first four were discovered in Europe by an American collector. The fifth piece, a table lamp (Hum 202), turned up later. These discoveries filled in gaps in the mold number sequence previously designated closed numbers, the term Goebel applies to pieces never placed in production. At least three complete sets of the five pieces are positively known to exist: one set in the company archives and two others in private collections. There have been other single pieces found and there are reports of three or more sets in the U.S. There is little doubt that some others do exist, either singly or in sets, but the number is likely to be extremely small. They were made in samples only and apparently rejected by the Siessen Convent as atypical of Hummel art. Collector value is about $20,000 for each.

THE MAMAS AND PAPAS. Left: Hum 181, OLD MAN READING NEWSPAPER, 6-3/8". Right: Hum 189, OLD WOMAN KNITTING, 6-13/16".

Hum 181	OLD MAN READING NEWSPAPER
Hum 189	OLD WOMAN KNITTING
Hum 190	OLD WOMAN WALKING TO MARKET
Hum 191	OLD MAN WALKING TO MARKET
Hum 202	Hum 181 above as TABLE LAMP

HUM 182: GOOD FRIENDS

Released around the late 1940s, Good Friends remains in production today. Produced in one size only, there are no variations influencing the regular collector value for the various trademarked pieces.

Hum No.	Basic Size	Trademark	Current Value ($)
182	4"	TMK-1, CM	350-425
182	4"	TMK-2, FB	250-280
182	4"	TMK-3, Sty. Bee	215-240
182	4"	TMK-4, 3-line	185-210
182	4"	TMK-5, LB	175-185
182	4"	TMK-6, MB	175-185

GOOD FRIENDS, Hum 182. Left: Stylized Bee (TMK-3), donut base, 4". Right: Missing Bee (TMK-6), 4-1/4".

HUM 183: FOREST SHRINE

This figure was released some time around the late 1940s. Apparently the figures were produced in limited quantities because those with early trademarks are in short supply. They were removed from production some time around the end of the Stylized Bee (TMK-3) period, but put back in 1977. This is probably the reason they are not found bearing the Three Line Mark (TMK-4).

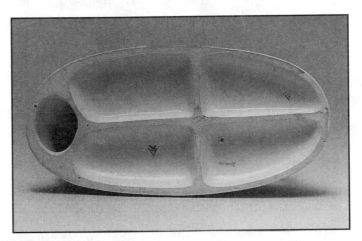

FOREST SHRINE, Hum 183. showing the base split in quarters.

Hum No.	Basic Size	Trademark	Current Value ($)
183	7"x9"	TMK-1, CM	1000-1200
183	7"x9"	TMK-2, FB	800-900
183	7"x9"	TMK-3, Sty. Bee	600-700
183	7"x9"	TMK-5, LB	500
183	7"x9"	TMK-6, MB	500

FOREST SHRINE, Hum 183. Left: Decimal designator with mold number, 183., incised Crown mark (TMK-1) and stamped Full bee (TMK-2) mark, black "Germany," split base, 9". Right: Missing Bee (TMK-6), 9".

HUM 184: LATEST NEWS

First produced about 1946, the older pieces have square bases and wide-open eyes. The figures are found with a variety of newspaper names. For a time the figures were produced with any name requested by merchants (i.e. their hometown newspapers). The figure was remodeled in the 1960s and given a round base and lowered eyes so the boy appears more like he is reading his paper. Later models bear the newspaper names "Das Allerneuste," "Latest News" and "Munchener Presse." As of 1985 the only newspaper name used was "Latest News." These three titles are the most common. Some of the rarer titles can range in value from $750 to $1,500. Be careful in cleaning these items: if you rub too hard or use harsh cleaners you may rub off the titles. The figures were also produced for a time with no titles.

In 1996 Goebel began producing a special limited edition of Latest News. This design used the U.S. Armed Forces newspaper masthead *Stars and Stripes* on the front page and a drawing of the famous Checkpoint Charlie of the Berlin Wall on the back page. The edition is limited to 20,000.

Another special edition produced in 1996 is entitled The Chancellor's Visit. A special backstamp identifies it as such. This figure was accompanied by a wooden base with a brass plate reading: "In commemoration of Chancellor Dr. Helmut Kohl's historic meeting with President Bill Clinton, Milwaukee, Wisconsin, May 23 1996." The newspaper is imprinted with the *Milwaukee Journal-Sentinel* masthead and the headline reads "Clinton and Chancellor Helmut Kolb Meet in Milwaukee Today." An undisclosed number (probably very few) of these figures were produced in a limited edition for Mader's Tower Gallery.

Goebel announced the production of Personal Touch figurines in 1996. Four figurines in the line lend themselves well to this application: Latest News is one of these. The other three are Bird Duet (Hum 169), The Guardian (Hum 455) and For Father (Hum 87).

LATEST NEWS, Hum 184. Left to right (A through D): A. Daily Mail. Has the decimal designator in the mold number 184., Crown Mark (TMK-1), U.S. ZONE Germany in a rectangular box beneath. B. Bermuda News, 1909-1959. C. Latest News. Stylized Bee (TMK-3) mark in an incised circle, black "Western Germany." D. "LB Goebel - NACH." Last Bee (TMK-5) trademark. Note the round base. All four measure 5-1/8".

Hum No.	Basic Size	Trademark	Current Value ($)
184	5-1/4"	TMK-1, CM	520-650
184	5-1/4"	TMK-2, FB	375-425
184	5-1/4"	TMK-3, Sty. Bee	300-350
184	5-1/4"	TMK-4, 3-line	275-300
184	5-1/4"	TMK-5, LB	260-275
184	5-1/4"	TMK-6, MB	260

HUM 185: ACCORDION BOY

First released sometime around the late 1940s, this model remains in the line today. Produced in only one size through the years, there have been no significant variations in the mold or the finish that would affect value.

Hum No.	Basic Size	Trademark	Current Value ($)
185	5-1/4"	TMK-1, CM	360-450
185	5-1/4"	TMK-2, FB	260-290
185	5-1/4"	TMK-3, Sty. Bee	225-250
185	5-1/4"	TMK-4, 3-line	190-225
185	5-1/4"	TMK-5, LB	180-190
185	5-1/4"	TMK-6, MB	180

ACCORDION BOY, Hum 185. Left: 185., Incised Full Bee mark, black "Germany," donut base, 5-1/2". Right: Stylized Bee mark, 5-3/8".

HUM 186: SWEET MUSIC

This piece appeared in the collection around the late 1940s. The most significant variation of Sweet Music is the striped slippers shown on the figure in the accompanying photo. It is found on the Crown Mark (TMK-1) figures and will bring $1,000-1,200, depending upon condition. The plain painted slippers are also found on Crown Mark era figures.

Hum No.	Basic Size	Trademark	Current Value ($)
186	5-1/4"	TMK-1, CM	360-450
186	5-1/4"	TMK-2, FB	260-290
186	5-1/4"	TMK-3, Sty. Bee	225-250
186	5-1/4"	TMK-4, 3-line	190-225
186	5-1/4"	TMK-5, LB	180-190
186	5-1/4"	TMK-6, MB	180

SWEET MUSIC, Hum 186. Left: Full Bee mark, black "Germany," 5-1/4". Right: Stylized Bee mark, black "Western Germany," 5".

SWEET MUSIC , Hum 186 (with striped slippers). Left: Full Bee mark, black "Germany," 5-1/4". Right: Stylized Bee mark, black "Western Germany," 5".

HUM 187: DEALER PLAQUES and DISPLAY PLAQUES

The 187 mold number was used on all dealer plaques until 1986, when it was taken out of production (see Hum 460). The older pieces have the traditional bumblebee perched on top. The piece was redesigned in 1972 to have a raised round area known as the "moon top" in place of the traditional bumblebee and was imprinted with the Stylized Bee trademark. The plaques in current production do not have this round medallion-like area. Some plaques have been found with the mold numbers 187/A and 187/C.

The accompanying picture is of a special edition of the display plaque made available for a short time to local chapter members of the Goebel Collectors' Club. As you

STORE or DISPLAY PLAQUE, Hum 187, Full Bee mark, "© W. Goebel".

A specially customized Hum 187 Dealer Plaque. Goebel has been known to do this for dealers from time to time.

STORE or DISPLAY PLAQUE, Hum 187.

STORE or DISPLAY PLAQUE, Hum 187. A special edition commemorating 100 years of service by the Army and Air Force Exchange Service (AAFES).

STORE or DISPLAY PLAQUES, Hum 187. Left to right (A through D): A. Stylized Bee in the "moon top," plaque bears the Three Line Mark and an incised 1947 MID on the base, 3-3/4". B. 187/A, Last Bee mark, incised 1976 MID, 3-5/8". C. 187/A, Missing Bee mark, incised 1976 MID, 3-5/8". D. Last Bee mark, incised 1947 MID, 3-5/8".

can see they were personalized with chapter and member name.

A number of the 187-mold plaques in existence in Europe were made specifically for individual stores and displayed the store name, in addition to the traditional wordings.

Please see the description of the Goebel Employee Service Plaque in chapter 5.

Hum No.	Basic Size	Trademark	Current Value ($)
187	4"x5 1/2"	TMK-1, CM	650
187	4"x5 1/2"	TMK-2, FB	550
187	4"x5 1/2"	TMK-3, Sty. Bee	450
187 (with bumblebee)	4"x5 1/2"	TMK-4, 3-line	600
187 (with Moon Top)	4"x5 1/2"	TMK-4, 3-line	325-375
187*	4"x5 1/2"	TMK-5, LB	125-150
187*	4"x5 1/2"	TMK-6, MB	125-150

*A suggested retail price list from a few years ago indicates the availability of a "Display Plaque Retailer" and a "Display Plaque Collector." The list suggested that each bore the 187 mold number. Neither are offered anymore.

STORE or DISPLAY PLAQUES. Left to right (A through D): A. Hum 187, but there is no apparent mold number or trademark. Measures 3-3/4". B. Hum 187, Full Bee mark, 3-3/4". "SCHMID BROS. Inc. BOSTON" *painted* on the satchel. The rare variation is in bas-relief, molded in. C. Hum 211, Full Bee, white overglaze, 3-7/8". D. Hum 213, Spanish language, Full Bee mark, "(R)," 4".

HUM 188: CELESTIAL MUSICIAN

Until 1983 this piece was made only in the 7" size, with a mold number of 188. Beginning in 1983 a smaller size was produced. The smaller size is 5-1/2" and bears the mold number 188/0. At the same time the mold number of the 188 was changed to 188/I on the TMK-7, current production pieces, to reflect the difference.

This figure has reportedly surfaced in white overglaze. Other than that, there have been no significant variations that would influence normal values for the various trademarked pieces.

Hum No.	Basic Size	Trademark	Current Value ($)
188/4/0	3-1/8"	TMK-6, MB	90
188/0	5"	TMK-5, LB	195
188/0	5"	TMK-6, MB	195
188	7"	TMK-1, CM	500-650
188	7"	TMK-2, FB	355-405
188	7"	TMK-3, Sty. Bee	300-355
188	7"	TMK-4, 3-line	260-290
188	7"	TMK-5, LB	250-260
188	7"	TMK-6, MB	250

CELESTIAL MUSICIAN, Hum 188. Left: Three Line Mark, incised 1948 MID, 6-3/4". Right: Missing Bee mark, incised 1948 MID, 7".

HUM 189, 190, 191: OLD PEOPLE "THE MAMAS AND THE PAPAS"

(See description under HUM 181.)

HUM 192: CANDLELIGHT

There are two distinct versions of this piece. The chief difference is found in the candle receptacle. This variation is found on the Crown Mark (TMK-1) and Full Bee (TMK-2) figurines. The transition from this older style to the newer one where the candle socket is held in the hand (no extension) took place in the Stylized Bee (TMK-3) era, so you may also find the old design so marked.

Hum No.	Basic Size	Trademark	Current Value ($)
192 (long candle)	6-1/4"	TMK-1, CM	700-800
192 (long candle)	6-3/4"	TMK-2, FB	500-600
192 (long candle)	6-3/4"	TMK-3, Sty. Bee	350
192 (regular)	6-3/4"	TMK-3, Sty. Bee	250-275
192 (regular)	6-3/4"	TMK-4, 3-line	220-250
192 (regular)	6-3/4"	TMK-5, LB	210-220
192 (regular)	6-3/4"	TMK-6, MB	210

CANDLELIGHT, Hum 192. Left: Incised Full Bee mark (TMK-2). "© W. Goebel," black "Germany," donut base, 6-3/4". Right: Last Bee mark (TMK-5), incised 1948 MID, 6-3/4".

HUM 193: ANGEL DUET (Candleholder)

Essentially the same design as Hum 261 except that the 261 is not a candleholder. Figure 193 has been produced in two variations, noticeable in the rear view of the figure. One shows the angel not holding the song book and with an arm around the waist of the other. In the other design one angel has a hand on the shoulder of the other angel. Both versions are found in Crown Mark (TMK-1) and Full Bee (TMK-2) Mark. The transition to the new arm-around-waist figure took place during the Full Bee trademark period.

This piece has been found in white overglaze. The value of this variation is $1,200-1,500.

Hum No.	Basic Size	Trademark	Current Value ($)
193	5"	TMK-1, CM	400-500
193	5"	TMK-2, FB	275-325
193	5"	TMK-3, Sty. Bee	235-275
193	5"	TMK-4, 3-line	210-235
193	5"	TMK-5, LB	200-210
193	5"	TMK-6, MB	200

ANGEL DUET candleholder, Hum 193. Missing Bee mark (TMK-6), 5".

HUM 194: WATCHFUL ANGEL

Once called "Angelic Care," this figurine entered the line around the late 1940s. There are no significant mold or finish variations reported.

WATCHFUL ANGEL, Hum 194. Three Line mark, incised 1948 MID, 6-1/2".

Hum No.	Basic Size	Trademark	Current Value ($)
194	6-1/2"	TMK-1, CM	580-725
194	6-1/2"	TMK-2, FB	410-460
194	6-1/2"	TMK-3, Sty. Bee	350-385
194	6-1/2"	TMK-4, 3-line	305-345
194	6-1/2"	TMK-5, LB	290-305
194	6-1/2"	TMK-6, MB	290

HUM 195: BARNYARD HERO

Introduced into the line in the late 1940s. This figure has undergone some major mold changes over the years, but most were associated with a trademark change or a change in the finish of the entire collection. None has had a significant influence on collector values.

Hum No.	Basic Size	Trademark	Current Value ($)
195/2/0	4"	TMK-2, FB	300-375
195/2/0	4"	TMK-3, Sty. Bee	180-220
195/2/0	4"	TMK-4, 3-line	160-180
195/2/0	4"	TMK-5, LB	150-160
195/2/0	4"	TMK-6, MB	150
195	5-3/4"-6"	TMK-1, CM	700-800
195	5-3/4"-6"	TMK-2, FB	500-550
195/I	5-3/4"-6"	TMK-2, FB	450-500
195/I	5-3/4"	TMK-3, Sty. Bee	375-400
195/I	5-3/4"	TMK-4, 3-line	310-350
195/I	5-3/4"	TMK-5, LB	290-310
195/I	5-3/4"	TMK-6, MB	290

BARNYARD HERO, Hum 195. Left: Incised Crown mark and a stamped Full Bee mark, split base, black "Germany," blue "© W. Goebel," 5-3/4". Right: 195/1, Three Line mark, incised 1948 MID, 5-3/4".

HUM 196: TELLING HER SECRET

This figurine was introduced sometime in the late 1940s in a 6-3/4" basic size. During the Full Bee (TMK-2) trademark period a second, smaller size, 196/0, was introduced. With this came a change of the mold number for the larger one, from 196 to 196/I. The Full Bee (TMK-2) can be found with either mold number.

Hum No.	Basic Size	Trademark	Current Value ($)
196/0	5-1/4"	TMK-2, FB	375-425
196/0	5-1/4"	TMK-3, Sty. Bee	325-375
196/0	5-1/4"	TMK-4, 3-line	280-325
196/0	5-1/4"	TMK-5, LB	270-280
196/0	5-1/4"	TMK-6, MB	270
196	6-3/4"	TMK-1, CM	900-1400
196/I	6-3/4"	TMK-2, FB	700-800
196/I	6-3/4"	TMK-2, FB	600-700
196/I	6-3/4"	TMK-3, Sty. Bee	470-485
196/I	6-3/4"	TMK-4, 3-line	450-470
196/I	6-3/4"	TMK-5, LB	430-450
196/I	6-3/4"	TMK-6, MB	430

TELLING HER SECRET, Hum 196. Left: 196/1, Full Bee mark in an incised circle, incised 1948 MID, black "Western Germany," 6-1/2". Right: 196/0, Missing Bee mark, incised 1948 MID, 5-1/2". White overglaze.

HUM 197: BE PATIENT

There are no important mold or finish variations to be found on this late 1940s release. There is, however, a mold number variation that is significant. The figure was first produced in only one size with an incised mold number of 197. When a smaller size, 197/2/0, was produced in the Stylized Bee\ (TMK-3) period, the mold number on the larger one was changed to 197/I.

Attendees of the 1994 Disneyana Convention were given the opportunity to purchase a limited edition set of figurines on a wooden base. A regular-production Be Patient (Hum 197/2/0) bearing TMK-7 was paired with a Minnie Mouse figurine posed the same way. Minnie bears the incised mold number 17324, a limited edition indicator and TMK-7. The issue price for the set was $395. It can now bring around $500-650.

Hum No.	Basic Size	Trademark	Current Value ($)
197/2/0	4-1/4"	TMK-2, FB	300-375
197/2/0	4-1/4"	TMK-3, Sty. Bee	180-220
197/2/0	4-1/4"	TMK-4, 3-line	160-180
197/2/0	4-1/4"	TMK-5, LB	150-160
197/2/0	4-1/4"	TMK-6, MB	150
197	6-1/4"	TMK-1, CM	700-800
197	6-1/4"	TMK-2, FB	500-550
197/I	6-1/4"	TMK-2, FB	450-500
197/I	6-1/4"	TMK-3, Sty. Bee	375-400
197/I	6-1/4"	TMK-4, 3-line	310-350
197/I	6-1/4"	TMK-5, LB	290-310
197/I	6-1/4"	TMK-6, MB	290

BE PATIENT, Hum 197. Left: Full Bee mark "© W. Goebel," black "Germany," 6-1/2". Right: 197/I, Last Bee mark, incised 1948 MID, 6".

HUM 198: HOME FROM MARKET

There are no important mold or finish variations to be found on this late 1940s release. There is, however, a mold number variation that is significant. The figure was first produced in only one size with the incised mold number 198. When a smaller size, 198/2/0, was issued in the Stylized Bee (TMK-3) period, the mold number of the larger figure was changed to 198/I.

Hum No.	Basic Size	Trademark	Current Value ($)
198/2/0	4-3/4"	TMK-2, FB	180-225
198/2/0	4-3/4"	TMK-3, Sty. Bee	155-180

Hum No.	Basic Size	Trademark	Current Value ($)
198/2/0	4-3/4"	TMK-4, 3-line	140-150
198/2/0	4-3/4"	TMK-5, LB	130-140
198/2/0	4-3/4"	TMK-6, MB	130
198	5-3/4"	TMK-1, CM	290-500
198	5-3/4"	TMK-2, FB	300-350
198/I	5-3/4"	TMK-2, FB	275-315
198/I	5-3/4"	TMK-3, Sty. Bee	240-260
198/I	5-3/4"	TMK-4, 3-line	210-230
198/I	5-3/4"	TMK-5, LB	195-210
198/I	5-3/4"	TMK-6, MB	195

HOME FROM MARKET, Hum 198. Left: Full Bee mark in an incised circle, 1948 MID, black "Germany," © by W. Goebel, 5-7/8". Right: 198/1, Three Line mark (TMK-4), 1948 MID, donut base, 5-1/2".

HOME FROM MARKET, Hum 198, with a red line on the base. This indicates that this particular piece was a master model at one time. Note the archive medallion wired and sealed around the legs.

HUM 199: FEEDING TIME

There are no major mold or finish variations outside the normal evolution of this figurine. There is, however, a mold number variation that is important. This piece was first produced in the late 1940s in only one size with the incised mold number 199. It was also sometimes found as "199." with the decimal designator. When a new smaller size, 199/0, was introduced during the Stylized Bee (TMK-3) era, the trademark on the larger size was changed to 199/I.

The older pieces have blonde hair and the newer ones dark hair.

FEEDING TIME, Hum 199. Left: Full Bee mark, black "Germany," "© W. Goebel," donut base, 5-1/2". Right: 199/1. Full Bee in an incised circle, black "Germany," "© W. Goebel," incised 1948 MID, donut base, 5-1/2".

Hum No.	Basic Size	Trademark	Current Value ($)
199/0	4-1/4"	TMK-2, FB	250-275
199/0	4-1/4"	TMK-3, Sty. Bee	210-250
199/0	4-1/4"	TMK-4, 3-line	185-215
199/0	4-1/4"	TMK-5, LB	175-185
199/0	4-1/4"	TMK-6, MB	175
199 or 199.	5-3/4"	TMK-1, CM	480-600
199 or 199.	5-3/4"	TMK-2, FB	325-400
199/I	5-3/4"	TMK-2, FB	325-400
199/I	5-3/4"	TMK-3, Sty. Bee	275-325
199/I	5-3/4"	TMK-4, 3-line	250-275
199/I	5-3/4"	TMK-5, LB	240-250
199/I	5-3/4"	TMK-6, MB	240

HUM 200: LITTLE GOAT HERDER

There are no important mold or color variations outside those occurring during the normal evolution of the figure. There is, however, a mold number variation that is significant. This figure was first produced in only one size, with the incised mold number 200. It also sometimes appeared as "200." with the decimal designator. When a new smaller basic size of 4-3/4" was introduced in the Stylized Bee (TMK-3) era, the mold number on the larger size was changed to 200/I.

LITTLE GOAT HERDER, Hum 200. Both of these are the same basic size, according to their mold numbers, though they differ in actual measurement. The larger one on the left is the 200/I measuring 5-3/4", has a Full Bee (TMK-2) trademark in an incised circle, a "© by W. Goebel," a black "Germany" and a 1948 MID. The one on the right is the 200/I measuring 5-1/4", has a Three Line Mark (TMK-4) piece and also has an incised 1948 MID.

Hum No.	Basic Size	Trademark	Current Value ($)
200/0	4-3/4"	TMK-2, FB	250-275
200/0	4-3/4"	TMK-3, Sty. Bee	210-250
200/0	4-3/4"	TMK-4, 3-line	185-215
200/0	4-3/4"	TMK-5, LB	175-185
200/0	4-3/4"	TMK-6, MB	175
200 or 200.	5-1/2"	TMK-1, CM	440-550
200 or 200.	5-1/2"	TMK-2, FB	325-400
200/I	5-1/2"	TMK-2, FB	300-350
200/I	5-1/2"	TMK-3, Sty. Bee	250-300
200/I	5-1/2"	TMK-4, 3-line	230-250
200/I	5-1/2"	TMK-5, LB	220-230
200/I	5-1/2"	TMK-6, MB	220

IIUM 201: RETREAT TO SAFETY

There are no important mold or finish variations outside those occurring during the normal evolution of this figure. There is, however, a significant mold number variation. The figure was first produced in one size only with the incised mold number 201. It also sometimes appeared with the decimal point designator. When a new smaller size of 4" was introduced during the Stylized Bee (TMK-3) era, the mold number on the 5-1/2" size was changed to 201/I.

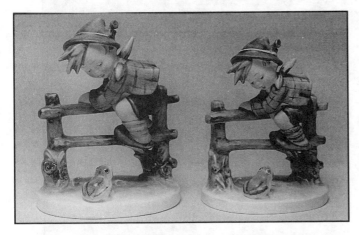

RETREAT TO SAFETY, Hum 201. Left: Full Bee mark with a "(R)" associated, "© W. Goebel," black "Germany," split base, 6". Right: 201/I, 3-line mark, incised 1948 MID, 5-3/8".

Hum No.	Basic Size	Trademark	Current Value ($)
201/2/0	4"	TMK-2, FB	300-375
201/2/0	4"	TMK-3, Sty. Bee	180-220
201/2/0	4"	TMK-4, 3-line	160-180
201/2/0	4"	TMK-5, LB	150-160
201/2/0	4"	TMK-6, MB	150
201. or 201	5-1/2"	TMK-1, CM	700-800
201. or 201	5-1/2"	TMK-2, FB	500-550
201/I	5-1/2"	TMK-2, FB	450-500
201/I	5-1/2"	TMK-3, Sty. Bee	375-400
201/I	5-1/2"	TMK-4, 3-line	310-350
201/I	5-1/2"	TMK-5, LB	290-310
201/I	5-1/2"	TMK-6, MB	290

HUM 202: OLD MAN READING NEWSPAPER (Table Lamp) (Closed Number)

(See description under HUM 181.)

HUM 203: SIGNS OF SPRING

Released about 1950, there is a significant mold variation in the 4" basic size, 203/2/0. This size was introduced in the Full Bee (TMK-2) period, when the figure had both feet on the ground and was wearing shoes. At some point during this period, it was remodeled so that her right foot is raised above the ground and the foot has no shoe on. The first variation is the more scarce and is valued at about $600-750.

Another mold variation is worthy of note. One version of this figure has four fence pickets instead of the usual three, and there are more flowers present. The mold number of the example in the photo appears to have been scratched into the figure by hand before firing. This is probably a prototype, for no more have surfaced.

There is also a variation in mold numbering. This figure was first released in the 201 mold number in only the 5" size. When the smaller 4" size, 203/2/0, was released in the Full Bee era, the mold number of the larger size was changed to 203/I. The earlier "203" is also occasionally found with the decimal designator. Both sizes have been permanently retired.

Base of the four picket variation showing the unusual split base. Stamped Full Bee, "© W. Goebel," black "Germany." The mold number appears to have been rendered by hand.

Hum No.	Basic Size	Trademark	Current Value ($)
203/2/0	4"	TMK-1, CM	360-430
203/2/0	4"	TMK-2, FB	225-325
203/2/0	4"	TMK-3, Sty. Bee	175-200
203/2/0	4"	TMK-4, 3-line	150-175
203/2/0	4"	TMK-5, LB	140-150
203/2/0	4"	TMK-6, MB	140
203 or 203.	5"	TMK-1, CM	400-500
203 or 203.	5"	TMK-2, FB	325-375
203/I	5"	TMK-2, FB	275-325
203/I	5"	TMK-3, Sty. Bee	225-275
203/I	5"	TMK-4, 3-line	210-230
203/I	5"	TMK-5, LB	200-210
203/I	5"	TMK-6, MB	200

SIGNS OF SPRING, Hum 203/1. Three Line Mark (TMK-4), 1948 MID, 5".

SIGNS OF SPRING, Hum 203. This is a very rare and unusual variation. Note the fourth fence post and additional flowers.

HUM 204: WEARY WANDERER

There is a major variation associated with this figurine. The normal figurine has eyes painted with no color. The variation has blue eyes. There are only five blue-eyed pieces presently known to be in collectors' hands. These are valued at about $5,000 each.

This figure was introduced sometime in the early 1950s. There are no other significant variations affecting values.

Hum No.	Basic Size	Trademark	Current Value ($)
204	6"	TMK-1, CM	450-575
204	6"	TMK-2, FB	325-380
204	6"	TMK-3, Sty. Bee	275-300
204	6"	TMK-4, 3-line	240-275
204	6"	TMK-5, LB	225-240
204	6"	TMK-6, MB	225

WEARY WANDERER, Hum 204. Left: Incised Full Bee (TMK-2) mark, black "Germany," © W. Goebel, 5-7/8". Right: Stamped Full Bee (TMK-2), black "Germany," © W. Goebel,

HUM 205: DEALER PLAQUES or DISPLAY PLAQUES

The following list is of merchant display plaques used by dealers. Each has a large bumblebee perched atop the plaque and a Merry Wanderer figure attached to the right side. All are 5-1/4" x 4-1/4" in basic size. Variations are noted at each listing. See also Hum 187.

Hum 205 (German Language) occurs in the Crown, Full Bee, Stylized Bee and 3-line trademarks. Valued at $1,000 to $1,200.

Hum 208 (French Language) occurs in the Crown, Full Bee and Stylized Bee trademarks. Valued at about $3,500 to 5,000.

Hum 209 (Swedish Language) occurs in the Crown, Full Bee and Stylized Bee trademarks. Valued at about $3,500 to 5,000. Two distinctly different lettering designs have been found.

Hum 210 (English Language) is the Schmid Brothers display plaque, made specifically for this distributor. "Schmid Bros., Boston" is found molded in bas-relief on the suitcase. There are only four pieces presently known to exist. If found, this significant piece would likely bring about $12,000.

Hum 211 (English Language). There are only two presently known to exist in collectors' hands. One is in white overglaze with no color and one is in full color. This is the only dealer plaque to use the word "Oeslau" as the location of Goebel in Bavaria. The name has since been changed to Rodental, but this is not found on any plaques. (See photo.)

Hum 213 (Spanish Language) occurs in the Crown, Full Bee and Stylized Bee trademarks. Valued at $5,000-7,500. (See photo.)

STORE or DISPLAY PLAQUES. Left: Hum 205, German language, incised Crown mark and a Stylized Bee mark, 4". Center: Hum 208, French language, Full Bee mark, 3-3/4". Right: Hum 209, Swedish language, Full Bee mark, 3-3/4".

HUM 206: ANGEL CLOUD (Holy Water Font)

ANGEL CLOUD Font, Hum 206. Three Line mark, incised 1949 MID, 4-3/4".

Released in the early 1950s, this figure has been redesigned several times. It has been in and out of production since the beginning but apparently in very limited quantities each time. The older trademarks have always been in short supply.

Hum No.	Basic Size	Trademark	Current Value ($)
206	2-1/4"x4-3/4"	TMK-1, CM	200-250
206	2-1/4"x4-3/4"	TMK-2, FB	100-150
206	2-1/4"x4-3/4"	TMK-3, Sty. Bee	90-100
206	2-1/4"x4-3/4"	TMK-4, 3-line	60-80
206	2-1/4"x4-3/4"	TMK-5, LB	50
206	2-1/4"x4-3/4"	TMK-6, MB	50

HUM 207: HEAVENLY ANGEL (Holy Water Font)

First released in the early 1950s, this piece has the distinction of the highest mold number in the collection that can be found with the Crown Mark (TMK-1). There are a number of variations to be found, but none have any significant impact on collector value.

Hum No.	Basic Size	Trademark	Current Value ($)
207	2"x4-3/4"	TMK-1, CM	200-250
207	2"x4-3/4"	TMK-2, FB	100-150
207	2"x4-3/4"	TMK-3, Sty. Bee	90-100
207	2"x4-3/4"	TMK-4, 3-line	60-80
207	2"x4-3/4"	TMK-5, LB	50
207	2"x4-3/4"	TMK-6, MB	50

HEAVENLY ANGEL Font, Hum 207. Three Line mark, incised 1949 MID, 5".

HUM 208-211: DEALER PLAQUES

(See description under HUM 205.)

HUM 212: UNKNOWN (Closed Number)

This was previously suspected to be another dealer plaque. Then it was thought that this number was intended to be utilized with the letters A through F as mold numbers for a set of musician pieces called Orchestra. It is now known that this mold number was used for a short time merely as an inventory designation for the Band Leader (Hum 129) and several of the musical figurines. The number was not incised on the figures.

HUM 214: NATIVITY SET

In the early Hum 214 sets the Madonna and infant Jesus were molded as one piece. The later figures are found as two separate pieces. Hum 366 (the Flying Angel) is frequently used with this set. One old model camel and two more recently issued camels are also frequently used with the set, but these are not Hummel pieces.

Collectors may note the omission of 214/I in the listing below. It has long been assumed that the mold number was never used because of the possible confusion that might result from the similarity of the "I" and the "1" when incised as a mold number. The existence of a Hum 214/I has now been substantiated. The piece found is in white overglaze and is of two connected geese similar to the geese in the Goose Girl figure. It has the incised M.I. Hummel signature.

Hum No.	Size	Figure	TMK-2($)	TMK-3($)	TMK-4($)	TMK-5($)	TMK-6($)
214/A	6-1/2"	Madonna & Jesus	815-1000	140-160	110-140	110-140	110-140
214/A/K	1-1/2"	Infant Jesus	None	45-65	40-45	40-45	35-40
214/B	7-1/2"	Joseph	175	140-160	130-140	100-105	100-105
214/C	3-1/2"	Goodnight	100-150	75-90	75-90	75-90	75-90
214/D	3"	Angel Serenade	100-150	75-90	75-95	75-95	75-95
214/E	3-1/4"	We Congratulate	200-300	170-200	170-200	170-200	170-200
214/F	7-1/2"	Shepherd With Sheep	195-225	140-170	130-140	100-110	100-110
214/G	3-3/4"	Shepherd Boy	185-290	170-200	90-105	75-100	75-80
214/H	3-3/4"	Little Tooter	125-150	100-125	100-125	100-125	100
214/J	5-1/4"	Donkey	75-105	60-75	50-65	50-65	50-60
214/K	6-1/2"	Cow	75-105	60-70	50-60	50-60	50-60
214/L	8-1/2"	Moor King	150	140-160	135-140	100-105	100-105
214/M	5-3/4"	King (Kneeling on one knee)	150	140-160	135-140	100-105	100-105
214/N	5-1/2"	King (Kneeling on both knees)	150	140-160	110-115	95-100	95-100
214/O	2-1/4"	Lamb	25	10-15	10-15	10-15	10-15

In 1988 Goebel began a three-year program to introduce a smaller, third size of the Nativity Set. These are offered as three- or four-piece sets in the initial years of the offer and as separate pieces subsequently. They were offered as follows: *(Cont'd. next page)*

The number 214 size NATIVITY SET.

Hum No.	Size	Figure	Current Value ($)
214/A/M/0	5-1/4"	Madonna	75-85
214/J/0	6-1/8"	Joseph	75-85.99
214/K/0	2-7/8"	Jesus	25-30

Hum No.	Size	Figure	Current Value ($)
214/L/0	6-1/2"	King (standing)	90-100
214/M/0	4"	King (on one knee)	80-90
214/N/0	4-1/2"	King (on both knees)	80-85

Hum No.	Size	Figure	Current Value ($)
366/0	2-3/4"	Flying Angel	60-65
214/J/0	3-7/8"	Donkey	30-35
214/K/0	2-3/4"	Ox	30-35
214/O/0	1-1/2"	Lamb	10-15

Hum No.	Size	Figure	Current Value ($)
214/F/0	5-3/4"	Shepherd (w/sheep)	90-100
214/G/0	4"	Shepherd Boy	70-75
214/H/0	3"	Little Tooter	20-25

HUM 215: UNKNOWN (Closed Number)

Not likely to be found. Records indicate it could possibly be a standing child Jesus holding a lamb in his arms.

HUM 216: UNKNOWN (Closed Number)

Not likely to be found. No known examples anywhere. Records indicate it might be a Joyful (Hum 53) ashtray, if it exists.

HUM 217: BOY WITH TOOTHACHE

This figure, released in the 1950s, has no significant mold or finish variations affecting the normal values. Older models of the figure will have the "WG" after the M.I. Hummel incised signature. This mark is illustrated and discussed in the trademark section at the front of the book.

Hum No.	Basic Size	Trademark	Current Value ($)
217	5-1/2"	TMK-2, FB	400-600
217	5-1/2"	TMK-3, Sty. Bee	225-275
217	5-1/2"	TMK-4, 3-line	210-225
217	5-1/2"	TMK-5, LB	200-210
217	5-1/2"	TMK-6, MB	200

BOY WITH TOOTHACHE, Hum 217. Three Line mark, incised 1951 MID, 5-3/8".

HUM 218: BIRTHDAY SERENADE

The most significant variation found of this figure is the "reverse mold variation." In the older versions of this double figure piece the girl plays the concertina and the boy plays the flute. In the newer models the instruments are the other way around.

The older, Full Bee (TMK-2) pieces with the reverse mold were changed beginning in the next trademark period, the Stylized Bee (TMK-3), so you can find the old design in that mark as well. There must have been many of the old design left in stock, for you can even find them bearing the Three Line Mark (TMK-4). Note that the boy lost his kerchief when he was given the concertina or accordion.

Hum No.	Basic Size	Trademark	Current Value ($)
218/2/0 (reverse mold)	4-1/4"	TMK-2, FB	500-550
218/2/0 (reverse mold)	4-1/4"	TMK-3, Sty. Bee	400-450
218/2/0	4-1/4"	TMK-3, Sty. Bee	225-250
218/2/0 (reverse mold)	4-1/4"	TMK-4, 3-line	350-400
218/2/0	4-1/4"	TMK-4, 3-line	200-225
218/2/0	4-1/4"	TMK-5, LB	160
218/2/0	4-1/4"	TMK-6, MB	160
218/0 (reverse mold)	5-1/4"	TMK-2, FB	600-700
218/0 (reverse mold)	5-1/4"	TMK-3, Sty. Bee	450-550
218/0	5-1/4"	TMK-3, Sty. Bee	275-300
218/0 (reverse mold)	5-1/4"	TMK-4, 3-line	400-450
218/0	5-1/4"	TMK-4, 3-line	275-300
218/0	5-1/4"	TMK-5, LB	275
218/0	5-1/4"	TMK-6, MB	275

Reversed instruments variations, BIRTHDAY SERENADE, Hum 218. Left: Full Bee mark, black "Germany," "© W. Goebel," 5-3/8". Right: 218/0, Last Bee mark, incised 1952 MID, 5-1/4".

HUM 219/2/0: LITTLE VELMA

This figure bears a number with the "Closed Number" designation, supposedly meaning a number that never has been and never will be used to designate a Hummel figurine. It is a girl sitting on a fence, looking down at a frog on the ground. It was never officially released by the factory, although it has turned up due to a no-longer practical policy of distributing pre-production samples. It was never placed in production due to its similarity to Hum 195 and Hum 201. The owner of the first example of this figure to be uncovered has named it Little Velma. It was designed in 1952. At least 15-20 examples have been found to date, so far only in the Full Bee (TMK-2). Collector value is $4,000-5,000 depending on condition.

LITTLE VELMA, Hum 219.
219/2/0, Full Bee (TMK-2) with
registered trademark symbol,
"© W. Goebel," 3-15/16".

HUM 220: WE CONGRATULATE

A very similar figure to Hum 214/E (Nativity Set piece) except this figure is on a base and 214/E is not, and the girl has no wreath of flowers in her hair.

This piece was introduced in the 1950s and has been produced with one variation of some significance. At first the piece was produced with a 220/2/0 designator. It was soon dropped, leaving only the mold number 220 incised on the base.

WE CONGRATULATE, Hum 220. Three Line Mark (TMK-4), 3-7/8".

Hum No.	Basic Size	Trademark	Current Value ($)
220/2/0	4"	TMK-2, FB	200-250
220	4"	TMK-3, Sty. Bee	175-200
220	4"	TMK-4, 3-line	150-175
220	4"	TMK-5, LB	145-150
220	4"	TMK-6, MB	145

HUM 221: HAPPY PASTIME (Candy Box) (Closed Number)

Previously listed as unknown, it is now known that this is a pre-production sample never released. At least two examples are known to be in private collections. A photograph of this piece appears on page 276 of the *M.I. Hummel Album*, copyright 1992, Portfolio Press Corporation. A want ad in a leading national collectible periodical in mid-1996 offered $7,000 for this piece.

HUM 222: MADONNA (Wall Plaque)

An extremely rare piece out of current production. It is unique in that a metal frame surrounds it. The basic size is 4" x 5". This piece has been found with several different designs of wire frame around it. Most were originally made with a felt backing. Each may be found with any design of the wire frame or no frame at all.

Hum No.	Basic Size	Trademark	Current Value ($)
222	4"x5"	TMK-2, FB	700-800
222	4"x5"	TMK-3, Sty. Bee	600-700

MADONNA, Plaque, Hum 222. No apparent mark other than mold number. Measures 4" x 5". The wire frame is detachable.

HUM 223: TO MARKET (Table Lamp)

First introduced in the 1950s, this lamp was temporarily withdrawn from production in 1989 with no reinstatement date given. There are no mold or finish variations significant enough to affect normal values. See the Hum 101 entry for a description of a lamp of similar design.

TO MARKET table lamp, Hum 223. Stylized Bee mark (TMK-3), 8-3/4", without the light fixture.

Hum No.	Basic Size	Trademark	Current Value ($)
223	9-1/2"	TMK-2, FB	425-475
223	9-1/2"	TMK-3, Sty. Bee	375-400
223	9-1/2"	TMK-4, 3-line	320-340
223	9-1/2"	TMK-5, LB	290-300
223	9-1/2"	TMK-6, MB	290-300

HUM 224: WAYSIDE HARMONY (Table Lamp)

First introduced as a redesign of the Hum 111 lamp in the 1950s, this lamp was produced in two sizes. Both were temporarily withdrawn from production in 1989 with no published date of reinstatement.

There are no finish or mold variations that have an impact on normal values.

WAYSIDE HARMONY table lamp, Hum 224/II. Missing Bee mark (TMK-6), 9" without the light fixture.

Hum No.	Basic Size	Trademark	Current Value ($)
224/I	7-1/2"	TMK-2, FB	360-400
224/I	7-1/2"	TMK-3, Sty. Bee	300-325
224/I	7-1/2"	TMK-4, 3-line	260-285
224/I	7-1/2"	TMK-5, LB	250-260
224/I	7-1/2"	TMK-6, MB	250-260
224	9-1/2"	TMK-2, FB	500-575
224	9-1/2"	TMK-3, Sty. Bee	425-500
224/II	9-1/2"	TMK-2, FB	425-475
224/II	9-1/2"	TMK-3, Sty. Bee	350-400
224/II	9-1/2"	TMK-4, 3-line	320-340
224/II	9-1/2"	TMK-5, LB	300-325
224/II	9-1/2"	TMK-6, MB	290-300

HUM 225: JUST RESTING (Table Lamp)

First released in the 1950s as a redesign of the Hum 112, it was listed as temporarily withdrawn from production by Goebel in 1989. No reinstatement date was given.

Hum No.	Basic Size	Trademark	Current Value ($)
225/I	7-1/2"	TMK-2, FB	350-400
225/I	7-1/2"	TMK-3, Sty. Bee	300-325
225/I	7-1/2"	TMK-4, 3-line	260-285
225/I	7-1/2"	TMK-5, LB	250-260
225/I	7-1/2"	TMK-6, MB	250-260
225	7-1/2"	TMK-2, FB	500-575
225	7-1/2"	TMK-3, Sty. Bee	425-500
225/II	9-1/2"	TMK-2, FB	425-475
225/II	9-1/2"	TMK-3, Sty. Bee	350-400

Hum No.	Basic Size	Trademark	Current Value ($)
225/II	9-1/2"	TMK-4, 3-line	320-340
225/II	9-1/2"	TMK-5, LB	290-300
225/II	9-1/2"	TMK-6, MB	290-300

JUST RESTING table lamp, Hum 225/II. Missing Bee mark (TMK-6), 8-7/8" without the lamp fixture.

HUM 226: THE MAIL IS HERE

THE MAIL IS HERE, Hum 226. This example is an older piece with a Full Bee (TMK-2) trademark in an incised circle. It also has a "by W. Goebel," a black "West Germany" and measures 4-1/2" x 6-1/2".

First introduced into the line in the 1950s, it was known as "Mail Coach." This name is still favored by many collectors. Incidentally, this figure was preceded by a wall plaque utilizing the same motif (Hum 140).

There are no major variations affecting normal values. The figure remains in production today.

Hum No.	Basic Size	Trademark	Current Value ($)
226	4-1/4"x6-1/4"	TMK-2, FB	700-800
226	4-1/4"x6-1/4"	TMK-3, Sty. Bee	600-650
226	4-1/4"x6-1/4"	TMK-4, 3-line	525-575
226	4-1/4"x6-1/4"	TMK-5, LB	505-515
226	4-1/4"x6-1/4"	TMK-6, MB	505

HUM 227: SHE LOVES ME, SHE LOVES ME NOT (Table Lamp)

This figure is a 7-1/2" lamp base utilizing Hum 174 as part of the design.

It was listed by Goebel in 1989 as temporarily withdrawn from production. No reinstatement date was given.

Hum No.	Basic Size	Trademark	Current Value ($)
227	7-1/2"	TMK-2, FB	350-400
227	7-1/2"	TMK-3, Sty. Bee	300-350
227	7-1/2"	TMK-4, 3-line	265-290
227	7-1/2"	TMK-5, LB	250-260
227	7-1/2"	TMK-6, MB	250

HUM 228: GOOD FRIENDS (Table Lamp)

This piece is a 7-1/2" lamp base utilizing Hum 182 as part of the design.

It was listed by Goebel as temporarily withdrawn from production in 1989. No date for reinstatement was given.

Hum No.	Basic Size	Trademark	Current Value ($)
228	7-1/2"	TMK-2, FB	360-390
228	7-1/2"	TMK-3, Sty. Bee	300-340
228	7-1/2"	TMK-4, 3-line	260-290
228	7-1/2"	TMK-5, LB	250-260
228	7-1/2"	TMK-6, MB	250

HUM 229: APPLE TREE GIRL (Table Lamp)

This 7-1/2" base utilized Hum 141 as part of the design.

It was listed as temporarily out of production by Goebel in 1989. No date of reinstatement was given.

Hum No.	Basic Size	Trademark	Current Value ($)
229	7-1/2"	TMK-2, FB	600-750
229	7-1/2"	TMK-3, Sty. Bee	300-340
229	7-1/2"	TMK-4, 3-line	260-290
229	7-1/2"	TMK-5, LB	250-260
229	7-1/2"	TMK-6, MB	250

HUM 230: APPLE TREE BOY (Table Lamp)

This 7-1/2" lamp base utilized Hum 142 as part of the design.

This piece was listed by Goebel as temporarily withdrawn from production in 1989. No reinstatement date was given.

Hum No.	Basic Size	Trademark	Current Value ($)
230	7-1/2"	TMK-2, FB	600-750
230	7-1/2"	TMK-3, Sty. Bee	300-340
230	7-1/2"	TMK-4, 3-line	260-290
230	7-1/2"	TMK-5, LB	250-260
230	7-1/2"	TMK-6, MB	250

HUM 231: BIRTHDAY SERENADE (Table Lamp)

This particular lamp was out of production for many years. It utilizes the Hum 218 (Birthday Serenade) as its design. The old model is found in the Full Bee trademark and reflects the same old mold (girl with accordian and boy with flute) design. These old mold design lamps measure about 9-3/4" tall and are fairly scarce. The Hum 231 was reissued in the late 1970s with the instruments reversed. Now the girl plays the flute and the boy, the accordian. The newer pieces are found with the Last Bee (TMK-5) and the Missing Bee (TMK-6) trademarks. (See Hum 234.)

Goebel listed this lamp as temporarily withdrawn from production as of December 31, 1989, and no reinstatement date was given.

BIRTHDAY SERENADE table lamp, Hum 231. Missing Bee mark (TMK-6), measures 8-7/8" without the light fixture.

Hum No.	Basic Size	Trademark	Current Value ($)
231	9-3/4"	TMK-2, FB	1200-1500
231	9-3/4"	TMK-5, LB	450
231	9-3/4"	TMK-6, MB	400

HUM 232: HAPPY DAYS (Table Lamp)

The 9-3/4" Happy Days table lamp was placed in production in the 1950s. It was apparently made in limited numbers in the early days because those with the Full Bee (TMK-2) trademark have always been in short supply. For a while the figures were available in the Last Bee (TMK-5) and the Missing Bee (TMK-6) marks, but the factory listed them as temporarily withdrawn from production in late 1989.

Hum No.	Basic Size	Trademark	Current Value ($)
232	9-3/4"	TMK-2, FB	800-1000
232	9-3/4"	TMK-5, LB	450
232	9-3/4"	TMK-6, MB	400

HUM 233: UNKNOWN (Closed Number)

This figure is unlikely to be found. There is evidence to suggest that this is a preliminary design for Bird Watcher (Hum 300). No known examples anywhere.

HUM 234: BIRTHDAY SERENADE (Table Lamp)

This lamp, like the larger Hum 231, was apparently also removed from or limited in production for a time. Unlike the Hum 231 lamp, however, it can be found in all trademarks beginning with the Full Bee. It was redesigned in the late 1970s with the instruments reversed, just as the Hum 231 was. It can be found in the old or new styles in the Full Bee.

Hum No.	Basic Size	Trademark	Current Value ($)
234 (reverse mold)	7-3/4"	TMK-2, FB	1000-1200
234	7-3/4"	TMK-2, FB	500-750
234 (reverse mold)	7-3/4"	TMK-3, Sty. Bee	500-750
234	7-3/4"	TMK-3, Sty. Bee	350-400
234 (reverse mold)	7-3/4"	TMK-4, 3-line	350-450
234	7-3/4"	TMK-4, 3-line	325-340
234	7-3/4"	TMK-5, LB	290-300
234	7-3/4"	TMK-6, MB	290-300

HUM 235: HAPPY DAYS (Table Lamp)

This is a smaller size (7-3/4") of the Hum 232 lamp. It too was placed in production in the 1950s and removed shortly thereafter. It was reissued in a new design in the late 1970s, as was the larger lamp. Unlike the larger lamp, however, this one can be found in all trademarks starting with the Full Bee.

Hum No.	Basic Size	Trademark	Current Value ($)
235	7-3/4"	TMK-2, FB	500-750
235	7-3/4"	TMK-3, Sty. Bee	400-450
235	7-3/4"	TMK-4, 3-line	300-400
235	7-3/4"	TMK-5, LB	280-300
235	7-3/4"	TMK-6, MB	280-300

HAPPY DAYS table lamp, Hum 235. Missing Bee Mark (TMK-6), 1954 MID, measures 7-1/2" without the light fixture.

HUM 236A and HUM 236B: NO NAME (Closed Number)

Only one example of each of these is known to exist at this time. The figures are two angels, one at the base of a tree and the other seated on a tree limb. Hum 236A has one angel playing a harp at the base of a tree and the other seated on a tree limb above singing. The Hum 236B has the tree angel blowing a horn and the seated angel playing a lute. No known examples exist outside the factory archives.

HUM 237: STAR GAZER (Wall Plaque) (Closed Number)

This piece is a plaque using "Star Gazer" in white overglaze as its design. None are known to be in private collections. Factory archives only.

HUM 238/A : ANGEL WITH LUTE, HUM 238/B: ANGEL WITH ACCORDION, HUM 238/C: ANGEL WITH HORN (Angel Trio Set)

ANGEL TRIO. Left: Angel with Lute, Hum 238A, paper sticker with the Last Bee mark, incised 1967 MID, 2-3/8". Center: Angel with Accordian, Hum 238B, paper sticker with the Last Bee mark, incised 1967 MID, 2-3/8". Right: Angel with Horn, Hum 238C, paper sticker with the Last Bee mark, 2-3/8".

These three pieces are usually sold as a set. In current production, they can be found in the current-use Missing Bee (TMK-6), Last Bee (TMK-5) and the 3-line (TMK-4) trademarks. Each is 2" to 2-1/2" high. They are essentially the same set as the Angel Trio, (Hum 38, 39 and 40) but the three Hum 238 are not candleholders.

Hum No.	Basic Size	Trademark	Current Value ($) (each piece)
238/A,B,C	2", 2-1/2"	TMK-4, 3-line	55-60
238/A,B,C	2", 2-1/2"	TMK-5, LB	50-55
238/A,B,C	2", 2-1/2"	TMK-6, MB	50

HUM 239/A: GIRL WITH NOSEGAY, HUM 239/B: GIRL WITH DOLL, HUM 239/C: BOY WITH HORSE (Children Trio)

These three are usually sold as a set. Placed in production in the 1960s, they are essentially the same as the Hum 115, Hum 116 and Hum 117, except that the three Hum 239 have no receptacle for holding a candle.

Hum No.	Basic Size	Trademark	Current Value ($) (each piece)
239/A,B,C	3-1/2"	TMK-4, 3-line	55-60
239/A,B,C	3-1/2"	TMK-5, LB	50-55
239/A,B,C	3-1/2"	TMK-6, MB	50

CHILDREN TRIO SET. Left: Hum 239/A. Center: Hum 239/B. Right: Hum 239/C. All three measure 3-1/2", have 1967 MIDs and Last Bee Trademarks on silver paper stickers attached beneath the base.

HUM 240: LITTLE DRUMMER

Placed into production in the 1950s. This figure is usually found with an incised MID of 1955. There are no variations significant enough to affect normal values for this piece.

LITTLE DRUMMER, Hum 240. This piece bears the Last Bee (TMK-5) mark, measures 4-1/2" tall and has an incised 1955 MID.

Attendees at the 1993 Disneyana Convention were given the opportunity to purchase a pair of figurines on a wooden base. The figurines were a normal production model of the Little Drummer (Hum 240), and a matching Donald Duck figurine in the same pose. The Donald Duck drummer is marked with an incised mold number of 17323, TMK-7 trademark and a limited edition notation. The edition was limited to 1,500. They were original sold for $300 and are now valued at $450-600.

Hum No.	Basic Size	Trademark	Current Value ($)
240	4-1/4"	TMK-2, FB	200-225
240	4-1/4"	TMK-3, Sty. Bee	160-180
240	4-1/4"	TMK-4, 3-line	145-160
240	4-1/4"	TMK-5, LB	135-145
240	4-1/4"	TMK-6, MB	135

HUM 241: ANGEL JOYOUS NEWS WITH LUTE
(Holy Water Font) (Closed Number)

The mold number 241 was used by mistake on the next piece listed (Angel Lights). This design was produced only in sample form and never put into regular production. There is only one presently known to exist outside the factory archives. If sold, this unique piece would bring about $10,000. It is in the Don Stephens Collection, soon to be a part of the Goebel Gallery and M.I. Hummel Museum in Rosemont, Illinois.

ANGEL WITH LUTE
Font, Hum 241.

HUM 241: ANGEL LIGHTS (Candleholder)

ANGEL LIGHTS
candleholder, Hum 241.
Last Bee mark (TMK-5),
incised 1977 MID.

This was a new release in 1978. It is in the form of an arch placed on a plate. A figure sits attached to the top of the arch, with candle receptacles down each side of the arch. It is not attached to the plate base.

This figure occurs in the Last Bee (TMK-5) trademark only. Usually sells for around $225-300. Suspended from production since January 1, 1990.

HUM 242: ANGEL JOYOUS NEWS WITH TRUMPET
(Holy Water Font) (Closed Number)

This piece was produced as a sample only and never put into production. It is not likely to ever find its way into a private collection. As far as is known, the only example is in the Goebel archives.

HUM 243: MADONNA AND CHILD (Holy Water Font)

Even though this piece was apparently not released until the 1960s, it can be found in all trademarks starting with the Full Bee (TMK-2).

There are no significant variations affecting normal values for this figure.

MADONNA AND
CHILD Font, Hum 243.
Three Line Mark, incised
1955 MID, 4".

Hum No.	Basic Size	Trademark	Current Value ($)
243	3-1/4"x4"	TMK-2, FB	70-80
243	3-1/4"x4"	TMK-3, Sty. Bee	60-70
243	3-1/4"x4"	TMK-4, 3-line	55-60
243	3-1/4"x4"	TMK-5, LB	50-55
243	3-1/4"x4"	TMK-6, MB	50

HUM 244: UNKNOWN (Open Number)

HUM 245: UNKNOWN (Open Number)

HUM 246: HOLY FAMILY (Holy Water Font)

This font was released into the line in the mid-1950s. There are no significant mold or finish variations affecting normal values. It is usually found with the incised MID of 1955.

HOLY FAMILY, Hum 246. Full Bee Mark, incised 1955 MID, black "Western Germany," 4-1/2".

Hum No.	Basic Size	Trademark	Current Value ($)
246	3"x4"	TMK-2, FB	70-80
246	3"x4"	TMK-3, Sty. Bee	60-70
246	3"x4"	TMK-4, 3-line	55-60
246	3"x4"	TMK-5, LB	50-55
246	3"x4"	TMK-6, MB	50

HUM 247: STANDING MADONNA WITH CHILD (Closed Number)

This beautiful piece was designed in 1961 but apparently rejected by the Siessen Convent. It exists in sample form only in the factory archives.

STANDING MADONNA AND CHILD.
Photo courtesy M.I. Hummel Club

HUM 248: GUARDIAN ANGEL (Holy Water Font)

This piece is a redesigned version of Hum 29, which is no longer in production. When placed in the collection it was a 2-1/4" x 5-1/2". The mold number is 248/0. When first produced (Full Bee era), there was a larger version made, the 248/I, but this was never placed into regular production.

LITTLE DRUMMER, Hum 240. This piece bears the Last Bee (TMK-5) mark, measures 4-1/2" tall and has an incised 1955 MID.

Hum No.	Basic Size	Trademark	Current Value ($)
248/I	2-1/4"x5-1/2"	TMK-3, Sty. Bee	1000-1500
248/0	2-1/4"x5-1/2"	TMK-3, Sty. Bee	60-70
248/0	2-1/4"x5-1/2"	TMK-4, 3-line	55-60
248/0	2-1/4"x5-1/2"	TMK-5, LB	50-55
248/0	2-1/4"x5-1/2"	TMK-6, MB	50

HUM 249: MADONNA AND CHILD (Plaque in Relief) (Closed Number)

Molded as a sample only, this plaque was never put in the line. It is essentially the same design as the Hum 48 Madonna Plaque with the background cut away. No known examples outside the Goebel archives.

HUM 250/A, 250/B: LITTLE GOAT HERDER and FEEDING TIME (Bookends)

These were placed in the line in the mid-1960s. If the figurines are removed from the wooden bookend bases, they are indistinguishable from the regular pieces.

These figures were temporarily withdrawn from production at the end of 1989. No date for reinstatement was given.

Hum No.	Basic Size	Trademark	Current Value ($)
250/A&B	5-1/2"	TMK-2, FB	400-450
250/A&B	5-1/2"	TMK-3, Sty. Bee	300-325
250/A&B	5-1/2"	TMK-5, LB	225-300
250/A&B	5-1/2"	TMK-6, MB	225-300

LITTLE GOAT HERDER (Hum 250A) and FEEDING TIME (Hum 250B) bookends. Left figure measures 4-1/2" and the right 4-3/4". Both bear the Missing Bee Mark (TMK-6).

HUM 251/A, 251/B: GOOD FRIENDS and SHE LOVES ME, SHE LOVES ME NOT (Bookends)

GOOD FRIENDS (Hum 251A) and SHE LOVES ME, SHE LOVES ME NOT (Hum 251B) bookends. Both bear the Stylized Bee mark (TMK-3).

These bookends were entered into the line in the mid-1960s. If the figurines are removed from the wooden bookend bases, they are indistinguishable from the regular production figurines.

Goebel listed these pieces as temporarily withdrawn from production in 1989. No reinstatement date was given at the time.

Hum No.	Basic Size	Trademark	Current Value ($)
251/A&B	5-1/2"	TMK-2, FB	400-450
251/A&B	5-1/2"	TMK-3, Sty. Bee	300-325
251/A&B	5-1/2"	TMK-5, LB	225-300
251/A&B	5-1/2"	TMK-6, MB	225-300

HUM 252/A, 252/B: APPLE TREE BOY and APPLE TREE GIRL (Bookends)

These bookends were placed in the collection in the mid-1960s. If the figures are removed from the bookends they are indistinguishable from the regular figurines.

The bookends were temporarily withdrawn from production at the end of 1989 with no stated reintroduction date.

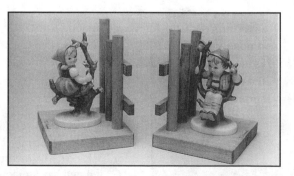

Hum No.	Basic Size	Trademark	Current Value ($)
252/A&B	5-1/4"	TMK-3, Sty. Bee	300-325
252/A&B	5-1/4"	TMK-5, LB	225-300
252/A&B	5-1/4"	TMK-6, MB	225-300

APPLE TREE GIRL and APPLE TREE BOY bookends, Hum 252A and Hum 252B. Each bears the Stylized Bee mark (TMK-3) and measures 3-7/8" tall.

HUM 253: UNKNOWN (Closed Number)

Goebel records indicate that this piece was a design much like the girl in Hum 52 (Going to Grandma's). There is no evidence that it was ever produced and there are no known examples in the archives or anywhere else.

HUM 254: UNKNOWN (Closed Number)

Goebel records indicate that this piece was a design much like the girl figure in Hum 150 (Happy Days). There is no evidence that it was ever produced and there are no examples in the archives or anywhere else.

HUM 255: A STITCH IN TIME

A STITCH IN TIME, Hum 255. Three Line Mark (TMK-4), incised 1963 MID, donut base, 5-3/4".

First released in the mid-1960s, there are no significant variations that might affect normal values.

In 1990 a smaller size, 3", was added as part of a four-figurine series matching mini-plates in the same series. When this figure was introduced, the mold number for the larger size was changed to 255/0.

Hum No.	Basic Size	Trademark	Current Value ($)
255/4/0	5"	TMK-6, MB	85
255	6-3/4"	TMK-3, Sty. Bee	600-750
255	6-3/4"	TMK-4, 3-line	275-300
255	6-3/4"	TMK-5, LB	260-275
255/0	5-3/4"	TMK-5, LB	260-270
255/0	6-3/4"	TMK-6, MB	260

HUM 256: KNITTING LESSON

Introduced in the mid-1960s, Knitting Lesson has no significant variations that might affect normal values. It has an incised MID of 1963.

Hum No.	Basic Size	Trademark	Current Value ($)
256	7-1/2"	TMK-3, Sty. Bee	750-1000
256	7-1/2"	TMK-4, 3-line	500-550
256	7-1/2"	TMK-5, LB	475-500
256	7-1/2"	TMK-6, MB	475

KNITTING LESSON, Hum 256. Missing Bee (TMK-6), 1967 MID, 7-3/8".

HUM 257: FOR MOTHER

Introduced into the collection in the mid-1960s, this figure has no significant mold or finish variations.

A new smaller-size figurine was released as a part of a four-piece series with matching mini-plates in 1985. When this was done the mold number for the larger size was changed to 257/0.

Hum No.	Basic Size	Trademark	Current Value ($)
257/5/0	2-3/4	TMK-7	HM 55
257/2/0	3"	TMK-5, LB	110-120
257/2/0	3"	TMK-6, MB	110
257	5-1/4"	TMK-3, Sty. Bee	600-750
257	5-1/4"	TMK-4, 3-line	195-225
257 or 257/0	5-1/4"	TMK-5, LB	185-195
257/0	5-1/4"	TMK-6, MB	185

FOR MOTHER, Hum 257. Left: Missing Bee (TMK-6), 1963 MID, 5-1/8". Right: 257 2/0, Missing Bee (TMK-4), 1984 MID, 4".

HUM 258: WHICH HAND?

There are no mold or finish variation that would affect normal values. Released in the mid-1960s, this figure has an incised MID of 1963.

Hum No.	Basic Size	Trademark	Current Value ($)
258	5-1/4"	TMK-3, Sty. Bee	600-750
258	5-1/4"	TMK-4, 3-line	190-215
258	5-1/4"	TMK-5, LB	180-190
258	5-1/4"	TMK-6, MB	180

WHICH HAND, Hum 258. Missing Bee Mark (TMK-6). Incised 1963 MID, 5-3/8".

HUM 259: GIRL WITH ACCORDION (Closed Number)

This is almost exactly the same design as that of the girl with concertina or accordion in the Hum 218 (Birthday Serenade). It was produced in sample form only and never placed into production. Only one is known to reside in a private collection.

HUM 260: NATIVITY SET (Large)

There was only sketchy information concerning complete nativity sets in this size and little more about the individual pieces in any of the many price lists studied. Below is a listing of each piece in the Hum 260 Nativity Set. The set has been temporarily withdrawn from production. The set is found in 3-line (TMK-4) and Last Bee (TMK-5) trademarks as well as the Missing Bee mark (TMK-6). The 16-piece set, including the wooden stable, is valued at about $4,000-5,000.

Hum No.	Basic Size	Figure
260/A	9-3/4"	Madonna
260/B	11-3/4"	Joseph
260/C	5-3/4"	Infant Jesus

Hum No.	Basic Size	Figure
260/D	5-1/4"	Goodnight (Angel Standing)
260/E	4-1/4"	Angel Serenade (Kneeling)
260/F	6-1/4"	We Congratulate
260/G	11-3/4"	Shepherd
260/H	3-3/4"	Sheep and Lamb
260/J	7"	Shepherd Boy (Kneeling)
260/K	7-1/2"	Little Tooter
260/L	7-1/2"	Donkey
260/M	6"x11"	Cow
260/N	12-3/4"	Moor King
260/O	12"	King (Standing)
260/P	9"	King (Kneeling)
260/R	3-1/4"x4"	Sheep

HUM 261: ANGEL DUET

This figure is essentially the same design as Hum 193 but does not have a provision for a candle. It was apparently produced in very limited quantities, for it is somewhat difficult to find bearing the older, 3-line mark (TMK-4).

There are no major variations affecting value. There is no reverse mold variation as in the Hum 193 candleholder. Released in the late 1960s, these figures bear a 1968 incised MID.

ANGEL DUET, Hum 261. Last Bee Mark, incised 1968 MID, 5".

Hum No.	Basic Size	Trademark	Current Value ($)
261	5-1/2"	TMK-4, 3-line	210-236
261	5-1/2"	TMK-5, LB	195-210
261	5-1/2"	TMK-6, MB	195

HUM 262: HEAVENLY LULLABY

HEAVENLY LULLABY, Hum 262. 3-1/2" high, this figure bears the Last Bee (TMK-5) trademark and an incised 1968 MID.

First released in the late 1960s, this figure had undergone no significant mold variations. It bears an incised MID of 1968.

This figure is the same design as Hum 24 but does not have a provision for a candle. It was apparently produced in very limited quantities, for it is very difficult to locate in older trademarks. Current production pieces sell for about $170.

Hum No.	Basic Size	Trademark	Current Value ($)
262	3-1/2"x5"	TMK-3, Sty. Bee	210-250
262	3-1/2"x5"	TMK-4, 3-line	180-210
262	3-1/2"x5"	TMK-5, LB	170-180
262	3-1/2"x5"	TMK-6, MB	170

HUM 263: MERRY WANDERER (Plaque in Relief)

A very rare plaque of the familiar Merry Wanderer motif. There is only one known to be outside the factory collection and in a private collection. As far as can be determined there are no more on the collector market. It is known to bear the 3-line trademark (TMK-4). It appears to have been made from a regular Merry Wanderer mold with the base cut off and the back side flattened. It is valued at upwards of $10,000.

MERRY WANDERER, Hum 263, plaque in relief.

MERRY WANDERER, Hum 263, back of plaque.

ANNUAL PLATES

In 1971 the factory produced its first annual plate. This plate utilized the Heavenly Angel (Hum 21) design and was released to the Goebel factory workers to commemorate the 100th anniversary of the W. Goebel firm. The plate was subsequently produced for regular sales without the factory worker inscription. It was received so well in the United States it was decided that a similar plate would be released annually from then on. The 1971 plate was not released to European dealers.

Since 1971 the firm has released one new design per year in a series of 25, each bearing a traditional Hummel figurine motif. The plates and their current market value are listed on the following pages.

HUM 264: 1971 HUMMEL ANNUAL PLATE

There are three versions of this plate. The first is the "normal version." The second differs from the first only in that it has no holes for hanging. It was exported to England where tariff laws in 1971 placed a higher duty on the plate if it had holes than if not. The law states that holes make it a decorative object, subject to a higher duty rate. The third variation is the special original edition produced only for the Goebel factory workers. There is an inscription on the back side of the lower rim. It reads in German as follows: "Gewidmet Aller Mitarbeitern Im Jubilaumsjahr. Wirdanken ihnen fur ihre mitarbeit." Roughly translated this means thanks to the workers for their fine service. This last plate is the least common of the three, hence the most sought after.

HUM 265: 1972 GOEBEL ANNUAL PLATE

There are three known versions of the 1972 plate. The first is the "normal" one with the regular backstamp and the current Goebel trademark. The second has the same backstamp but bears the 3-line mark instead of the current mark. The third is exactly the same as the second but does not bear the inscription "Hand Painted," and the "2nd" is omitted from the identification of the plate as an annual plate.

Hum No.	Size	Plate Design	Year	Current Value ($)
264	7-1/2"	Heavenly Angel	1971	450-650
265	7-1/2"	Hear Ye, Hear Ye (TMK-3)	1972	50-60
265*	7-1/2"	Hear Ye, Hear Ye (TMK-4)	1972	45-60
266	7-1/2"	Globe Trotter	1973	80-105
267	7-1/2"	Goose Girl	1974	50-70
268**	7-1/2"	Ride into Christmas	1975	50-60
269***	7-1/2"	Apple Tree Girl	1976	50-60
270	7-1/2"	Apple Tree Boy	1977	70-80
271	7-1/2"	Happy Pastime	1978	30-40
272	7-1/2"	Singing Lesson	1979	25-30
273	7-1/2"	School Girl	1980	35-45
274	7-1/2"	Umbrella Boy	1981	55-70
275	7-1/2"	Umbrella Girl	1982	130-135
276	7-1/2"	Postman	1983	180-195
277	7-1/2"	Little Helper	1984	65-75
278	7-1/2"	Chick Girl	1985	75-85
279	7-1/2"	Playmates	1986	120-155
283	7-1/2"	Feeding Time	1987	300-360
284	7-1/2"	Little Goat Herder	1988	130-140
285	7-1/2"	Farm Boy	1989	120-140
286	7-1/2"	Shepherd's Boy	1990	150-165
287	7-1/2"	Just Resting	1991	150-160
288	7-1/2"	Wayside Harmony	1992	150-160
289	7-1/2"	Doll Bath	1993	150-165
290	7-1/2"	Doctor	1994	150-165
291	7-1/2"	Come Back Soon	1995	180-195

Annual Plates: 1971-1973, Hum 264, 265, 266.

*Made at the same time as the Last Bee marked plate and represents a transition. Not appreciably more valuable.

**Late in 1983 an unusual plate was found in Germany. It was a 1975 Annual Plate but instead of the Ride Into Christmas motif it was a Little Fiddler. No doubt that this was a prototype plate considered for 1975, but obviously not selected. How it managed to find its way out of the factory is anybody's guess. It may have been the only one.

***Somehow a number of the 1976 Annual Plates were inadvertently given the incorrect backstamp "Wildlife Third Edition, Barn Owl" and they were released. How many got out is anybody's guess. It has no value significance.

Annual Plates: 1974-1976, Hum 267, 268, 269.

Annual Plates: 1977-1979, Hum 270, 271, 272.

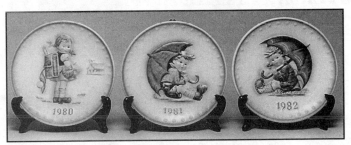

Annual Plates: 1980-1982, Hum 273, 274, 275.

Annual Plates: 1983-1985, Hum 276, 277, 278.

Annual Plates: 1986-1988, Hum 279, 283, 284.

Annual Plates: 1989-1990, Hum 287, 288.

Annual Plates: 1991-1992, Hum 288, 286.

DOLL BATH, Hum 289, 1993 Annual Plate.

DOCTOR, Hum 290, 1994 Annual Plate.

COME BACK SOON, Hum 291. The Final Edition (1995)

White Overglaze Annual Plates. Left: Hum 271, 1978, HAPPY PASTIME, Last Bee trademark incised 1972 MID. Right: Hum 272, SINGING LESSON, Last Bee trademark, incised 1972 MID.

HUM 280: 1975 ANNIVERSARY PLATE

This larger plate (10") utilizes the Stormy Weather (Hum 71) design. Presently valued at $80-110.

Anniversary Plates. Left to right: STORMY WEATHER 1975, Hum 280; SPRING DANCE 1980, Hum 281; AUF WIEDERSEHEN 1986, Hum 282.

HUM 281: 1980 ANNIVERSARY PLATE

This plate is called "Spring Dance" but utilizes only one figure from the Spring Dance piece. The second girl in the plate design is taken from the "Ring Around the Rosie" figurine. This plate presently sells for $60-80.

HUM 282: 1985 ANNIVERSARY PLATE

As are the previous anniversary plates, this last one is 10" in diameter. It uses as its design the figurine Auf Wiedersehen (Hum 153). It is presently selling at $150-250.

HUM 292, 293, 294, 295: FRIENDS FOREVER (Plate Series)

This is a four-plate series introduced in 1992. At 7" diameter the plates are smaller than the annual plates and have a decorative border.

Year	Hum No.	Design	Current Value ($)
1992	Hum 292	Meditation	150-160
1993	Hum 293	For Father	150-160
1994	Hum 294	Sweet Greetings	205 (release price)
1995	Hum 295	Surprise	210 (release price)

SWEET GREETINGS, Hum 294 (1994).

MEDITATION, Hum 292 (1992).

FOR FATHER, Hum 293 (1993).

SURPRISE, Hum 295 (1995).

HUM 296, 297, 298, 299: FOUR SEASONS (Plate Series)

This series began in 1996. The plates measure 7-1/2" in diameter and contrary to the norm, the plate design elements are three-dimensional: less than figural and more than bas-relief. The first in the series was issued at $195. It bears a 1996 MID and a First Issue backstamp.

WINTER MELODY, Hum 296 (1996).

Year	Hum No.	Design
1996	Hum 296	Winter Melody
1997	Hum 297	Summertime Stroll
1998	Hum 298	Autumn Glory
1999	Hum 299	Springtime Serenade

HUM 300: BIRD WATCHER

BIRD WATCHER, Hum 300. Missing Bee mark, incised 1956 MID, 5".

First known as Tenderness, this figure was released in 1979. It was originally designed in the Full Bee (TMK-2) trademark period. Samples in that trademark have an incised MID of 1954.

Far more easy to locate are the regular production pieces bearing the 1956 MID. They start with the Last Bee (TMK-5) and have been in continuous production since.

Hum No.	Basic Size	Trademark	Current Value ($)
300	5"	TMK-2, FB	4000-5000
300	5"	TMK-5, LB	205-225
300	5"	TMK-6, MB	205

HUM 301: CHRISTMAS ANGEL

A new release in 1989, this piece was originally designed in the Stylized Bee (TMK-3) period. It was made in prototype with that trademark and given an incised MID of 1957. Then it was redesigned, made slightly smaller than the sample and released with the Missing Bee (TMK-6) and the same 1957 MID. It remains in production.

Hum No.	Basic Size	Trademark	Current Value ($)
301	6-1/4"	TMK-3, Sty. Bee	4000-5000
301	6"	TMK-6, MB	230-250

CHRISTMAS ANGEL, Hum 301. Missing Bee mark, incised 1957 MID, 4-3/4".

HUM 302: CONCENTRATION (Possible Future Edition)

This figure was first designed and made in sample form in the Full Bee (TMK-2) era, but regular production has not yet begun. The example in the accompanying photograph has the Full Bee trademark and a 1956 MID.

CONCENTRATION, Hum 302, PFE.

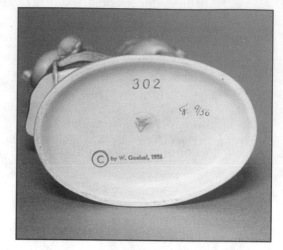

Base of the figurine showing the Full Bee (TMK-2) trademark in an incised circle.

HUM 303: ARITHMETIC LESSON (Possible Future Edition)

ARITHMETIC LESSON, Hum 303, PFE.

First designed and made in sample form in the Full Bee (TMK-2) era, this figure appears to be a combination of one boy and one girl from Hum 170 (School Boys) and Hum 177 (School Girls). The boy in this figure is also much like the boy in the Dealer Plaque (Hum 460). Note the line around the base in the accompanying photograph: a red line like that indicates that this is a sample figurine. The figurine measures 5-1/4". Collector value: $4,000-5,000.

HUM 304: THE ARTIST

This figurine was placed in regular production about 1970. There is reason to believe it may have been made in extremely limited quantities in the Full Bee (TMK-2) era and somewhat limited in the Stylized Bee (TMK-3) era. The figure in the accompanying photograph bears that mark and a 1955 incised MID.

THE ARTIST, Hum 304. Left: Missing Bee trademark (TMK-6), incised 1955 MID. Right: Inked-in incised mold number indicating that this is a master model. It bears a stamped Full Bee trademark and "© by W. Goebel, 1955." Note the paint drip on the base. This feature has never made it to the production piece.

Hum No.	Basic Size	Trademark	Current Value ($)
304	5-1/4"	TMK-2, FB	4000-5000
304	5-1/4"	TMK-3, Sty. Bee	2000-3000
304	5-1/4"	TMK-4, 3-line	240-260
304	5-1/4"	TMK-5, LB	220-240
304	5-1/4"	TMK-6, MB	220

THE ARTIST, Hum 304. Three Line Mark, incised 1955 MID, 5-1/4".

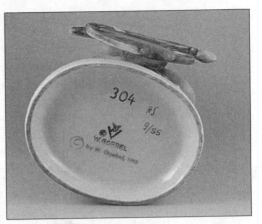

Base of THE ARTIST, showing the inked-in incised mold number indicating that this a figurine from the Mother Mold, a master model.

HUM 305: THE BUILDER

The first sample of this figure was made in the Full Bee (TMK-2) period and bears that trademark. It was originally introduced into the line in 1963 and remains in production today.

There are no significant mold or finish variations affecting the normal values, but a Full Bee trademarked piece is rare.

THE BUILDER, Hum 305. Three Line Mark, incised 1955 MID, 5-3/8".

Hum No.	Basic Size	Trademark	Current Value ($)
305	5-1/2"	TMK-2, FB	4000-5500
305	5-1/2"	TMK-3, Sty. Bee	1000-1200
305	5-1/2"	TMK-4, 3-line	240-260
305	5-1/2"	TMK-5, LB	220-240
305	5-1/2"	TMK-6, MB	220

HUM 306: LITTLE BOOKKEEPER

The first example of this figure was made in the Full Bee (TMK-2) era and those prototypes bear that trademark.

There are no significant mold or finish variations affecting normal values, but a Full Bee trademarked example is rare.

LITTLE BOOKKEEPER, Hum 306. Left: Three Line Mark (TMK-4), 1955 MID. Right: Last Bee (TMK-5) trademark, 1955 MID. Both measure 4-1/2". Shows head position variation.

Hum No.	Basic Size	Trademark	Current Value ($)
306	4-3/4"	TMK-2, FB	4000-5000
306	4-3/4"	TMK-3, Sty. Bee	1000-1200
306	4-3/4"	TMK-4, 3-line	280-300
306	4-3/4"	TMK-5, LB	260-280
306	4-3/4"	TMK-6, MB	260

HUM 307: GOOD HUNTING

This figure was first made in the 1960s, in the Full Bee (TMK-2) era, but figures with the Stylized Bee (TMK-3) trademark and later are the most common.

In older versions of this piece the boy holds the binoculars significantly lower than they are held in the figure made today, but this and any other mold and finish variations have no effect on normal values. The variations merely reflect the normal changes in the evolution of the figurine.

GOOD HUNTING, Hum 307. Left: Three Line Mark (TMK-4), 1955 MID, 5". Right: Missing Bee (TMK-6) mark, 1955 MID, 5-1/8".

Hum No.	Basic Size	Trademark	Current Value ($)
307	5-1/4"	TMK-2, FB	4000-5000
307	5-1/4"	TMK-3, Sty. Bee	600-800
307	5-1/4"	TMK-4, 3-line	240-260
307	5-1/4"	TMK-5, LB	220-240
307	5-1/4"	TMK-6, MB	220

HUM 308: LITTLE TAILOR

LITTLE TAILOR, HUM 308. This photo shows the difference between the old style (left) with an incised 1955 MID and the new (right), 1972 MID. The left measures 5-1/4" and the right, 5-5/8". Both bear the Last Bee trademark (TMK-5).

This figure was first produced in the Full Bee (TMK-2) era, but not placed in the line until the 1970s. There are a few of the Full Bee and Stylized Bee (TMK-3) pieces around, but they are rare.

There was a major mold redesign in the Last Bee (TMK-5) era and the old and new figures may be found in that trademark. See the accompanying photograph for the differences between the two.

Hum No.	Basic Size	Trademark	Current Value ($)
308	5-1/2"	TMK-2, FB	4000-5000
308	5-1/2"	TMK-3, Sty. Bee	2000-2500
308	5-1/2"	TMK-4, 3-line	240-260
308	5-1/2"	TMK-5, LB	220-240
308	5-1/2"	TMK-6, MB	220

HUM 309: WITH LOVING GREETINGS

When first released in 1983 the suggested retail price for this piece was $80. It now sells for $175. The basic size is 3-1/2". Take a look at the left-hand figure in the accompanying photograph. When you compare it to the other two, you will see that the sample piece is a good bit more complex. This is a good illustration of how a figure can evolve from sample to production. Obviously the paintbrush under the boy's arm was judged too vulnerable to breakage and was removed from the production model.

When first introduced into the line in 1983, the ink pot was colored blue, and the writing on the tablet turquoise. In late 1987 the color of the ink pot was changed

WITH LOVING GREETINGS, Hum 309. Left: Full Bee in an incised circle, "© by W. Goebel," 1955 MID, 3-1/2". This is the blue inkwell with stopper variation. Note brush under left arm. Center: Missing Bee mark, 1955 MID, 3 1/2". Blue inkwell. The brush is now missing. Right: Missing Bee mark, 1955 MID, 3-1/2". Purplish brown inkwell.

to brown and the color of the writing to blue. This change was made during the Missing Bee (TMK-6) period and can be found with the old or the new color in that trademark.

Hum No.	Basic Size	Trademark	Current Value ($)
309	3-1/2"	TMK-2, FB	4000-5000
309	3-1/2"	TMK-5, LB	175-190
309	3-1/2"	TMK-6, MB	175

HUM 310: SEARCHING ANGEL (Wall Plaque)

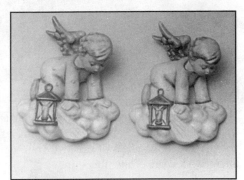

SEARCHING ANGEL Plaque, Hum 310. Left: Full Bee mark in an incised circle, incised 1955 MID, 3-3/8" x 4-1/4". Right: Last Bee Mark, incised 1955 MID, 4-1/4" x 4-1/8".

This piece was first fashioned in the Full Bee (TMK-2) period, but was not released for sale until 1979. It is very rare but it has been found bearing this mark.

Hum No.	Basic Size	Trademark	Current Value ($)
310	4"x2-1/2"	TMK-2, FB	2000-2500
310	4"x2-1/2"	TMK-5, LB	115-125
310	4"x2-1/2"	TMK-6, MB	115

HUM 311: KISS ME

Kiss Me was first designed and made in the Full Bee (TMK-2) era, but it was not released for sale until the Stylized Bee (TMK-3) period. A few of these Full Bee pieces have made their way into the collectors' market. They are very rare.

The mold was reworked in the 3-line trademark (TMK-4) period so that the doll no longer wears any socks. The figures can, therefore, be found either way in that trademark.

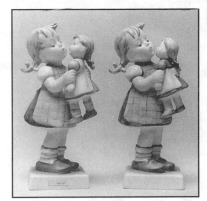

KISS ME, Hum 311. Left Three Line Mark (TMK-4), 1955 MID, 6-1/8". Right: Missing Bee (TMK-6), 6-1/4".

Hum No.	Basic Size	Trademark	Current Value ($)
311	6"	TMK-2, FB	4000-5000
311	6"	TMK-3, Sty. Bee	750-1000
311(socks)	6"	TMK-4, 3-line	450-550
311(no socks)	6"	TMK-4, 3-line	280-300
311	6"	TMK-5, LB	260
311	6"	TMK-6, MB	260

HUM 312: HONEY LOVER

This piece was first found illustrated in the Golden Anniversary Album as a possible future edition (PFE) when the book was released in 1984. At that point in time, a few had somehow already made their way into collectors' hands. The figure is now officially on the market, having been released as a special M.I. Hummel Club exclusive offering. Released at $190, it is available to members after the fifteenth anniversary of their club membership.

Photo of the underside of the base of Hum 312/I HONEY LOVER, showing the special club backstamp.

Hum No.	Basic Size	Trademark	Current Value ($)
312	3-3/4"	FB	TMK-2, FB 7000-8000
312	3-3/4"	MB	TMK-6, MB 350
312	3-3/4"	HM	TMK-7, HM 210

HONEY LOVER, Hum 312. Left: This 3-7/8" figure has a Full Bee mark and a hand lettered mold number along with the frequently found normal "© by W. Goebel". Additionally there is a painted red "Z," indicating that this particular piece is a prototype. Right: Also a Full Bee marked piece, this 4" figure bears a 1955 incised mold induction date (MID).

HONEY LOVER, Hum 312/I. Hummel Mark (current use or TMK-7), incised 1955 MID, 3-3/4". This issue is available exclusively to members of the M.I. Hummel Club who have attained 15 years of membership.

HUM 313: SUNNY MORNING (Possible Future Edition)

This piece was designed and the first examples made in the mid-1950s, but it has not yet been placed in production. Somehow this one and two others have made it into the collectors' market. They are valued at up to $8,000.

SUNNY MORNING, Hum 313. Inked in incised 313 mold number, Full Bee trademark in an incised circle, 1955 MID, "© by W. Goebel, 1956," 4-1/4".

HUM 314: CONFIDENTIALLY

CONFIDENTIALLY, Hum 314, Left: Last Bee mark (TMK-5), incised 1955 MID, 5-3/8". Right: Last Bee mark (TMK-5), incised 1972 MID, 5-7/8".

Even though this figure was first introduced into the line in 1972, the Last Bee (TMK-5) period, it can also be found in the Full Bee (TMK-2), Stylized Bee (TMK-3) and the Three Line (TMK-4) eras.

Apparently Goebel redesigned the figure shortly after releasing it. The new and old styles are evident in the accompanying photograph. The old and new styles can be found with the Last Bee trademark.

Hum No.	Basic Size	Trademark	Current Value ($)
314	5-1/2"	TMK-2, FB	4000-5000
314	5-1/2"	TMK-3, Sty. Bee	1000-1500
314	5-1/2"	TMK-4, 3-line	500-650
314 (old)	5-1/2"	TMK-5, LB	400-500
314 (new)	5-1/2"	TMK-5, LB	260-275
314	5-1/2"	TMK-6, MB	260

HUM 315: MOUNTAINEER

Released during the Stylized Bee (TMK-3) trademark period, this figure is also found, albeit rarely, with the Full Bee (TMK-2) trademark.

There are no mold or finish variations that would have any effect on the normal values.

MOUNTAINEER, Hum 315. This example is 5" in height, has the Three Line Mark (TMK-4) and bears an incised 1955 MID.

Hum No.	Basic Size	Trademark	Current Value ($)
315	5-1/4"	TMK-2, FB	4000-5000
315	5-1/4"	TMK-3, Sty. Bee	1000-1200
315	5-1/4"	TMK-4, 3-line	210-230
315	5-1/4"	TMK-5, LB	195-210
315	5-1/4"	TMK-6, MB	195

HUM 316: RELAXATION (Possible Future Edition)

This piece was designed and produced in prototype in the mid-1950s, in the Full Bee (TMK-2) period. The figures have not yet been put into production, but at least two bearing the Full Bee trademark have somehow made their way into the collectors' market. No trade data was found from which to derive a realistic collector value. However, using data on other figures in this mold number group an educated guess can be made, putting this figure's value at $4,000-5,000.

RELAXATION, Hum 316, PFE.

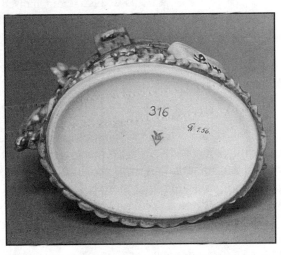

Base of Hum 316 showing the markings.

HUM 317: NOT FOR YOU

Even though this figurine was not released for sale until the early 1960s (the Stylized Bee (TMK-3) period), it is occasionally found bearing the Full Bee (TMK-2) trademark.

There are no mold or finish variations that affect the normal values for the figures with the various trademarks.

NOT FOR YOU, Hum 317. Has an incised mold induction date (MID) of 1955. It is 5-5/8" tall and bears the Missing Bee (TMK-6) trademark.

Hum No.	Basic Size	Trademark	Current Value ($)
317	6"	TMK-2, FB	4000-5000
317	6"	TMK-3, Sty. Bee	700-900
317	6"	TMK-4, 3-line	235-260
317	6"	TMK-5, LB	220-235
317	6"	TMK-6, MB	220

HUM 318: ART CRITIC

ART CRITIC, Hum 318. Missing Bee mark (TMK-6), incised 1955 MID, 5-1/4", first issue backstamp dated 1991.

This figure was first designed and produced in prototype back in the 1950s during the Full Bee (TMK-2) era, but was not released until 1991. At least two of these figures, marked with the Full Bee trademark, have found their way into the collectors' market.

There are no significant mold or finish variations affecting the normal value for the figures.

Hum No.	Basic Size	Trademark	Current Value ($)
318	5-3/4"	TMK-1, FB	5000-6000
318	5-3/4"	TMK-6, MB	260-275

THE ART CRITIC, Hum 318. Demonstration piece with only the flesh tones and brown base color on the coat painted. Current-use trademark (TMK-7), First Issue backstamp, incised 1955 MID, 5-1/4". Valued at about $400.

HUM 319: DOLL BATH

This figure was first designed and produced during the Full Bee (TMK-2) trademark period, but was not released until 1962, during the Stylized Bee (TMK-3) period. It is possible that there are some pieces out there with the Full Bee trademark.

In the 1970s the entire collection underwent a change from the old smooth surface finish to a textured finish. Unlike many of the other figures in the collection, this one made a clean break from the old style finish (found only in the Three Line (TMK-4) trademarked pieces) to the new textured finish (found on the Last Bee (TMK-5) pieces and all thereafter).

Hum No.	Basic Size	Trademark	Current Value ($)
319	5-1/4"	TMK-2, FB	4000-5000
319	5-1/4"	TMK-3, Sty. Bee	600-800
319	5-1/4"	TMK-4, 3-line	275-300
319	5-1/4"	TMK-5, LB	260-275
319	5-1/4"	TMK-6, MB	260

DOLL BATH, Hum 319. Both figures bear the Three Line mark (TMK-5). The one on the left has an incised 1956 MID and the other has an MID of 197?. It was impossible to discern the fourth digit.

DOLL BATH, Hum 319. Both figures bear the Three Line mark (TMK-5). The one on the left has an incised 1956 MID and the other has an MID of 197?. It was impossible to discern the fourth digit.

HUM 320: THE PROFESSOR

First produced in prototype in the mid-1950s during the Full Bee (TMK-2) era, this figure was not released until 1992. The new pieces bear the mold number 320/0, but the Full Bee pieces have the mold number 320 with no size designator. These pieces are considerably larger than the production pieces.

There are no significant variations affecting the normal collector values.

Hum No.	Basic Size	Trademark	Current Value ($)
320	5-3/4"	TMK-2, FB	8000-10,000
320/0	4-3/4"	TMK-5, LB	195-210
320/0	4-3/4"	TMK-6, MB	195

THE PROFESSOR, Hum 320. Hummel mark (current use or TMK-7), incised 1989 MID, 4-7/8", first issue backstamp dated 1992.

THE PROFESSOR, Hum 320. This is a master model. Note the red line around the base.

THE PROFESSOR, Hum 320. The base of the Hum 320 master model. Note the inked incised mold number. This is routinely done on pieces made from the mother or master mold.

HUM 321: WASH DAY

WASH DAY, Hum 321. Three Line Mark, incised 1957 MID, 5-3/4".

In the first sample figurines, made in the 1950s, the laundry being held up was much longer and attached to the rest of the laundry down in the basket. This was the Full Bee period. It is possible though unlikely that you will find this figure. The only known examples are in the factory archives. These are marked with the Full Bee (TMK-2) trademark.

In 1989 a new smaller version of this piece was issued as a part of a four-piece series with matching mini-plates. These versions do not have the laundry basket. They have an incised mold number of 321 4/0. When this mold was issued Goebel changed the number on the larger piece to 321/0. You may find it either way on those figures with the Missing Bee (TMK-6) trademark.

Hum No.	Basic Size	Trademark	Current Value ($)
321/4/0	3"	TMK-6, MB	90-100
321	5-3/4"	TMK-2, FB	4000-5000
321	5-3/4"	TMK-3, Sty. Bee	300-350
321	5-3/4"	TMK-4, 3-line	275-300
321	5-3/4"	TMK-5, LB	260-275
321	5-3/4"	TMK-6, MB	260

HUM 322: LITTLE PHARMACIST

This figurine was first designed and produced in the 1950s and those samples bear the Full Bee (TMK-2) trademark. The only known examples of the figure are in the factory archives.

There are several variations in the labeling of the medicine bottle at the figure's feet. The version written in German (see photo) was temporarily withdrawn from production as of December 31, 1984. One of the most difficult pieces to find is the version with "Castor Oil" on the bottle in Spanish. When found, it is on the Three Line Mark (TMK-4) pieces. It is valued at $4,000-5,000.

In 1988 Little Pharmacist was redesigned, and all subsequent production of the figure reflects the following changes. The base was made more shallow with rounded corners, which made the figure shorter than its former 6" size (now 5-3/4"). The coat is now curved in front at the button line. A breast pocket was added, the strap (in back) was made wider and a second button was added. The figure's bow tie was straightened and the eyeglass stems made to disappear into his hair.

Somehow in 1990 an unknown (but probably very small) number of these figures were produced with the bottle label in German ("Rizinusol") and the prescription in English ("Recipe"). A TMK-6 Little Pharmacist with these words has a collector value of about $1,000.

Hum No.	Basic Size	Trademark	Current Value ($)
322	6"	TMK-2, FB	4000-5000
322	6"	TMK-3, Sty. Bee	750-1000
322	6"	TMK-4, 3-line	230-250
322	6"	TMK-5, LB	220-230
322	6"	TMK-6, MB	220

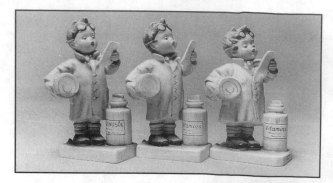

LITTLE PHARMACIST, Hum 322. Left: Last Bee (TMK-5) trademark, 1955 MID, 5-3/4", the word "REZEPT" is found on the prescription pad in his left hand. Center: Missing Bee (TMK-6) trademark, 1955 MID, 5-3/4", "RECIPE" is on the pad. Right: The same as the center figure except this one measures 5-5/8" and has a different hair style. Other variations are discussed in the accompanying text.

HUM 323: MERRY CHRISTMAS (Wall Plaque)

Designed and made in sample form during the 1950s in the Full Bee (TMK-2) period, this plaque was not offered for sale until 1979. It was initially issued bearing the Last Bee (TMK-5) and continues in the line with the present use trademark, the Hummel Mark (TMK-7).

Hum No.	Basic Size	Trademark	Current Value ($)
323	4"x5-1/4"	TMK-2, FB	2000-2500
323	4"x5-1/4"	TMK-5, LB	120-130
323	4"x5-1/4"	TMK-6, MB	120

MERRY CHRISTMAS Plaque, Hum 323. Last Bee mark, 3-1/8" x 5-1/4".

HUM 324: AT THE FENCE (Possible Future Edition)

This figure was designed and produced in sample form in the 1950s, but has not yet been put into regular production and offered for sale. The one in the picture is marked with the Full Bee (TMK-2), as you can see. Somehow it managed to make it onto the collectors' market. Notice the line painted around the base: this denotes a painter's sample, a model that the Goebel painters try to duplicate when producing the figurines. Collector value: $4,000-5,000.

AT THE FENCE,
Hum 324, PFE.

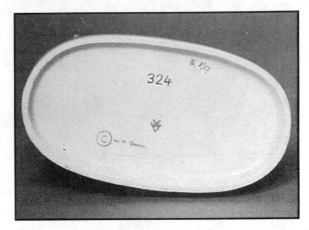

Base of Hum 324 showing the markings.

HUM 325: HELPING MOTHER (Possible Future Edition)

Originally designed and produced in prototype during the Full Bee (TMK-2) trademark era of the 1950s, this figure exists in at least two private collections with the Full Bee trademark. Collector value: $7,000-9,000.

HELPING MOTHER, Hum 325, PFE.

HUM 326: BEING PUNISHED

The original design and prototype figure was made in the mid-1950s. Those figures have an incised 1955 MID and bear the Full Bee (TMK-2) trademark. Although the piece has not yet been released, more than one has made its way onto the collector market. The figure has reportedly been found with the Stylized Bee (TMK-3) trademark also. Collector value: $5,000-7,500 for either one.

BEING PUNISHED,
Hum 326.

HUM 327: THE RUN-A-WAY

THE RUN-A-WAY, Hum 327. Left: Last Bee mark (TMK-5), incised 1955 MID, 5-1/8". Right: Last Bee Mark (TMK-5), incised 1972 MID, 5-1/2".

Originally designed and produced in the 1950s, this figure was not released until 1972.

There exist at least two variations of Hum 327. Significantly they have both been found with the Last Bee (TMK-5) trademark, although each bears a different mold induction date (MID). The older design (1955 MID) has flowers in the basket, gray jacket, gray hat, and the crook on the cane is turned more sideways. The newer design (1972 MID) has no flowers, a green hat, blue jacket, and the cane is situated with the crook pointing up.

Hum No.	Basic Size	Trademark	Current Value ($)
327	5-1/4"	TMK-2, FB	4000-5000
327	5-1/4"	TMK-4, 3-line	1000-1200
327 (old style)	5-1/4"	TMK-5, LB	750-900
327 (new style)	5-1/4"	TMK-5, LB	225-240
327	5-1/4"	TMK-6, MB	225

HUM 328: CARNIVAL

The original design and samples of this figure were made in the mid-1950s. Those sample pieces have a MID of 1955 and bear the Full Bee trademark. When the piece was put into regular production and offered for sale in the 1960s it had the Three Line Mark (TMK-4), but a few have been found bearing the Stylized Bee (TMK-3) as well.

There are no major mold or finish variations affecting the normal values.

Hum No.	Basic Size	Trademark	Current Value ($)
328	6"	TMK-2, FB	4000-5000
328	6"	TMK-3, Sty. Bee	800-1200
328	6"	TMK-4, 3-line	215-240
328	6"	TMK-5, LB	205-215
328	6"	TMK-6, MB	205

CARNIVAL, Hum 328. Three Line Mark (TMK-4), incised 1957 MID, 5-3/4".

HUM 329: OFF TO SCHOOL (Possible Future Edition)

This figure was originally designed and samples made in the 1950s. None are known to be outside the factory archives. Release date unknown.

The figure consists of a boy and girl walking along. The girl has a book satchel in the crook of her left arm. The boy figure is substantially similar to Hum 82 (School Boy).

HUM 330: BAKING DAY

This figure was first made in sample form in the 1950s. These early examples bear the 1955 MID, as do they today. The figure was not released until 1985, during the Missing Bee (TMK-6) period.

There are no significant mold or finish variations affecting normal values.

Hum No.	Basic Size	Trademark	Current Value ($)
330	5-1/4"	TMK-2, FB	4000-5000
330	5-1/4"	TMK-5, LB	240-250
330	5-1/4"	TMK-6, MB	240

BAKING DAY,
Hum 330.
Missing Bee
mark, incised
1955 MID,
5-1/4".

HUM 331: CROSSROADS

This piece was first made and released in the 1950s. It has been reported that there is a variation regarding the position of the trombone. It is not terribly obvious in the photo here but if you look closely, you can see the end of the horn protruding above the boy's head. The reported variation is that the horn is reversed so that it points down instead of up as in the one pictured here. This is an abberation and can't really be regarded as a legitimate variation. It is the result of a mistake in the assembly of the parts at the factory and is likely to be the only one in existence.

In 1990, Goebel issued a special edition of Crossroads to commemorate the demise of the Berlin Wall. Limited to 20,000 worldwide, it is the same figure except the "HALT" sign on the post is placed at the base of the post as if it had fallen or been torn down. Production of this edition took place during the transition from the Missing Bee (TMK-6) trademark to the Hummel Mark (TMK-7) currently being used. Interestingly, it has been reported that only about 3,500 of the 20,000 were given the Hummel Mark (TMK-7).

The newest variation is another edition created for the U.S. military forces. As with the special "Desert Storm" edition of Hum 50 (Volunteers), this one was sold through military base exchange stores only. The edition consists of three pieces. The figure is the regular production model with the sign on the post, but it has an American and German flag beneath the glaze under the base. A second piece is a representation of a piece of the wall with "Berlin Wall" on it in bas-relief. It also has the flags underneath along with the inscription "With esteem and grateful appreciation to the United States Military Forces for the preservation of peace and freedom." That same inscription is found on a brass plate on the front of the third piece, a wooden display base. The Berlin Wall piece is limited to 20,000 worldwide and sequentially hand-numbered beneath the base in the traditional manner of marking limited editions. The initial release price in 1992 was $265 for the set. It is valued at about $700 today.

CROSSROADS, Hum 331. Left: Last Bee mark (TMK-5), incised 1955 MID, 6-3/8". Right: Missing Bee mark (TMK-6), incised 1955 MID, 6-5/8". Special Backstamp reading "M.I. Hummel 1990 a Celebration of Freedom." Note the "HALT" sign is now on the ground.

Hum No.	Basic Size	Trademark	Current Value ($)
331	6-3/4"	TMK-2, FB	4000-5000
331	6-3/4"	TMK-3, Sty. Bee	2500-3500
331	6-3/4"	TMK-4, 3-line	800-1000
331	6-3/4"	TMK-5, LB	380-400
331	6-3/4"	TMK-6, MB	380-400
331 (sign down)	6-3/4"	TMK-6, MB	700-900
331 (sign down)	6-3/4"	TMK-7, HM	900-1100
331 (Desert Storm)	6-3/4"	TMK-7, HM	600-750

HUM 332: SOLDIER BOY

Originally designed and produced in prototype in the 1950s, this figure was not released for sale to the general public until the early 1960s.

There is a variation on the color of the cap medallion. It is painted red on older pieces and blue on the newer ones. The transition from red to blue took place in the Three Line Mark (TMK-4) period and can be found both ways bearing that trademark.

Goebel released a special limited edition in 1994 consisting of the figurine, a small porcelain replica of the shack at Checkpoint Charlie of Berlin Wall fame and a wooden base with a sign and brass ID plate (see accompanying photograph). The edition was limited to 20,000 and the pieces each bear a special backstamp identifying them appropriately. The release price was $330 and is still valued at about the same today.

Hum No.	Basic Size	Trademark	Current Value ($)
332	6"	TMK-2, FB	4000-5000
332	6"	TMK-3, Sty. Bee	800-1000
332 (red)	6"	TMK-4, 3-line	400-500
332 (blue)	6"	TMK-4, 3-line	205-225
332	6"	TMK-5, LB	195-205
332	6"	TMK-6, MB	195

SOLDIER BOY, Hum 332. Left: Three Line Mark (TMK-4), 1957 MID, red cap medallion, 5-3/4". Right: All is now the same except this one has a blue cap medallion.

The special edition Checkpoint Charlie SOLDIER BOY display.

The bases of the SOLDIER BOY and CHECKPOINT CHARLIE shack showing the special markings.

HUM 333: BLESSED EVENT

This figure was designed and produced as samples in the 1950s, but not released until 1964 during the Three Line (TMK-4) trademark era.

No significant variations have been reported.

There have been no examples found outside the factory archives with the Full Bee (TMK-2) and Stylized Bee (TMK-3) trademarks, but it would not be unreasonable to suspect they may be out there.

BLESSED EVENT, Hum 333. Three Line Mark, donut base, 5-1/4".

Hum No.	Basic Size	Trademark	Current Value ($)
333	5-1/2"	TMK-2, FB	*
333	5-1/2"	TMK-3, Sty. Bee	*
333	5-1/2"	TMK-4, 3-line	320-350
333	5-1/2"	TMK-5, LB	300-320
333	5-1/2"	TMK-6, MB	300

*Existence assumed but unsubstantiated.

HUM 334: HOMEWARD BOUND

This figurine was first made in sample form in the mid-1950s but not released until 1971. Older models of this design have a support molded in beneath the goat. The newer versions do not have this support.

The transition from the old, molded support model to the newer design took place during the Last Bee (TMK-5) period and can be found either way in that trademark.

Hum No.	Basic Size	Trademark	Current Value ($)
334	5"	TMK-2, FB	4000-5000
334	5"	TMK-4, 3-line	500-600
334 (old style)	5"	TMK-5, LB	375-500
334 (new style)	5"	TMK-5, LB	320-340
334	5"	TMK-6, MB	320

HOMEWARD BOUND, Hum 334. Left: Last Bee (TMK-6) mark, 1975 MID, split base, 5-1/2". Right: Last Bee (TMK-6), 1955 MID, donut base.

HUM 335: LUCKY BOY

Produced in sample form in the Stylized Bee (TMK-3) period, this figurine was reported as a possible future edition in the last edition of this book. The example in the accompanying photograph has a red line painted around the base, used by the factory to denote a figure that is used as a sample model for the factory artists.

Lucky Boy was released in special limited edition in a 4-1/2" size for $200. It was part of Goebel's 1995 celebration of 60 years of Hummel figurines. Two hundred and fifty U.S. dealers participated in Goebel's M.I.Hummel 60th Anniversary Open House. The figurine was limited to 25,000 worldwide with 15,000 of them bearing a special 60th anniversary backstamp. Collectors could only purchase figurines from participating dealers during the year. The other 10,000 pieces were made available in 1996 with the Goebel 125th anniversary backstamp. None will ever again be produced in this size. The release price was $190.

LUCKY BOY, Hum 335/0. The special limited edition. It measures 2-1/2", bears an incised MID of 1989 and the sixtieth anniversary backstamp.

Factory sample of LUCKY BOY, Hum 335. It has a 1956 MID and measures 5-3/4".

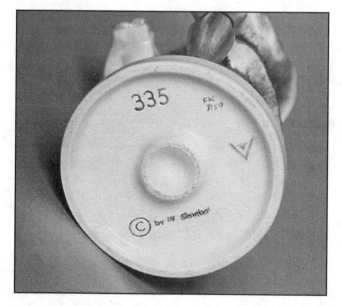

Base showing the Stylized Bee (TMK-3) trademark.

HUM 336: CLOSE HARMONY

This figure was first produced in sample form in the Full Bee (TMK-2) era, but not released until the early 1960s.

Inexplicably, this piece can be found with any one of three mold induction dates (MID): 1955, 1956 or 1957.

CLOSE HARMONY, Hum 336. Left: Three Line Mark (TMK-4), incised 1957 MID, donut base, 5-3/8". Right: Three Line Mark (TMK-4), incised 1955 MID, 5-1/4".

There is a 1962 MID that is explained by a redesign in that year. Even more peculiar is that those in production currently are yet another redesign, but they bear the 1955 MID. This strange circumstance makes the pieces with the later MID of 1962 more valuable than those with the 1955 MID that are currently in production. This is the only figure in the collection that can be found with four different MID's.

Hum No.	Basic Size	Trademark	Current Value ($)
336	5-1/2"	TMK-2, FB	4000-5000
336	5-1/2"	TMK-3, Sty. Bee	1000-1500
336	5-1/2"	TMK-4, 3-line	600-700
336 (old)	5-1/2"	TMK-5, LB	350-475
336 (new)	5-1/2"	TMK-5, LB	260-275
336	5-1/2"	TMK-6, MB	260

HUM 337: CINDERELLA

Produced first in the Full Bee (TMK-2) era as samples, this figure was not placed in the collection until 1972, during the Last Bee (TMK-5) period. Any with marks older than Last Bee will bring premium prices.

In the first versions of this figure the eyes are open. Newer figures have the eyes closed. These variations represent two entirely different molds. Both versions have appeared bearing the Last Bee trademark (TMK-5).

Hum No.	Basic Size	Trademark	Current Value ($)
337	5-1/2"	TMK-2, FB	4000-5000
337	5-1/2"	TMK-4, 3-line	1500-1700
337 (old style)	5-1/2"	TMK-5, LB	900-1200
337 (new style)	5-1/2"	TMK-5, LB	260-275
337	5-1/2"	TMK-6, MB	260

Last Bee 1952 MID, eyes closed.

CINDERELLA, Hum 337. Left: Full Bee mark in an incised circle, "© by W. Goebel," 4-5/8". Note the fourth bird (on the left shoulder). From the collection of Katherine Stephens. Right: Last Bee mark, incised 1958 MID, 4-1/2".

HUM 338: BIRTHDAY CAKE (Candleholder)

Birthday Cake was added to the line in the winter of 1988. It measures 3-3/4" and has a receptacle for a candle as you can see by the photo on the next page. It has an incised mold induction date of 1956.

BIRTHDAY CAKE candleholder, Hum 338. Missing Bee mark, incised 1956 MID, 3-9/16".

There are two versions to be found. The differences are with regard to the texture of the top of the cake surface. It is reported that about the first 2000 were produced with a smooth texture. This was changed to a rough texture ostensibly to correspond to the style of today.

It does exist in the Full Bee (TMK-2) prototype and has recently turned up in the Stylized Bee (TMK-3) trademark.

Hum No.	Basic Size	Trademark	Current Value ($)
338	3-3/4"	TMK-2, FB	4000-5000
338	3-3/4"	TMK-3, Sty. Bee	3000-4000
338	3-3/4"	TMK-6, MB	130

HUM 339: BEHAVE

The sample figurine in the photo bears a 1956 mold induction date (MID), indicating that it was designed then or prior (in the Full Bee (TMK-2) era). This one has the Stylized Bee (TMK-3) trademark and a collector value of $4,000-5,000.

The figurine was released in 1996 as a M.I. Hummel Club exclusive for the club year 1996-97. It has a special club backstamp in commemoration of twenty years of membership. It measures 5-1/2". The release price was $350. Notice the considerable differences between the sample piece and the regular production figurine.

Factory "Sample" of BEHAVE!, Hum 339.

Base of the factory sample.

Current production figurine, Hum 339.

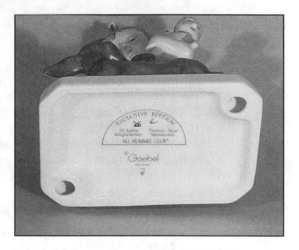

Base of the current production BEHAVE!.

HUM 340: LETTER TO SANTA CLAUS

LETTER TO SANTA, Hum 340. This particular figurine measures 7-1/8", has an incised 1957 MID and bears the Three Line Mark (TMK-4).

The first sample models produced had a tree trunk instead of a milled lumber post for the mailbox. The post was the final design approved for production. It was first released in the early 1970s. It was restyled with a new textured finish. This was a general change throughout the collection in the Last Bee Mark (TMK-5) period and can be found either way bearing that trademark. The old pieces sport gray-green pants and the newer ones have red-orange pants.

Hum No.	Basic Size	Trademark	Current Value ($)
340 (tree trunk post)	6"	TMK-2, FB	10,000-20,000
340	7"	TMK-2, FB	4000-5000
340	7"	TMK-3, Sty. Bee	3500-4000
340	7"	TMK-4, 3-line	600-750
340	7"	TMK-5, LB	305-325
340	7"	TMK-6, MB	305

HUM 341: BIRTHDAY PRESENT

This piece, in 5" sample form bearing the Three Line (TMK-4) trademark, was found on the collectors' market long before its release in 1994. This early sample model has a collector value of $4,000-5,000.

The production figurine is smaller at 4" and bears the First Issue backstamp and the Special Event backstamp, as it was part of a district manager promotion during 1994. It was available in this configuration during that year only. The release price was $140. It is in general production now at $155.

BIRTHDAY PRESENT, Hum 341. The figure on the left is an early factory sample model measuring 5-1/4" and bearing the Stylized Bee (TMK-3) trademark. The one on the right is the smaller (4") current production piece. The MID is 1989.

HUM 342: MISCHIEF MAKER

First made in sample form in the mid-1950s, this figure was not released for sale until 1972. There are no significant variations affecting normal values.

Hum No.	Basic Size	Trademark	Current Value ($)
342	4-15/16"	TMK-2, FB	4000-5000
342	4-15/16"	TMK-4, 3-line	600-750
342	4-15/16"	TMK-5, LB	240-250
342	4-15/16"	TMK-6, MB	240

MISCHIEF MAKER, Hum 342. Has an incised MID of 1960, is 4-7/8" tall and bears the Missing Bee (TMK-6) trademark.

HUM 343: CHRISTMAS SONG

CHRISTMAS SONG,
Hum 343. Missing Bee
1957 MID, 6-3/8".

This is one of the six new designs released by Goebel in 1981. There is at least one example of this piece known to exist bearing the Stylized Bee trademark.

All others found so far have later trademarks, but because there were five others designed and released at the same time that have been found with the Full Bee (TMK-2) trademark, it would not be unreasonable to assume there are some out there somewhere.

Hum No.	Basic Size	Trademark	Current Value ($)
343/4/0	3-1/2	TMK-7, HM	115
343	6-1/4"	TMK-2, FB	--
343	6-1/4"	TMK-3, Sty. Bee	2000-3000
343	6-1/4"	TMK-4, 3-line	600-750
343	6-1/4"	TMK-5, LB	195-210
343	6-1/4"	TMK-6, MB	195

HUM 344: FEATHERED FRIENDS

First designed and made in sample form in the mid-1950s, this piece was not released until 1972 during the Last Bee (TMK-5) era. Figurines have been found on the collectors' market, however, that bear the three earlier marks: Full Bee (TMK-2), Stylized Bee (TMK-3) and Three-Line (TMK-4).

There are no major mold or finish variations to be found that affect normal collector values.

FEATHERED FRIENDS, Hum 344. Missing Bee (TMK-6) mark, 1956 MID, 4-1/2".

Hum No.	Basic Size	Trademark	Current Value ($)
344	4-3/4"	TMK-2, FB	4000-5000
344	4-3/4"	TMK-3, Sty. Bee	2000-3000
344	4-3/4"	TMK-4, 3-line	750-1000
344	4-3/4"	TMK-5, LB	240-250
344	4-3/4"	TMK-6, MB	240

HUM 345: A FAIR MEASURE

This figure was first made as samples in the mid-1950s but was not released until the early 1960s.

At least two variations of this figure exist. It is important to note that both have been found bearing the current trademark and different mold induction dates (MID). The older design (1956 MID) shows the boy with his eyes wide open. In the newer design (1972 MID) the boy is looking down so that it appears that he is looking at his work. See the accompanying photograph. This transition from eyes up to eyes down took place during the Last Bee (TMK-5) and can be found both ways with that trademark.

Hum No.	Basic Size	Trademark	Current Value ($)
345	4-3/4"	TMK-2, FB	4000-5000
345	4-3/4"	TMK-3, Sty. Bee	2000-3000
345	4-3/4"	TMK-4, 3-line	900-1000
345 (old style)	4-3/4"	TMK-5, LB	550-750
345 (new style)	4-3/4"	TMK-5, LB	260-275
345	4-3/4"	TMK-6, MB	260

A FAIR MEASURE, Hum 345. Left: Last Bee mark, incised 1956 MID, donut base, 5-3/8". Center: Last Bee mark, incised 1972 MID, split base, 5-5/8". Right: Missing Bee mark, incised 1972 MID, split base, 5-5/8".

HUM 346: SMART LITTLE SISTER

Samples of Smart Little Sister were first made in the 1950s, but not released for sale until the early 1960s. It is nevertheless found with the earlier Full Bee (TMK-3) trademark, albeit rarely. The Stylized Bee (TMK-3) figures are not so rare; they seem to be available in a somewhat limited quantity.

There are no significant variations affecting normal values.

Hum No.	Basic Size	Trademark	Current Value ($)
346	4-3/4"	TMK-2, FB	4000-5000
346	4-3/4"	TMK-3, Sty. Bee	1200-1500
346	4-3/4"	TMK-4, 3-line	235-270
346	4-3/4"	TMK-5, LB	225-235
346	4-3/4"	TMK-6, MB	225

THE SMART LITTLE SISTER, Hum 346. Left: Three Line Mark, incised 1956 MID. Right: Last Bee mark, incised 1956 MID. Both measure 4-3/8".

HUM 347: ADVENTURE BOUND (SEVEN SWABIANS)

This large, complicated multi-figure piece was first made as a sample in the mid-1950s but was not released for sale until 1971-72. It has been made continuously since, but it is produced in limited numbers because it is a difficult and time-consuming piece to make.

There are at least three Full Bee (TMK-2) trademarked pieces known to be in private collections. No significant variations affect normal collector value.

Hum No.	Basic Size	Trademark	Current Value ($)
347	7-1/4"x8"	TMK-2, FB	10,000-12,000
347	7-1/4"x8"	TMK-4, 3-line	4000-5000
347	7-1/4"x8"	TMK-5, LB	3500-4000
347	7-1/4"x8"	TMK-6, MB	3500

ADVENTURE BOUND, Hum 347. Three Line Mark, incised 1957 MID, 8" long x 7" high.

HUM 348: RING AROUND THE ROSIE

RING AROUND THE ROSIE, Hum 348 with Full Bee mark (TMK-2) in an incised circle and "© by W. Goebel, Oeslau 1957." There is a painted red "X" beneath the base, making it probable that this particular piece is a prototype.

This figure was first molded in 1957 but was not released until 1960. Sizes found in various price lists range from 6-1/4" to 7-1/4". The older ones tend to be the larger ones. They all bear a 1957 mold induction date (MID).

There are no significant variations affecting normal values.

Hum No.	Basic Size	Trademark	Current Value ($)
348	6-3/4"	TMK-2, FB	10,000-12,000
348	6-3/4"	TMK-3, Sty. Bee	3200-3500
348	6-3/4"	TMK-4, 3-line	2700-2800
348	6-3/4"	TMK-5, LB	2500
348	6-3/4"	TMK-6, MB	2500

HUM 349: FLORIST (Possible Future Edition)

This figure is a standing boy wearing a bib apron. He holds a flower in his left hand and appears to be examining it closely. More flowers grow at his feet.

Only one example is known to be in a private collection. It is a 7-1/2" figure and bears the Three Line (TMK-4) trademark.

HUM 350: ON HOLIDAY

First made in the Stylized Bee (TMK-3) period, this figurine was a new release in 1981. Apparently a few samples were made in the Stylized Bee (TMK-3) and the Three Line (TMK-4) trademarks, for there have been a few uncovered. The remainder are found in the Last Bee (TMK-5) or later trademarks.

No significant mold or finish variations affect normal collector values.

ON HOLIDAY, Hum 350. Missing Bee (TMK-6), 1965 MID, 4-1/4".

Hum No.	Basic Size	Trademark	Current Value ($)
350	4-1/4"	TMK-3, Sty. Bee	2000-3000
350	4-1/4"	TMK-4, 3-line	1700-2000
350	4-1/4"	TMK-5, LB	1200-1500
350	4-1/4"	TMK-6, MB	160

HUM 351: THE BOTANIST

The basic size of this 1982 design release is 4". There is a very rare example of The Botanist known to exist with the Three Line Mark and a 1965 mold induction date. This is apparently an early sample and too unusual to be given a realistic market value. Another sample recently found with a 1965 mold induction date (MID) has the Last Bee (TMK-5) on it. All the newer pieces bear the 1972 MID.

Hum No.	Basic Size	Trademark	Current Value ($)
351	4"	TMK-4, 3-line	2000-3000
351	4"	TMK-5, LB	1500-1800
351	4"	TMK-6, MB	195

THE BOTANIST, Hum 351. Missing Bee mark, incised 1972 MID, 4-5/8".

HUM 352: SWEET GREETINGS

SWEET GREETINGS, Hum 352. Missing Bee mark, 1964 MID, 4-1/4".

Sweet Greetings was among the six new designs to be released in 1981. Its basic size is 4-1/8". Like a few other new releases it was apparently produced in limited numbers as a sample in the Three Line Mark era, for at least one figure is known to exist bearing that mark. Both the sample piece and the new release have a mold induction date of 1965.

Hum No.	Basic Size	Trademark	Current Value ($)
352	4-1/8"	TMK-4, 3-line	2000-3000
352	4-1/8"	TMK-5, LB	1500-1800
352	4-1/8"	TMK-6, MB	195

HUM 353: SPRING DANCE

This figure first appeared in the 1960s. The smaller size, 353/0, was released in the Last Bee trademark era. The 353/0 with a Three Line Mark is quite rare.

The larger size, 353/I, was temporarily withdrawn from production. No reinstatement date was disclosed. There are no significant variations that affect normal collector value.

SPRING DANCE, Hum 353. Left: 353/0, Last Bee mark (TMK-5) 1963 MID, 5-3/8". Right: 353/I, Three Line Mark (TMK-4), 1963 MID, 6-3/4".

Hum No.	Basic Size	Trademark	Current Value ($)
353/0	4-3/4"	TMK-4, 3-line	2500-3000
353/0	4-3/4"	TMK-5, LB	280-300
353/0	4-3/4"	TMK-6, MB	280
353/1	6-1/2"	TMK-4, 3-line	600-750
353/1	6-1/2"	TMK-5, LB	550
353/1	6-1/2"	TMK-6, MB	500

HUM 354/A: ANGEL WITH LANTERN, HUM 354/B: ANGEL WITH TRUMPET, HUM 354/C: ANGEL WITH BIRD (Holy Water Fonts)

This figure has a closed number designation. Three fonts exist in the Goebel archives as factory samples only.

Apparently they were never produced.

HUM 355: AUTUMN HARVEST

First produced as a sample in the Stylized Bee (TMK-3) era, this figurine was not released for sale in any quantity until the early 1970s. The earliest production pieces bear the Three Line Mark (TMK-4), but they are apparently in fairly short supply.

The figures have an incised MID of 1971. There are no significant variations affecting normal collector values.

Hum No.	Basic Size	Trademark	Current Value ($)
355	4-3/4"	TMK-4, 3-line	800-1000
355	4-3/4"	TMK-5, LB	195-205
355	4-3/4"	TMK-6, MB	195

AUTUMN HARVEST,
Hum 355. Left: Three Line Mark,
incised 1964 MID,
4-7/8". Right: Missing
Bee mark, incised 1964 MID, 5".

HUM 356: GAY ADVENTURE

This figure was first produced as a sample in the 1960s and was known as Joyful Adventure at the time. It was released for sale in the early 1970s bearing a 1971 incised MID. There are no significant variations affecting normal collector values.

GAY ADVENTURE,
Hum 356. Last Bee
(TMK-5), 1971 MID,
4-3/4".

Hum No.	Basic Size	Trademark	Current Value ($)
356	4-15/16"	TMK-4, 3-line	800-1000
356	4-15/16"	TMK-5, LB	190
356	4-15/16"	TMK-6, MB	175

HUM 357, 358 and 359: GUIDING ANGEL, SHINING LIGHT and TUNEFUL ANGEL

Originally molded around 1960 with a 1960 MID, these were not released until the early 1970s. They are usually sold as a set.

There are no significant variations affecting normal values.

Hum No.	Basic Size	Trademark	Current Value ($)
357	2-3/4"	TMK-4, 3-line	85-95
357	2-3/4"	TMK-5, LB	80-85
357	2-3/4"	TMK-6, MB	80
358	2-3/4"	TMK-4, 3-line	80
358	2-3/4"	TMK-5, LB	85-95
358	2-3/4"	TMK-6, MB	80-85
359	2-3/4"	TMK-4, 3-line	80
359	2-3/4"	TMK-5, LB	85-95
359	2-3/4"	TMK-6, MB	80-85

GUIDING ANGEL, Hum 357. Missing Bee (TMK-6) mark, 1960 MID, 2-7/8".
SHINING LIGHT, Hum 358. Missing Bee (TMK-6) mark, 1960 MID, 2-3/4".
TUNEFUL ANGEL, Hum 359. Missing Bee (TMK-6) mark, 1960 MID, 2-5/8".

M 360/A, 360/B and 360/C: BOY, GIRL and BOY AND GIRL (Wall Vases)

Stylized Bee trademarked wall vases are considered rare. They were first produced around 1955 and discontinued about 1960. Of the three, the Boy and Girl (Hum 360/A) seems to be the most easily found. All three appear with the earliest and rarest Stylized Bee (TMK-3) trademark. Their basic size is 4-1/2"x6-1/4".

All three figures were restyled and reissued in 1979 with the Last Bee trademark and continued in production in the Missing Bee (TMK-6) trademark. They were temporarily withdrawn from production once again on December 31, 1989. No reinstatement date was disclosed.

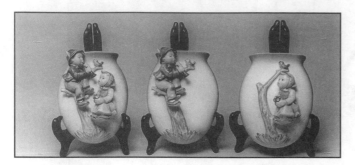

WALL VASES, Hum 360/A, Hum 360/B, Hum 360/C. All three bear an incised Stylized Bee trademark (TMK-3), "© by W. Goebel," black "Western Germany," incised 1958 MID and measure 5-3/4".

Hum No.	Basic Size	Trademark	Current Value ($)
360 A,B&C	4-1/2"x6-1/4"	TMK-3, Sty. Bee	350-500 each
360 A,B&C	4-1/2"x6-1/4"	TMK-5, LB	150-200 each
360 A,B&C	4-1/2"x6-1/4"	TMK-6, MB	125-140 each

HUM 361: FAVORITE PET

First made in prototype about 1960, this figure was released for sale in the mid-1960s. There are no significant variations affecting normal collector values.

Hum No.	Basic Size	Trademark	Current Value ($)
361	4-1/4"	TMK-3, Sty. Bee	800-1000
361	4-1/4"	TMK-4, 3-line	275-300
361	4-1/4"	TMK-5, LB	260-275
361	4-1/4"	TMK-6, MB	260

FAVORITE PET, Hum 361. Three Line Mark (TMK-4), 1960 MID, donut base, 4-1/4".

HUM 362: I FORGOT (Possible Future Edition)

Made in sample form in the late 1950s, this figure has not yet been released for sale. It bears the Last Bee (TMK-5) trademark and a mold induction date of 1959.

I FORGOT, Hum 362, PFE.

Base of Hum 362 showing the markings.

HUM 363: BIG HOUSECLEANING

The original sample models of this figure were made during the Stylized Bee (TMK-3) era. The figures have been in continuous production since their release at the end of the Three Line (TMK-4) era. Some were made bearing this trademark, but they are fairly scarce. There are no significant variations affecting normal value for the figures.

BIG HOUSECLEANING, Hum 363. Missing Bee mark, incised 1980 MID, 4".

Hum No.	Basic Size	Trademark	Current Value ($)
363	3-15/16"	TMK-4, 3-line	800-1000
363	3-15/16"	TMK-5, LB	260-275
363	3-15/16"	TMK-6, MB	260

HUM 364: SUPREME PROTECTION

This piece is a 9" full-color Madonna and child and is the first limited edition figurine ever offered to the general public by Goebel. Released in 1984, it was scheduled to be produced during that year only, in commemoration and celebration of what would have been Sister M.I. Hummel's 75th birthday. The figure has a special backstamp identifying it as such. As the first figures became available it was discovered that some 3,000 to 3,500 of them were released with a mistake in the stamp. The M.I. Hummel came out as M.J. Hummel. The factory tried at first to correct the mistake by modifying the "J" in the decal to appear as an "I." However, they attempted to change it by cutting the decal and unfortunately the modification didn't come off too well: the result demonstrated their attempt quite obviously. As a consequence there are three backstamp versions to be found: the correct backstamp, the poorly modified backstamp, and the "M.J. Hummel" incorrect backstamp. This particular backstamp variation is apparently in strong demand.

These Hum 364's have been found bearing the Three Line (TMK-4) trademark, but these are rare. They were probably sample pieces never meant to be sold.

Hum No.	Basic Size	Trademark	Current Value ($)
364	9"	TMK-4, 3-line	2500-3500
364 (regular signature)	9"	TMK-6, MB	250-275
364 (M.J. variation)	9"	TMK-6, MB	400-500
364 (M.J. altered version)	9"	TMK-6, MB	500-600

SUPREME PROTECTION, Hum 364. Missing Bee (TMK-6) mark, 1964 MID, 9-1/8".

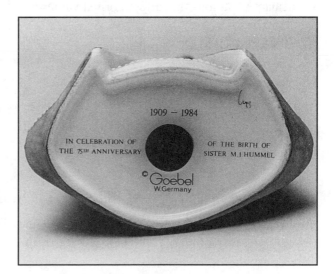

SUPREME PROTECTION, Hum 364. Base photo showing the special inscription.

HUM 365: LITTLEST ANGEL (Possible Future Edition)

THE LITTLEST ANGEL, Hum 365. This particular example bears the Three Line mark and measures 2-3/4".

This beautiful little angel was first made in prototype in the early 1960s and has not yet been put into production. The one in the accompanying photo bears the Three Line (TMK-4) trademark.

HUM 366: FLYING ANGEL

This figure is commonly used with the nativity sets and has been produced in painted versions as well as white overglaze. The white ones are rare and valued at $200-250.

This piece was first released in the Three Line (TMK-4) trademark period and has remained in production throughout the years. The new smaller version was introduced in 1989. There are no significant variations affecting normal values.

FLYING ANGEL, Hum 366.

Hum No.	Basic Size	Trademark	Current Value ($)
366/0	2-3/4"	TMK-5, LB	85-95
366/0	2-3/4"	TMK-6, MB	85
366	3-1/2"	TMK-4, 3-line	125-135
366	3-1/2"	TMK-5, LB	115-125
366	3-1/2"	TMK-6, MB	115

HUM 367: BUSY STUDENT

First made and released in the mid-1960s, this figure has been continuously available since then. There are no significant variations that affect normal values.

Hum No.	Basic Size	Trademark	Current Value ($)
367	4-1/4"	TMK-3, Sty. Bee	700-1000
367	4-1/4"	TMK-4, 3-line	160-175
367	4-1/4"	TMK-5, LB	150-160
367	4-1/4"	TMK-6, MB	150

BUSY STUDENT, Hum 367. Three Line mark (TMK-4), incised 1963 MID, 4-1/4".

HUM 368: LUTE SONG (Possible Future Edition)

The figure is a standing girl playing the lute. This design is substantially similar to the girl in Close Harmony (Hum 336).

HUM 369: FOLLOW THE LEADER

This figurine was first made in prototype in the mid-1960s, but not released for sale until the early 1970s. There are no significant variations to affect the normal values.

FOLLOW THE LEADER, Hum 369. Missing Bee mark (TMK-6), 1964 MID, 7".

Hum No.	Basic Size	Trademark	Current Value ($)
369	6-15/16"	TMK-4, 3-line	1200-1500
369	6-15/16"	TMK-5, LB	1100-1200
369	6-15/16"	TMK-6, MB	1100

HUM 370: COMPANIONS (Possible Future Edition)

This design is much like To Market (Hum 49) except that the girl has been replaced with a boy that is remarkably like the boy of Hum 51 (Village Boy).

HUM 371: DADDY'S GIRLS

Daddy's Girls was a new addition to the line in 1989. It measures 4-7/8" tall and has an incised mold induction date of 1964 on the underside of the base. Because it was first made as a sample in the Three Line (TMK-4) period there is good reason to suspect there may be one or two out there with that trademark.

These figures are commonly found in the Missing Bee (TMK-6) and Hummel Mark (TMK-7). They are valued at about $180-200 and are in current production.

DADDY'S GIRLS, Hum 371. Missing Bee mark, incised 1964 MID, 4-3/4".

HUM 372: BLESSED MOTHER (Possible Future Edition)

This figure is a standing Madonna and child.

HUM 373: JUST FISHING

This is a new figure released in early 1985 at a suggested retail price of $85. It measures 4-1/4" x 4-1/2". Early Goebel promotional materials referred to this piece as an ash tray. This was in error; probably due to the tray-like base representing the pond. Interestingly it was once more identified as an ashtray in the Goebel price list, but in the 1993 list it is called as a figurine.

This piece is found in the Missing Bee (TMK-6) and the Hummel Mark (TMK-7) trademarks and valued at about $180-200. It is in current production.

JUST FISHING, Hum 373. Missing Bee (TMK-6) mark, 1965 MID, measures 4-1/8" with the pole.

HUM 374: LOST STOCKING

Made as a sample in the mid-1960s, this figurine was not released for sale until 1965 (in the Three Line (TMK-4) trademark period). No significant variations affect normal values.

Hum No.	Basic Size	Trademark	Current Value ($)
374	4-3/8"	TMK-4, 3-line	800-1000
374	4-3/8"	TMK-5, LB	130-140
374	4-3/8"	TMK-6, MB	130

LOST STOCKING, Hum 374. This piece bears the Last Bee (TMK-5) trademark, measures 4-1/2" and has an incised MID of 1965.

HUM 375: MORNING STROLL

First produced in sample form with the Three Line (TMK-4) trademark, this figurine was placed in production and released to the market in 1994. It measures 3-3/4" (a full 3/4" smaller than the pre-production sample). Those produced in 1994 bear a First Issue backstamp. The production piece Hum 375/3/0 is found with TMK-7 and is listed for $195 in the Goebel price list.

MORNING STROLL, Hum 375. This is an early factory sample piece.

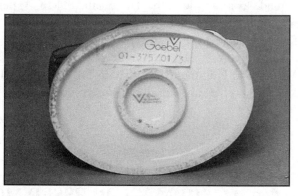

The base of the sample MORNING STROLL showing the Three Line (TMK-4) trademark.

HUM 376: LITTLE NURSE

This piece is one of the two designs released in 1982. Although most of them are found with TMK-5, it is known that at least one exists bearing the Last Bee mark (TMK-5) with a 1965 mold induction date. The Last Bee (TMK-6) or later trademarked pieces have a 1972 MID.

LITTLE NURSE, Hum 376. Bears the Missing Bee mark (TMK-6), is 4-1/8" tall and has an incised 1972 MID.

Hum No.	Basic Size	Trademark	Current Value ($)
376	4"	TMK-5, LB	3000-3500
376	4"	TMK-6, MB	225-250

HUM 377: BASHFUL

This figure was first made in sample form in the Three Line Mark (TMK-4), but production models in that mark are fairly scarce. Later marks are more easily found.

There are no significant variations that affect normal values. The older pieces generally have a 1966 mold induction date (MID) and sometimes a 1971 MID, but the new production figurines do not have an incised MID at all.

Hum No.	Basic Size	Trademark	Current Value ($)
377	4-3/4"	TMK-4, 3-line	800-1000
377	4-3/4"	TMK-5, LB	180-200
377	4-3/4"	TMK-6, MB	180

BASHFUL, Hum 377. Last Bee mark, incised 1966 MID, 4-5/8".

HUM 378: EASTER GREETINGS

The early sample models of Easter Greetings were made during the Three Line Mark (TMK-4) period of production, but regular production figurines bearing this mark are scarce. They have an incised MID of 1971. There are no significant mold or finish variations affecting normal collector values.

EASTER GREETINGS, Hum 378. Last Bee mark, incised 1971 MID, 5".

Hum No.	Basic Size	Trademark	Current Value ($)
378	5-1/2"	TMK-4, 3-line	800-1000
378	5-1/2"	TMK-5, LB	195-210
378	5-1/2"	TMK-6, MB	195

HUM 379: DON'T BE SHY (Possible Future Edition)

This figure is a little girl with a kerchief on her head. She is feeding a bird perched on a fence post.

HUM 380: DAISIES DON'T TELL

DAISIES DON'T TELL, Hum 380. Missing Bee mark, incised 1972 MID, 5".

This is the Goebel Collectors' Club Special Edition figure offered exclusively to club members in 1981. As with all the others it could be purchased by current members with redemption cards for $80 in the U.S. and $95 in Canada. As of May 31, 1985, it was no longer available on the secondary market. It is available only in the Missing Bee (TMK-6) trademark and valued at $170-180.

The mold induction date is 1972. There is at least one known to exist bearing the Three Line Mark (TMK-4) and one MID of 1966. This latter piece is exceedingly rare and cannot be assigned a realistic collector value.

HUM 381: FLOWER VENDOR

This figurine was released in the early 1970s at the end of the Stylized Bee (TMK-3) and Three Line Mark (TMK-4) eras, but can only be found in the latter (which are fairly scarce). There are no significant variations affecting values.

FLOWER VENDOR, Hum 381. Last Bee (TMK-5) mark, 1971 MID, 5-1/8".

Hum No.	Basic Size	Trademark	Current Value ($)
381	5-1/2"	TMK-4, 3-line	800-1000
381	5-1/2"	TMK-5, LB	220
381	5-1/2"	TMK-6, MB	220

FLOWER VENDOR, Hum 381. Demonstration piece with only the facial features painted. The flesh tones are applied before the face details in demonstrations. In early demonstrations it was not always done, as in this case. Last Bee trademark (TMK-5), incised 1971 MID, donut base, 5-1/4". Valued at about $450-500.

HUM 382: VISITING AN INVALID

This figurine was released first in the Three Line (TMK-4) era but is scarce and hard to find with that trademark. There are no significant variations to report.

VISITING AN INVALID, Hum 382. Last Bee mark, incised 1971 MID, 4-7/8".

Hum No.	Basic Size	Trademark	Current Value ($)
382	4-15/16"	TMK-4, 3-line	800-1000
382	4-15/16"	TMK-5, LB	195-210
382	4-15/16"	TMK-6, MB	195

HUM 383: GOING HOME

This new piece for 1985 was released at a suggested retail price of $125. Basic size is 5". The first examples were apparently made in the prototype phase in the previous trademark, the Last Bee (TMK-5). One item bearing that trademark has recently surfaced.

There are no significant variations that influence collector values.

Hum No.	Basic Size	Trademark	Current Value ($)
383	5"	TMK-5, LB	3000-3500
383	5"	TMK-6, MB	280

GOING HOME, Hum 383. Missing Bee (TMK-6). 1972 MID, donut base, 4-15/16".

HUM 384: EASTER TIME

EASTER TIME,
Hum 384. Last Bee
trademark, incised
1971 MID, 4".

Occasionally called Easter Playmates, this figure was first produced in sample form in the Three Line Mark (TMK-4). It was first released for sale at the very end of that period so the figures are fairly scarce in that trademark.

There are no significant variations that affect collector value.

Hum No.	Basic Size	Trademark	Current Value ($)
384	3-15/16"	TMK-4, 3-line	800-1000
384	3-15/16"	TMK-5, LB	240-250
384	3-15/16"	TMK-6, MB	240

HUM 385: CHICKEN-LICKEN

This one of the 25 pieces first released in 1971-72 with the Three Line Mark. It has a mold induction date (MID) of 1971 and has been in production since. In 1990 Goebel released a smaller size, 3-1/4", with the incised mold number 385/4/0. The recommended retail price at release time was $85.

There are no significant variations affecting collector value.

CHICKEN LICKEN,
Hum 385. Last Bee
mark, incised 1971
MID, 4-11/16".

Hum No.	Basic Size	Trademark	Current Value ($)
385/4/0	3-1/4"	TMK-5, LB	90-100
385/4/0	3-1/4"	TMK-6, MB	90
385	4-3/4"	TMK-4, 3-line	800-1000
385	4-3/4"	TMK-5, LB	260-275
385	4-3/4"	TMK-6, MB	260

HUM 386: ON SECRET PATH

ON SECRET PATH, Hum 386.
Last Bee (TMK-5), 1971 MID,
3-3/8".

This is one of the 25 pieces first released in 1971-72 in the Three Line (TMK-4) trademark. It has a mold induction date (MID) of 1971 and has been in production since it was introduced.

There are no significant variations affecting the collector value.

Hum No.	Basic Size	Trademark	Current Value ($)
386	5-3/8"	TMK-4, 3-line	800-1000
386	5-3/8"	TMK-5, LB	225-240
386	5-3/8"	TMK-6, MB	225

HUM 387: VALENTINE GIFT

VALENTINE GIFT, Hum 387, with the matching M.I. Hummel Club exclusive miniature as a pendant. Last Bee mark (TMK-5), incised 1972 MID, 5-3/4". An M.I. Hummel Club exclusive.

This rather special figure was the first special edition figurine available only to members of the Goebel Collectors Club (now the M.I. Hummel Club), an organization sponsored by and a division of the Goebel firm. The figure was originally released in 1977 at $45 with a redemption card obtained through membership in the club. The size is 5-3/4". The most commonly found piece bears the Last Bee mark (TMK-5) and sells at $350-400. Older pieces (TMK-4) have brought as much as $2,000. As of May 31, 1984, the piece was no longer available except on the secondary market.

HUM 388: LITTLE BAND (Candleholder)

This is a three-figure piece utilizing Hum 389, 390 and 391 on one base. It contains a candle receptacle. It was released in the Three Line (TMK-4) period and was in continuous production until the company placed it on a list of figurines that were temporarily withdrawn from production on December 31, 1990. Goebel disclosed no reinstatement date.

LITTLE BAND music box and candleholder, Hum 388/M. Three Line mark (TMK-4), 1968 MID.

Hum No.	Basic Size	Trademark	Current Value ($)
388	3"x4-3/4"	TMK-4, 3-line	235-260
388	3"x4-3/4"	TMK-5, LB	220-235
388	3"x4-3/4"	TMK-6, MB	220

HUM 388/M: LITTLE BAND (Candleholder and Music Box)

This is the same piece as Hum 388 but is mounted on a wooden base with a music box inside. When the music box plays, the Little Band figure rotates.

Goebel placed this figure on a list of pieces taken out of production temporarily on December 31, 1990. There was no reinstatement date disclosed. No significant variations affect collector values.

Hum No.	Basic Size	Trademark	Current Value ($)
388/M	4-3/4"x5"	TMK-4, 3-line	325-350
388/M	4-3/4"x5"	TMK-5, LB	300-325
388/M	4-3/4"x5"	TMK-6, MB	300

LITTLE BAND music box and candleholder, Hum 388 M.

LITTLE BAND candleholder, Hum 388.

HUM 389: GIRL WITH SHEET MUSIC, HUM 390: BOY WITH ACCORDION, HUM 391: GIRL WITH HORN (Little Band)

These three pieces are the same figures used on Hum 388, 388/M, 392 and 392/M. They are on current suggested price lists as available in a set of three or separately.

No significant variations affect collector values for the various trademarked pieces.

CHILDREN TRIO. Hum 389, Girl with Sheet Music, Last Bee (TMK-5) mark, 2-5/8".
Hum 390, Boy with Accordion, Three Line Mark (TMK-4), 2-3/4". Hum 391, Girl with Horn, Last Bee (TMK-5) mark, 1968 MID, 2-3/4".

Hum No.	Basic Size	Trademark	Current Value ($)
389	2-1/2"-2-3/4"	TMK-3, Sty. Bee	90-100
389	2-1/2"-2-3/4"	TMK-4, 3-line	80-90
389	2-1/2"-2-3/4"	TMK-5, LB	75-80
389	2-1/2"-2-3/4"	TMK-6, MB	75
390	2-1/2"-2-3/4"	TMK-3, Sty. Bee	90-100
390	2-1/2"-2-3/4"	TMK-4, 3-line	80-90
390	2-1/2"-2-3/4"	TMK-5, LB	75-80
390	2-1/2"-2-3/4"	TMK-6, MB	75
391	2-1/2"-2-3/4"	TMK-3, Sty. Bee	90-100
391	2-1/2"-2-3/4"	TMK-4, 3-line	80-90
391	2-1/2"-2-3/4"	TMK-5, LB	75-80
391	2-1/2"-2-3/4"	TMK-6, MB	75

HUM 392: LITTLE BAND

The same as Hum 388 except that this piece has no provision for a candle. Little Band is listed as having been temporarily withdrawn from current production status with no reinstatement date given. There are no significant variations affecting collector value.

Hum No.	Basic Size	Trademark	Current Value ($)
392	4-3/4"x3"	TMK-4, 3-line	235-260
392	4-3/4"x3"	TMK-5, LB	220-235
392	4-3/4"x3"	TMK-6, MB	220

TIMID LITTLE SISTER, Hum 394.
Missing Bee mark, 1972 MID, 6-3/4", base is split laterally beneath.

HUM 389/M: LITTLE BAND (Music Box)

This is the same piece as Hum 392, but it is placed atop a base with a music box inside. When the music plays the piece revolves.

There are no significant mold or finish variations affecting values.

Hum No.	Basic Size	Trademark	Current Value ($)
392/M	4-1/4"x5"	TMK-4, 3-line	325-350
392/M	4-1/4"x5"	TMK-5, LB	300-325
392/M	4-1/4"x5"	TMK-6, MB	300-325

LITTLE BAND music box, Hum 392/M. Three Line mark (TMK-4), 1968 MID. Two of three styles of bases found.

HUM 393: DOVE (Holy Water Font) (Possible Future Edition)

The design of this figure includes a flying dove and a banner with the inscription "+ KOMM + HEILIGER + GEIST +". This translates into English as "Come Holy Spirit." Only one known example exists outside Goebel archives. It bears the Three Line Mark (TMK-4).

HUM 394: TIMID LITTLE SISTER

TIMID LITTLE SISTER, Hum 394. Missing Bee mark, 1972 MID, 6-3/4", base is split laterally beneath.

This two-figure piece was a new design released with five others in 1981. It has been found with the Last Bee trademark (TMK-5). Both the older vintage pieces and the commonly found current-use trademarked pieces bear the 1972 mold induction date. When released in 1981 the price was $190

There are no significant variations that affect collector value.

Hum No.	Basic Size	Trademark	Current Value ($)
394	7"	TMK-5, LB	3000-3500
394	7"	TMK-6, MB	390-400

HUM 395: SHEPHERD BOY

This 6-3/4" figurine was first made as a sample in the early 1970s and released in late 1995. An early sample has been found bearing the Last Bee (TMK-5) with a 1989 MID. The first year's figures will be marked with the First Issue backstamp. The latest Goebel suggested retail price for the figure in a current trademark (TMK-7) is $295.

SHEPHERD BOY, Hum 395.

HUM 396: RIDE INTO CHRISTMAS

RIDE INTO CHRISTMAS, Hum 396/I. Missing Bee mark, 1971 MID, 6".

This figurine remains quite popular and is in great demand by collectors. Perhaps this is why Goebel released a smaller version in 1982. The release of the smaller piece necessitated a change in the mold number of the larger one from 396 to 396/1.

The larger size bears a mold induction date (MID) of 1971 and the smaller has a 1981 MID. There are no significant production variations that affect collector values for this piece.

Hum No.	Basic Size	Trademark	Current Value ($)
396/2/0	4-1/4"	TMK-5, LB	135-165
396/2/0	4-1/4"	TMK-6, MB	135
396	5-3/4"	TMK-4, 3-line	1600-2200
396	5-3/4"	TMK-5, LB	250-315
396	5-3/4"	TMK-6, MB	220

RIDE INTO CHRISTMAS, Hum 396. Demonstration piece with only the flesh tones painted on the face. Missing Bee trademark, incised 1971 MID, 6". Valued at about $700-800.

HUM 397: THE POET

THE POET, Hum 397.

The Poet was released in 1994 in a 6" size. Those produced in 1994 bear the First Issue backstamp. Any production subsequent to 1994 bears the current-use trademark (TMK-7). The figure was first made in sample form with the Three Line Mark (TMK-4). The suggested retail price from Goebel lists is $250.

HUM 398: SPRING BOUQUET (Possible Future Edition)

This figure is a girl picking flowers. She holds a bouquet in her left arm. No known examples exist outside the company archives.

HUM 399: VALENTINE JOY

This is the fourth special edition offered exclusively to the members of the Goebel Collector's Club (now the M.I. Hummel Club). Issued in 1980-81, the figures bear a 1979 mold induction date, measure 5-5/8" and were available for $95 with the club redemption card. Although it is known that there are existing examples with the Last Bee trademark (TMK-5), the piece is normally found with the Missing Bee (TMK-6). Available only on the secondary market.

VALENTINE JOY, Hum 399. Left: Last Bee mark, incised 1973 MID, split base, 6-1/4". Note the grass and bird on the base. Old style. Right: Missing Bee mark, incised 1979 MID, 5-3/4".

Hum No.	Basic Size	Trademark	Current Value ($)
399	5-3/4"	TMK-5, LB	10,000
399	5-3/4"	TMK-6, MB	200-250

HUM 400: WELL DONE! (Possible Future Edition)

This is a figure of two standing boys. The one wearing shorts pats the other, who wears long pants, on the shoulder. No known examples exist outside the company archives.

HUM 401: FORTY WINKS (Possible Future Edition)

This girl is seated with a small boy next to her. He is asleep with his head on her right shoulder. No known examples exist outside the company archives.

HUM 402: TRUE FRIENDSHIP (Possible Future Edition)

In this figurine, a seated girl eats porridge from bowl held in her left hand. Her right hand holds a spoonful and a bird is perched on her right forearm.

HUM 403: AN APPLE A DAY

AN APPLE A DAY, Hum 403. Missing Bee mark, incised 1974 MID, 6-1/2".

An Apple a Day was released in 1988. It is 6-1/2" tall and carries an incised 1974 mold induction date. The price at the time of release was $195.

The fact that the design was copyrighted in the Last Bee (TMK-5) trademark era makes it possible that the figure exists, at least as a sample, with that trademark.

Presently it is available only in the Hummel Mark (TMK-7), which is listed in the latest Goebel suggested retail price list at $300. There are no known examples in private collections and no significant variations that affect collector value

HUM 404: SAD SONG (Possible Future Edition)

This figure is a standing boy singing. He looks as if he is about to cry and holds the sheet music at back with his right hand. No known examples exist outside the company archives.

HUM 405: SING WITH ME

This piece was first released in 1985. The basic size is 5". The one in the accompanying photo measures slightly bigger at 5-1/8" tall. A mold induction date of 1974 is found incised on the underside of the base. The figure is found in the Missing Bee (TMK-6) and the Hummel Mark (TMK-7).

There are no significant variations that affect collector value.

SING WITH ME, Hum 405. Missing Bee mark (TMK-6), incised 1974 MID, 5".

Hum No.	Basic Size	Trademark	Current Value ($)
405	5"	TMK-6, MB	280

HUM 406: PLEASANT JOURNEY

Released in 1987, this piece has a basic size of 6-1/2" long by 6-1/4" high. This piece, like the Chapel Time clock, is limited to those produced in 1987. The figures will not be produced again in the twentieth century. The release price was $500 and the current value is about $1,500-2,500. Early samples in the Goebel archives bear the Last Bee Mark (TMK-5). The production figure is found only with the Missing Bee (TMK-6) trademark. There are no variations affecting the figure's value.

PLEASANT JOURNEY, Hum 406. Missing Bee mark, incised 1976 MID, 7-3/8" long x 6-3/8" high. Century Collection, 1987.

HUM 407: FLUTE SONG (Possible Future Edition)

In this figure a seated boy plays the flute for the lamp standing in front of him. The boy is seated on what appears to be a stump.

HUM 408: SMILING THROUGH

This is the tenth redemption piece available only to members of the Goebel Collector's Club. It was released in 1985 at $125 to those with a redemption card. The mold number incised on the bottom of this figurine is actually 408/0. The reason for this is that a larger model was molded but never released in 1976. It was made as a sample only and resides in the factory archives now. This larger version was 6" while the one released to club members is only 4-3/4". As of May 31, 1987, the figures are available only on the secondary market and are found only in the Missing Bee (TMK-6) trademark. Collector value: $190-220. There are no significant variations that affect value.

SMILING THROUGH, Hum 408/0. Missing Bee mark (TMK-6), incised 1983 MID, 4-3/4".

HUM 409: COFFEE BREAK

This is the ninth special edition piece available exclusively to members of the Goebel Collector's Club. It was available to members with a redemption card until May 31, 1986. The issue price for Coffee Break was $90. Now available only on the secondary market and only in the Missing Bee (TMK-6), it is valued at $100-125.

COFFEE BREAK, Hum 409. Missing Bee mark (TMK-6), incised 1976 MID, 3-15/16".

HUM 410: LITTLE ARCHITECT

New for 1993, this figure (also known as Truant) has a basic size of 6" and bears the mold number 410/I. The suggested retail price is $330.

HUM 411: DO I DARE? (Possible Future Edition)

This figure is a standing girl holding a flower in her left hand and a basket in the crook of her right arm.

HUM 412: BATH TIME

BATH TIME, Hum 412. Missing Bee, 1978 MID, 6-1/8".

This figure was released for sale in 1990 during the Missing Bee (TMK-6) trademark era. It is found in that trademark and the current-use trademark, the Hummel Mark (TMK-7). There are no significant variations that affect the collector value of $410.

HUM 413: WHISTLER'S DUET

This figure was released in late 1991 and is found only in the Hummel Mark (TMK-7). It is listed with the basic size of 4-3/8" and a price of $310 in the latest suggested retail price list from Goebel. No significant variations affect the collector value.

WHISTLER'S DUET, Hum 413. Hummel Mark (current use or TMK-7), incised 1979 MID, 4", first issue backstamp dated 1992.

HUM 414: IN TUNE

IN TUNE, Hum 414. Missing Bee (TMK-6), 1979 MID, 4".

This figure is one of six designs released by Goebel in 1981. Its basic size is 4" and it is a matching figurine to the 1981 Annual Bell.

It was released during the Missing Bee (TMK-6) era and is found in that mark and in the current-use trademark, the Hummel Mark (TMK-7). It is valued at $2,500-3,000 in the Last Bee trademark and is $310 in the current suggested retail price list.

There are no significant variations that affect the collector value.

HUM 415: THOUGHTFUL

This is another of the six new designs released by Goebel in 1981. Its basic size is 4-1/2" and it is a matching piece to the 1980 Annual Bell. Thoughtful has a 1980 mold induction date (MID) and has been found only with the Missing Bee (TMK-6) and the Hummel Mark (TMK-7). Those pieces bearing the Missing Bee trademark are valued at $205-220.

In 1996 Goebel issued a special edition of Thoughtful in conjunction with the release of their Master Sculptor Gerhard Skrobek's new book *Hummels and Me*. The title page of the book in the figurine is the same as Skrobek's book and it bears the 125th anniversary backstamp. The edition was limited to 2,000. Collectors who bought that particular figurine in that year received the book for no extra charge.

THOUGHTFUL, Hum 415, Missing Bee mark (TMK-6), incised 1980 MID, 4-1/2".

HUM 416: JUBILEE

Beginning in January of 1985 this very special figurine was made available to collectors. Production was limited to the number sold during 1985. The figure has a special backstamp reading "50 Years, M.I. Hummel Figurines, 1935-1985, The Love Lives On," in celebration of the golden anniversary of Hummel figurines. It is 6-1/4" high and the factory recommended retail price was $200.

At least two of these figures are found with "75" instead of "50" on the golden anniversary figure. The speculation is that this piece was originally designed to celebrate the 75th anniversary or perhaps M.I. Hummel's birthday. Whatever the reason, the figures exist and their value would be in the mid to high five-figure range.

Another unusual variation is one where the circle around the "50" is a shiny gold gilt. This particular piece, one of only two known to be in private collections, bears the Last Bee (TMK-5) trademark. Apparently Goebel had an idea for the golden anniversary, but the gilt didn't come out to their satisfaction after being fired and they scrapped the idea. These figures are unique, and there is no way to realistically assign a value to them.

The normal Jubilees are found only with the Missing Bee (TMK-6) and are valued at $250-300 on the collector market.

JUBILEE, Hum 416. Missing Bee (TMK-6), 1980 MID, 6-1/4".

JUBILEE, Hum 416. This is the figurine with the unique gold gilt "50" discussed in the accompanying text.

JUBILEE, Hum 416. Shows the special inscription backstamp beneath the base.

HUM 417: WHERE DID YOU GET THAT? (Possible Future Edition)

This is a figure of a standing boy and girl. The boy holds his hat in both hands. It has three apples in it. The girl dangles her doll in her left hand.

HUM 418: WHAT'S NEW?

Added to the line in 1990, What's New? is 5-1/4" tall. The suggested retail price was $200. It can be found with the Missing Bee (TMK-6) and the current-use Hummel (TMK-7) marks. There are no variations that affect the collector value.

WHAT'S NEW?, Hum 418. Missing Bee mark, 1981 MID, 5".

The figure is found only in the Missing Bee (TMK-7). The collector value for the Missing Bee trademarked pieces is $200-230.

The M.I. Hummel Club announced a new edition of What's New? to honor its twentieth anniversary. It is an exclusive members-only edition for the club year 1996-97. The newspaper the girl reads has the M.I. Hummel Club newsletter masthead (*Insights: North American Edition*) with an American or Canadian flag and the club dates. The inside also pictures the club's exclusive anniversary piece, Celebrate with Song, in full color. It was released to club members at $310.

HUM 419: GOOD LUCK (Possible Future Edition)

In this figure a standing boy has his left hand in his pocket. He holds an umbrella in his right arm.

HUM 420: IS IT RAINING?

The figure was added to the line in 1989. The one in the accompanying photo measures 6" tall. It has a mold induction date of 1981 and its retail price at release was $175. The current suggested retail price is $280.

This piece is found bearing only the Missing Bee (TMK-6) trademark and the current-use trademark, the Hummel Mark (TMK-7).

There are no significant variations to affect the collector value of $240-250.

IS IT RAINING?, Hum 420. Missing Bee (TMK-6) mark, 1981 MID, 6".

HUM 421: IT'S COLD

IT'S COLD, Hum 421. Missing Bee mark (TMK-7), incised 1981 MID, 5-1/8".

This is the sixth in a series of special offers made exclusively to members of the Goebel Collectors' Club. It is available only from them initially, requiring a special redemption card issued to members. Each of these special editions have shown themselves to be good candidates for fairly rapid appreciation in collector value. This figurine bears a 1981 MID and was sold with redemption card for $80.

It is found only bearing the Missing Bee (TMK-6) trademark and valued at $180-190. There are no significant variations that affect the collector value of this figurine.

HUM 422: WHAT NOW?

This is the seventh special edition issued for members of the Goebel Collectors' Club. The usual redemption card was required for purchase of this figurine at $90. What Now? stands 5-1/4" high and since May 31, 1985 has been available only on the secondary market. The piece is valued at $180-200.

There are no variations that affect this figure's value.

WHAT NOW?, Hum 422, with the matching M.I. Hummel exclusive miniature as a pendant. Missing Bee mark, incised 1981 MID, 5-1/2". An M.I. Hummel Club exclusive.

HUM 423: HORSE TRAINER

Horse Trainer was added to the line in 1990 at 4-1/2" and a suggested retail price of $155. It can be found with the Missing Bee (TMK-6) and the current-use Hummel (TMK-7) marks. The collector value is presently $175-190 for the figures with the Last Bee trademark. There are no variations that affect this value.

HORSE TRAINER, Hum 423. Missing Bee, 1981 MID, 4-5/8".

HUM 424: SLEEP TIGHT

A 1990 release, this piece can be found with the Missing Bee (TMK-6) and the current-use Hummel (TMK-7) trademarks. At 4-1/2" Sleep Tight has a collector value range of $170-200 for the pieces bearing the Missing Bee trademark.

SLEEP TIGHT, Hum 424. Missing Bee mark, 1981 MID, 4-3/4".

HUM 425: PLEASANT MOMENT (Possible Future Edition)

This figure has two seated girls. One holds flowers in her left hand. The other reaches down with her right hand toward a yellow butterfly.

HUM 426: PAY ATTENTION (Possible Future Edition)

This girl is sitting on a fence. She holds flowers and a basket and is looking away from a crowing black bird perched on the fence post behind her.

HUM 427: WHERE ARE YOU? (Possible Future Edition)

In this figure a boy sits on a fence and holds a bouquet of flowers. A bird is perched on a fence post.

HUM 428: I WON'T HURT YOU (Possible Future Edition)

A boy with a hiking staff in his left hand looks down at a ladybug in his right hand.

HUM 429: HELLO WORLD

HELLO WORLD, Hum 429. Missing Bee mark, incised 1983 MID, 5-5/8".

Released in 1989 as a special edition available to members of the Goebel Collectors' Club with redemption cards on which the expiration date was May 31, 1990. There are already two variations to be found. In 1989 the club changed from the Goebel Collectors' Club to the M.I. Hummel Club. Apparently a few figures were released with the old special edition backstamp before the error was discovered. All those subsequently released will bear the M.I. Hummel Club backstamp. The piece stands 5-1/2" high.

These figures can be found with either club inscription, and in either the Missing Bee (TMK-6) trademark or the current-use trademark, the Hummel (TMK-7). The collector value for either variation and either trademark is the same, at $130-140.

HUM 430: IN D MAJOR

This 1988 release is listed at 4-3/8" tall. The one in the photo measures 4-1/8" and carries a 1981 mold induction date incised beneath the base. It was released at $135.

There are no significant variations to affect the value. Found with the Missing Bee (TMK-6) trademark and the current-use trademark, the Hummel (TMK-7) only. The value for the Missing Bee figure is $160-180.

IN D MAJOR, Hum 430. Missing Bee (TMK-6) mark, 1981 MID, 4-1/8".

HUM 431: THE SURPRISE

THE SURPRISE, Hum 431. Missing Bee mark, incised 1981 MID, 5-1/2".

This figure, introduced in 1989, is the twelfth special edition for members of the Goebel Collectors' Club (now M.I. Hummel Club). The expiration date on the redemption card was May 31, 1990. The Surprise bears the incised mold induction date of 1981 as well as the same date in decal beneath the current trademark. This figure is the first to also bear the little bumblebee that is to appear on all future special editions for club members. The figure is 5-3/8" high, is found only with the Missing Bee (TMK-6) and is valued at $130-150. There are no significant variations.

HUM 432: KNIT ONE, PURL ONE

This figure was a new addition to the line in 1981. It was made to go with the 1982 Annual Bell of the same motif. Note that it has no base.

It is found only with the Missing Bee (TMK-6) trademark and the current-use trademark, the Hummel (TMK-7). The collector value for the Missing Bee trademarked figurine is $105-115. There are no significant variations to affect this value.

KNIT ONE, PURL ONE, Hum 432. Missing Bee (TMK-6), 1982 MID, 6".

HUM 433: SING ALONG

SING ALONG, Hum 433. Missing Bee mark, incised 1982 MID, 4-1/4".

Released in 1987 at $145, this figure measures 4-3/8" tall and bears an incised mold induction date of 1982.

It can be found only in the Missing Bee (TMK-6) and the current-use Hummel (TMK-7) trademarks. There are no variations to affect the collector value of $260-275.

HUM 434: FRIEND OR FOE

This 4" figure was released in 1991 at a $195 suggested retail price. It bears an incised 1982 mold induction date.

The piece is found only in the Missing Bee (TMK-6) trademark and the current-use Hummel Mark (TMK-7). There are no variations to affect the price of the normal production pieces, which are valued at $195-205.

FRIEND OR FOE, Hum 434. Missing Bee trademark, incised 1982 MID, 3-3/4". Has the first issue backstamp dated 1991.

FRIEND OR FOE, Hum 434. Demonstration piece with only the flesh tones and dress painted. Current use trademark, incised 1982 MID, 3-7/8". Valued at about $300.

HUM 435: DELICIOUS

DELICIOUS, Hum 435.

Hum 435/3/0 was released in 1996 in a 3-7/8" size. It has an incised 1988 MID and two special backstamps: the First Issue and the 125th anniversary backstamps. Both appear only on those pieces produced in 1996. The issue price was $155.

HUM 436: AN EMERGENCY (Possible Future Edition)

This figure is a boy with a bandage on his head. He is about to push the button on the doctor's gate.

HUM 437: TUBA PLAYER

This figure was released in the winter of 1988. It is listed as 6-1/4", but the one in the photo here actually measures 6-1/8" high. It carries a 1988 mold induction date and the Missing Bee (TMK-6) trademark. The pieces continue to be produced with the current-use trademark, the Hummel Mark (TMK-7).

There are no variations to affect the value of the Missing Bee pieces at $240-250.

THE TUBA PLAYER, Hum 437. Missing Bee mark, 1983 MID, 6-1/8".

HUM 438: SOUNDS OF THE MANDOLIN

SOUNDS OF THE MANDOLIN, Hum 438. Missing Bee mark (TMK-6), incised 1984 MID, measures 3-5/8".

This 3-3/4" figure was released in 1987 as one of three musical angel pieces. The other two are Song of Praise (Hum 454) and The Accompanist (Hum 453).

The figurine was originally produced with the Missing Bee (TMK-6) trademark and today is produced with the current-use trademark, the Hummel Mark (TMK-7).

The collector value for the Missing Bee pieces is $110-120. There are no variations to affect that value.

HUM 439: A GENTLE GLOW (Candleholder)

Released in 1987, this piece is a small standing child. The candle receptacle appears to be resting on greenery that the child holds up with both hands.

The figurine is found only in the Missing Bee (TMK-6) and the Hummel Mark (TMK-7). There are no variations to affect the collector value of the Missing Bee trademarked figures, which stands at $190-200.

A GENTLE GLOW candleholder, Hum 439. Missing Bee (TMK-6), 5-1/4".

HUM 440: BIRTHDAY CANDLE (Candleholder)

BIRTHDAY CANDLE candleholder, Hum 440. Missing Bee mark (TMK-6), incised 1983 MID, 5-1/4".

This 5-1/2" candleholder is the tenth special edition available to members of the Goebel Collectors' Club only. It bears the following inscription on the base: "EXCLUSIVE SPECIAL EDITION NO. 10 FOR MEMBERS OF THE GOEBEL COLLECTORS' CLUB". It was released at $95, and the redemption card cut-off date was May 31, 1988. The figure was released in conjunction with the tenth anniversary celebration of the founding of the club.

This piece is found in the Missing Bee (TMK-6) only and is valued at $130-150. There are no variations affecting value.

HUM 441: CALL TO WORSHIP (Clock)

This is only the second clock ever made from a Hummel design. It stands 13" tall and chimes every hour. You can choose from two tunes by moving a switch beneath the figure. The tunes are Ave Maria and the Westminster Chimes. This is the second offering in what Goebel calls the Century Collection, a group of pieces produced in the twentieth century with a one-year limited production. Figures in the collection bear the Roman numeral XX on their base. The suggested retail price in 1988 (the year of production) was $600.

These figures can be found in the Missing Bee trademark only. They are valued at $800-1,000. There are no variations that affect value.

CALL TO WORSHIP clock, Hum 441. Missing Bee mark (TMK-6), incised 1988 MID, 13". Century Collection, 1988.

HUM 442: CHAPEL TIME (Clock)

This is the first clock to be put into production and released by Goebel. It was limited to one year of production (1986) and will not be made again in this century. Included with the artist's mark and date on the bottom is the Roman numeral XX, indicating the twentieth century. The base also bears the current-use Missing Bee (TMK-6) trademark and a blue M.I. Hummel signature with the inscription "The Love Lives On."

There are several variations of this piece, mostly having to do with the windows in the chapel building. So far the most common version has all windows closed and painted except for the four in the belfry. As of this writing, the rarest is a version with all windows closed and painted. According to Goebel this version was a pre-production run numbering 800-1,000. Reportedly a few of these have been found with the two small round windows in the gables open. A third version has the gable and the belfry windows all open. There are other variations with regard to the base and size of the hole in the bottom (to replace battery), but these are not presently considered significant.

The clock is 11-1/2" tall. The following is a breakdown of the values of the three variations:

Belfry windows and gable windows open..........$2,500-2,800
Belfry windows and gable windows painted......$1,200-1,500
Belfry windows open, gable windows painted....$2,000-2,500

CHAPEL TIME clock, Hum 442. Missing Bee mark (TMK-6), incised 1983 MID, 11-1/8".

HUM 443: COUNTRY SONG (Clock) (Possible Future Edition)

This figure is a boy blowing the horn. He is seated on a flower-covered mound. Blue flowers are used instead of numbers on the clock face.

HUM 444 and 445: UNKNOWN (Possible Future Editions)

HUM 446: A PERSONAL MESSAGE (Possible Future Edition)

This figure is a girl on her knees using a large pen to write on paper. There is an ink well to her left. This piece looks somewhat like Hum 309 (With Loving Greetings).

HUM 447: MORNING CONCERT

MORNING CONCERT, Hum 447. No apparent marks other than an incised 1984 MID. It is from the Missing Bee mark period and is an M.I. Hummel Club exclusive offer.

This is the eleventh special edition piece made and offered exclusively for members of the Goebel Collectors' Club (now the M.I. Hummel Club). They were available to members until the expiration date of May 31, 1989. Morning Concert has a mold induction date of 1984 incised beneath the base and the special edition club backstamp in decal underglaze. It stands 5" tall and was available to members for $98.

This figure is available only in the Missing Bee (TMK-6) and is valued at $110-125. There are no significant variations.

HUM 448: CHILDREN'S PRAYER (Possible Future Edition)

This is a figure of a boy and girl standing, looking up at a roadside shrine of Jesus on the Cross.

HUM 449: THE LITTLE PAIR

In 1990 the M.I. Hummel Club began offering special figures to those members who had passed certain milestones in their membership. This particular piece is made available to only those members who have attained or surpassed their tenth year of membership. Each bears a special backstamp commemorating the occasion. The tenth year club exclusive is available to qualified members for $200. The secondary market value is about $250.

These figures are found only in the Missing Bee (TMK-6) and the current-use trademark, the Hummel Mark (TMK-7).

THE LITTLE PAIR, Hum 449. Missing Bee mark, incised 1985 MID, 5-1/2". Available xclusively to members of the M.I. Hummel Club who have attained 10 years of membership.

HUM 450: WILL IT STING? (Possible Future Edition)

This is a figure of a girl looking at a bee perched on a plant at her feet.

HUM 451: JUST DOZING

Released in 1995, this figure measures 4-1/8" and has an incised 1984 mold induction date. Those produced in 1995 bear the First Issue backstamp. Released at $220, the suggested retail price is listed at $240.

JUST DOZING, Hum 451.

HUM 452: FLYING HIGH

This is the first in a series of hanging ornaments. It is not, however, the first Hummel hanging ornament. The first was the Flying Angel (Hum 366), commonly used with the nativity sets. Flying High was introduced in late 1987 as the 1988 (first edition) ornament at $75. It measures 3-1/2" x 4-1/8".

There are three variations with regard to additional marks. When first released there were no additional markings. The second variation is the appearance of a decal reading "First Edition" beneath the skirt. The third is the appearance of the "First Edition" mark and "1988" painted on the back of the gown.

The value of the regular dated version is $100-125. The undated and unmarked variation is $125-150. These are found only with the Missing Bee (TMK-6) trademark and the current-use trademark, the Hummel Mark (TMK-7).

FLYING HIGH, Hum 452. 1988 Christmas ornament, Missing Bee (TMK-6) mark, no other apparent markings. This is one of the early undated ornaments.

HUM 453: THE ACCOMPANIST

THE ACCOMPANIST, Hum 453. Missing Bee mark (TMK-6), incised 1984 MID, 3-1/4".

This piece, along with Hum 454 (Song of Praise) and Hum 438 (Sounds of the Mandolin), was introduced in 1987 as a trio of angel musicians. It was released at $39. The figurine measures 3-1/4" high and has an incised mold induction date of 1984.

It is not found with any earlier trademark than the Missing Bee (TMK-6) and is valued at $90-100 in that mark.

HUM 454: SONG OF PRAISE

This piece is one of three angel musician figures introduced in 1987. The others are Hum 453 (The Accompanist) and Hum 438 (Sounds of the Mandolin). Song of Praise stands 3" high.

This figure is not found with any earlier trademark than the Missing Bee (TMK-6) and is valued at $90-100 in that mark.

SONG OF PRAISE, Hum 454, Missing Bee Mark, 1984 MID, 2-7/8".

HUM 455: THE GUARDIAN

A 1991 release, The Guardian is a 3-1/2" figure. The suggested retail price at the time of release was $145. It bears an incised mold induction date of 1984, and those made in 1991 bear the First Issue backstamp dated 1991. These are not found in trademarks earlier than the Missing Bee (TMK-6). Collector value: $155-165.

In 1996 Goebel announced Personal Touch figurines. There are four figurines in the line that lend themselves well to this application. The Guardian is one of these. The other three are Bird Duet (Hum 69), Latest News (Hum 184) and For Father (Hum 87).Goebel will fire onto the figure a permanent personalization of your choice. (The bird is removed for the inscription.)

THE GUARDIAN, Hum 455. Missing Bee mark, 1985 MID, 2-3/4", first issue backstamp dated 1991.

HUM 456: UNKNOWN (Open Number for Possible Future Edition)

HUM 457: SOUND THE TRUMPET

SOUND THE TRUMPET, Hum 457. Missing Bee mark, 1984 MID, 2-13/16".

This figure was introduced in 1987 at a price of $45. It measures 2-3/4" high and has an incised mold induction date of 1984.

The piece is not found in trademarks earlier than the Missing Bee (TMK-6) and it is valued at $90-100 in that mark.

HUM 458: STORYBOOK TIME

This piece was introduced as new for 1992 in the fall 1991 issue of *Insights*, the M.I. Hummel Club newsletter, with the name Story Time. Inexplicably, all references to the piece have subsequently referred to it as Storybook Time. It is listed as 5" tall and the release price was $330.

It is found only in the current-use trademark, the Hummel Mark (TMK-7), and its current Goebel suggested retail price is $420.

STORYBOOK TIME, Hum 458. Hummel mark (current use or TMK-7), incised 1985 MID, 5-1/8", first issue backstamp dated 1992.

HUM 459: IN THE MEADOW

IN THE MEADOW, Hum 459. Missing Bee (TMK-6) mark, 1985 MID, 4".

This was released in 1987 as one of five 1987 releases. The size is 4" and the release price was $110. It has an incised mold induction date of 1985 beneath the base.

It is found only with the current-use trademark, the Hummel mark (TMK-7). It is listed in the Goebel suggested retail price list at $220.

HUM 460: TALLY (Retail Dealer Plaque)

The retail dealer plaque, TALLY, Hum 460. Left to right the languages are Italian, Swedish and Dutch.

The retail dealer plaque TALLY, Hum 460. Left to right the countries are United States, Great Britain, Germany, France, Spain.

This dealer plaque was introduced in 1986. Many assumed it was to replace the Hum 187 (Merry Wanderer) dealer plaque, but in 1990 the Merry Wanderer style was reissued. When Tally was first introduced there was apparently a shortage and dealers were limited to one figure each, but the shortage was soon alleviated. The boy on the plaque is, as you can see, very similar to the center figure in School Boys (Hum 170). The base of the plaque bears an incised mold induction date of 1984.

There are no structural or color variations presently known, but there are variations in the language used on the front of the plaque. German, Swedish, French, Italian, Spanish and Dutch are used on the plaques, in addition to a version for British dealers and one for the American market, for a total of eight different versions. The plaque was released at $85 in the U.S. and is presently valued at about $100-120. The British version is valued at about $350-400.

The various language plaques are valued as follows:

Dutch	600-800
French	800-900
German	600-800
Italian	600-800
Spanish	800-1000
Swedish	800-1000

HUM 461, 462: UNKNOWN (Possible Future Editions)

HUM 463: MY WISH IS SMALL

This is a M.I. Hummel Club exclusive offering for the 1992-93 club year available only in the current-use trademark, the Hummel Mark (TMK-7). The figure was available exclusively to members with redemption cards. It is 5-1/2" tall and the current collector value is $130-150. This piece was permanently retired on May 31, 1994, and the mold was destroyed.

MY WISH IS SMALL, Hum 463/0. An M.I. Hummel members only exclusive offering. It is 5-1/2" tall, bears the current use trademark (TMK-7), the special club backstamp and an incised 1985 MID.

HUM 464, 465, 466: UNKNOWN (Possible Future Editions)

HUM 467: THE KINDERGARTNER

A new release in 1987, this figure stands 5" high. The release price was $100. The actual measurement of the figurine in the photo here is 5-3/8" and it bears a mold induction date of 1986 incised beneath the base.

This figure is not found with trademarks earlier than the Missing Bee (TMK-6). It is listed at $220 in the Goebel suggested retail list It is not valued at any more than that in either TMK-6 or TMK-7.

THE KINDERGARTNER, Hum 467. Missing Bee (TMK-6), 1985 MID, 5-3/8".

HUM 468, 469, 470: UNKNOWN (Possible Future Editions)

HUM 471: HARMONY IN FOUR PARTS

HARMONY IN FOUR PARTS, Hum 471. Missing Bee mark, incised 1987 MID, 9-1/8" long x 9-15/16" high. Century Collection dated 1989.

This is the 1989 addition to the Century Collection. These pieces are limited to one production year and will not be produced again in the twentieth century. They each bear a special backstamp indicating this. The stamp on this figure is 1989 underlined, with the Roman numeral XX beneath it in the center of a circle made up of the M.I. Hummel signature and the words "CENTURY COLLECTION." The piece measures 9" wide and 10" high. The mold induction date is 1987. The lamp post was originally made of the same fine earthenware used to render Hummel pieces, but it was soon noted that the post was very easily broken. To alleviate this problem Goebel began using a metal post. Although there is presently no difference in the value of the figures, it is reasonable to assume that the earthenware post version may become rarer and thus more desirable to serious collectors and more valuable. Only time will tell. Hum 471 was released at $850.

This piece is not found with trademarks earlier than the Missing Bee (TMK-6) mark and is valued at $1,300-1,800 in that mark.

HUM 472: ON OUR WAY

ON OUR WAY, Hum 472. Hummel Mark (current use or TMK-7), incised 1987 MID, 8", Century Collection, 1992.

This unusual piece was introduced as new for 1992 in the fall 1991 issue of *Insights*, the M.I. Hummel Club newsletter. On Our Way is the Century Collection piece for 1992, which means its availability is limited by the number produced during the one year of production. The figures bear a special identifying backstamp and are accompanied by a certificate of authenticity. Size is 6-1/2" x 5-1/2" x 8" and the release price was $950.

It is available only in the current-use trademark, the Hummel Mark (TMK-7), and was still listed at $950 in the 1993 Goebel suggested retail price list.

HUM 473, 474: UNKNOWN

Open numbers for possible future editions.

HUM 475: MAKE A WISH

This piece was a new release in 1989. The basic size is 4-1/4" and bears a 1987 incised mold induction date.

There are no significant variations. These figures cannot be found with trademarks earlier than the Missing Bee (TMK-6) and are valued at $175 in that mark.

MAKE A WISH, Hum 475. This example stands 4-1/2", has the Missing Bee (TMK-6) trademark and a 1987 mold induction date (MID).

HUM 476: WINTER SONG

WINTER SONG, Hum 476. Missing Bee trademark, incised 1987 MID, 4".

This figure was a 1987 release. It stands 4-1/2" tall and was priced at $45 when introduced. It bears an incised mold induction date of 1987 and appears with the Missing Bee (TMK-6) or later trademarks. It is valued at $100-120 in the Missing Bee.

HUM 477: A BUDDING MAESTRO

This figure measures 3-7/8" tall. It was released in 1987 at $45 and is found with the Missing Bee (TMK-6) or later trademarks. It is valued at $95-115 in the Missing Bee and there are no significant variations.

A BUDDING MAESTRO, Hum 477. Missing Bee mark, incised 1987 MID, 3-15/16".

HUM 478: I'M HERE

I'm Here was released in 1988 as a new addition to the line. The figure in the photo measures 3" but is described in price lists as 2-3/4". It carries a 1987 incised mold induction date.

This piece is not found with trademarks earlier than the Missing Bee (TMK-6) and is valued at $95-115 in that mark. There are no significant variations.

I'M HERE, Hum 478. Missing Bee (TMK-6) mark, 3-1/8".

HUM 479: I BROUGHT YOU A GIFT

Left: I BROUGHT YOU A GIFT, Hum 479, Missing Bee mark, incised 1987 MID, 4". Right: LUCKY FELLOW, Hum 560, Hummel Mark (current use or TMK-7), 5-5/8".

On June 1, 1989, the 4" bisque plaque with the Merry Wanderer motif, which had been given to every new member of the Goebel Collectors' Club, was officially retired. On the same date the club became the M.I. Hummel Club, and a new membership premium, I Brought You a Gift, was introduced. At the time of transition each renewing and new member was given the new premium. Hum 479 is 4" high and has the incised mold induction date of 1987 on the underside of the base. There are two variations with regard to the club special edition backstamp. If you will look at the accompanying photograph of the base you will note one old club name underneath the bumblebee. This is found on the early examples. Newer ones have the M.I. Hummel Club name on them.

The figures are found with the Last Bee (TMK-6) trademark and the current-use trademark, the Hummel Mark (TMK-7), and are valued at $75 in either mark.

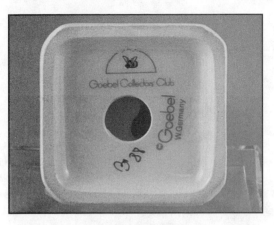

I BROUGHT YOU A GIFT, Hum 479. M.I. Hummel Club offering exclusively for members. It is 4" tall, bears the Missing Bee trademark (TMK-6), the club backstamp and an incised 1987 MID.

The base of I BROUGHT YOU A GIFT showing the old "Goebel Collectors' Club" name.

HUM 480: HOSANNA

Released in 1989, this figure stands 4" tall. It has a 1987 mold induction date incised under the base. The suggested retail price at the time of the release was $68.

Hum 480 is not found with trademarks earlier than the Missing Bee (TMK-6). It is valued at $110 in the current Goebel suggested retail list.

HOSANNA, Hum 480. Missing Bee (TMK-6) mark, 1987 MID, 4".

HUM 481: LOVE FROM ABOVE (1989 Christmas Ornament)

This is the second edition in the hanging ornament series that began with the 1988 Flying High (Hum 452). Hum 481 bears the Missing Bee (TMK-6) trademark and was released at $75. It is now valued at about $100.

LOVE FROM ABOVE, Hum 481. 1989 Christmas ornament, Missing Bee (TMK-6) mark, 1987 MID, 3-1/4".

HUM 482: ONE FOR YOU, ONE FOR ME

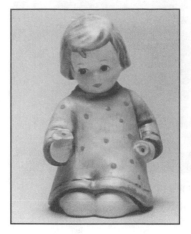

This piece was a new release in 1988. It is 3-1/8" high and carries a 1987 incised mold induction date. It was originally priced at $50 and is $110 in the current Goebel suggested retail price list.

The figure is not found with trademarks earlier than the Missing Bee (TMK-6) and is valued at $95-115 in that mark.

ONE FOR YOU, ONE FOR ME, Hum 482. No apparent markings of any sort, 3-3/16".

HUM 483: I'LL PROTECT HIM

New in 1989, this figure stands 3-3/4" high. It bears an incised mold induction date of 1987 on the underside of the base.

Hum 483 is not found with trademarks earlier than the Missing Bee (TMK-6) and is valued at $75-90 in that mark.

I'LL PROTECT HIM, Hum 483, Missing Bee (TMK-6) mark, 1987 MID, 3-3/4".

HUM 484: PEACE ON EARTH (1990 Christmas Ornament)

The third in an annual series of M.I. Hummel Christmas ornaments, this one was released at a suggested retail price of $80. The size is 4".

It is found only in the Missing Bee (TMK-6) trademark and is valued at about $100.

PEACE ON EARTH, Hum 484. 1990 Christmas ornament, Missing Bee

HUM 485: A GIFT FROM A FRIEND

This little 4-3/8" fellow was offered exclusively to members of the M.I. Hummel club in the club year 1991-92. Its availability to members at $160 was subject to the cut-off date of May 31, 1993.

Hum 485 is found only with the current-use trademark, the Hummel Mark (TMK-6). There are no significant variations, and it is still valued at $160.

A GIFT FROM A FRIEND, Hum 485. Hummel mark (current use or TMK-7), incised 1988 MID, 5". An M.I. Hummel Club exclusive offer.

HUM 486: I WONDER

This was a club exclusive offered only to members of the M.I. Hummel Club during the club year of June 1, 1990, to May 31, 1991. The figures were offered at $140. The size is listed as 5-1/4" and each piece bears the Bumble Bee club backstamp.

Hum 486 is found in both the Missing Bee (TMK-6) and the current use trademark, the Hummel Mark (TMK-7). It is still valued at $140, but the older mark is slightly more valuable than the new.

Somehow an estimated 300 of these escaped the factory with the erroneous year date "1991/92" on the backstamp, according to Goebel. Only time will tell if this variation becomes significant.

I WONDER, Hum 486. Missing Bee (TMK-6), incised 1988 MID, 5-1/4".

I WONDER, Hum 486. Demonstration piece with only flesh tones painted. Current use trademark (TMK-7), M.I. Hummel Club special backstamp, incised 1988 MID, 5-1/8". Valued at about $300-400.

HUM 487: LET'S TELL THE WORLD

LET'S TELL THE WORLD, Hum 487. Missing Bee mark, 1988 MID, 8" x 10-7/16" high, Century Collection dated 1990. 1935-1990 55 Years of M.I. Hummel Figurines.

Released in 1990 as part of the Century Collection, Let's Tell the World is 10-1/2" tall. Production was limited to one year (1990) and the edition is listed as closed in the 1992 Goebel price list. No price is listed, so presumably they are no longer available. The actual number of figures produced is not presently known. Each piece bears a special backstamp commemorating the 55th anniversary of M.I. Hummel figurines. Released at $875, they are available only in the Missing Bee (TMK-6) trademark and are valued at $900-1,000.

HUM 488: THAT'S THAT (Possible Future Edition)

HUM 489: PRETTY PLEASE

This figurine is part of an informal series of paired pieces called Cozy Companions. The figurine paired with this one is No Thank You (Hum 535). Pretty Please has an incised mold induction date of 1988 and will bear both the First Issue and the 125th anniversary backstamps during the initial year of production. The issue price was $120.

PRETTY PLEASE, Hum 489.

HUM 490: CAREFREE

CAREFREE, Hum 490.

Recently Goebel began releasing paired figurines in an informal annual series called Cozy Companions. Hum 490 is paired with Free Spirit (Hum 564). Carefree measures 3-3/4" and bears an incised mold induction date of 1988. Released in 1996, it has the First Issue backstamp and is valued at about $100.

HUM 491, 492: OPEN NUMBERS

HUM 493: TWO HANDS, ONE TREAT

This special 4" figure is an M.I. Hummel Club exclusive. It was made available as a renewal premium, a gift, to those members renewing their membership in the club year 1991-92. The club placed a $65 value on the piece at that time.

These figures are found only with the current-use trademark, the Hummel Mark (TMK-7). Their value is still about the same.

TWO HANDS, ONE TREAT, Hum 493. Hummel mark (current use mark or TMK-7), incised 1988 MID, 4".

HUM 494: OPEN NUMBER (Possible Future Edition)

HUM 495: EVENING PRAYER

EVENING PRAYER, Hum 495. Hummel mark (current use or TMK-7), incised 1988 MID, 3-7/8", first issue backstamp dated 1992.

Introduced as "New for '92" in the fall 1991 issue of the M.I. Hummel Club newsletter, this figure is listed at 3-3/4" tall and was released at a price of $95.

It has an incised 1988 mold induction date and is found only in the current-use trademark, the Hummel Mark (TMK-7). It is valued at $105-120.

HUM 496-499: UNKNOWN

Open numbers for possible future editions.

HUM 500: FLOWERS FOR MOTHER (Mother's Day Plate) (Possible Future Edition)

This plate was listed in the index of the *M.I. Hummel: The Golden Anniversary Album*. Little else is known at this time. The plate was not illustrated.

HUM 501-511: DOLL PARTS

These mold numbers were utilized to identify the heads, arms and legs of the eight porcelain dolls released by Goebel starting in 1984. There were eight different heads and the left and right hands were the same on each doll, which accounts for the ten mold numbers used.

HUM 512-519: DOLL PARTS

These are the mold numbers used to identify the parts of the dolls made by the Danbury Mint. There were eight dolls in all.

HUM 521: LITTLE SCHOLAR (by Goebel), HUM 522: SCHOOL GIRL (by Goebel) (Doll Parts)

HUM 523-529: OPEN NUMBERS

HUM 530: LAND IN SIGHT

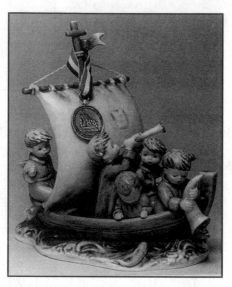

LAND IN SIGHT, Hum 530. Hummel mark (current use mark or TMK-7), incised 1988 MID, 9" long x 9-1/8" high, #1, 112 of 30,000. The medallion that accompanies the figure is hanging from the mast. It is not attached.

This large, complicated piece is very special. Land in Sight is a sequentially numbered limited edition of 30,000 worldwide, released in 1992 to commemorate Columbus' discovery of America. It is 9-1/8" x 8-3/8" x 5-7/8". The special backstamp reads "1492 - The Quincentennial of America's Discovery." A medallion accompanies the piece.

These pieces are found only in the current-use Hummel Mark (TMK-7). Land in Sight is still valued at about $900-1,000.

HUM 531, 532, 533: OPEN NUMBERS

HUM 534: A NAP

This piece was introduced as new for 1991 in the fall issue of the M.I. Hummel Club newsletter, *Insights*. A Nap is listed as 2-1/4" in size, and it was released at $100.

It is found only with the Hummel trademark (TMK-7) and is listed in the current suggested retail price list at $130.

A NAP, Hum 534, Missing Bee (TMK-6) mark, 1988 MID, First Issue paper sticker, 2-1/2".

HUM 535: NO THANK YOU

This piece is part of an informal series of paired figurines called Cozy Companions. Its companion piece is Pretty Please (Hum 489). The 1996 release carried the 125th anniversary backstamp. Those issued during the first year of production also carry the First Issue backstamp. The issue price was $120.

HUM 536, 537: OPEN NUMBERS

HUM 538: SCHOOL'S OUT

This is a new piece for 1997. It is 4" and has a 1988 mold induction date. The first year of production will have the First Issue backstamp. The suggested retail price is $170.

SCHOOL'S OUT, Hum 538.

HUM 539, 540: OPEN NUMBERS

HUM 541: SWEET AS CAN BE

SWEET AS CAN BE, Hum 541. 1993/94 club exclusive "Preview Edition."

A special preview edition of this figure (basic size 4") was offered only to members of the M.I. Hummel Club for the 1993-94 club year. The figures were given the standard club exclusive backstamp for the year and were put into regular production with the regular trademark afterward.

Goebel placed a value of $125 on the figure in the spring of 1993. As of 1996 it had not yet been listed as available as a regular production figurine.

HUM 542, 543, 544: OPEN NUMBERS

HUM 545: COME BACK SOON

This figure was first released in 1995 and can be found in TMK-6 and TMK-7. In the first year of production each figure was given the special First Issue backstamp. These pieces have a 1989 mold induction date and the TMK-7. For some inexplicable reason those produced after the first year are a very slightly different style from an obviously different mold. These bear a 1988 mold induction date and the earlier TMK-6. It appears that Goebel produced many of the regular figurines in advance of the "First Issue" pieces released in 1995.

COME BACK SOON, Hum 545. Left: The regular production figure with TMK-6. Right: The 1995 "First Issue" version with TMK-7.

Bases of the Hum 545 showing the trademarks and backstamps.

HUM 546, 547: OPEN NUMBERS

HUM 548: FLOWER GIRL

FLOWER GIRL, Hum 548. Missing Bee mark, incised 1989 MID, 4-1/2". An M.I. Hummel Club exclusive offer.

This is a special figure available only to members of the M.I. Hummel Club and then only upon or after the fifth anniversary of their membership. It is 4-1/2" high and bears a special backstamp to indicate its unique status.

The figure is currently available to members in the Hummel Mark (TMK-7) at $130. Goebel began producing them in the previous trademark era, that of the Missing Bee (TMK-6), and those marked with TMK-6 are worth about the same today.

HUM 549: A SWEET OFFERING

This is an M.I. Hummel Club exclusive for members only. Free to members renewing their membership, it carries the mold number 549/3/0 and has a basic size of 3-1/2". Goebel valued the piece at $80 in the spring of 1993.

A SWEET OFFERING, Hum 549 3/0. 1993/94 club renewal gift, 3-1/2".

HUM 550, 551, 552: OPEN NUMBERS

HUM 553: SCAMP

This was a new figure in 1992. It has a basic size of 3-1/2" and is found only in the current-use Hummel Mark (TMK-7) at $105. Hum 553 has an incised mold induction date of 1989. There are no known significant variations. It is listed at $120 in the Goebel suggested retail price list.

SCAMP, Hum 553. Hummel mark (current use or TMK-7), incised 1989 MID, 3-5/8", first issue backstamp dated 1992.

HUM 554: CHEEKY FELLOW

This figure was offered in a special preview edition exclusively to members of the M.I. Hummel Club for the 1992-93 club year. Figures produced in that year were given the standard club exclusive backstamp. Those produced later became regular production pieces and no longer had the special marking. Goebel placed a value of $120 on the figure in the spring of 1992, and it is still worth about the same.

Left: CHEEKY FELLOW, Hum 554, Hummel mark (current-use or TMK-7), incised 1989 MID, 4-3/16". Right: MY WISH IS SMALL, Hum 463/0, Hummel mark (current-use or TMK-7), incised 1985 MID, 5-1/2".

CHEEKY FELLOW, Hum 554. Incised 1989 MID, 4-1/8".

HUM 555: ONE, TWO, THREE

ONE, TWO, THREE,
Hum 555.

This small figurine measures 4" and has an incised mold induction date of 1989. It is an exclusive edition available to members of the M.I. Hummel Club only. The 1997 companion piece is What's That? (Hum 488). One, Two, Three was released at $145.

HUM 556: ONE PLUS ONE

This figure was first made available in a limited form. Although it was released in 1993 it was not made available through normal channels, but rather only at authorized dealer promotions that were billed as a "district manager promotion" in the United States and a "Canadian artist promotion" in Canada. The figures were made available for purchase by anyone interested, on a first-come, first-served basis. These pieces bear a special marking on the base, along with the regular markings, to indicate they were part of the promotion. The figures sold for $115 at these events and are now in regular production at a suggested retail price of $145.

HUM 557: OPEN NUMBER

HUM 558: LITTLE TROUBADOUR

Released in 1994, this figurine measures 4" high and has an incised 1989 mold induction date. It was an exclusive edition reserved for members of the M.I. Hummel Club, and it bears the special club backstamp. For some reason Goebel decided to reserve the right to reissue this figurine at a later date without, of course, the club markings. This is an unusual measure. The original issue price was $130 and it is still worth about the same today.

LITTLE TROUBADOUR,
Hum 558.

HUM 559: HEART AND SOUL

This is part of an informal annual series of paired figurines called Cozy Companions. It is paired with From the Heart (Hum 761). Released in 1996, Heart and Soul measures 3-5/8". Those produced in 1996 will bear both the First Issue and the 125th anniversary backstamps. The suggested retail price at release was $120.

HEART AND SOUL,
Hum 559.

HUM 560: LUCKY FELLOW

This figure was given free to members who renewed their membership in the club year 1992-93. Lucky Fellow has a basic size of 3-1/2" and Goebel valued it at $75 in the summer of 1992. It is presently worth about the same.

LUCKY FELLOW, Hum 560. An M.I. Hummel Club members only exclusive offering. It is 3-5/8" tall, bears the current use trademark (TMK-7), the special club backstamp and an incised 1989 MID.

HUM 561: GRANDMA'S GIRL

In 1993, on the day after the First Annual M.I. Hummel Club Convention, a special meeting was held for local chapter members from all over the United States and Canada. Each member of the 650 attending was given either a Hum 561 (Grandma's Girl) or a Hum 562 (Grampa's Boy). On the side of the each base was the inscription "1993 - M.I. Hummel Club Convention." Each figure was also signed by Goebel's Master Sculptor Gerhard Skrobek.

The regular piece is in the suggested retail price list at $160 and the Missing Bee piece is valued at about the same. The convention edition is valued at about $500.

GRANDMA'S GIRL, Hum 561. Missing Bee mark, 1989 MID incised, 4". Has the first issue backstamp dated 1991.

GRANDMA'S GIRL, Hum 561, showing the convention inscription.

HUM 562: GRANDPA'S BOY

GRANDPA'S BOY, Hum 562. Missing Bee mark, 1989 MID incised, 4-1/4". Has the first issue backstamp dated 1991.

GRANDPA'S BOY, Hum 562, showing the convention inscription.

In 1993, on the day after the First Annual M.I. Hummel Club Convention, a special meeting was held for local chapter members from all over the United States and Canada. Each member of the 650 attending was given either a Hum 561 (Grandma's Girl) or a Hum 562 (Grampa's Boy). On the side of the each base was the inscription "1993 - M.I. Hummel Club Convention." Each figure was also signed by Goebel's Master Sculptor Gerhard Skrobek.

The regular production piece is listed in the suggested retail price list at $160. The Last Bee (TMK-6) pieces are valued at about the same. The convention edition is valued at about $200-300.

HUM 563: LITTLE VISITOR

This figure has the mold number 563/0, indicating that another size might be in the offing. This one measures 5-1/4" and has an incised 1991 mold induction date. Little Visitor is a M.I. Hummel Club exclusive, available only to club members. It was released in 1994 and bears the special club backstamp. The price to members was $180 and it is valued at about the same today.

LITTLE VISITOR, Hum 563.

HUM 564: FREE SPIRIT

FREE SPIRIT, Hum 564.

Free Spirit is part of an informal annual series of paired figurines. The pair for this piece is Carefree (Hum 490). Free Spirit measures 3-3/4" and has an incised mold induction date of 1988 and a First Issue backstamp. Both figures were released in 1996. The collector value is about $100

HUM 565: OPEN NUMBER

HUM 566: THE ANGLER

This figure was released in 1995 at $320. It measures 6" and bears a 1989 mold induction date. Each figure produced during 1995 will be found bearing the First Issue backstamp. The current suggested retail price is $350.

THE ANGLER, Hum 565.

HUM 567, 568: OPEN NUMBERS

HUM 569: A FREE FLIGHT

This figure was released in late 1992. Its basic size is 4-3/4". It is not found in trademarks earlier than the Missing Bee (TMK-6). There are no significant variations. It continues in production today and is valued at $215 in the Goebel suggested price list.

A FREE FLIGHT, Hum 569. Hummel mark (TMK-7), 4-3/4".

HUM 570: OPEN NUMBER

HUM 571: ANGELIC GUIDE (1991 Christmas Ornament)

This figure is found no earlier than the Missing Bee (TMK-6) trademark era and is valued at about $100 in that mark.

ANGELIC GUIDE, Hum 571. 1991 Christmas ornament, Missing Bee (TMK-6) mark, 1989 MID, 3-1/2".

HUM 574: ROCK-A-BYE

This is the Century Collection piece for 1994. Production in the twentieth century was limited to only that one year. The figure has a special Century Collection backstamp, measures 7-1/2" and has an incised 1991 mold induction date. The suggested retail price is $1150.

ROCK-A-BYE,
Hum 574.

HUM 575-582, 585, 586: ANGELS OF CHRISTMAS
(Christmas Ornament Series)

This series of ornaments was made by Goebel in 1990 for mail order distribution by Danbury Mint. The figures were made in full color for Danbury.

In 1992 Goebel made these pieces available as the Christmas Angels, but the finish is different. These small ornaments appear to have been made from the same molds as the Danbury Mint pieces, but they are rendered in white overglaze with only their eyes and lips painted in color (in the same fashion as the Expressions of Youth series). The wing tips are flashed in 14K gold. The following figures are listed at $33 each in the 1996 Goebel suggested retail price list.

Hum No.	Design	Size
Hum 575	Heavenly Angel	3"
Hum 576	Festival Harmony with Mandolin	3"
Hum 577	Festival Harmony with Flute	3"
Hum 578	Celestial Musician	3"
Hum 579	Song of Praise	2-1/2"
Hum 580	Angel with Lute	2-1/2"
Hum 581	Prayer of Thanks	3"
Hum 582	Gentle Song	3"
Hum 585	Angel in Cloud	2-1/2"
Hum 586	Angel with Trumpet	2-1/2"

A wreath decorated with Angels of Christmas ornaments. Photo courtesy M.I. Hummel Club.

Christmas Angel CELESTIAL MUSICIAN, Hum 578, with its box, 3".

HUM 583, 584, 587-595: OPEN NUMBERS

HUM 596: THANKSGIVING PRAYER (Christmas Ornament)

THANKSGIVING PRAYER,
Hum 596.

See entries for Hum 641 and Hum 645.

HUM 597, 598, 599: OPEN NUMBERS

HUM 600: WE WISH YOU THE BEST

This figure is not found with trademarks earlier than the Missing Bee (TMK-6). It is valued at $1,400 in that mark. Those examples bearing the current-use trademark, the Hummel Mark (TMK-7), are worth about $1,000.

WE WISH YOU THE BEST, Hum 600. Missing Bee mark, incised 1989 MID, 9-5/8" wide x 9-1/4" high, Century Collection dated 1991.

HUM 601-607: OPEN NUMBERS

HUM 608: BLOSSOM TIME

A 1996 release, this piece has the 125th anniversary and the First Issue backstamps. It measures 3-1/8" and has an incised mold induction date of 1990. The release price was $155 suggested retail.

BLOSSOM TIME,
Hum 608.

HUM 609-615: OPEN NUMBERS

HUM 616: PARADE OF LIGHTS

This 6" figurine, released in 1993, seems to be a cousin of Carnival (Hum 328). It is in the 1996 suggested retail price list at $275.

PARADE OF LIGHTS, Hum 616. Hummel mark (TMK-7), 6".

HUM 617, 618, 619: OPEN NUMBERS

HUM 620: A STORY FROM GRANDMA

Goebel introduced this relatively large, complicated 9" figurine as an M.I. Hummel Club exclusive in 1995. It was a companion piece to the Hum 621, which was introduced a year earlier. If you bought At Grandpa's, you were given the opportunity to reserve A Story from Grandma with the same sequential limited edition number as the first. Once these reserved pieces were sold, the figurine was released to the general membership of the club. Like Hum 621, Hum 620 was limited to 10,000 pieces worldwide. It was released at $1,300 and is worth about the same today.

A STORY FROM GRANDMA, Hum 620.

HUM 621: AT GRANDPA'S

AT GRANDPA'S, Hum 621.

In 1994 Goebel announced production of the first M.I. Hummel figurine to feature an adult. Hum 621 was introduced in a limited edition of 10,000 sequentially numbered pieces for exclusive sale to members of the M.I. Hummel Club. The edition was limited in sale "... from June 1, 1994 until May 31, 1995, or unless the edition is sold out," according to the brochure. Each bears the club exclusive backstamp, measures 9" and was released at $1300. Currently it is worth about the same.

HUM 622: LIGHT UP THE NIGHT (1992 Christmas Ornament)

This is another in the annual series of ornaments. It has a collector value of about $75-100.

LIGHT UP THE NIGHT, Hum 622. 1992 Christmas ornament, Hummel mark (TMK-7), 1990 MID, 3-1/4".

HUM 623: HERALD ON HIGH (1993 Christmas Ornament)

This is another in the annual series of ornaments. It appeared in the 1993 suggested retail price list at $155 and is now valued a bit higher, at $165-175.

HERALD ON HIGH, Hum 623. 1993 Christmas ornament.

HUM 624, 625: OPEN NUMBERS

HUM 626: I DIDN'T DO IT

This figure with a basic size of 5-1/2" was the M.I. Hummel club exclusive offering for the club year 1993-94. It was available for $175 to members with redemption cards. It has the special club exclusive backstamp.

I DIDN'T DO IT, Hum 626. 1993/94 club exclusive, 5-5/8". The thing he holds behind himself is an archery bow.

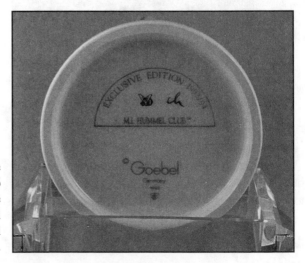

Base of the Hum 626 showing the M.I. Hummel Club special backstamp.

HUM 627: OPEN NUMBER

HUM 628: GENTLE FELLOWSHIP

This is the third and final figurine issued in the UNICEF Commemorative Series. This piece bears the special UNICEF backstamp, measures 5-5/8" and has an incised 1992 mold induction date. It is the only M.I. Hummel figurine to date that depicts two black children. The design was taken from a drawing made during the 1930s when the Siessen Convent was beginning to develop missionary work in Africa. The figurine is limited in production to 25,000 sequentially numbered pieces. The suggested retail price at release in 1995 was $550. As for the two previous figures in the series, for each one sold a $25 donation was made to the United States Committee for UNICEF.

GENTLE FELLOWSHIP, Hum 628.

Base of Hum 628 showing the special backstamp.

HUM 629: FROM ME TO YOU

This figure was given to each member of the M.I. Hummel Club who renewed their membership for the 1995-96 club year. It measures 3-1/2" and has a 1992 incised mold induction date. At the time of release the club valued it at $85.

FROM ME TO YOU, Hum 629.

HUM 630: FOR KEEPS

This figurine measures 3-5/8" and bears an incised mold induction date of 1992. It was the renewal premium given free to members of the M.I. Hummel Club when they renewed their membership for the year 1995-95. Its value is about $60.

FOR KEEPS, Hum 630.

HUM 631, 632: OPEN NUMBERS

HUM 633: I'M CAREFREE

Released in 1994, this figure carries an incised mold induction date of 1990 and measures 4-3/4" high. When the piece was first released the M.I. Hummel signature was located on the rear of the wagon. Later the signature was moved to the back side of the piece, beneath the bird. It is thought that fewer than 1,000 of these were produced with the signature on the rear end of the wagon. All those produced in 1994 will bear the First Issue backstamp. The price is $410 in the latest suggested retail price list. The rear signature variation will bring about 25% more.

I'M CAREFREE,
Hum 633.

HUM 634: OPEN NUMBER

HUM 635: WELCOME SPRING

This is the 1993 Century Collection piece. Production is limited to that one year during this century. The figure is marked so on the base and comes with a certificate of authenticity.

The release price was $1,085 in the suggested retail price list from Goebel.

WELCOME SPRING,
Hum 635. Hummel mark
(TMK-7), 12-1/4", 1993
Century Collection piece.

HUM 636-640: OPEN NUMBERS

HUM 641: THANKSGIVING PRAYER

This is a mini-size figurine with the mold number 641/0. Several pieces are released each year, each with the same theme, to form a Christmas group consisting of a mini-figurine, a Christmas tree ornament, a bell and a plate. This mini-size figurine measures 4", has a 1991 mold induction date and if produced during the first year it will bear the 1995 Limited Issue backstamp. (Compare Hum 596.)

THANKSGIVING
PRAYER, Hum 641.

HUM 642, 643, 644: OPEN NUMBERS

HUM 645-648: CHRISTMAS TREE ORNAMENTS

CELESTIAL MUSICIAN,
Hum 646. 1993 Annual
Christmas Ornament.

A new series of Christmas tree ornaments was initiated in 1993. Each ornament matches a miniature figurine and a Christmas plate design.

Year	Theme	Size	Mold	Release Price($)
1993	Celestial Musician	2-7/8"	Hum 646	90
1994	Fest. Harmony w/ Mand.	2-3/4"	Hum 647	95
1995	Fest. Harmony w/ Flute	2-3/4"	Hum 648	100
1996	Christmas Song	3-1/8"	Hum 645	115
1997	Thanksgiving Prayer	2-3/4"	Hum 596	125

HUM 649-659: OPEN NUMBERS

HUM 660: FOND GOODBYE

This is the twelfth piece in the Century Collection. During the twentieth century the edition will be limited to those produced in 1997. The figures are marked with the Century Collection backstamp and accompanied with a certificate of authenticity. The figure measures 6-7/8" high. The suggested retail price at the time of release was $1450.

FOND
GOODBYE,
Hum 660.

HUM 661, 663-667: OPEN NUMBERS

HUM 662: FRIENDS TOGETHER

This figurine was released in the summer of 1993 in two basic sizes. The smaller of the two, Hum 662/0 at 4", will be the regular production figure. It will bear a special Commemorative Edition backstamp and will be sold through regular channels. The larger size, Hum 662/1, 6", is a limited edition. This is the first of three cooperative fund-raising efforts between Goebel and the U.S. Committee for UNICEF, the United Nations Children's Fund. The art from which the figurine is taken was done by Sister Maria Innocentia Hummel in connection with her convent at Siessen and their African missionary work during the 1930s. The figurines were not released to the public until September 3, 1993, but were available exclusively to members of the M.I. Hummel Club on a first-come, first-served basis for roughly one month prior to the general release. These figures were not marked with the special club exclusive backstamp and are not considered club pieces.

The 6" size will be limited in production to 25,000 worldwide. That seems a large number at first, but considering the millions of collectors, the number is small. Each will be hand-numbered with the special markings.

The suggested retail price for the 4" size at release was $260. The release price for the limited edition, 6" size, was $475, with $25 of that amount being contributed to UNICEF.

FRIENDS TOGETHER, Hum 662.

HUM 668: STRIKE UP THE BAND

STRIKE UP THE BAND,
Hum 668.

This figure, released in 1995, is the tenth piece in the Century Collection. All figures in the Century Collection are limited in number to those produced in one designated year of the twentieth century. This figurine measures 7-3/8" and has an incised mold induction date of 1992. The suggested retail price is $1,200.

HUM 669-674: KITCHEN MOLDS

These mold numbers are used to identify the kitchen molds sold by the Danbury Mint. Please refer to the section on kitchen molds in chapter 6.

HUM 676-679: CANDLEHOLDERS

These mold numbers are used to identify four candleholders sold by the Danbury Mint. Please refer to the section on candleholders in chapter 6.

HUM 680-689: OPEN NUMBERS

HUM 690: SMILING THROUGH (Wall Plaque)

This is the second special edition produced exclusively for members of the Goebel Collectors' Club. It was available through membership in the club only. Members received a redemption certificate upon receipt of their annual dues, and they could purchase the piece for $55 through dealers who are official representatives of the club. The figure bears the Last Bee trademark (TMK-5) only. It is 5-3/4" in diameter and is presently valued at about $65-75. As of May 31, 1984, it was no longer available as a redemption piece.

SMILING THROUGH plaque, Hum 690, in the optional frame. Last Bee mark, 5-3/4" diameter. M.I. Hummel Club exclusive.

HUM 691: OPEN NUMBERS

HUM 692, 693, 694: ANNUAL CHRISTMAS PLATES

This is a series of four Christmas plates that began in 1995. The figures on the latest are three-dimensional and listed as "figural" plates by Goebel. There is a mini-figurine and a Christmas tree ornament to match each plate.

Year	Theme	Mold	Release Price ($)
1995	Festival Harmony with Flute	Hum 693	125
1996	Christmas Song	Hum 692	130
1997	Thanksgiving Prayer	Hum 694	135
1998	final edition	unknown	unknown

FESTIVAL HARMONY WITH FLUTE. Christmas grouping for 1995 comprising the mini-figurine, Hum 173/4/0, the plate and the ornament, Hum 647.

A CHRISTMAS SONG grouping for 1996 comprising the mini-figurine, Hum 343/0, the plate and the ornament, Hum 645.

THANKSGIVING PRAYER figural plate, Hum 694.

HUM 695-699: OPEN NUMBERS

HUM 700: 1978 ANNUAL BELL

This is the first edition of a bell that the factory has started producing each year. This first bell utilized the Let's Sing (Hum 110) motif. It is a first of its kind and like the first edition annual plate it experienced quite a rapid rise in value for a time. It was first released at $50 and is presently bringing about $40.

Annual Bells (left to right): 1978, 1979, 1980, 1981, 1982.

HUM 701: 1979 ANNUAL BELL

This is the second edition bell, released in 1979. It utilized the Hum 65 (Farewell) design motif. The suggested retail release price was $70 and it now sells for about $20.

HUM 702: 1980 ANNUAL BELL

The third edition in the series of annual bells. This bell utilizes the design motif of a boy seated and reading from a large book in his lap. It is somewhat similar to Hum 3 or 8, The Girl Book Worm. The design is named Thoughtful. The issue price was $85, and it now sells for abut $30.

HUM 703: 1981 ANNUAL BELL

The fourth bell in the series uses the design from Hum 414 (In Tune). Released at $115, it is now selling for about $40-45.

HUM 704: 1982 ANNUAL BELL

This fifth bell in the series matches the design of Hum 174 (She Loves Me, She Loves Me Not). Released at $85 and now selling at $65-70.

HUM 705: 1983 ANNUAL BELL

This is the sixth bell in the series. The design is called Knit One. The release price was $90 and it is presently widely advertised at about $55-60.

Annual Bells (left to right): 1983, 1984, 1985, 1986, 1987.

HUM 706: 1984 ANNUAL BELL

The seventh bell in the annual series derives its design from the figurine Mountaineer. The release price was $90 and it is presently selling at about $65.

HUM 707: 1985 ANNUAL BELL

The eighth bell in the series matches the design of the figurine Girl with Sheet Music. The release price was $90 and it is presently advertised for sale at $60.

HUM 708: 1986 ANNUAL BELL

The ninth bell in the series. Uses the figurine Sing Along (Hum 433) as its design. Release price: $100. It is presently selling at $95-100.

HUM 709: 1987 ANNUAL BELL

The tenth bell in the series. Uses With Loving Greetings (Hum 309) as its design. Release price. $110. It is presently selling at $150.

HUM 710: 1988 ANNUAL BELL

The eleventh bell in the series. Uses Busy Student (Hum 367) as its design. Release price: $120. It is presently selling at about $105.

Annual Bells (left to right): 1988, 1989, 1990, 1991, 1992.

HUM 711: 1989 ANNUAL BELL

The twelfth bell in the series, Hum 711 uses Latest News (Hum 184) as its design. It was released at a suggested retail price of $135. A few of these Hum 711 bells were produced with the mold number 710 before the mistake was discovered. The present collector value is $110-115.

HUM 712: 1990 ANNUAL BELL

Hum 712 is the thirteenth bell in the series. It uses What's New? (Hum 418) as its design. The release price was $140 and it is presently selling at about $150.

HUM 713: 1991 ANNUAL BELL

The fourteenth bell in the series, Hum 713, uses Favorite Pet (Hum 361) as its design. It is presently selling at $130-140.

HUM 714: 1992 ANNUAL BELL

The fifteenth bell in the series uses Whistler's Duet (Hum 413) as its design motif. Released at $165, it is now widely advertised for $115-120. This was the final edition in the series.

HUM 717: VALENTINE GIFT (Display Plaque)

This figure was an M.I. Hummel Club exclusive. It is 5-1/4" high and utilizes the first club exclusive figurine design, Valentine Gift (Hum 387). It was available to any member during the year 1996 for $250. For an extra $20 the purchase could have it personalized

HUM 721: A TRIO OF WISHES

A TRIO OF WISHES, Hum 721.

This is the second (1997) in a series of three called the Trio Collection. It measures 4-1/4" and comes with a hardwood display base. Production was limited to 20,000 sequentially numbered pieces. The other two figures are Tuneful Trio (Hum 757) and Traveling Trio (mold number not yet released). A Trio of Wishes was released at $475 suggested retail price.

HUM 730: ANNIVERSARY BELL

Although this figure has been announced it will probably not be produced. It is listed but not illustrated in the index of the book *M.I. Hummel: Golden Anniversary Album*. The original intention was to release it as a companion piece for a plate in the Anniversary Plate Series, but since the series was cancelled so went the bell.

HUM 735-738: CELEBRATION PLATE SERIES

A series of four 6" plates was made available exclusively to members of the Goebel Collectors' Club (now the M.I. Hummel Club). One plate was released each year starting in 1986.

Hum No.	Year	Design	Trademark	Collector Value ($)
738	1986	Valentine Gift	TMK-6, MB	120
736	1988	Daisies Don't Tell	TMK-6, MB	120
737	1987	Valentine Joy	TMK-6, MB	120
735	1989	It's Cold	TMK-6, MB	120

CELEBRATION PLATE SERIES (left to right): It's Cold, Daisies Don't Tell, Valentine Joy, Valentine Gift.

HUM 739/I: CALL TO GLORY

This figurine was released in 1994. All pieces produced that year bear the First Issue backstamp. The figure has an incised mold induction date of 1992, measures 5-3/4" and comes with three flags: the German, the European Common Market and the U.S. The suggested retail price at time of release was $250 and is listed at $275 today.

A special edition of this figurine was made for attendees of the M.I. Hummel Club Convention in Orlando.

CALL TO GLORY,
Hum 739/I.

HUM 740: OPEN NUMBER

HUM 741-744: LITTLE MUSIC MAKERS (Mini-Plate Series)

This is a four-plate series of 4" diameter plates. At the time the plates were issued, small figurines in matching motifs were also issued. The plates were limited in number to the amount produced during each year of the release. They are all found with the Missing Bee (TMK-6) trademark. There is no explanation for the non-sequential mold number/year of release situation.

LITTLE MUSIC MAKERS Plate Series (left to right): Serenade, Band Leader, Soloist, Little Fiddler. Plates are accompanied by the corresponding figurines.

Hum No.	Year	Design	Collector Value ($)
741	1985	Serenade	25-40
742	1987	Band Leader	40-55
743	1986	Soloist	35-50
744	1984	Little Fiddler	25-40

HUM 745-748: LITTLE HOMEMAKERS (Mini-Plate Series)

This four-piece mini-plate series was started in 1988. The plates are 4" in diameter, and a small matching figure was issued every year along with each plate. Each plate was limited to the number produced in the year of issue. All but the last one in the series bear the Last Bee (TMK-6) trademark. The last one, produced in 1991, is found with the current-use trademark, the Hummel Mark (TMK-7).

LITTLE HOMEMAKERS Plate Series (left to right): Little Sweeper, Wash Day, Stitch in Time, Chicken Licken. Plates are accompanied by the corresponding figurines.

Mold	Year	Design	Collector Value ($)
745	1988	Little Sweeper	35-50
746	1989	Wash Day	40-50
747	1990	A Stitch in Time	35-45
748	1991	Chicken-Licken	60-70

HUM 750: GOOSE GIRL (Anniversary Clock)

This is one of the most unusual Hummel items ever to be produced. The face of the clock is approximately 4" in diameter and is the "Goose Girl" rendered in bas-relief. The overall height, including the dome, is 12". The release price was $200. According to the current price list, the value is $225.

GOOSE GIRL
anniversary clock,
Hum 750.

HUM 751: LOVE'S BOUNTY

LOVE'S BOUNTY,
Hum 751.

Hum 751 is the eleventh piece in the Century Collection. Production of this figure will be limited to one year only in the twentieth century. This particular piece is in commemoration of Goebel's 125th anniversary and each figure is so marked. In addition, they each bear the Century Collection backstamp. Hum 751 measures 6-1/2" without the wooden base and has an incised mold induction date of 1993. It appears in the January '97 Goebel suggested retail price list at $1200.00.

HUM 754: WE COME IN PEACE

This figure, released in 1994, is a special commemorative UNICEF piece. It is quite similar to Hum 31 and Hum 113, but was redesigned especially for this release. It measures 3-1/2" and has a 1994 mold induction date and a special backstamp identifying it as a UNICEF piece. The price at release was $350. A $25 donation was made to the United States Committee for UNICEF for each figurine sold.

WE COME IN PEACE, Hum 754.

HUM 755: HEAVENLY ANGEL (Tree Topper)

This is another very unusual M.I. Hummel item. The familiar Heavenly Angel (Hum 21) theme has been rendered as a topmost ornament for a Christmas tree. It is open from the bottom so that it may be placed at the treetop, or it can be slipped over a wood base for display. The figure is 7" tall and was released in 1994. Those produced during that first year will have the First Issue backstamp. It has an mold induction date of 1992 and was issued at $450.

HEAVENLY ANGEL
tree topper, Hum 755.

HUM 756: THE ARTIST (Display Plaque)

In 1993 Goebel released The Artist (Hum 304) in display plaque form to commemorate the opening of the M.I. Hummel Museum in New Braunfels, Texas. At the time it sold for $260. It was available with the "Grand Opening" wording in 1993 only. Thereafter it has been made without that inscription. The museum uses the plaque as their logo on letterheads, etc. The plaque is listed at $295 in the suggested retail price list.

There are two more "Artist" display plaques, both produced for German consumption and in very limited quantities. Each has a 1973 mold induction date (see accompanying photo).

THE ARTIST display plaque, Hum 756.

THE ARTIST display plaque, Hum 756, one of the variations produced for the German market.

THE ARTIST display plaque, Hum 756, another variation produced for the German market.

HUM 757: TUNEFUL TRIO

This is the first edition in a trio of trios called the Trio Series. Issued on a hardwood base in 1996 in a limited edition of 20,000, each figure bears a 125th anniversary backstamp. The figurine measures 4-3/4". The post, a separate part, measures 6-3/4". The suggested retail price at release was $450. The second in the series is A Trio of Wishes (Hum 721) and the third is Traveling Trio, for which the mold number is not yet known.

TUNEFUL TRIO,
Hum 757.

HUM 758: NIMBLE FINGERS

This is the second figurine in the collection to be fashioned in such a way as it must be seated. Seen in the photo here with its companion piece To Keep You Warm (Hum 759), which came out a year before, it measures 4-3/4" and has a 1993 mold induction date. Those made in 1995, the year of release, will bear the First Issue backstamp. The suggested retail price is $225.

Left: NIMBLE FINGERS, Hum 758. 4-3/4" high, 1993 incised MID, First Issue 1995. Right: TO KEEP YOU WARM, Hum 759.

HUM 759: TO KEEP YOU WARM

TO KEEP YOU WARM, Hum 759. First Issue and 125th anniversary backstamps.

Released in 1994, this is the first M.I. Hummel figurine to be fashioned so that it must be seated. As you can see from the photo, a wooden chair was provided with the figure. It is 5" high and bears a 1993 mold induction date. It will have both the "First Issue" and the 125th anniversary backsstamps if made during 1994. The suggested retail price list assigns this piece a value of $215.

HUM 760: COUNTRY SUITOR

This figurine was released as an M.I. Hummel Club exclusive with a cut-off purchase date of May 31, 1997. It measure 5-9/16" and has an incised mold induction date of 1993. The release price was $195 and it is still valued at about the same.

COUNTRY SUITOR, Hum 760.

HUM 761: FROM THE HEART

FROM THE HEART, Hum 761.

This figure is part of an informal annual series of paired figurines called Cozy Companions. The other figurine in this pair is Heart and Soul (Hum 559). Both were released in 1996. From the Heart has an incised 1993 mold induction date and measures 3-3/4". Those produced in 1996 will bear both the "First Issue" and the 125th anniversary backstamps. From the Heart was released at a suggested retail price of $120.

HUM 767: SIXTY YEAR ANNIVERSARY (Display Plaque)

This plaque is a special edition created to celebrate the sixtieth anniversary of the making of Hummel figurines. It features Puppy Love, the first in the series of original figurines released in 1935. The plaque in the accompanying photograph has a 1993 mold induction date and measures 4-5/8" in height. Available only during 1995, it was assigned a value of $265 in the suggested retail price list of that year.

SIXTY YEAR ANNIVERSARY display plaque, Hum 767.

HUM 768: PIXIE

This figurine was released in 1995. Each piece made that year will have the First Issue backstamp. The piece measures 3-1/2" and has an incised 1994 mold induction date. Pixie is part of an informal series of paired figurine called Cozy Companions. Its companion piece is Scamp (Hum 553). The suggested retail price for Pixie is $115.

PIXIE, Hum 768.

HUM 771: PRACTICE MAKES PERFECT

One of only three figures in the collection that is fashioned so as to be seated on something. In this case a rocking chair is supplied with the figurine. It was issued in 1996 and measures 4-5/8". The first year of production will bear the First Issue backstamp. Suggested retail price at time of issue was $250.

PRACTICE MAKES PERFECT, Hum 771.

CHRISTMAS BELLS, left to right: 1989, Hum 775, Ride Into Christmas; 1991, Hum 777, Hear Ye, Hear Ye; 1992, Hum 778, Harmony in Four Parts.

1990 CHRISTMAS BELLS. The one on the right is the reverse side of the regular 1990 bell, Letter to Santa Claus, in a soft pastel blue color. The bell on the left is rendered in a greenish yellow color in a limited edition of 295.

HUM 775-783: CHRISTMAS BELL SERIES

Christmas bells are being released in three four-year series: 1989-1992, 1993-1996, and 1997-2000. The bells are rendered in a soft blue and each has a clapper in the shape of a pine cone. They are 3-1/4" in height.

The only significant variation to be found is with regard to color. Some 250-300 of the 1990 bell, Ride into Christmas, were made in greenish yellow color and given to company representatives as a Christmas present from Goebel.

Hum No.	Year	Design	Collector Value ($)
775	1989	Ride into Christmas	50
776	1990	Letter to Santa Claus	50
777	1991	Hear Ye, Hear Ye	50
778	1992	Harmony in Four Parts	50
779	1993	Celestial Musician	50
780	1994	Festival Harmony with Mandolin	50
781	1995	Festival Harmony with Flute	55
782	1996	Christmas Song	55
783	1997	Thanksgiving Prayer	55

CELESTIAL MUSICIAN bell showing the location of the markings in the bells.

CELESTIAL MUSICIAN, Hum 779. The 1993 Christmas Bell.

THANKSGIVING PRAYER, Hum 783. The 1997 Christmas Bell.

The 1994, 1995 and 1996 Christmas Bells: FESTIVAL HARMONY WITH MANDOLIN, FESTIVAL HARMONY WITH FLUTE and CHRISTMAS SONG. They are colored lavender, yellow and pink, respectively.

HUM 784-787: OPEN NUMBERS

HUM 788/A: HELLO, HUM 788/B: SURPRISE (Perpetual Calendars)

Released in the summer of 1995, both of theses pieces bear an incised 1995 mold induction date. Hello measures 6" x 7-7/8" and Surprise measures 5-3/4" x 7-7/8". The suggested retail price is $295 for each.

HELLO, Perpetual Calendar, Hum 788A.

SURPRISE, Perpetual Calendar, Hum 788B.

HUM 789: OPEN NUMBER

HUM 790: CELEBRATE WITH SONG

CELEBRATE WITH SONG, Hum 790. M.I. Hummel Club member exclusive.

This unusual figurine was issued as an exclusive M.I. Hummel Club piece. Sold only to those with redemption certificates from the club, it celebrates the twentieth anniversary of the club. It measures 4-1/2" (7" with the flag), has an incised 1994 mold induction date and was priced at $295 at the time of release. It is still worth about the same.

HUM 793: FOREVER YOURS

Hum 793 measures 4" and bears a 1994 incised mold induction date. It was the renewal gift for members of the M.I. Hummel Club who renewed their membership for the club year 1996-97. The figure has the special club backstamp as well as the First Issue backstamp and medallion. The collector value is about $60.

FOREVER YOURS, Hum 793. Renewal gift for M.I. Hummel Club members.

HUM 795: FROM MY GARDEN

From My Garden has a mold number of 795/0, which suggests that there may be another size in the offing. It measures 5" and has a mold induction date of 1994. It bears the First Issue backstamp and has a suggested retail price of $180.

FROM MY GARDEN, Hum 795.

HUM 2002: MAKING NEW FRIENDS

The highest mold number used in a production piece by Goebel before this was 795. Why this sudden jump to 2002 is anybody's guess. Whatever the reason, it is a most attractive figurine. Released in September of 1996, it measures 6-5/8" and has a 1996 mold induction date. Those produced in 1996 will have the First Issue and the 125th anniversary backstamps. The issue price was $595.

MAKING NEW FRIENDS, Hum 2002.

PHOTOGRAPHING YOUR COLLECTION

There are two very good reasons for taking good photographs of your collection. The most important is to have a record of what you had in the unfortunate event of a theft, fire or any other disaster that may result in the loss or destruction of your collection. Insurance companies are loathe to take your word that you had a Hum 1, Puppy Love worth ten times the normal value just because its head was tilted in a different direction. A photograph would prove it. In the case of theft you have little chance of identifying your collection in the event of a recovery in some instances. Law enforcement authorities often recover stolen property that can't be identified as to owner. If you have photographs and documentation such as detailed descriptions of marks, etc., they can help you positively identify what is yours. The second reason for this section is to help you also, but it is to help me as well. I get hundreds of photos each year, most of which are useless. You send me the photograph(s) with your questions and all I can see is what looks like a scarecrow out in the middle of a four acre field or a fuzzy Feathered Friends figurine due to its being out of focus. Can't help you much there. So, ready for your photography lesson?

This will be simple and fun for most of you. It won't make you America's next Ansel Adams, but it will make you a better photographer of figurines. You experts and pros can move on to the next section now.

THE CAMERA

The two most common cameras most of us use today are the 35mm single lens reflex (SLR) and the automatic "point and shoot" cameras that use the mini negative disc or regular 35mm film. The method for taking the kind of photographs we are looking for here differs between the the types so we will go through the basic set-up to get your figurines ready to shoot and then describe the method for each of the camera types.

SETTING

I employ a light blue or gray paper background normally that starts flat on a table top and is rolled up behind the figurine forming a curved background so there is no horizontal line to distract from the figure. You probably won't want to get that elaborate so go out and get a sheet of poster board. I recommend a light gray, pale blue or a beige for a neutral background. First try to set it up as I described before, rolling it up. If you are not successful that way, try cutting it in half, putting one piece flat on the table top and the other propped up somehow behind it as in the diagram. The diagram is overly simple and out of scale, but illustrates the idea.

If this to is more than you want to try, a simple table top or any flat surface will suffice. Try to avoid any with a patterned surface.

LIGHTING

There are two types of light: natural (or available) light and artificial light.

Natural Light

The simplest and best light is natural light outdoors, on an overcast day or in the shade on a bright sunshiny day. This eliminates harsh shadows. You can get almost the same light indoors if you shoot your picture at a large window that is admitting much light but not letting direct sunlight in.

Artificial Light

If you wish to shoot inside under artificial light you can do so in a bright, well-lighted room. You must be careful, however, about the type of light you have. Fluorescent lighting will produce pictures with a decidedly greenish cast. Incandescent lighting, ordinary light bulbs, will cause your pictures to come out with a yellowish or red cast. This is true when using ordinary, daylight color film designed for use outdoors or with a flash. Most modern photo processing labs can filter this color distortion out, but you must tell them about the type of light you used beforehand.

Using a flash is the third possibility, but under ordinary circumstances produces a severe, flat picture with harsh shadows.

If you can devise a way of filtering the flash, diffusing it or bouncing it off the ceiling or any other reflector you can devise, results are generally much more satisfying. The best use of flash is for "fill light" when shooting outdoors. It fills in shadows, eliminating them if done right.

CHOICE OF FILM

Film comes in different speeds (ASA ratings). The higher the ASA the faster the speed. The faster the speed, the less light needed to take a good photograph. There is a trade-off, however. The faster the speed the grainier the picture. This should not be of concern to you unless you are going to enlarge the picture or submit it for publication. I recommend that you use film with an ASA or 100 or 200, but if you have a poor light situation the ASA 400 would give you satisfactory pictures. Those of you with the modern automatic cameras shouldn't need to worry about switching these ASA's because your camera will automatically adjust to the ASA. Be sure to read your manual about this (You did read your manual didn't you?). Those of you with the more complicated SLR's know what to do.

GENERAL TECHNIQUES

First, you have a choice of methods. It your are shooting the pictures for insurance purposes you may choose to make a gang shot; that is shooting of two or three or more at the same time, or shooting your display cabinets or shelves (if there is a glass door, be sure to open it first). The latter is less desirable because you lose the detail you may need for identification later. If you don't wish to shoot each individual piece, then shoot them in groups of no more than three or four and try to match sizes as best you can.

When you take your pictures get in as close as you can, filling the frame with the figures. Try to hold the camera as low and level with the pieces as you can unless this causes a hand or some other part of the figure to obscure or cast a shadow on a face or other important feature. Sometimes adjusting the position of the figure can alleviate this problem. Remember, you want to show it at its best. If your camera is capable of close-up photography or there is a close-up lens attachment for it, take shots of the underside of the base of each piece or at least of the most valuable ones. These close-up attachments are usually quite inexpensive and come in sets of three lens.

TECHNIQUE FOR AUTOMATIC CAMERAS

Most of the automatic cameras of today come with a fixed focus lens or an automatic focus feature. Some even have a "macro" feature allowing you to get a little closer than normal to your subject. This feature allows somewhat nicer close-up portraiture, but is not of much use for our purposes here. Most automatic cameras will not allow you to get any closer than three feet from your subject. Any closer and everything will be out of focus. The field of view at three feet will be about 20" x 24". If you put one 6" figurine in the middle of that, take the picture and process it, you will get a photo about 4" x 5" in size and the figurine will be less than 1-1/4" tall, a lonesome trifling tidbit in the center (Remember the Scarecrow in the forty acre field?). It would be of little use in identification. A few of these cameras have close-up attachments available so check your manual to see if yours is one of them. If not then you will at best, only be able to make group pictures. You might want to experiment with one roll of film. Some of the automatic cameras will do much more than others and some will do better than the manual indicates. If your experiment is a failure, I suggest you prevail upon a friend or relative who has a better camera to help you out. Better yet, go out and buy one. The single lens reflex cameras are not nearly as complicated to use as they appear, and some of the new, electronic ones make it almost impossible to take a bad picture.

TECHNIQUE FOR THE SINGLE LENS REFLEX (SLR) CAMERA

Chances are many of you who have SLRs have never tried to do macro work. That is what small object photography is called. If you have perfected that art, you have permission to skip the rest of this section.

Macrophotography is a big word for a relatively simple technique, the results of which can be quite rewarding. In fact many of the photos in this book were shot with a Honeywell Pentax SLR with a standard 55mm lens that I bought many years ago. Many of you will probably have much newer and better cameras than mine. Your camera should do as well as the one I have. Mine will focus down to about 13" from the subject with a 5" x 7" field of view and with a set of inexpensive close-up lens (less than $25.00), you can get spectacular close-ups. Remember though, the more magnification you get, the less depth of field is available. I may have lost some of you there. Depth of field is simply the area in front of the camera that will photograph with acceptable sharpness. Said another way, it is the difference between the nearest and the furthest point of acceptable sharpness or focus in the scene to be photographed.

Focusing and Depth of Field

The depth of field you will be concerned with here is a function of the f-stop for the photograph and to a lesser extent, the distance from the lens to the subject. Simply put, the higher the f-stop selected, the more depth of field you have. It varies with the lens but the depth of field on my camera at f-16 is about 3" when it is focused as close as possible. When I focus on a figurine I try to focus about midway into its depth. This is entirely sufficient to keeping all parts of the figurine in focus in most cases. You may be able to do a little better or a little worse depending on your lens. Although you will likely be working as close to the subject as you can get, you should know that the further you get from the subject, the more the depth of field.

Shutter Speeds and f-stops

We have already noted that you will want to use a high f-stop number, f-11 or higher. Well the higher the f-stop, the smaller the aperture (the hole through which the reflected light passes on its way to the film). The smaller that hole is the longer it takes enough light reflected from your subject to form a good image on the film. So it follows that the smaller the hole the longer the shutter must remain open. Since we want enough depth of field so that all the figurine is in focus we'll have to trade off for time. That means the shutter speed will be too slow for you to hand hold your camera. That is why you will need to buy or borrow a tripod. Some folks are clever enough to jury-rig one. It would also be a good idea to have a cable release to insure that you do not shake the camera when tripping the shutter. They are inexpensive and available anywhere good cameras are sold.

Shooting the Picture

Here is a typical set-up in sufficient light to take your pictures:

Film speed	ASA 100 to 200
Shutter speed	1/8 to 1/30
f-stop	f-11 to f-16
Focal distance	14" to 18" approx. As close as

you can or need to be.

You will likely need to experiment a little until you are happy with the results. There are 12 print rolls of film available if you don't wish to waste film. The best way to find the ideal set-up for your light conditions is to shoot at different f-stops, leaving everything else constant, and place a piece of paper with your subject with the setting written on it or do the same thing varying any setting you want. You then will have a set of photos from which to pick the best and have the best camera setting right there in the picture.

Some Last Notes On Photographing Your Collection

Now you have your photograph(s). First, especially if this is an insurance inventory, you should have two sets of photographs. One set for you to keep at home to work with when you need to and the other in a safe deposit box or a separate location in case of fire or other happenstance resulting in the loss of your photographs. Second, you should have a written record either on the back of the photos or separate from them, of the date of purchase, the amount of the purchase, where or from whom you obtained it, the size, the trademark and every other mark to be found on the piece. This data along with the photo can leave no doubt as to ownership. This is especially true when, as in the case of Hummel, each piece is hand painted therefore slightly different from any other like piece; same as people. One last comment: If you are photographing the piece to send to me — give me the same information.

CURRENT PRICE LIST

This listing is taken from the *Suggested Retail Price List* issued by the Goebel company. Dated January 1, 1997, it is the published suggested retail price for the figures and other items which bear the trademark presently being used by the company. The appearance of a particular piece on this list is not necessarily an indication that it is available from dealers. Few dealers have the wherewithal to pick their stock and even fewer have the ability to have a large, comprehensive stock.

The abbreviation "TW" in the place of a retail price means that the item has been "Temporarily Withdrawn" from current production with no stated date for reinstatement. Other pieces may be absent from the list. Those have been removed from production or retired.

NAME	MOLD NUMBER	APPROX. SIZE	PRICE ($)
Accompanist, The	453	3-1/4"	115
Adoration	23/I	6-1/4"	380
Adoration	23/III	9"	595
Adventure Bound	347	7-1/2"x8-1/4"	3980
An Apple A Day	403	6-3/8"	310
Angel Duet	261	5"	245
Angel Serenade	214/D/I	3"	100
Angel Serenade	260/E	4-1/4"	TW
Angel Serenade with Lamb	83	5-1/2"	245
Angel with Accordion	238/B	2"	60
Angel with Lute	238/A	2"	60
Angel with Trumpet	238/C	2"	60
Angelic Song	144	4"	165
Angler, The	566	5-7/8"	350
Apple Tree Boy	142/3/0	4"	160

NAME	MOLD NUMBER	APPROX. SIZE	PRICE ($)
Apple Tree Boy	142/I	6"	310
Apple Tree Boy	142/V	10"	1,350
Apple Tree Boy	142/X	33"	24,000
Apple Tree Girl	141/3/0	4"	160
Apple Tree Girl	141/I	6"	310
Apple Tree Girl	141/V	10"	1,350
Apple Tree Girl	141/X	33"	24,000
Art Critic	318	5-1/2"	315
Artist, The	304	5-1/2"	275
Auf Wiedersehen	153/0	5"	270
Auf Wiedersehen	153/I	7"	330
Autumn Harvest	355	4-3/4"	225
Baker	128	4-3/4"	225
Baking Day	330	5-1/4"	310
Band Leader	129/4/0	3"	(TW)115
Band Leader	129	5"	225
Barnyard Hero	195/2/0	4"	185
Barnyard Hero	195/I	5-1/2"	350
Bashful	377	4-3/4"	225
Bath Time	412	6-1/8"	485
Be Patient	197/2/0	4-1/4"	225
Be Patient	197/I	6-1/4"	330
Begging His Share	9	5-1/2"	280
Best Wishes	540	4-5/8"	180
Best Wishes (personalized)	540	4-5/8"	200

NAME	MOLD NUMBER	APPROX. SIZE	PRICE ($)
Big Housecleaning	363	4"	315
Bird Duet	169	4"	160
Bird Duet (personalized	169	4"	180
Bird Watcher	300	5-1/4"	240
Birthday Cake	338	3-1/2"	160
Birthday Present	341/3/0	4"	160
Birthday Serenade	218/2/0	4-1/4"	190
Birthday Serenade	218/0	5-1/2"	330
Blessed Event	333	5-1/2"	350
Blossom Time	608	3-1/8"	155
Book Worm	8	4"	245
Book Worm	3/I	5-1/2"	335
Boots	143/0	5-1/2"	225
Boots	143/I	6-1/2"	360
Botanist, The	351	4-1/2"	200
Boy With Accordion	390	2-1/4"	100
Boy With Horse	239/C	3-1/2"	60
Boy With Toothache	217	5-1/2"	230
Brother	95	5-1/2"	230
Budding Maestro, A	477	4"	120
Builder, The	305	5-1/2"	275
Busy Student	367	4-1/4"	180
Call to Glory	738/I	5-3/4"	275
Carefree	490	3-1/2"	120
Carnival	328	6"	240

NAME	MOLD NUMBER	APPROX. SIZE	PRICE ($)
Celestial Musician	188/4/0	3-1/8"	115
Celestial Musician	188/0	5-1/4"	245
Celestial Musician	188/I	7"	295
Chick Girl	57/2/0	3-1/4"	160
Chick Girl	57/0	3-1/2"	185
Chick Girl	57/I	4-1/4"	310
Chicken Licken	385/4	3-1/8"	(TW)115
Chicken Licken	385	4-1/4"	310
Chimney Sweep	12/2/0	4"	130
Chimney Sweep	12/I	5-1/2"	245
Christ Child	18	6" x 2"	160
Christmas Angel	301	6-1/4"	280
Christmas Song	343/4/0	3-1/2"	110
Christmas Song	343	6-1/2"	245
Cinderella	337	4-1/2"	315
Close Harmony	336	5-1/2"	330
Come Back Soon	545	4-1/4"	160
Confidentially	314	5-1/2"	325
Congratulations	17	6"	225
Coquettes	179	5"	325
Crossroads	331	6-3/4"	450
Culprits	56/A	6-1/4"	325
Daddy's Girls	371	4-3/4"	250
Delicious	435/3/0	3-7/8"	155
Doctor	127	4-3/4"	170

NAME	MOLD NUMBER	APPROX. SIZE	PRICE ($)
Doll Bath	319	5"	315
Doll Mother	67	4-3/4"	230
Easter Greetings	378	5-1/4"	225
Easter Time	384	4"	275
Evening Prayer	495	4"	120
Eventide	99	4-3/4"x 4-1/4"	360
Fair Measure, A	345	5-1/2"	325
Farm Boy	66	5"	260
Favorite Pet	361	4-1/4"	315
Feathered Friends	344	4-3/4"	310
Feeding Time	199/0	4-1/4"	225
Feeding Time	199/I	5-1/2"	315
Festival Harmony w/ Flute	173/4/0	3-1/8"	115
Festival Harmony w /Flute	173/0	8"	350
Festival Harmony w/ Mandolin	172/4/0	3-1/8"	115
Festival Harmony w/ Mandolin	172/0	8"	350
Flower Vendor	381	5-1/4"	275
Follow The Leader	369	7"	1,320
For Father	87	5-1/2"	240
For Mother	257/2/0	4"	130
For Mother	257	5"	225
Forest Shrine	183	9"	595
Free Flight, A	569	4-3/4"	200
Free Spirit	564	3-1/2"	120
Friend or Foe?	434	3-7/8"	245

NAME	MOLD NUMBER	APPROX. SIZE	PRICE ($)
Friends	136/I	5"	230
Friends	136/V	10-3/4"	1,320
Friends Together (Commemorative Edition)	662/0	4"	300
Friends Together (Limited Edition)	662/I	6"	550
From My Garden	795/0	4-7/8"	180
From the Heart	761	3-1/2"	120
Gay Adventure	356	5"	220
Gentle Fellowship (Limited Edition)	628	5-3/4"	550
Gentle Glow, A	439	5-1/4"	230
Girl With Doll	239/B	3-1/2"	60
Girl With Nosegay	239/A	3-1/2"	60
Girl With Sheet Music	389	2-1/4"	100
Girl With Trumpet	391	2-1/4"	100
Going Home	383	4-3/4"	350
Going To Grandma's	52/0	4-3/4"	275
Good Friends	182	5"	225
Good Hunting	307	5"	270
Good Night	214/C/I	3-1/2"	100
Good News	539	4-1/2"	180
Good News (personalized)	539	4-1/2"	200
Good Shepherd	42	6-1/4"	280
Goose Girl	47/3/0	4"	185
Goose Girl	47/0	4-3/4"	260
Goose Girl (sampler)	47/3/0	4"	200

NAME	MOLD NUMBER	APPROX. SIZE	PRICE ($)
Grandma's Girl	561	4"	160
Grandpa's Boy	562	4-1/8"	160
Guardian, The	455	2-3/4"	180
Guardian, The (personalized)	455	2-3/4	200
Guiding Angel	357	2-3/4"	100
Happiness	86	4-3/4"	150
Happy Birthday	176/0	5-1/2"	240
Happy Birthday	176/I	6"	330
Happy Days	150/2/0	4-1/4"	190
Happy Days	150/0	5-1/4"	330
Happy Days	150/I	6-1/4"	500
Happy Traveler	109/0	5"	165
Hear Ye! Hear Ye!	15/2/0	4"	170
Hear Ye! Hear Ye!	15/0	5"	225
Hear Ye! Hear Ye!	15/I	6"	280
Heart and Soul	559	3-1/2"	140
Heavenly Angel	21/0	4-3/4"	140
Heavenly Angel	21/0/1/2	6"	245
Heavenly Angel	21/I	6-3/4"	295
Heavenly Lullaby	262	5" x 3-1/2"	210
Heavenly Protection	88/I	6-3/4"	495
Heavenly Protection	88/II	9"	800
Hello	124/0	6-1/4"	245
Holy Child	70	6-3/4"	280
Home From Market	198/2/0	4-3/4"	170

NAME	MOLD NUMBER	APPROX. SIZE	PRICE ($)
Home From Market	198/I	5-1/2"	240
Homeward Bound	334	5-1/4"	360
Horse Trainer	423	4-1/2"	245
Hosanna	480	3-7/8"	120
I'll Protect Him	483	3-1/4"	100
I'm Carefree	633	4-3/4"	400
I'm Here	478	3-1/8"	120
In D Major	430	4-1/4"	225
In The Meadow	459	4"	225
In Tune	414	4"	310
Is It Raining?	420	6-1/8"	300
Joyful	53	4"	140
Joyous News	27/III	4-1/4"x 4-3/4"	245
Just Dozing	451	4-1/4"	240
Just Fishing	373	4-1/4"	250
Just Resting	112/3/0	4"	165
Just Resting	112/I	5"	310
Kindergartner, The	467	5-1/4"	225
Kiss Me	311	6"	315
Knit One, Purl One	432	3"	135
Knitting Lesson	256	7-1/2"	525
Latest News	184	5"	320
Latest News (personalized	184	5"	340
Let's Sing	110/0	3"	140
Let's Sing	110/I	4"	185

NAME	MOLD NUMBER	APPROX. SIZE	PRICE ($)
Letter To Santa Claus	340	7-1/4"	360
Little Architect, The	410/I	6"	330
Little Bookkeeper	306	4-3/4"	315
Little Cellist	89/I	6"	240
Little Drummer	240	4-1/4"	165
Little Fiddler	2/4/0	3"	(TW)115
Little Fiddler	4	4-3/4"	225
Little Fiddler	2/0	6"	245
Little Gabriel	32	5"	165
Little Gardener	74	4"	130
Little Goat Herder	200/0	4-3/4"	225
Little Goat Herder	200/I	5-1/2"	260
Little Guardian	145	4"	165
Little Helper	73	4-1/4"	130
Little Hiker	16/2/0	4-1/2"	130
Little Hiker	16/I	6"	245
Little Nurse	376	4"	270
Little Pharmacist	322/E	6"	270
Little Scholar	80	5-1/2"	240
Little Shopper	96	5-1/2"	160
Little Sweeper	171/4/0	3-1/8"	(TW) 115
Little Sweeper	171/0	4-1/4"	160
Little Tailor	308	5-1/2"	275
Little Thrifty	118	5"	170
Lost Stocking	374	4-1/4"	165

NAME	MOLD NUMBER	APPROX. SIZE	PRICE ($)
Mail Is Here, The	226	6"x 4-1/2"	595
Make A Wish	475	4-1/2"	225
Making New Friends	2002	6-3/4"	595
March Winds	43	5"	170
Max And Moritz	123	5"	245
Meditation	13/2/0	4-1/2"	160
Meditation	13/0	5-1/2"	245
Merry Wanderer	11/2/0	4-1/4"	160
Merry Wanderer	11/0	4-3/4"	225
Merry Wanderer	7/0	6-1/4"	310
Merry Wanderer	7/X	33"	24,000
Mischief Maker	342	5"	310
Morning Stroll	375/3/0	3-3/4"	195
Mother's Darling (retires in 1997)	175	5-1/2"	240
Mother's Helper	133	5"	225
Mountaineer	315	5"	240
Nap, A	534	2-1/2"	130
Nimble Fingers w/ wooden bench	758	4-1/2"	230
Not For You!	317	6"	270
No Thank You	535	3-1/2"	120
One For You, One For Me	482	3-1/8"	120
One Plus One	556	4"	145
Ooh, My Tooth	533	3"	125
On Holiday	350	4-1/4"	170
On Secret Path	386	5-1/4"	275

NAME	MOLD NUMBER	APPROX. SIZE	PRICE ($)
Out of Danger	56/B	6-1/4"	325
Parade of Lights	616	6"	275
Photographer, The	178	5"	315
Pixie	768	3-1/2"	120
Playmates	58/2/0	3-1/4"	165
Playmates	58/0	4"	185
Playmates	58/I	4-1/4"	310
Poet, The	397/I	6"	250
Postman	119/2/0	4-1/2"	160
Postman	119	5"	225
Postman (sampler)	119/2/0	4-1/2"	160
Practice Makes Perfect (w/ wooden rocker)	771	4-3/4"	250
Prayer Before Battle	20	4-1/4"	185
Pretty Please	489	3-1/2"	120
Professor, The	320	4-3/8"	225
Retreat to Safety	201/2/0	4"	180
Retreat to Safety	201/I	5-1/2"	350
Ride Into Christmas	396/2/0	4-1/4"	260
Ride Into Christmas	396/I	5-3/4"	485
Ring Around The Rosie	348	6-3/4"	2, 860
Run-a-way, The	327	5-1/4"	280
St. George	55	6-3/4"	350
Scamp	553	3-1/2"	120
School Boy	82/2/0	4"	160
School Boy	82/0	5"	225

NAME	MOLD NUMBER	APPROX. SIZE	PRICE ($)
School Boy	82/II	7-1/2"	500
School Boys	170/I	7-1/2"	1,320
School Girl	81/2/0	4-1/4"	160
School Girl	81/0	5"	225
School Girls	177/I	7-1/2"	1,320
School's Out	538	4 '	170
Sensitive Hunter	6/2/0	4"	165
Sensitive Hunter	6/0	4-3/4"	225
Sensitive Hunter	6/I	5-1/2"	280
Serenade	85/4/0	3"	(TW)115
Serenade	85/0	4-3/4"	150
Serenade	85/II	7-1/2"	500
She Loves Me, She Loves Me Not	174	4-1/2"	220
Shepherd Boy	395/0	4-3/8"	295
Shepherd's Boy	64	5-1/2"	260
Shining Light	358	2-3/4"	100
Sing Along	433	4-3/8"	310
Sing With Me	405	4-3/4"	350
Singing Lesson	63	2-3/4"	135
Sister	98/2/0	4-3/4"	160
Sister	98/0	5-1/2"	230
Skier	59	5"	225
Sleep Tight	424	4-1/2"	245
Smart Little Sister, The	346	4-3/4"	275
Soldier Boy	332	6"	240

NAME	MOLD NUMBER	APPROX. SIZE	PRICE ($)
Soloist	135/4/0	3"	(TW)115
Soloist	135	4-3/4"	150
Song of Praise	454	3"	115
Sound the Trumpet	457	3"	120
Sounds of Mandolin	438	3-3/4"	140
Spring Dance	353/0	5-1/4"	350
Star Gazer	132	4-3/4"	230
Stitch In Time	255/4/0	3-1/4"	(TW)115
Stitch In Time	255/I	6-3/4"	325
Stormy Weather	71/2/0	4-3/4"	330
Stormy Weather	71/I	6-1/4"	495
Storybook Time	458	5-1/8"	440
Street Singer	131	5"	220
Surprise	94/3/0	4"	170
Surprise	94/I	5-1/2"	325
Sweet Greetings	352	4-1/4"	200
Sweet Music	186	5"	225
Telling Her Secret	196/0	5"	330
Thanksgiving Prayer	641/4/0	3-1/4"	120
Thanksgiving Prayer	641/0	4-3/4"	180
Thoughtful	415	4-1/4"	245
Timid Little Sister	394	6-3/4"	485
To Keep You Warm w/ wooden chair	759	5"	230
To Market	49/3/0	4"	175
To Market	49/0	5-1/2"	325

NAME	MOLD NUMBER	APPROX. SIZE	PRICE ($)
Trio of Wishes (limited edition)	721	6-3/8"	475
Trumpet Boy	97	4-3/4"	150
Tuba Player	437	6-1/8"	300
Tuneful Angel	359	2-3/4"	100
Tuneful Trio, A (limited edition)	757	4-7/8"	475
Umbrella Boy	152/A/0	4-3/4"	650
Umbrella Boy	152/A/II	8"	1,600
Umbrella Girl	152/B/0	4-3/4"	650
Umbrella Girl	152/B/II	8"	1,600
Village Boy	51/3/0	4"	130
Village Boy	51/2/0	5"	165
Village Boy	51/0	6"	280
Visiting an Invalid	382	5"	225
Volunteers	50/2/0	5"	245
Volunteers	50/0	5-1/2"	330
Waiter	154/0	6"	240
Waiter	154/I	7"	325
Wash Day	321/4/0	3-1/8"	(TW)115
Wash Day	321	6"	325
Watchful Angel	194/I	6-3/4"	340
Wayside Devotion	28/II	7-1/2"	450
Wayside Devotion	28/III	8-1/4"	600
Wayside Harmony	111/3/0	4"	165
Wayside Harmony	111/I	5"	310
We Come in Peace (Commemorative Edition)	754	3-1/2"	385

NAME	MOLD NUMBER	APPROX. SIZE	PRICE ($)
Weary Wanderer	204	6"	280
We Congratulate	214/E/I	3-1/2"	180
We Congratulate	220	4"	170
What's New?	418	5-1/4"	310
Which Hand?	258	5-1/2"	225
Whistler's Duet	413	4-3/8"	310
Whitsuntide	163	7"	330
Winter Song, A	476	4-1/4"	125
With Loving Greetings	309	3-1/2"	220
Worship	84/0	5"	180

ANNUAL SERIES

Christmas Bells

NAME	MOLD NUMBER	APPROX. SIZE	PRICE ($)
1996 Christmas Song	782	3-1/4"	65
1997 Thanksgiving Prayer	783	3-1/4"	68

Figural Christmas Plates

NAME	MOLD NUMBER	APPROX. SIZE	PRICE ($)
1996 Christmas Song	692	5-7/8"	130
1997 Thanksgiving Prayer	694	6"	140

Four Seasons Plate Series

NAME	MOLD NUMBER	APPROX. SIZE	PRICE ($)
1996 Winter Melody	296	7-5/8"	195
1997 Spring Time Serenade	297	7-5/8"	195

Miniature Ornaments

NAME	MOLD NUMBER	APPROX. SIZE	PRICE ($)
1996 Christmas Song	645	3-1/8"	115
1997 Thanksgiving Prayer	596	3"	120

CALENDARS/PERPETUAL

NAME	MOLD NUMBER	APPROX. SIZE	PRICE ($)
Hello	788/A	7-1/2" x 6-3/8"	295
Sister	788/B	7-1/2" x 6-3/8"	295

BAVARIAN VILLAGE COLLECTION

Houses

NAME	MOLD NUMBER	APPROX. SIZE	PRICE ($)
All Aboard	-	4-3/4"	60
Angel's Duet	-	8"	60
The Village Bakery	-	5-1/2"	60
Company's Coming	-	5-1/2"	60
Winter's Comfort	-	5-1/2"	60
Christmas Mail	-	5-1/2"	60

NAME	MOLD NUMBER	APPROX. SIZE	PRICE ($)
Shoe Maker Shop	-	5-1/4"	60
Off for the Holidays	-	5-1/2"	60

Accessories

NAME	MOLD NUMBER	APPROX. SIZE	PRICE ($)
The Village Bridge	-	5" long	30
The Wishing Well	-	2-1/4" long	30
The Bench and Pine Tree Set	-	1-1/2" + 1-1/2"	30
The Sled and Pine Tree Set	-	2-1/2 + 1-7/8"	30
Holiday Fountain	-	2-7/8"	35
Horse with Sled	-	2-1/8"	35

CANDLEHOLDERS

NAME	MOLD NUMBER	APPROX. SIZE	PRICE ($)
Angel w/ Accordion	I/39/0	2"	60
Angel w/ Lute	I/38/0	2"	60
Angel w/ Trumpet	I/40/0	2"	60
Boy with Horse	117	3-1/2"	60
Candlelight	192	6-3/4"	265
Girl w/ Fir Tree	116	3-1/2"	60
Girl w/ Nosegay	115	3-1/2"	60
Lullaby	240/I	5" x 3-1/2"	210
Silent Night	54	4-3/4" x 3-1/2"	360

CENTURY COLLECTION

NAME	MOLD NUMBER	APPROX. SIZE	PRICE ($)
1996 Love's Bounty	751	6-1/2"	1,200
1997 Fond Goodbye	660	6-7/8'	1,450

CHRISTMAS ANGELS

NAME	MOLD NUMBER	APPROX. SIZE	PRICE ($)
Angel In Cloud	585	2-1/2"	35
Angel With Lute	580	2-1/2"	35
Angel With Trumpet	586	2-1/2"	35
Celestial Musician	578	3"	35
Festival Harmony With Flute	577	3"	35
Festival Harmony With Mandolin	576	3"	35
Gentle Song	582	3"	35
Heavenly Angel	575	3"	35
Prayer of Thanks	581	3"	35
Song of Praise	579	2-1/2"	33

CLOCKS

NAME	MOLD NUMBER	APPROX. SIZE	PRICE ($)
Goose Girl	750	12"	220

DISPLAY PLAQUES

NAME	MOLD NUMBER	APPROX. SIZE	PRICE ($)
Artist, The (Hummel Museum)	304	4-3/4"	290

FIGURINE MINIATURES

NAME	MOLD NUMBER	APPROX. SIZE	PRICE ($)
Mail is Here Clock Tower	-	7-3/4"	575
Ring Around the Rosie Musical Vignette	-	9-1/2"	675

FONTS

NAME	MOLD NUMBER	APPROX. SIZE	PRICE ($)
Angel Cloud	206	4-3/4"	55
Angel Duet	146	4-3/4"	55
Angel Facing Left	91/A	4-3/4"	45
Angel Facing Right	91/B	4-3/4"	45
Angel Shrine	147	5"	55
Angel Sitting	22/0	3-1/2"	45
Angel With Bird	167	4-3/4"	55
Child Jesus	26/0	5"	45
Child With Flowers	36/0	4"	45
Good Shepherd	35/0	4-3/4"	45
Guardian Angel	248/0	5-1/2"	55
Heavenly Angel	207	4-3/4"	55
Holy Family	246	4-3/4"	55
Madonna & Child	243	4"	55
White Angel	75	3-1/2"	45
Worship	164	4-3/4"	55

MADONNAS

NAME	MOLD NUMBER	APPROX. SIZE	PRICE ($)
Flower Madonna, Color	10/I/11	8-1/4"	470
Madonna w/ Halo, Color	45/I/6	12"	140

NATIVITY FIGURINES

NAME	MOLD NUMBER	APPROX. SIZE	PRICE ($)
Madonna	214/A/M/O	5-1/4"	145
St. Joseph	214/B/O	6-1/8"	145
Infant Jesus	214/A/K/O	2-7/8" x 1-1/8"	45
Flying Angel	366/0	3-1/8"	115
King Kneeling	214/M/O	4-1/4"	155
King Kneeling w/Box	214/N/O	4-1/8"	150
King, Moorish	214/L/O	6-3/8"	165
Little Tooter	214/14/O	3-1/8"	110
Shepherd Kneeling	214/G/O	4"	130
Shepherd Standing	214/F/0	5-1/2"	165
Small Camel Standing	-	6-1/2"	220
Small Camel Lying	-	3-1/4" x 7-1/2"	220
Small Camel Kneeling	-	4" x 7-1/4"	220
Donkey	214/J/O	4"	55
Lamb	214/O/0	1-1/2" x 1"	22
Ox	214/K/0	2-3/4" x 5"	55
Madonna	214/a/M/I	6-1/2"	195
St. Joseph	214/B/I	7-1/2"	195
Infant Jesus	214/A/K/I	3-1/2" x 1-1/2"	70

NAME	MOLD NUMBER	APPROX. SIZE	PRICE ($)
Angel Serenade	214/D/I	3"	100
Flying Angel	366/I	3-1/2"	140
Good Night	214/C/I	3-1/2"	100
King, Moorish	214/L/I	8-1/4"	200
King Kneeling	214/M/I	5-1/2"	195
King Kneeling w/Box	214/N/I	5-1/2"	175
Little Tooter	214/H/I	4"	135
We Congratulate	214/E/I	3-1/2"	180
Shepherd w/Sheep-1 pc.	214/F/I	7"	195
Shepherd Boy	214/G/I	4-3/4"	145
Camel Standing	-	11-1/2"	275
Camel Kneeling	-	9"	275
Camel Lying	-	8"	275
Donkey	214/J/I	5"	75
Lamb	214/O/I	2" x 1-1/2"	22
Ox	214/K/I	6-1/4" x 3-1/2"	75

NATIVITY SETS

NAME	MOLD NUMBER	PRICE ($)
Holy Family, 3 Pcs. Color	214/A/M/I,B/I,A/K/I	460
12 piece set figurines only, Color	214/A/M/I,B/I,A/K/I,F/I,G/I,J/I, K/I,L/I,M/I,N/I, O/I,366/I	1,680
16 piece set figurines only, Color	214/A/M/I,B/I,A/K/I,F/I,G/I,J/I, K G/I,H/I,J/I,K/I, L/I,M/I,N/I,O/I,366/I	2,200

Porcelain Accessories

NAME	MOLD NUMBER	APPROX. SIZE	PRICE ($)
Featuring: The Lily of The Valley			
Bowl	-	5"	25
Pill Box	-	2" x 2-3/4" x 1/4"	20
Round Covered Box	-	2" x 1-1/4"	12.50
Round Covered Box (large)	-	3-3/4' x 2-1/4"	20
Vase	-	4"	17.50

Pen Pals

NAME	MOLD NUMBER	APPROX. SIZE	PRICE ($)
One For You, One For Me	482/5/0	2-3/4"	55
For Mother	257/5/0	2-3/4"	55
Soloist	135/5/0	2-3/4"	55
Sister	98/5/0	2-3/4"	55
Village Boy	51/5/0	2-3/4"	55
March Winds	43/5/0	2-3/4"	55

Tree Topper

NAME	MOLD NUMBER	APPROX. SIZE	PRICE ($)
Heavenly Angel	755	7-1/2" x 5"	495

Wall Plaques

NAME	MOLD NUMBER	APPROX. SIZE	PRICE ($)
Ba Bee Ring-Boy	30/A	4-3/4" x 5"	85

NAME	MOLD NUMBER	APPROX. SIZE	PRICE ($)
Ba Bee Ring-Girl	30/B	4-3/4" x 5"	85
Child In Bed	137	2-1/2" x 2-3/4"	60
Flitting Butterfly	139	2-1/2" x 2-1/2"	60
Merry Christmas	323	5-1/4"	120
Searching Angel	310	4-1/8" x 3-3/8"	115

M.I. HUMMEL CLUB® EXCLUSIVE COLLECTIBLES

Anniversary Figurines (prices subject to change)

NAME	MOLD NUMBER	APPROX. SIZE	PRICE ($)
Flower Girl (5 Year Figurine)	548	4-3/8"	140
The Little Pair (10 Year Figurine)	449	4-1/2"	220
Honey Lover (15 Year Figurine)	312	3-7/8"	230
Behave (20 Year Figurine)	339	5-1/2"	350

Club Figurines (available to current members only)

NAME	MOLD NUMBER	APPROX. SIZE	PRICE ($)
1995/96 Country Suitor	760	5-1/2"	195
1995/96 Strum Along	557	3-7/8"	135
1996/97 Celebrate with Song	790	5-7/8"	295
1996/97 One, Two, Three	555	3-7/8"	145
What's New?	418	5-1/4	310

SIZES INDICATED ARE ONLY APPROXIMATE
PRICES SUBJECT TO CHANGE WITHOUT NOTICE

INDEX

B

C

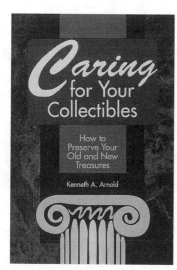
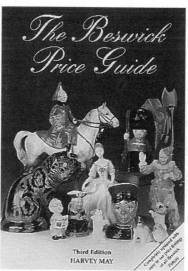